# Moodle Administration

An administrator's guide to configuring, securing, customizing, and extending Moodle

**Alex Büchner**

BIRMINGHAM - MUMBAI

Moodle Administration



First published: September 2008

Production Reference: 1190908

Published by Packt Publishing Ltd.
32 Lincoln Road
Olton
Birmingham, B27 6PA, UK.

ISBN 978-1-847195-62-3

www.packtpub.com

Cover Image by Vinayak Chittar (vinayak.chittar@gmail.com)

# Credits

**Author**

Alex Büchner

**Reviewer**

Derrin Kent

**Senior Acquisition Editor**

David Barnes

**Development Editor**

Nikhil Bangera

**Technical Editor**

Gaurav Datar

**Copy Editor**

Sneha Kulkarni

**Editorial Team Leader**

Mithil Kulkarni

**Project Manager**

Abhijeet Deobhakta

**Project Coordinator**

Brinell Lewis

**Indexer**

Rekha Nair

Monica Ajmera

**Proofreader**

Laura Booth

**Production Coordinator**

Aparna Bhagat

**Cover Work**

Aparna Bhagat

# About the Author

**Alex Büchner** is the co-founder and technical lead of Synergy Learning, UK's largest Moodle partner. He has been involved in system and database administration for two decades and has been administering virtual learning environments of all shapes and sizes since their advent on the educational landscape.

Alex holds a PhD in Computer Science and an MSc in Software Engineering. He has authored over 50 international publications, including two books, and is a frequent speaker on Moodle and related open-source technologies.

---


The best learning experience in Moodle is provided when communication and collaboration is utilized. The same applied to writing this book, which would not have been possible without the tremendous support of the Packt editorial team. Whatever time zone you were in, you certainly kept me on my toes 24/7.

I would also like to thank John Isner and Derrin Kent for their constructive feedback provided during the reviewing process. This book would not be the same without your comments and suggestions.

Special thanks must go to all my colleagues at Synergy Learning. Your input to the book content has been invaluable.

Last but not least, I have to thank all our customers. Without you we wouldn't be aware of all the Moodle hitches and glitches that are out there. Keep them coming!


---

# About the Reviewer

**Derrin Kent** describes himself as being a cross between a "trainer", a "manager" and a "geek". He lives in Worcestershire, UK and speaks Spanish at home with his Peruvian wife and two third-culture kids. Derrin has an NQF level 7 teaching qualification from Cambridge and is a member of the Association for Learning Technologies as well as being a **Linux-certified professional (LPI)**.

Derrin is the leader of The Development Manager Ltd. (`http://tdm.info`), a UK-based company which specializes in *improving e-learning and e-business with open source.*

# Table of Contents

# Preface

## What This Book Covers

### Part I: Getting Started

*Chapter 1* provides you with a brief overview and some background of Moodle. The Moodle business model and its development process is covered, along with the sectors in which Moodle is utilized. You will then learn about the job functions related to VLE administration alongside their responsibilities and skill sets, before some Moodle-specific administration tasks are covered.

*Chapter 2* tells you the most suitable Moodle setup for your organization, including software and hardware requirements. You will the learn how to install Moodle in three environments, namely LAMP/UNIX, Windows and Mac OS. Finally, Moodle manual and semi-automatic updates are covered in detail.

*Chapter 3* covers the building blocks of the learning platform. First, we cover the Moodle architecture, that is, the main Moodle components and where its data and code is stored. We then provide you with the skills to find your way round in Moodle via its intuitive user and administration interface. Finally, we deal with the management of files, which includes Moodle's standard file management and file management via web hosts, FTP and WebDAV.

### Part II: Moodle Configuration

*Chapter 4* tells you how to set up new courses and how to organize them in categories. This is followed by introducing meta-courses and course requests. The remainder of the chapter deals with an array of enrolment options, covering Moodle's internal enrolment, database-driven enrolment, for instance via LDAP and payment-driven enrolments.

*Chapter 5* explains how to manage users on your system. This includes browsing and filtering users as well as bulk user actions. We then cover a number of mechanisms of how to add users to Moodle, one-by-one, in bulk and by self-enrolment. Finally, you will learn about different authentication mechanisms provided by Moodle.

*Chapter 6* guides you regarding how to manage roles and grant permissions to users in different contexts. We will cover the assignment of roles, the modification of existing roles and the creation of new roles before we deal with any role-related settings.

*Chapter 7* tells you how to adapt your Moodle system to bring it in line with the corporate branding of your organization. We will cover the customization of the front page and the creation of Moodle themes.

*Chapter 8* brings you up-to-date with the vast array of Moodle options. The areas covered are accessibility, localization, module configuration, grades and gradebook settings, and miscellaneous parameters.

# Part III: Moodle Maintenance

*Chapter 9* will equip you with the tools you require to interpret and analyze the vast amounts of usage data Moodle is collecting. You will first learn about the monitoring facilities provided by Moodle that include activity reporting, user tracking and some basic statistics. Then, we will take a look at third-party monitoring tools that cover web log analyzers and live data trackers such as Google Analytics.

*Chapter 10* would focus on ensuring that the data in your Moodle system is protected from any misuse. You will learn about security notifications, user security, data and content security, and system security.

*Chapter 11* makes sure that your Moodle system runs to its full potential. We will cover configuring, monitoring and fine-tuning your virtual learning environment for maximum speed. You will learn how to optimize Moodle content before we focus on system parameters, namely path settings, caching settings, module settings and miscellaneous settings.

*Chapter 12* focuses on ensuring that in the event of a disaster, your data would not be lost. We are covering course backups, site backups, system backups and restoring data from the taken data archives.

## Part IV: Enhancing Moodle

*Chapter 13* explains in detail how to extend your Moodle system. You will be able to distinguish between good add-ons and not-so-good add-ons, before we cover extensions that are popular with other users. We will then cover how to install, configure and un-install third-party add-ons.

*Chapter 14* tells you how to connect disparate Moodle systems either in a peer-to-peer setup or via a community hub. You will also be able to apply the learned networking techniques to connect the popular open-source e-portfolio system Mahara to Moodle.

## Part V: Appendices

*Appendix I* equips you with a battery of over 100 diagnostic tests you should run against your system. It covers four main areas: performance (speed-related issues such as response times and load), security (covering all safety-related topics), functionality (enabling features and guaranteeing accessibility), and system settings (looking at Moodle's underlying components—operating system, database, PHP and web server).

*Appendix II* provides you with a list of parameters that can be modified in Moodle's *configuration file* and the impact each of the values will have. The areas covered are Administration Settings, System Settings and Theme Settings.

# What You Need for This Book

For Moodle, you must have the following components up and running on your server:

- Database: MySQL (version 4.1.6 or later), PostgreSQL (version 7.4 or later), Microsoft SQL Server (version 2005 or later), Oracle (version 8 or later).
- Web server: Apache is the preferred web server.
- PHP: PHP 4.30 is required to run Moodle. But it is advisable to use PHP 5.24 or higher, which will be necessary in the forthcoming 2.0 version of Moodle.
- PHP extensions: Moodle makes use of number of PHP extensions most of which are compiled into PHP by default.

Depending on your specific setup, additional software and hardware might be required.

# Who is This Book For

This book is written for technicians, systems administrators, as well as academic staff, that is, basically for anyone who has to administer a Moodle system. Whether you are dealing with a small-scale local Moodle system or a large-scale multi-site Virtual Learning Environment (VLE), this book will assist you with any administrative tasks. Some basic Moodle knowledge is helpful, but not essential.

# Conventions

In this book, you will find a number of styles of text that distinguish between different kinds of information. Here are some examples of these styles, and an explanation of their meaning.

Code words in text are shown as follows:

If the `cron.php` script is invoked over HTTP (either using `wget` or `curl`), more memory is used than calling directly via the `php -f` command.

Any command-line input and output is written as follows:

There are two ways you can create a so-called database dump from a MySQL database, either via command line or via Moodle's optional database interface.

The simplest syntax for the command line tool is:

```
mysqldump -u <user> -p <database> > backup.sql
```

**New terms** and **important words** are introduced in a bold-type font. Words that you see on the screen, in menus or dialog boxes for example, appear in our text like this:

There are two unrelated search settings in Moodle, both of which are still in an experimental stage. You can find them at **Miscellaneous | Experimental**

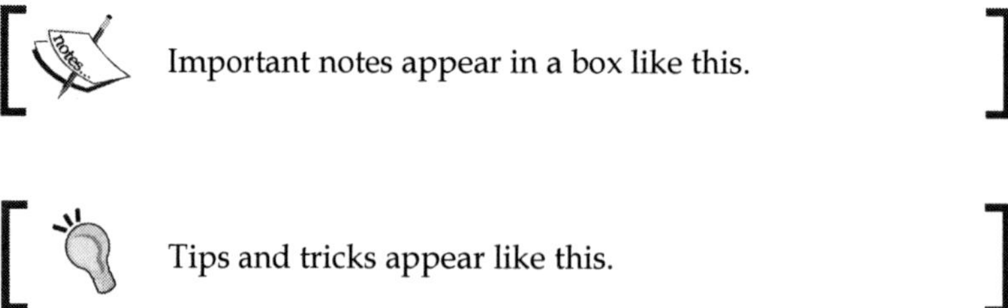

Important notes appear in a box like this.
Tips and tricks appear like this.

# Reader Feedback

Feedback from our readers is always welcome. Let us know what you think about this book, what you liked or may have disliked. Reader feedback is important for us to develop titles that you really get the most out of.

To send us general feedback, simply drop an email to `feedback@packtpub.com`, making sure to mention the book title in the subject of your message.

If there is a book that you need and would like to see us publish, please send us a note in the **SUGGEST A TITLE** form on `www.packtpub.com` or email `suggest@packtpub.com`.

If there is a topic that you have expertise in and you are interested in either writing or contributing to a book, see our author guide on `www.packtpub.com/authors`.

# Customer Support

Now that you are the proud owner of a Packt book, we have a number of things to help you to get the most from your purchase.

## Errata

Although we have taken every care to ensure the accuracy of our contents, mistakes do happen. If you find a mistake in one of our books—maybe a mistake in text or code—we would be grateful if you would report this to us. By doing this you can save other readers from frustration, and help to improve subsequent versions of this book. If you find any errata, report them by visiting `http://www.packtpub.com/support`, selecting your book, clicking on the **let us know** link, and entering the details of your errata. Once your errata are verified, your submission will be accepted and the errata added to the list of existing errata. The existing errata can be viewed by selecting your title from `http://www.packtpub.com/support`.

## Piracy

Piracy of copyright material on the Internet is an ongoing problem across all media. At Packt, we take the protection of our copyright and licenses very seriously. If you come across any illegal copies of our works in any form on the Internet, please provide the location address or website name immediately so we can pursue a remedy.

Please contact us at `copyright@packtpub.com` with a link to the suspected pirated material.

We appreciate your help in protecting our authors, and in our ability to bring you valuable content.

## Questions

You can contact us at `questions@packtpub.com` if you are having a problem with some aspect of the book, and we will do our best to address it.

# 1
# Introduction

Welcome to Moodle Administration!

**Moodle** stands for **Module Object-Oriented Dynamic Learning Environment**. We will begin with the principles of Moodle, followed by these introductory topics:

- A very brief overview of Moodle
- The Moodle model, covering development and business aspects of the software
- An overview of sectors in which Moodle is used, and the types of users who are using Moodle
- Job functions that have recently emerged in relation to VLE administration, their responsibilities, and the skill sets required
- Some Moodle-specific administration tasks

## Moodle's Rationale

Learning and teaching has been changing dramatically in the last decade. The shift from class-based environments to blended and online settings has been driven by the advent of new ubiquitous and internet-driven technologies such as cell phones, MP3 players, personal digital assistants, digital cameras, games consoles, interactive TV, and so on.

Marc Prensky has coined the terms **digital natives** (people who have grown up with these technologies) and **digital immigrants** (people who grew up without them and adapted them later). The problem that has arisen in educational settings is that the immigrants are often teaching the natives! This disconnection causes friction among all participants and now there is a need for technology to close this gap as much as possible.

A plethora of new assisting technologies has been introduced in recent years, which helps to supplement the existing learning and teaching environments. Examples are interactive whiteboards, classroom response/voting systems, rapid e-learning authoring tools, and **virtual learning environments**. Wikipedia defines a **Virtual Learning Environment** (**VLE**) as follows:

> *A virtual learning environment is a software system designed to support teaching and learning in an educational setting. [...] A VLE will normally work over the Internet and provide a collection of tools such as those for assessment (particularly of types that can be marked automatically, such as multiple choice), communication, uploading of content, return of students' work, peer assessment, administration of student groups, collecting and organizing student grades, questionnaires, tracking tools, etc.*

The following diagram depicts the schematic components of a typical virtual learning environment:

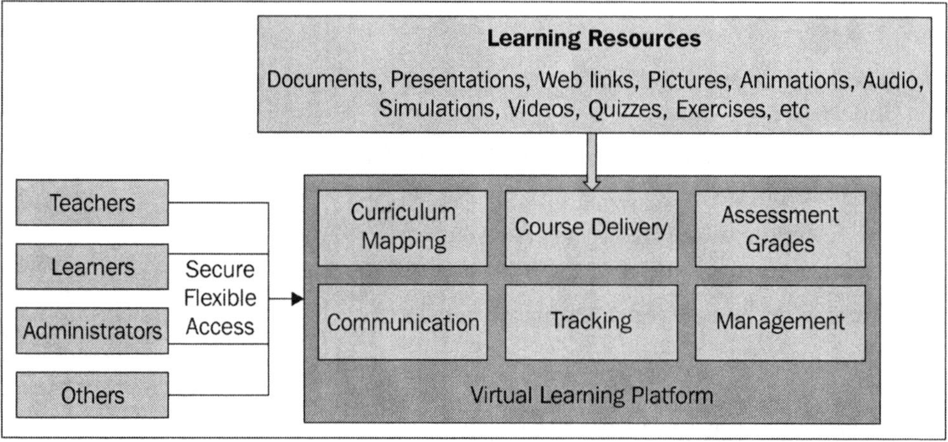


The figure shows the main building blocks of VLE, each of which has its counterpart in non-virtual settings. The key to a good learning experience is good learning resources; the same applies in physical learning environments. Secure and flexible access is granted to learners, teachers, and administrators as well as to other users such as parents, inspectors, visitors, and so on. VLE can also be described as: "a content management system with an educational and pedagogical wrapper".

Moodle is one of the most popular virtual learning environments in this vastly growing market. First of all, let's provide you with a very brief overview of Moodle.

# Moodle Overview

**Moodle** stands for **Modular Object-Oriented Dynamic Learning Environment**.

The section about Moodle on its website `www.moodle.org` also defines to moodle [verb]:

> *The process of lazily meandering through something, doing things as it occurs to you to do them, an enjoyable tinkering that often leads to insight and creativity. As such it applies both to the way Moodle was developed, and to the way a student or teacher might approach studying or teaching an online course.*

The original version of Moodle was developed by Martin Dougiamas as part of his research on social constructionist pedagogy or, for us mere mortals, learning by doing, communicating, and collaborating. If you wish to learn more about Moodle's underlying pedagogical framework, please refer to `http://docs.moodle.org/en/Philosophy`.

In a nutshell, Moodle is a web-based software system that facilitates learning and teaching. It is **learning-centered and not tool-centered**, which appeals to educationalists as well as learners. Moodle is now the most popular open-source virtual learning environment worldwide, and its uptake is growing steadily. Its modularity (remember, that's what the "M" stands for) allows us to configure the system flexibly and also to extend it if we wish to do so.

Before we cover Moodle in more detail, let's have a look at its unique development and business model.

# The Moodle Model

Moodle is open-source software that has been released freely under the GNU Public License. This means that you are allowed to copy, use, and modify Moodle, provided that you agree to: *provide the source to others; not modify or remove the original license and copyrights, and apply this same license to any derivative work.*

However, the name Moodle is copyrighted which means only authorized companies are allowed to sell related services.

The questions frequently asked are:

- How is Moodle being developed?
- How does Moodle make money?

Let us shed some light on these two valid questions. At the core is the Moodle Trust, set up by Martin Dougiamas, that manages the Moodle project.

# The Moodle Development Model

The Moodle Trust employs a number of full-time software developers who are implementing and co-ordinating the development of the software. Programmers around the globe contribute to the development. Some are core developers; some contribute through testing, while others offer small-scale patches and amendments. While some are paid by employers who benefit from Moodle such as universities or companies, others are volunteers who are enthusiastic about Moodle, or programming, or both.

A roadmap exists for Moodle, which is driven by feature requests from the Moodle community. These are users who either post requirements on `tracker.moodle.org` or who provide feedback at Moodle conferences called MoodleMoots. Some features are paid for (see Business Model section), for example, Microsoft part-financed the development of the XMLDB database abstraction layer.

# The Moodle Business Model

The Moodle trust has three main revenue-generating channels:

- Moodle Partners (`www.moodle.com`)

  Moodle Partners are companies that have been authorized by the Moodle Trust to carry out Moodle services (such as hosting, support, training, branding, development, and so on) in a particular territory, and use the Moodle trademark. It is similar to a franchise model, where each franchisee pays an annual fee and a commission on its revenue to the franchiser. There are approximately 40 Moodle partners world-wide, which displays the highest professional standards.

- Clients

  Institutions, companies, and individuals contract the Moodle Trust to implement functionality to its product. Most of these new features will then be made available to the community.

- Donations

  Many Moodle users including businesses, educational establishments, and individuals have funded the Moodle project through donations.

The two main expenses of the Moodle Trust are staff salaries and the maintenance of its community site `www.moodle.org`, which includes free forum-based support, full documentation, a bug tracking facility, and many more features.

If you want to deepen your knowledge on development and business models of open-source software, *The Cathedral & the Bazaar* by Eric S. Raymond is a must-read. For more information on the Moodle model, search for *Moodle: a case study in sustainability* by Martin Dougiamas who is Moodle's benevolent dictator.

# Moodle Usage

Like so many technologies related to teaching and learning, most VLEs, including Moodle, were initially tailored towards the needs and requirements of academia. While the core educational sector is still the largest consumer in the market, other verticals are now making use of Moodle. This has been reflected in the provision of a more flexible functionality. The main groups of users can be categorized in the following four sectors:

1. Core education

   Here core education means state-funded or private schools, colleges, academies, polytechnics, universities, and so on. Basically, any organization where learning and teaching (and optionally research and technology transfer) is at its core and qualifications in academic and vocational subjects are being offered.

   VLEs are crucial to these organizations whether they are used to supplement face-to-face learning in a blended environment or if a pure e-learning approach is taken. There exist very few core educational organizations today that do not have a VLE.

2. Industry

   There are two types of organizations in this group: The first type includes companies that specialize in delivering courses across industry sectors. This ranges from micro-businesses providing training in a niche sector such as helicopter maintenance (we have a Moodle customer who does exactly that!) to large corporations offering hundreds of courses (for example, languages, IT, and business subjects) to individuals and other companies. The second type involves businesses that use VLEs internally for their staff training.

   In both cases VLEs play a crucial role as they reduce cost, increase flexibility, and cater for a multitude of learning styles, pace, and methodologies.

3. Public sector

   More and more public sector organizations are using VLEs for a range of activities. Examples are continual professional development, dissemination of information, and citizen consultation. Special role play bodies that are responsible for organizations in the core educational sector such as education boards, qualifications and curriculum authorities, skills councils, and so on. In addition to using VLEs internally, they often act as an intermediary between policy makers and these individual organizations.

4. Not-for-profit organizations

   NPOs, voluntary organizations, and charities utilize VLEs to disseminate information, provide support to its service users, and offer self-help courses among other activities.

Independent of the sector in which VLEs are deployed, there are three main types of Moodle users:

1. Learners

   These are the most important users of Moodle! They are the **consumers** in any learning environment, whether it is physical or virtual. Depending on their status, they might be called pupils, students, participants, staff members, and so on.

   In addition to providing learning resources (text, audio, video, animation, simulation, and so on), good VLEs support a wide range of learning activities as well as collaboration and communication facilities for its learners.

2. Teachers

   These are the **producers** in a learning environment. There are two key roles: creation of learning content and the delivery thereof. Again, depending on the organization, you might call them teachers, lecturers, instructors, staff, trainers, coaches, and so on.

3. Administrators

   That's us! We are the ones who have to make sure that everything is working the way it is supposed to. Learners have to be given access to their courses or classes, and teachers have to be given facilities they need to carry out their duties. In addition to these key tasks, there is a plethora of responsibilities that have to be carried out. We will provide an overview in this introduction before we go into the details on a chapter-by-chapter basis.

There are additional types of users who will be able to access your Moodle system. Examples are external examiners, inspectors, parents, visitors, alumni, librarians, and so on. We will come across those user types later on while dealing with roles in Moodle.

# VLE Administration

A Moodle administrator is basically a VLE administrator who manages a Moodle system. We first look at the job functions, responsibilities, and necessary skill sets in general before understanding any Moodle-specific duties.

## VLE Job Functions

A quick search through recruitment agencies specializing in the educational sector reveal a growing number of dedicated job titles that are closely related to VLE administration. A few examples are:

- VLE Administrator (or LMS Administrator or MLE Administrator)
- VLE Support Officer
- VLE Architect
- VLE Engineer
- VLE Coordinator

The list does not include functions that regularly act in an administrative capacity such as IT support. It also does not include roles that are situated in the pedagogical field, but often take on the work of a VLE administrator such as learning technologists or e-learning coordinators.

A VLE administrator usually works very closely with the staff who have responsibility for the administration of IT systems, databases and networks. It has proven beneficial to have some basic skills in these areas. Additionally, links are likely in larger organizations where content management systems, student information management systems, and other related infrastructure is present.

Given this growing number of VLE administration-related roles, let us look at some key obligations of the job function and what skills are essential and desirable.

# Obligations and Skill Sets of a VLE Administrator

The responsibilities of the VLE administrator differ from organization to organization. However, there are some obligations that are common across installations and setups:

- User management (learners, teachers, and others)
- Course management (prospectus mapping)
- Module management (functionality provided to users)
- Look and feel of the VLE (sometimes carried out by a web designer)
- Year-end maintenance (if applicable)
- Beginning-of-year setup (if applicable)
- Support teaching staff and learners

In addition to these VLE-specific features, you are required to make sure that the virtual learning environment is secure, stable, and performs well. Backups have to be in place, monitoring has to be set up, reports about usage have to be produced, and regular system maintenance has to be carried out.

If you host your own system, you will be responsible for all of the listed tasks and many more. If your VLE is hosted in a managed environment, some of the tasks closer to system level will be carried out by the hosting provider. So it is important that they have a good understanding of Moodle. Either way, you will be the first person to be contacted by staff and learners if anything goes wrong, if they require new functionality, or if some administrative task has to be carried out.

While a range of e-learning related activities are now taught as part of some academic and vocational qualifications (for instance, instructional design or e-moderation), VLE administration per se is not. Most VLE administrators have a technical background and often have some system or database administration knowledge. Again, it entirely depends on whether you host your VLE locally or it is hosted externally. The administration skills of a remotely hosted system can be learned by anybody with some technical knowledge. However, for an internally hosted system you will require good working knowledge of the operating system on which the VLE is installed, the underlying database that is used, the network in which the VLE has to operate, and any further components that have to work with the learning system.

# Moodle Administration

Moodle administration essentially covers all the aspects mentioned in previous sections. But since Moodle is very open, flexible, and modular, it provides some additional layers of functionality that other systems lack. These extra options sometimes require further tasks to be carried out. Some examples are:

- Integration with other systems holding information about your learners and course participation (for example via LDAP).
- Installation of third-party add-ons: There are well over 350 non-core modules that can be installed and which will then have to be looked after.
- Networking: Moodle provides a unique feature to network Moodle systems across the Internet.
- Integration with ever more popular e-portfolio systems, for instance Mahara.
- Moodle can be skinned via themes. To create themes you need to have good HTML and CSS knowledge.

It is not necessary to have any programming skills to administer Moodle. However, if you wish to change any of the functionalities of VLE, it is necessary that you know PHP, the programming language in which Moodle has been developed. It is further recommended to be familiar with HTML and CSS. However, we won't cover any programming aspects of Moodle in this book.

Along with the tasks that have been mentioned in this introduction, some more will also be covered in great detail in this book.

# Summary

Moodle is a VLE that is innovative and flexible. It is able to cater to the needs of modern online learners. In this chapter we have provided a brief overview of Moodle per se as well as its development and business model, before describing the sectors in which Moodle is employed and the types of users that are using it.

Administering Moodle is not a straightforward task, which is why more and more organizations have dedicated resources to manage their learning environment. The first task of a Moodle administrator is to install the software, which we will go through step-by-step in the next chapter.

# 2

# Moodle Installation

Now that you have gathered some background knowledge about Moodle, let's get started by installing the virtual learning environment. After providing an overview that describes what setup is most suitable, software as well as hardware requirements are outlined. We will then cover the following installations:

- Installation of Moodle in a LAMP / Unix environment
- Installation of Moodle in a Windows environment
- Installation of Moodle in a Mac OS X environment
- Upgrading Moodle manually and via CVS

You will only need to study the section(s) of the operating system(s) you are planning to use. As mentioned in the Introduction, Moodle can be scaled from a single instructor to an entire institution. We will only be able to cover the most popular installations and present solutions to some common problems. We also have to assume that you are familiar with the basic system administration of the operating system on which you will be installing Moodle.

## Moodle Installation: An Overview

Before we start installing Moodle, you have to decide which setup is right for your organization. Once you have come to a conclusion, there are a number of prerequisites that you have to provide before we can get started.

### What is the Best Setup for Me?

There are quite a few different environments in which you can set up Moodle. The three main criteria that should dictate the choice of the correct setup are:

- Flexibility

  If you want to have full control over your system, be able to tweak system settings, and make frequent changes to the setup, you are best hosting your own server. However, if your preferred choice is to administer only your system while somebody else is looking after the operating system, the web server, and backups, you are better off with a professionally hosted setup.

- Scalability

  This is entirely driven by the number of concurrent users, that is, the number of learners and teachers logged in to Moodle at the same time. A Moodle on a USB memory stick or on a single processor desktop computer will not be able to cope with hundreds of simultaneously logged-in users. A load-balanced cluster, on the other hand, would be overkill for a small institution with a handful of learners. The following table provides some indicative setups for different types of educational organizations and is by no means complete:

| Organization | Likely Setup |
|---|---|
| Single Instructor | Desktop, laptop, memory stick |
| Small school | Shared server |
| Large school | Dedicated server |
| Medium to large college | Dedicated application and database servers |
| University | Load-balanced cluster |

  Organizations require a server (either dedicated or shared) that is either hosted in-house or externally. If you decide to go down the hosted route, it is highly recommended to avoid a "cheap hosting" package as its systems are not optimized for Moodle usage. It will have a significant impact on the performance of the system, especially with an increasing number of users.

- Cost

  Budgetary constraints will certainly play an important role in your setup. Unless you already have the appropriate infrastructure in place, it is likely to be more cost-effective to host your Moodle system externally. It saves you from purchasing servers and providing a 24x7 data connection that caters to your learners' needs. Licensing cost is significantly higher if you use commercial operating systems, web servers, and database systems; but your organization's IT policy might not allow the usage of Linux.

In addition to these three key criteria that usually influence the decision of the underlying infrastructure, there are other factors that will have an impact on your decision such as in-house expertise, compatibility with other systems, and existing resources.

We will cover the three most popular operating systems for hosting Moodle, that is, Linux, Windows, and Mac OS. For other setups such as on a memory stick or a larger multi-server cluster, please consult your local Moodle Partner (`http://www.moodle.com`). Some hosting companies offer quick one-click installations (often via the Fantastico installer, which usually doesn't contain the latest version). While the resulting Moodle system is sufficient for experimental sites, it is certainly unsuitable for production environments.

# Moodle Prerequisites

There are a number of hardware and software requirements that have to be satisfied before we can start installing Moodle.

## Hardware Requirements

These requirements apply if you host Moodle on your own, and if it is hosted on an external server (shared, virtual, dedicated, or clustered). Especially on cheaper hosting packages, the hardware requirements are often insufficient to run Moodle efficiently.

- Disk space

  Moodle takes up between 150 to 200MB disk space. However, this only provides you with an empty system and does not take into account the space you require for any learning resources. The faster the disks, the better the performance. RAIDed disks are recommended, but are not essential on smaller installations.

- Memory

  The minimum requirement is 256MB for a single-user instance, but more is necessary in a concurrent user setup. A good estimate is to have 1GB of RAM for each 50 concurrent users. You have to double this rule of thumb on Windows-based systems due to the higher overhead of the operating system.

The more the RAM the better, the faster the RAM the better!

- Network

  While Moodle can run on a standalone machine, its full potential is in a networked environment. A fast network card is essential, as is good upload and download speed, if the VLE is accessed over the Internet.

## Software Requirements

For Moodle 1.9, you must have the following components up and running on your server:

- Database

  Moodle supports a number of database systems including MySQL (version 4.1.6 or later), PostgreSQL (version 7.4 or later), Microsoft SQL Server (version 2005 or later), and Oracle (version 8 or later).

- Web server

  Apache is the preferred web server option, but Moodle works well with any other web server that supports PHP such as Microsoft Internet Information Server.

- PHP

  PHP 4.30 is required to run Moodle 1.9. But it is advisable to use PHP 5.24 or higher, which will be necessary in the forthcoming version 2.0 of Moodle. Also, some experimental features already in Moodle 1.9 such as global search will not work with PHP 4. There are a number of PHP settings that you might have to change in the `php.ini` or the `.htaccess` file (see `http://docs.moodle.org/en/Installing_Moodle` for more details).

- PHP extensions

  Moodle makes use of a number of PHP extensions, most of which are compiled into PHP by default.

  - Compulsory extensions: ctype, FreeType 2, and GD library
  - Recommended extensions: curl, iconv, mbstring, tokenizer, and zlib
  - Conditional extensions: mysql, pgsql, odbc (depending on database), ldap, and so on (depending on authentication mechanism used), openssl and xmlrpc (for networking).

Depending on your specific setup, additional software and hardware might be required. It is assumed that the database, web server, PHP, and its extensions have been installed correctly. Once this is the case, we are ready to go.

# Installation in a LAMP Environment

Moodle is developed in Linux using Apache, MySQL, and PHP (also known as the LAMP platform). If you have a choice, this is the preferred environment to be used.

# Downloading Moodle

Go to `http://download.moodle.org` to download Moodle. As you can see, there are quite a number of distributions to choose from:

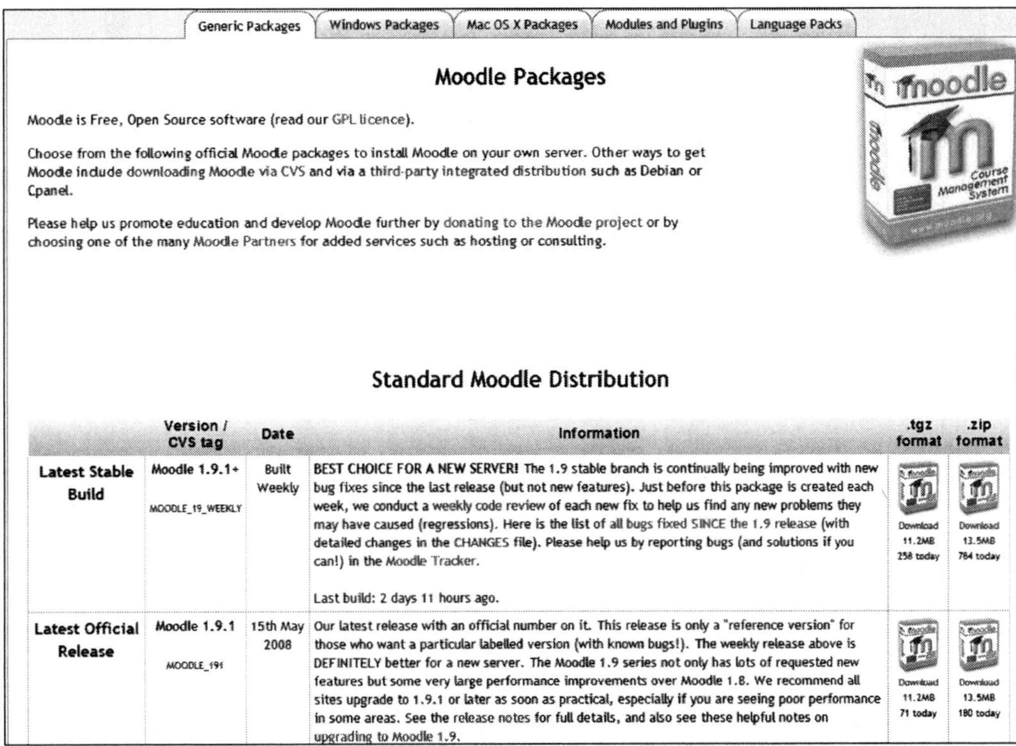


For the current version of Moodle, there are two releases: the latest stable build and the latest official release. The **latest stable version** is created weekly (every Wednesday) and is the best choice for a new server. The **latest official release** contains the stable build as well as new fixes, but the version will not have gone through the weekly code review and might contain unresolved issues.

Versions that are older than the current one are maintained by the Moodle development team, and bug fixes are back-ported. Sometimes newly added functionality is back-ported. Currently, the oldest supported version is 1.6, but this will certainly change in the future. For older versions, a stable build and the last release are made available.

Moodle (that is `http://download.moodle.org`) also offers you to download beta releases of the software (if available) and also the latest development release. These should only be downloaded for testing or development purposes, and never used in production environments.

Each version is made available in two compressed formats TGZ (use the tar command to uncompress) and ZIP (requires unzip). You can either download them by clicking on the respective link or, if you have (secure) shell access, retrieve the file directly using the `wget` command:

```
wget http://download.moodle.org/stable19/moodle-weekly-19.zip
```

[ The location where you install Moodle is referred to as **dirroot**. ]

Once you have moved the file to the location where you want to install it on your web server (dirroot), extract the file using the `unzip` command (or `tar -zxvf` if you downloaded the TGZ version). In a hosted environment, you might have to use the uncompressing method provided by the web administration interface (CPanel, Plesk, or any customized system).

If you place the entire folder in your web server documents directory, the site will be located at `http://www.yourwebserver.com/moodle`. To access your site from `http://www.yourwebserver.com`, copy the contents directly into the main web server's documents directory.

[ The URL via which Moodle is accessed is referred to as **wwwroot**. ]

```
synergy-learning:moodle>pwd
/srv/www/vhosts/synergy-learning.com/subdomains/packt/httpdocs/moodle
synergy-learning:moodle>wget http://download.moodle.org/download.php/stable19/moodle-weekly-19.tgz
--11:16:52--  http://download.moodle.org/download.php/stable19/moodle-weekly-19.tgz
           => `moodle-weekly-19.tgz'
Resolving download.moodle.org... 70.84.5.50
Connecting to download.moodle.org|70.84.5.50|:80... connected.
HTTP request sent, awaiting response... 200 OK
Length: unspecified [text/html]

    [ <=>                                                ] 6,186         --.--K/s

11:16:53 (45.00 KB/s) - `moodle-weekly-19.tgz' saved [6186]

synergy-learning:moodle>ls -la
total 12
drwxr-xr-x   2 synergy-learning psacln     33 2008-05-18 11:16 .
drwxr-x---  36 synergy-learning psaserv 4096 2008-05-18 11:09 ..
-rw-r--r--   1 synergy-learning psacln  6186 2008-05-18 11:16 moodle-weekly-19.tgz
synergy-learning:moodle>tar xvfz moodle-weekly-19.tgz
```

This screenshot is taken from a secure shell (SSH) in a hosted environment. Four commands were used:

- `Pwd`: To make sure we are in the correct path
- `wget`: To download Moodle
- `ls -la`: To verify that the file had been downloaded correctly
- `tar xvfz`: To unpack the archive.

Once this is successful, you have to create the database that Moodle uses to store its data.

# Creating the Moodle Database and the Data Directory

Moodle requires a database where it stores information. While it is possible to share an existing database, it is highly recommended to create a separate MySQL database for Moodle. This can either be done via a web interface as provided for hosted servers or via the Unix command line.

## Using a Hosted Server

Most hosting providers provide a dedicated web interface to carry out basic database operations. Alternatively, you can use phpMyAdmin, an open-source software that allows you to manage MySQL databases over the Web. It is a part of most Linux distributions, and also a part of many control panels such as CPanel or Plesk. (phpMyAdmin is often configured to stop new databases from being created. If this is the case, you have to create the database from the database manager in CPanel or Plesk).

Once you have started phpMyAdmin, go to the **Database** section and create a new database using the **UTF** collation. You don't need to create any tables; Moodle will be populating the database during the installation process.

While you can use an existing database user account, it is good practice to create a dedicated user for the Moodle database. This step is carried out in the **Privileges** section.

Do not use the MySQL root account for your Moodle database!

phpMyAdmin allows you to perform both steps—creating a database and adding a new user—in a single action, which is shown in the following screenshot. We create a user **book** and also a database with the same name granting all privileges:

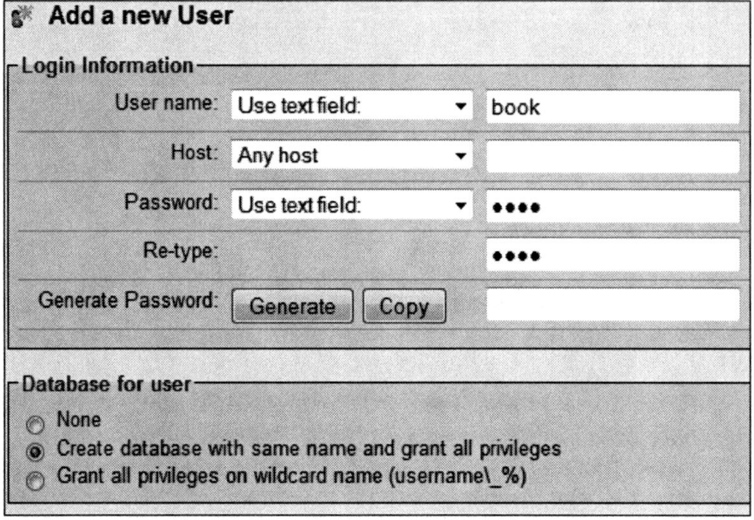


## Using the Command Line

If you don't have access to a web interface to create MySQL databases and user accounts, or if you prefer to use a Linux shell, you can perform the steps via the command line:

1. Start the database command line tool: `mysql -u root -p` and enter the password at the prompt
2. Create a database (here called **book**): `CREATE DATABASE book;` (all mysql commands have to be completed with a semicolon)
3. Set the default character set and collation order to UTF8: `ALTER DATABASE book DEFAULT CHARACTER SET utf8 COLLATE utf8_unicode_ci;`
4. Create a user and password (here both are **book**) and grant database access permissions:

   ```
   GRANT SELECT,INSERT,UPDATE,DELETE,CREATE,CREATE TEMPORARY
   TABLES,DROP,INDEX,ALTER ON book.* TO book@localhost IDENTIFIED
   BY 'book';
   ```

5. Exit the mysql command tool: `QUIT`

```
synergy-learning:moodle>mysql -u root
Welcome to the MySQL monitor.  Commands end with ; or \g.
Your MySQL connection id is 703223
Server version: 5.0.45-community MySQL Community Edition (GPL)

Type 'help;' or '\h' for help. Type '\c' to clear the buffer.

mysql> CREATE database book;
Query OK, 1 row affected (0.00 sec)

mysql> ALTER DATABASE book DEFAULT CHARACTER SET utf8 COLLATE utf8_unicode_ci;
Query OK, 1 row affected (0.00 sec)

mysql> GRANT SELECT,INSERT,UPDATE,DELETE,CREATE,CREATE TEMPORARY TABLES, DROP, INDEX, ALTER on book.*
    -> TO book@localhost IDENTIFIED BY 'book';
Query OK, 0 rows affected (0.00 sec)

mysql> QUIT
Bye
synergy-learning:moodle>
```

It is necessary to reload the grant tables using the following command line:

```
mysqladmin -u root -p reload
```

You have now completed the database setup. All we have to do now is to create Moodle's data directory before we are ready to start the installation of Moodle per se.

## Creating the Moodle Data Directory

Moodle stores most of its information in the database you have just created. However, any uploaded files such as assignments or pictures are stored in a separate directory. This data directory in Moodle is usually referred to as `moodledata`.

The location that holds your Moodle data files is referred to as **dataroot**.

Later on, the Moodle installer will attempt to create this directory, but in some setups this is not possible due to security restrictions. To be on the safer side, it is better to create `moodledata` manually or via a web-based file manager as provided by systems such as CPanel and Plesk.

1. Create the directory: `mkdir moodledata`
2. Change permissions recursively: `chmod -R 0770 moodledata` (if you use 0777, then everybody on the server will have access to the files)
3. Change user of the directory to that of your web server (usually Apache or www-data): `chown -R apache moodledata`

4. Change the group of the directory to that of your web server (usually nobody or www-data): `chgrp -R nobody moodledata`

```
synergy-learning:moodle>pwd
/home/booksyn
synergy-learning:moodle>mkdir moodledata
synergy-learning:moodle>chmod -R 770 moodledata
synergy-learning:moodle>chown -R apache moodledata
synergy-learning:moodle>chgrp -R nobody moodledata/
synergy-learning:moodle>cd moodledata
synergy-learning:moodle>ls -la
total 16
drwxrwx---  2 apache  nobody  4096 2008-06-02 14:40 .
drwx--x--x 10 booksyn booksyn 4096 2008-06-02 14:40 ..
synergy-learning:moodle>
```

It is important to create `moodledata` on your server where it cannot be accessed publicly, that is, outside your web directory! If you don't have permissions to create the data directory in a secure location, create the `.htaccess` file in your home directory containing the following two lines:

```
order deny,allow
deny from all
```

This will protect any files from being accessed without having permissions to do so.

# Running the Installer Script

The installer script performs two main actions: populating the database and creating the configuration file `config.php`. The Moodle installer is initiated by entering the URL of the `wwwroot` (the location where you copied Moodle) into your web browser. The installer will recognize that Moodle hasn't been installed yet and will start the process automatically.

The Moodle installer has to set a session cookie. If your browser has been configured to trigger a warning, make sure you accept that cookie.

The first installation screen lets you choose the language to be used during the installation. This is not the locale used for Moodle, but only the installation:

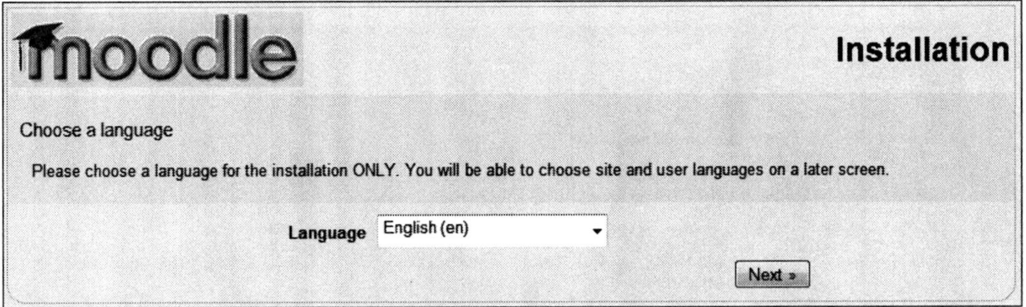


Before the Moodle installer continues, it checks that all your PHP settings are correct. If any of the tests are not passed, it is important that you go back to the software prerequisites section, resolve any problems, and restart the installation process after the issues have been fixed:

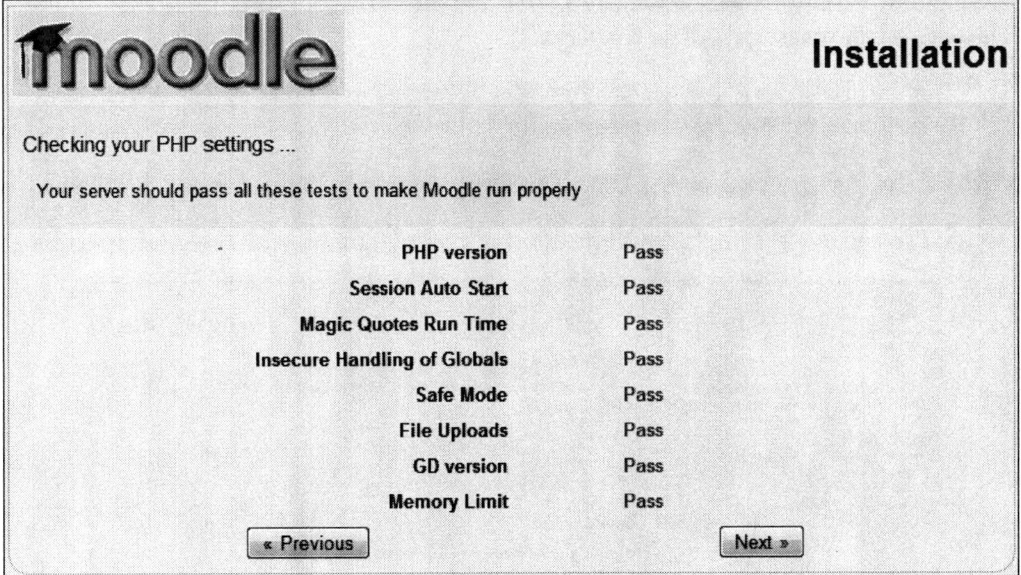

The next screen displays the expected values for the **Web address** of the site (`wwwroot`), the **Moodle Directory** (`dirroot`), and the **Data Directory** (`dataroot`). You might have to modify the data directory entry if the location of your moodledata differs:

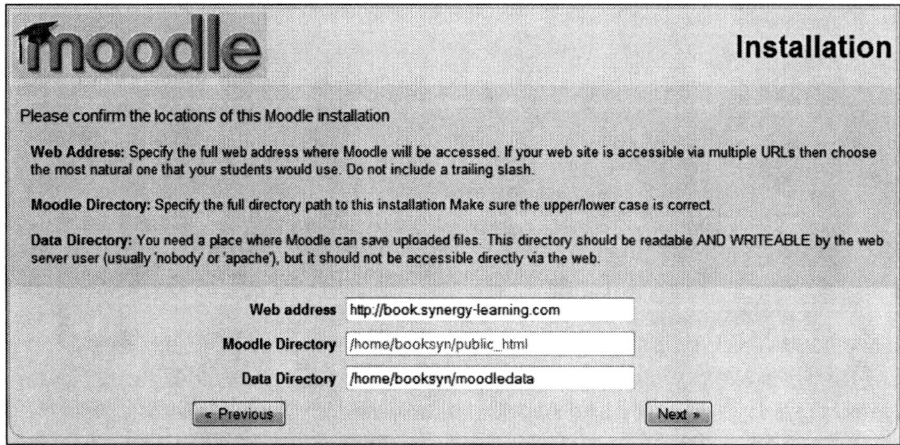


If `dataroot` cannot be located or does not have the correct permissions, the following error message will be displayed:

> "*The 'Data Directory' you specified could not be found or created. Either correct the path or create that directory manually.*"

If that is the case, go back to the **Data Directory** section to check for any problems.

The next screen deals with the configuration of your database, which we set up earlier:

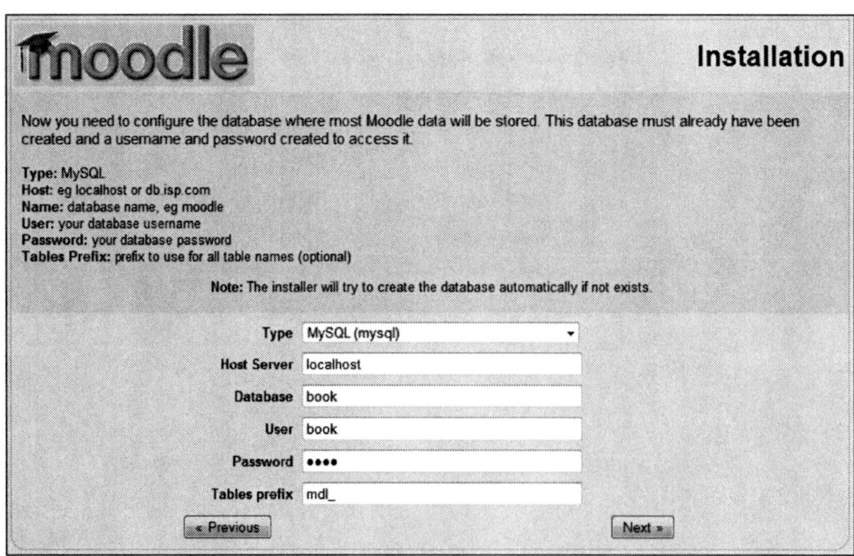

| Setting | Description |
|---|---|
| **Type** | This specifies the database type. The default is **MySQL**, which is used in this installation. If you use another database, select the appropriate choice. |
| **Host Server** | The default is localhost (or 127.0.0.1), which is correct if the database is located on the same server as the web server. If it is located on a separate server, specify the IP address (preferably unresolved to improve performance). |
| **Database** | The database name you entered when you ran the mysql command. |
| **User** | The username you entered when you ran the mysql command. |
| **Password** | The database password you entered when you ran the mysql command. |
| **Tables prefix** | All tables the Moodle installer is going to create will be prefixed with `mdl_`. This should only be changed if you run multiple Moodle installations using the same database. |

Once you are through the database details screen, the Moodle installer checks to see if a number of components are installed. Not all modules are compulsory (see the section on Prerequisites in this chapter).

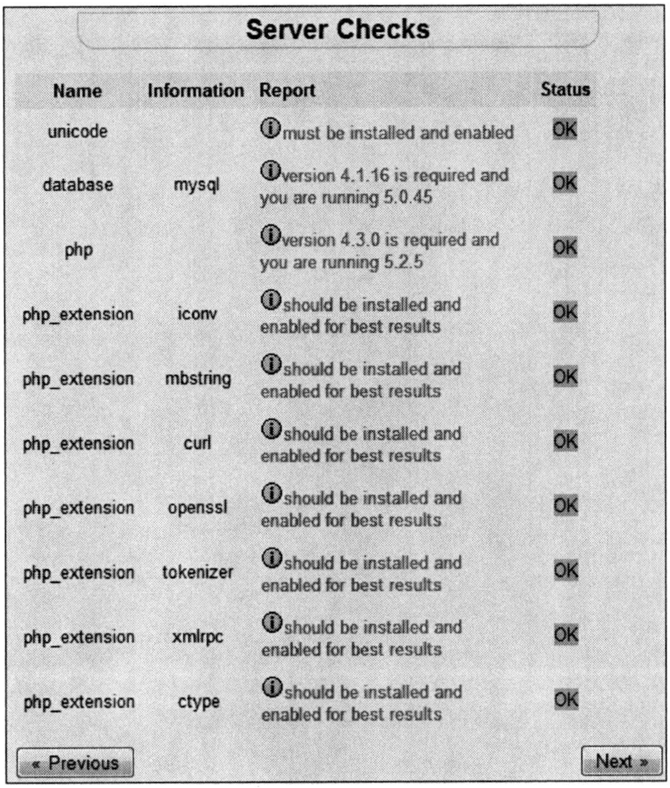

**Server Checks**

| Name | Information | Report | Status |
|---|---|---|---|
| unicode | | must be installed and enabled | OK |
| database | mysql | version 4.1.16 is required and you are running 5.0.45 | OK |
| php | | version 4.3.0 is required and you are running 5.2.5 | OK |
| php_extension | iconv | should be installed and enabled for best results | OK |
| php_extension | mbstring | should be installed and enabled for best results | OK |
| php_extension | curl | should be installed and enabled for best results | OK |
| php_extension | openssl | should be installed and enabled for best results | OK |
| php_extension | tokenizer | should be installed and enabled for best results | OK |
| php_extension | xmlrpc | should be installed and enabled for best results | OK |
| php_extension | ctype | should be installed and enabled for best results | OK |

« Previous Next »

The next screen allows you to install additional language packs that are required if you want to support languages other than the one selected for the installer. See Chapter 8 for details on language packs.

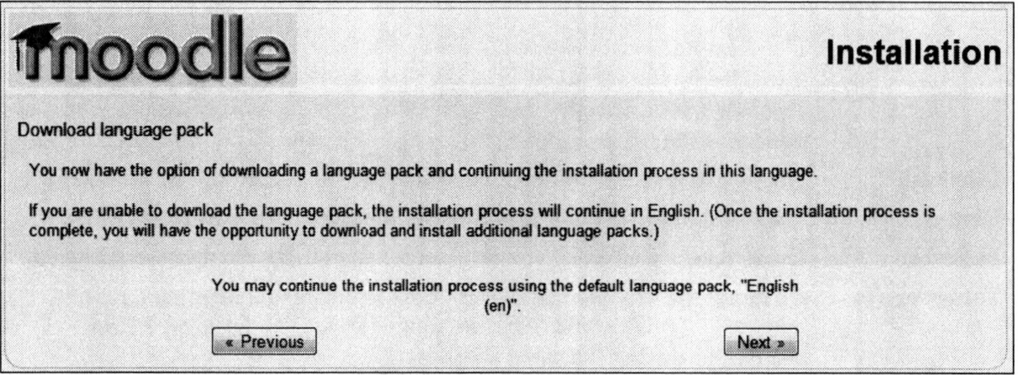


You will see in the next screen that the Moodle configuration file `config.php` has been successfully created. If the creation of the configuration file fails, the installer will let you download `config.php`. You will have to copy the text from the screen and paste it into a file called `config.php` in your `dirroot`:

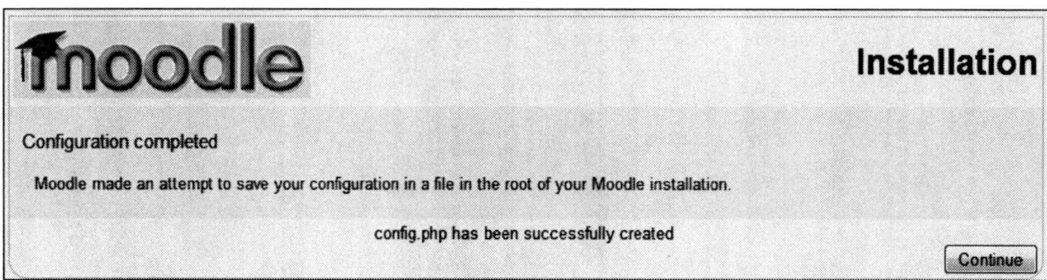


Before Moodle can proceed with the installation, you have to agree to the **GPL (General Public Licence)** agreement. You will find the full license text at `http://docs.moodle.org/en/License`:

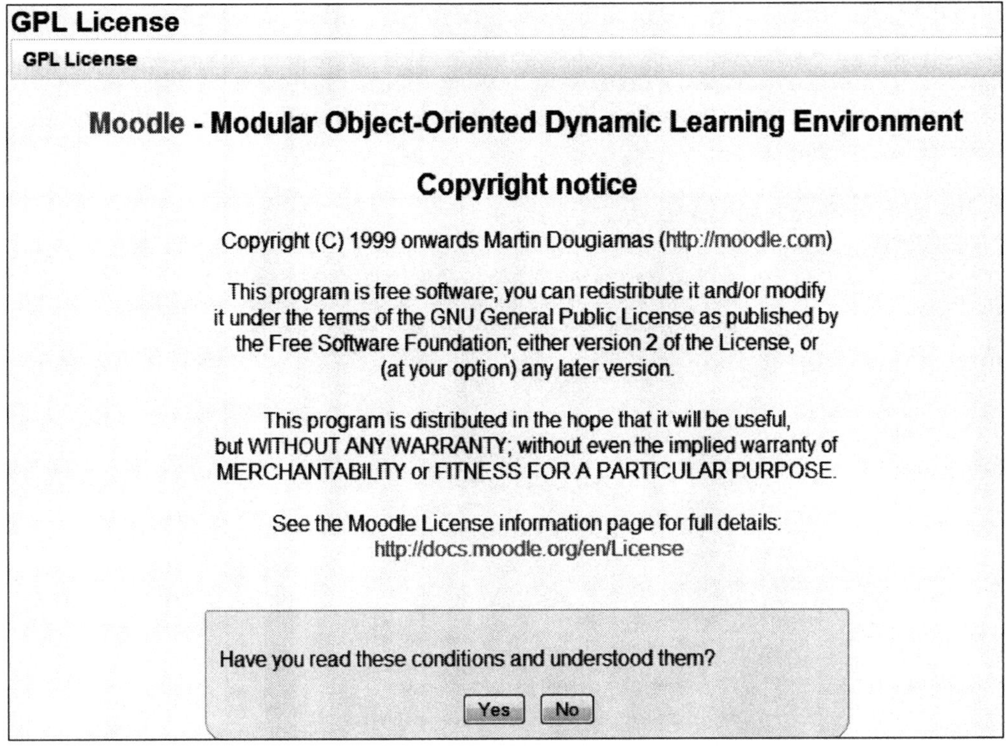

GPL License
GPL License
Moodle - Modular Object-Oriented Dynamic Learning Environment
Copyright notice
Copyright (C) 1999 onwards Martin Dougiamas (http://moodle.com)
This program is free software; you can redistribute it and/or modify it under the terms of the GNU General Public License as published by the Free Software Foundation; either version 2 of the License, or (at your option) any later version.
This program is distributed in the hope that it will be useful, but WITHOUT ANY WARRANTY; without even the implied warranty of MERCHANTABILITY or FITNESS FOR A PARTICULAR PURPOSE.
See the Moodle License information page for full details: http://docs.moodle.org/en/License
Have you read these conditions and understood them?
Yes
No


This screen is followed by the current release information that includes the version and built to be installed as well as a link to the current release notes.

Once this screen has been confirmed, the Moodle installer will create all tables in the database. If you untick the **Unattended operation** option, each screen will have to be confirmed. Unless this is your first installation or you have encountered problems with previous installations, it is usually not necessary to run the rest of the installation in attended operation mode:

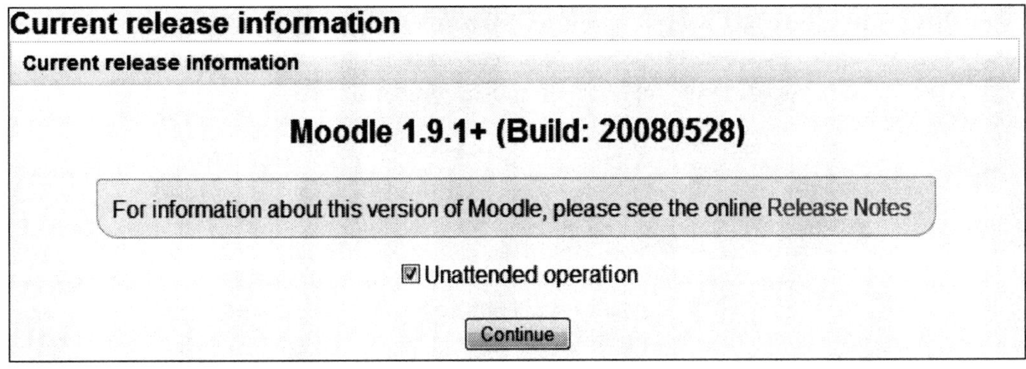

Once the table creation and population have been concluded, you will see the screen to set up the administrator account. The default username is **admin**, which can be changed. The self-explanatory fields you have to fill in are **password, First name**, **Surname, Email address, City/town**, and **country**. All other fields are explained in great detail in Chapter 5.

**Setup administrator account**

On this page you should configure your main administrator account which will have complete control over the site. Make sure you give it a secure username and password as well as a valid email address. You can create more admin accounts later on.

General

Show Advanced

| | |
|---|---|
| Username* | admin |
| New password* | ••••• Unmask |
| Force password change | |
| First name* | Alex |
| Surname* | Büchner |
| Email address* | packt@synergy-learning.com |
| Email display | Allow everyone to see my email address |
| Email activated | This email address is enabled |
| City/town* | Belfast |
| Select a country* | United Kingdom |
| Timezone | Server's local time |
| Preferred language | English (en) |

The last screen of the installation script asks you to enter some **Front Page settings**, namely the **Full site name**, the **Short name** of your site, and a **Site description**. These front page settings can be modified later on (see Chapter 7 for detailed explanation).

Once this information has been entered and the screen has been confirmed, you are ready to start using Moodle. However, it is recommended to finalize the installation and to set up the execution of the Moodle maintenance script.

# Finalizing the Installation

To make sure that Moodle is running without problems, go to **Notifications** in the **Site Administration** block. Your installation has been successful if the following screen is displayed:

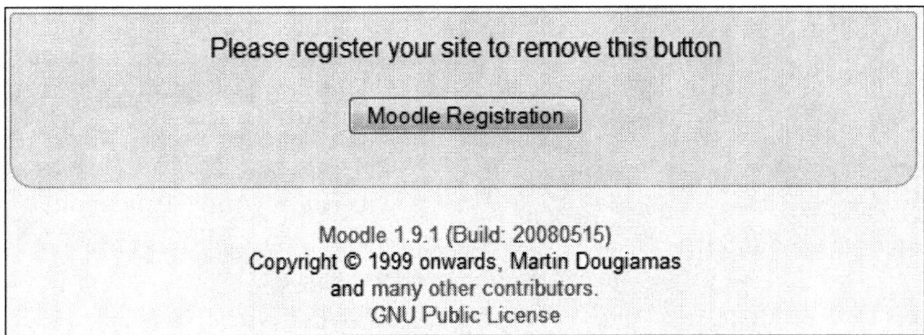

Please register your site to remove this button
Moodle Registration
Moodle 1.9.1 (Build: 20080515)
Copyright © 1999 onwards, Martin Dougiamas
and many other contributors.
GNU Public License


Moodle provides some statistics about its usage on `http://moodle.org/stats`. To be included in these figures, you have to register your Moodle site. Registration is optional and free, and you decide which information will be made public. You will get occasional notices from `moodle.org`, for example about advance security alerts.

Moodle states that once you are registered the **Moodle Registration** button will be removed, which is not the case. The fact that the button remains actually makes sense, as it is used to change any of your registration details at a later stage:

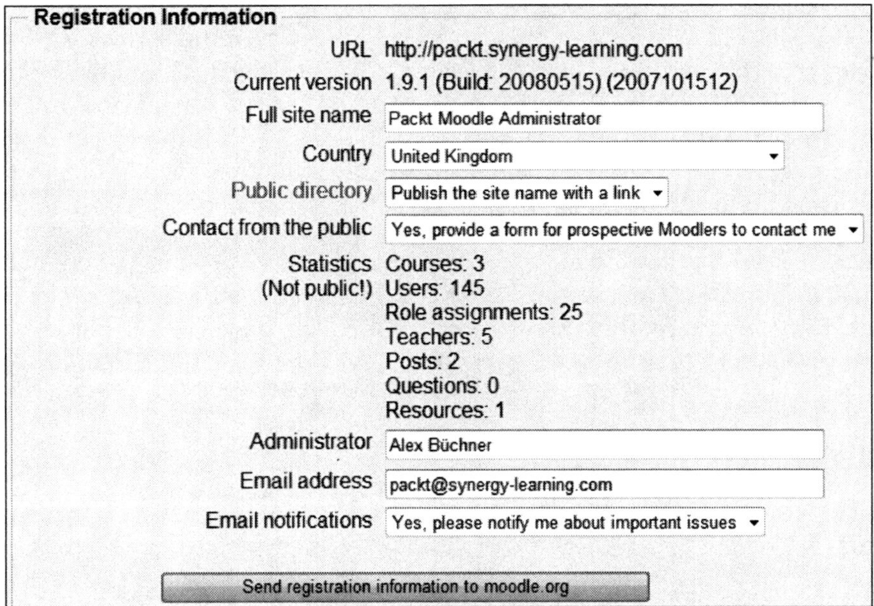

Registration Information
URL http://packt.synergy-learning.com
Current version 1.9.1 (Build: 20080515) (2007101512)
Full site name Packt Moodle Administrator
Country United Kingdom
Public directory Publish the site name with a link
Contact from the public Yes, provide a form for prospective Moodlers to contact me
Statistics (Not public!) Courses: 3
Users: 145
Role assignments: 25
Teachers: 5
Posts: 2
Questions: 0
Resources: 1
Administrator Alex Büchner
Email address packt@synergy-learning.com
Email notifications Yes, please notify me about important issues
Send registration information to moodle.org

The settings of the registration screen are as follows:

| Field | Description |
|---|---|
| **URL** | URL of your Moodle site. |
| **Current version** | Moodle version and build. |
| **Country** | Select the country in which your organization is located. |
| **Public directory** | You have the options to:<br>• Please do not publish this site.<br>• Publish the site name only.<br>• Publish the site name with a link (default). |
| **Contact from the public** | By default, Moodle creates a form for other Moodle users to contact you, which can be turned off. |
| **Statistics** | Some statistics regarding the number of courses, users, role assignments, teachers, forum posts, questions, and resources. This information will not be displayed to the public. |
| **Administrator** | Your name. |
| **Email address** | Your email address. |
| **Email notifications** | By default, Moodle emails you important information such as upgrades and security issues. |

# Setting up the Cron Process

Moodle has to perform a number of background tasks on a regular basis. The script that is performing these tasks is known as a cron script, which is executed by the so-called cron process. An entire page has been dedicated in the Moodle documentation and you can find it at `http://docs.moodle.org/en/Cron`. It is important that you set up the cron process. Otherwise, any timed Moodle features such as scheduled backups, sending forum notifications, statistics processing, and so on will not work.

The script `cron.php` is located in the admin directory and can be triggered manually through a web browser (unless your security settings have been changed). Once executed, the output from the script (`http://yoursite/admin/cron.php`) is shown on screen and you have to navigate back to your Moodle system manually.

Most control panels allow you to set up scheduled tasks via their interface. The following is a screenshot from the widely used Plesk system that executes the script every **5** minutes:



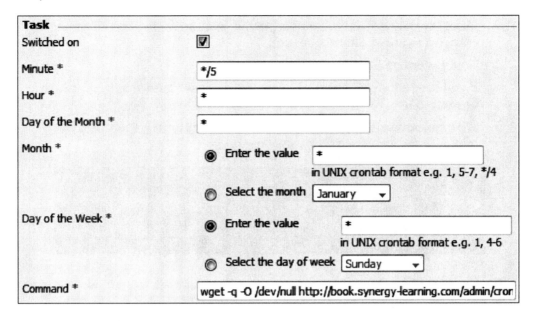

There are a number of ways to call the cron script. `wget -q -O /dev/null http://<yoursite>/admin/cron.php` is the most popular option in a Linux environment (see **Command** in the preceding screenshot). However, if this does not suit your environment, check out `http://docs.moodle.org/en/Cron` for alternatives.

The above interface creates an entry in the **crontab**, a file located in the `/etc` directory that contains all system-wide cron entries. This file can also be added manually using `crontab -e`, but be careful to get the syntax right.

This concludes the entire installation process of Moodle. If you have come across any problems that have not been covered in these instructions, or your setup differs from the one described, go to `http://docs.moodle.org/en/Installing_Moodle` where more installation details are provided along with exceptions covered in great detail.

# Installation in a Windows Environment

XAMPP is a free Apache distribution that contains MySQL and PHP (as well as Perl). It exists for a number of operating systems. The Moodle distribution for Windows makes full use of XAMPP, and is located at `http://download.moodle.org/windows`. The installation works on Windows XP, Windows Vista, and Windows Server 2003.

Once downloaded, follow these steps:

1. Copy the distribution to a directory on your PC and unzip the archive in your directory of choice.
2. Make sure any software that uses port 80 (such as Skype) is not running or change it to use an alternative port.
3. Double-click on **Start Moodle.exe**.
4. If you have a firewall installed, allow the database service `mysqld.exe` to be executed.
5. A command line window will appear, which has to stay open. You can minimize the window, but do not close it.

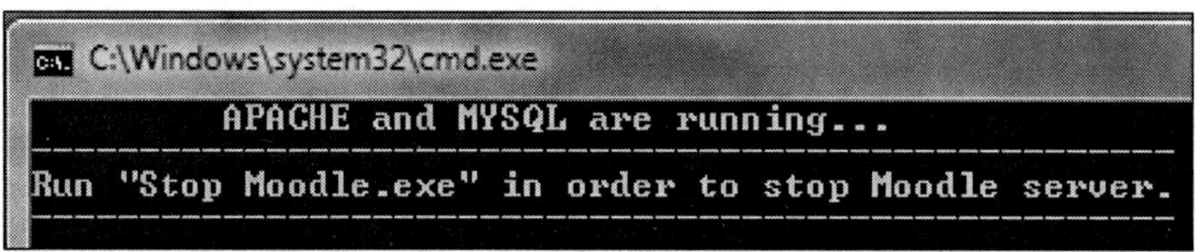
C:\Windows\system32\cmd.exe
APACHE and MYSQL are running...
Run "Stop Moodle.exe" in order to stop Moodle server.

6. Go to your web browser and enter `http://localhost` to your address bar.
7. You will see an installer being launched, which is the same one described for the LAMP environment. All values have already been populated; all you have to do is navigate through all the screens until you see the familiar **Setup administrator account**. This process will take a few minutes.
8. Enter the administrator details and select **Update Profile**.
9. Enter the **Front Page settings** for your site.
10. Check that no warnings are displayed in the **Notifications** area in the **Site Administration** block.

That's it! Your Moodle system is now up and running. You are now able to use Moodle locally or from a web browser on another machine as long as your IP address is accessible via the network you are in.

The XAMPP-based Moodle distribution is only suitable for servers with a small number of users. For larger Windows installations, you have to install Moodle manually or with Microsoft IIS (check out `http://download.moodle.org/windows` for details).

To stop using Moodle, double-click on **Stop Moodle.exe**. If you have a firewall installed, allow `myadmin.exe` to be executed.

```
C:\Windows\system32\cmd.exe
MySQL stop ...
Apache killed ...
apache.exe        (7504)
apache.exe        (3760)
Apache pid delete ... SHUTDOWN COMPLETE!
------------------------
Thanks for using Moodle.
------------------------
Press any key to continue . . .
```

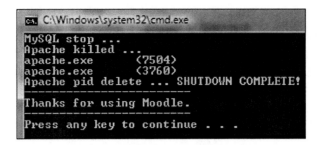

Instead of starting and stopping Moodle manually, you can start Apache and MySQL automatically as Windows services. In the `server` directory of your Moodle system you find an executable called `service.exe`, which you have to run with the `-install` parameter as administrator, for example:

```
C:/moodle/server/service.exe -install
```

# Installation in a Mac OS X Environment

MAMP is a free distribution that contains Apache, MySQL, and PHP for Mac OS X. The Moodle distributions for Mac OS X (10.4 or higher) are available as Intel and PPC versions, located at `http://download.moodle.org/macosx`. Once downloaded, follow these steps:

1. Double-click on the downloaded DMG file to start the installation. This will open a screen explaining the rest of the installation process.

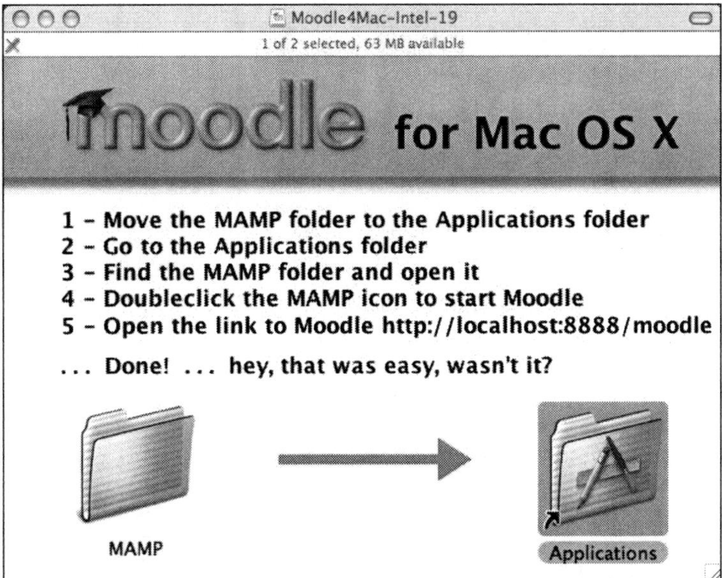

2. Drag the `MAMP` folder on this screen onto the **Applications** icon, which will copy the Moodle system and its required components.
3. Open the `MAMP` folder in **Applications** where you will find two relevant icons.

4. Double-click on the **MAMP** icon to start Apache and MySQL. There is also a **MAMP Control Widget** in the same directory, which you might want to install.

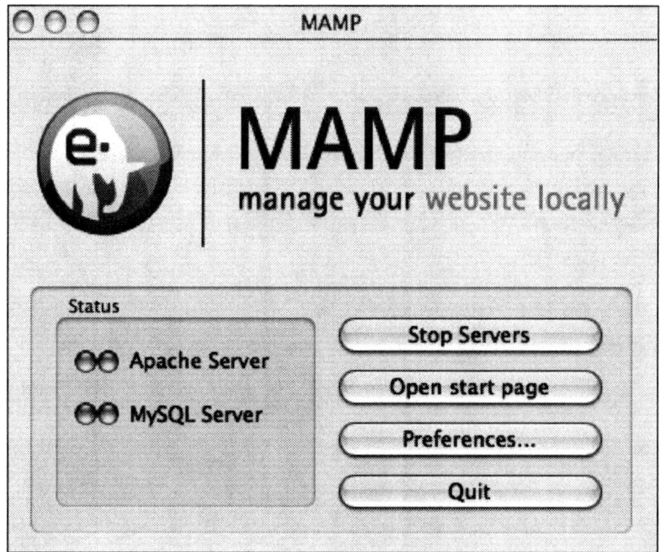


5. Double-click on the **Link to Moodle** icon, which opens `http://localhost:8888/moodle` on your default web browser.

And that's it! An installation cannot be easier than that. You don't even have to go through the installation process. Moodle is pre-configured and you are ready to go.

The default password for the admin account is **12345**. You should change this in the user profile.

The directory also includes a shell script called `UpdateMoodle19.sh` (requires CVS to be installed). When you double-click on the file, the script will be executed that downloads the latest version of Moodle and installs it on your Mac. On all other operating systems you will have to go through a more cumbersome update process, which is described next:

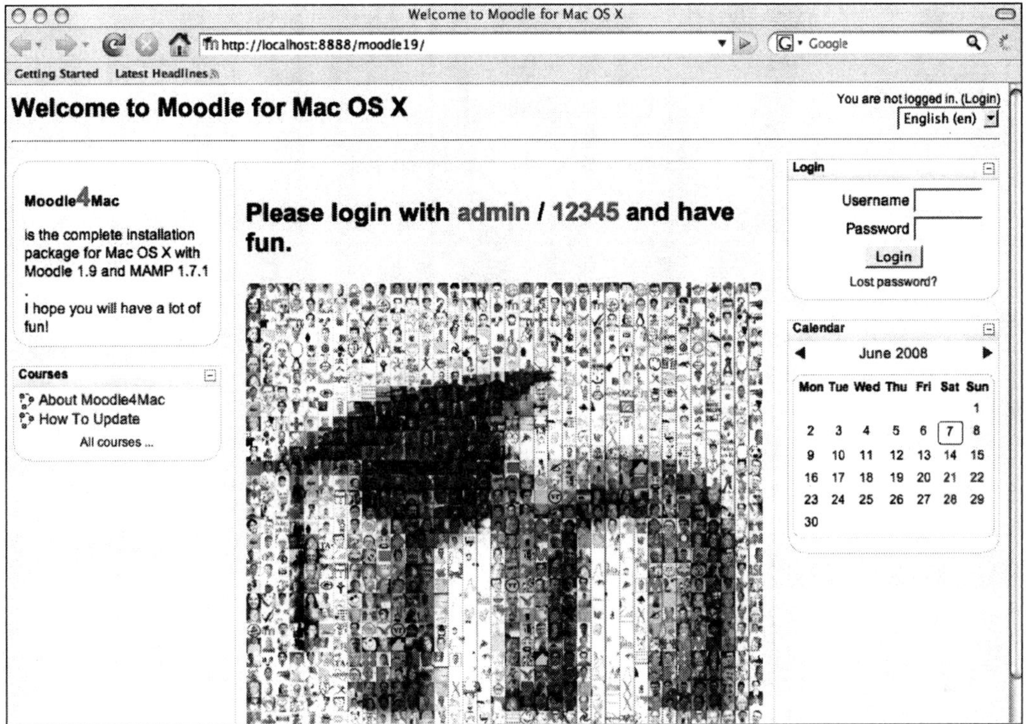


# Updating Moodle

Moodle is updated constantly. It is a common practice in open-source development environments. A new version is created every night and, as mentioned above, a fully tested version is released on a weekly basis. There is usually no need to install updates every week. However, there are a number of scenarios when you should upgrade your Moodle system:

- Security patches have been released
- New features have been added
- Bugs have been fixed that affect your setup
- A new version is released

There are principally two ways Moodle systems can be updated. You either run updates manually or stay up-to-date using the CVS command. Both procedures are described in this section.

Either way, before you start, make sure you put Moodle in **Maintenance mode** to ensure that no other user is logged in during the update. Go to **Server | Maintenance mode**, enter a maintenance message, and **Enable** the **Maintenance mode:**

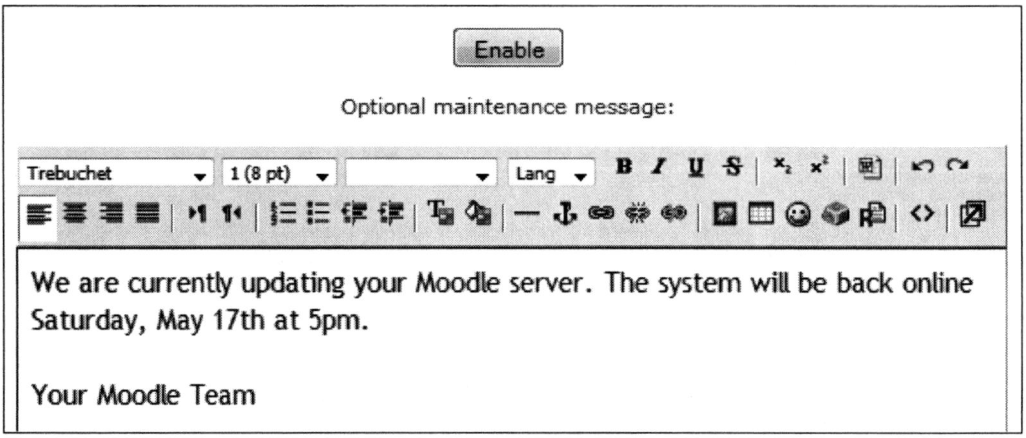


## Manual Update

The process for updating a Moodle system is as follows:

1. Create a backup.
2. Create new Moodle system.
3. Install update.

If you are updating from a previous version of Moodle, the process is the same. However, double-check the **Upgrading** document at `http://docs.moodle.org/en/Upgrading` for any version-specific issues.

> You cannot jump directly to any major version while updating Moodle.

For example, if your current Moodle system is on version 1.6 and you wish to update to version 1.9, you first have to update to version 1.7, then 1.8, and finally the latest version of 1.9. However, you can update from 1.9 straight to 1.9.2.

# Creating a Backup

Before you install a new update, it is highly recommended that you run a backup of your Moodle system. While most updates will run smoothly, the backup will be required if you have to revert back to the pre-update version. There are three parts that have to be backed up:

- Database

  There are two ways you can create a so-called database dump from a MySQL database, either via command line or via Moodle's optional database interface.

  The simplest syntax for the command line tool is:

  ```
  mysqldump -u <user> -p <database> > backup.sql
  ```

  If you have to restore the database, you have to use the mysql command line tool as follows:

  ```
  mysql -u <user> -p <database> < backup.sql
  ```

  The interface for the database tool is accessed via **Server | Database**. This is an optional module, and has to be installed separately (it is the MySQL Admin add-on—see Chapter 13 for more details).

  Click on the **Export** link on the front page, select the database to export, and press **Go**. The output of the command will be displayed on screen.

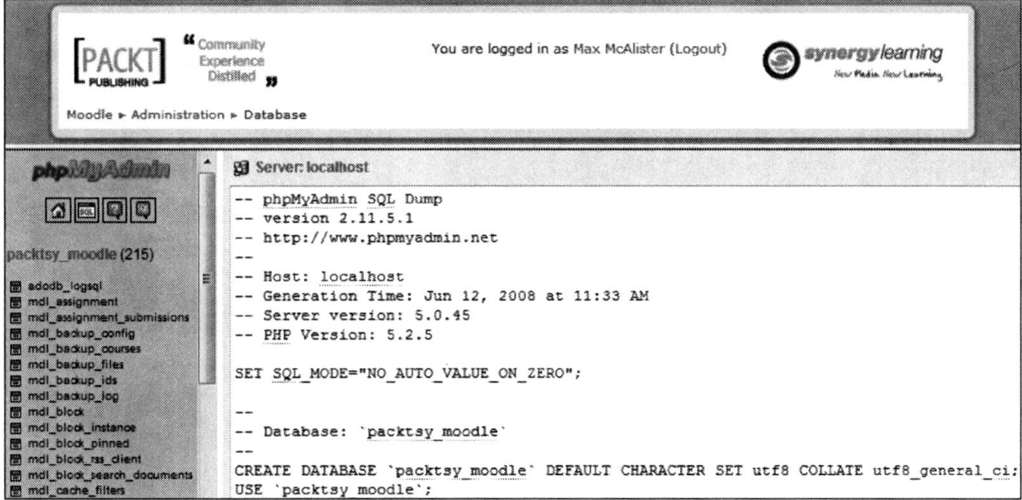


- Data directory

  This is the `moodledata` directory. Create a copy of this elsewhere on the server (using `cp -R`) or create an archive using the tar command (`tar -cvf moodledata`).

- Moodle

  This is the Moodle software. Create a copy of the directory elsewhere on the server. While only some parts of this backup are required (`config.php`, added themes, modified language packs, and so on), it is a good practice to create a backup of the entire software. Finally, rename your Moodle system from moodle to say, moodle.old. (`mv moodle moodle.old`).

## Creating New Moodle System

Once you have created a backup it is time to download the new version of Moodle. This is done in the same way as described during the installation process.

First, create a new moodle directory (`dirroot`) and copy the new version in that location (using the same unzip or tar command as during the installation). Also make sure the permissions as well as user and group are correct.

Now, copy the following files and directories from your `moodle.old` directory to your new `dirroot`. Existing files have to be overwritten:

- `config.php`
- `.htaccess` (only if present)
- Any theme folders that have been created
- Any modified language packs

That's it. Next time you start Moodle, the update script will kick in. We'll go through it next.

## Running the Update Script

Once you go to the location of your Moodle site and log in as adminstrator, the system will recognize that a new version is available and kick off the installer automatically.

The first screen displays the old and the new version of Moodle (here 1.9 and 1.9.1, respectively), and asks you to confirm that you wish to go ahead with the upgrade:

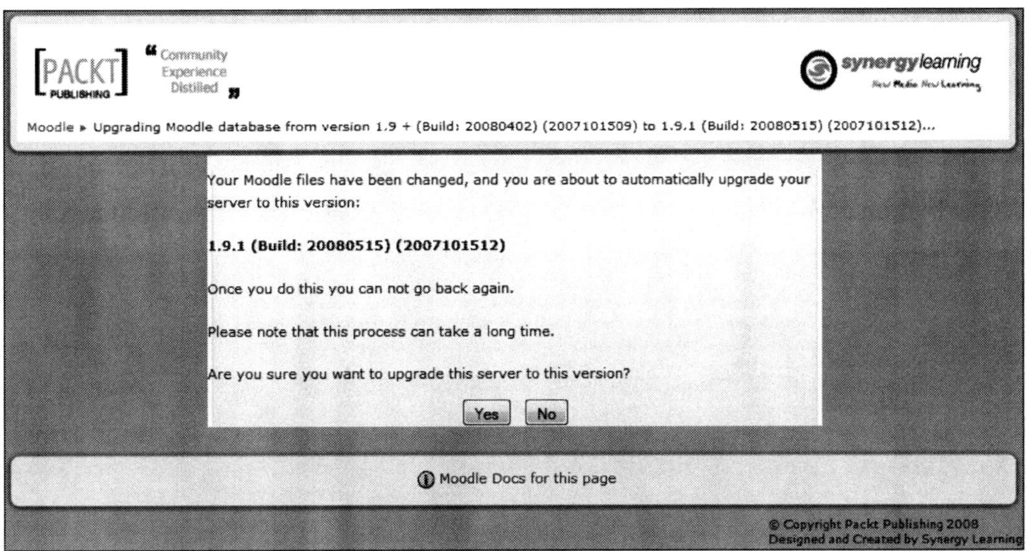

[PACKT] PUBLISHING
"Community Experience Distilled"
synergylearning
Moodle ▸ Upgrading Moodle database from version 1.9 + (Build: 20080402) (2007101509) to 1.9.1 (Build: 20080515) (2007101512)...
Your Moodle files have been changed, and you are about to automatically upgrade your server to this version:
1.9.1 (Build: 20080515) (2007101512)
Once you do this you can not go back again.
Please note that this process can take a long time.
Are you sure you want to upgrade this server to this version?
Yes
No
Moodle Docs for this page
© Copyright Packt Publishing 2008
Designed and Created by Synergy Learning


Next, a screen is displayed that provides a link to the release notes and performs the same server check as the one described during the installation:

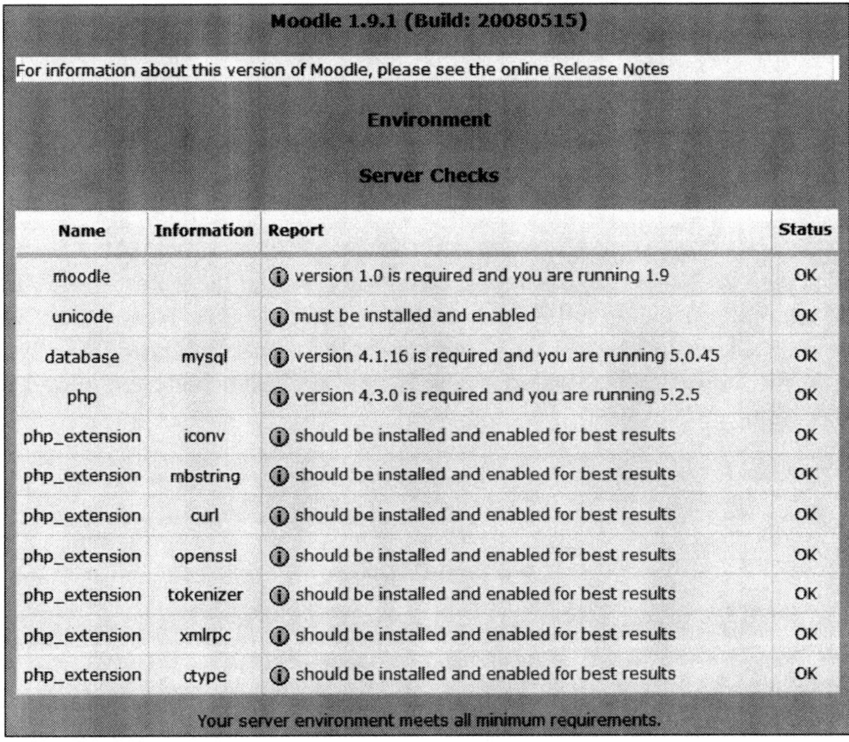

Moodle 1.9.1 (Build: 20080515)

For information about this version of Moodle, please see the online Release Notes

Environment

Server Checks

| Name | Information | Report | Status |
|---|---|---|---|
| moodle | | version 1.0 is required and you are running 1.9 | OK |
| unicode | | must be installed and enabled | OK |
| database | mysql | version 4.1.16 is required and you are running 5.0.45 | OK |
| php | | version 4.3.0 is required and you are running 5.2.5 | OK |
| php_extension | iconv | should be installed and enabled for best results | OK |
| php_extension | mbstring | should be installed and enabled for best results | OK |
| php_extension | curl | should be installed and enabled for best results | OK |
| php_extension | openssl | should be installed and enabled for best results | OK |
| php_extension | tokenizer | should be installed and enabled for best results | OK |
| php_extension | xmlrpc | should be installed and enabled for best results | OK |
| php_extension | ctype | should be installed and enabled for best results | OK |

Your server environment meets all minimum requirements.

Moodle plug-ins—core or third-party—sometimes cause problems while upgrading Moodle. The installer lists all components and states whether they are **Standard**, **Non-Standard**, or **Incompatible**. If the latter is the case, either replace the add-on with a compatible version, or remove it from the system via the provided **Delete** option. See Chapter 13 for more details.

At the bottom of the screen you can select the familiar **unattended operation** mode:

**Plugins check**

The following tables show the modules, blocks and filters that have been detected in your current Moodle installation; They indicate which plugins are standard, and which are not. All non-standard plugins should be checked and upgraded to their most recent versions before continuing with this Moodle upgrade.

**Activity module**

| Directory | Name | Status |
|---|---|---|
| mod/assignment | Assignment | Standard |
| mod/chat | Chat | Standard |
| mod/choice | Choice | Standard |
| mod/data | Database | Standard |
| mod/forum | Forum | Standard |
| mod/glossary | Glossary | Standard |
| mod/hotpot | Hot Potatoes Quiz | Standard |
| mod/journal | Journal | Standard |
| mod/label | Label | Standard |
| mod/lams | LAMS | Standard |
| mod/lesson | Lesson | Standard |
| mod/quiz | Quiz | Standard |
| mod/resource | Resource | Standard |

**Blocks**

| Directory | Name | Status |
|---|---|---|
| blocks/activity_modules | Activities | Standard |
| blocks/admin | Administration | Standard |
| blocks/admin_bookmarks | Admin bookmarks | Standard |
| blocks/admin_tree | Site Administration | Standard |
| blocks/blog_menu | Blog Menu | Standard |
| blocks/blog_tags | Blog Tags | Standard |
| blocks/calendar_month | Calendar | Standard |
| blocks/calendar_upcoming | Upcoming Events | Standard |
| blocks/course_list | Course List | Standard |
| blocks/course_summary | Course/Site Description | Standard |
| blocks/glossary_random | Random Glossary Entry | Standard |

**Filters**

| Directory | Name | Status |
|---|---|---|
| filter/activitynames | Activity Names Auto-linking | Standard |
| filter/algebra | Algebra Notation | Standard |
| filter/censor | Word Censorship | Standard |
| filter/emailprotect | Email Protection | Standard |
| filter/mediaplugin | Multimedia Plugins | Standard |
| filter/multilang | Multi-Language Content | Standard |
| filter/tex | TeX Notation | Standard |
| filter/tidy | Tidy | Standard |

Once this screen is confirmed, the actual installation starts. It creates new database fields and modifies any data fields as and when necessary. Any new system settings that have been added to Moodle are shown and can be changed straightaway. For example, in the following screenshot a new **Blogs** parameter has been added to the **Backups** section:

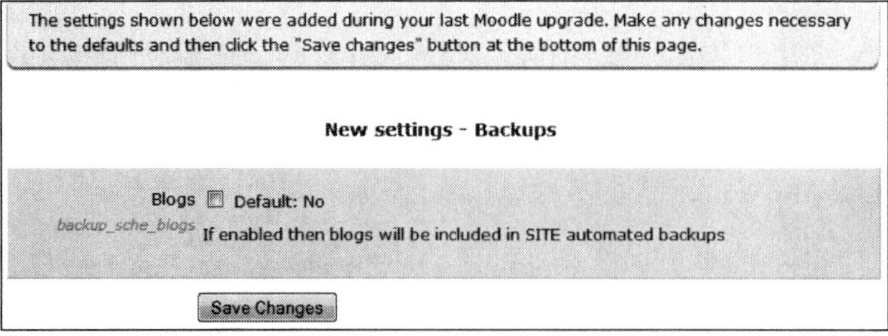
The settings shown below were added during your last Moodle upgrade. Make any changes necessary to the defaults and then click the "Save changes" button at the bottom of this page.
New settings - Backups
Blogs
Default: No
backup_sche_blogs
If enabled then blogs will be included in SITE automated backups
Save Changes

Once the upgrade process is completed, make sure you check the **Notifications** page as done under Windows environment installation. Also, don't forget to turn off the **Maintenance mode**.

# Update via CVS

An alternative approach exists to keep the current version up-to-date. It uses CVS, which is an open-source concurrent versioning system. All checked-in Moodle code is made available via this method, which allows you to update only the modules that have actually changed.

CVS has to be installed on your Moodle server. The first time you use CVS, you have to download the full version of Moodle:

```
cvs -z3 -d:pserver:anonymous@<mirror>:/cvsroot/moodle co -d
<directory> -r <version> Moodle
```

Select the nearest `<mirror>` from the following list. `<directory>` is the location where your Moodle system is installed. Specify the `<version>` you wish to install, for example MOODLE_19_WEEKLY or MOODLE_19_STABLE.

In addition to the main Moodle CVS repository, there are currently five CVS mirrors as shown in the list:

| Country | Server |
|---|---|
| Spain | es.cvs.moodle.org |
| UK | uk.cvs.moodle.org and eu.cvs.moodle.org |
| US | us.cvs.moodle.org and us2.cvs.moodle.org |

Once this has been successful, go to your Moodle site and you will be guided through the same update process as just explained. If this fails, check that the user and group permissions are set correctly and adjust them accordingly (`chown -R <user>:<group> moodle`).

For further updates, you should use the following command that remembers your previous settings such as the chosen mirror site:

```
cvs update -dP
```

For further options of how to use CVS from the command line and in operating systems other than Unix, check out `http://docs.moodle.org/en/CVS_for_Administrators`.

Because CVS is a shell command tool, it is possible to fully automate the updating process. However, if you have changed any core code, potential conflicts might arise that have to be resolved (CVS will prompt you to do so).

You might also come across some conflicting advice regarding whether to use CVS for production sites or not. The advantage is that your system is always up-to-date and that the updates are carried out automatically. The disadvantage is that the update process might require intervention to resolve any conflicts, or it might fail, especially when a lot of third-party add-ons have been employed.

# Summary

In this chapter, you have learned how to install Moodle on the most popular operating systems and also how to upgrade the VLE.

The fact that Moodle uses portable software architecture and facilitates standard open-source components allows the installation on multiple platforms. However, this also means that different idiosyncrasies have to be considered in different environments.

Now that your system is up and running, let's have a look at the components of Moodle that will provide you with a better understanding of the system and the ways to administer it.

# 3

# The Moodle System

Now that your Moodle system is up and running, we will look at the building blocks of the learning platform. The topics we will cover are:

- Moodle architecture:

  In this section, you will learn what the main components of Moodle are and where its data is stored.

- Finding your way around in Moodle:

  Moodle has an intuitive user interface that takes little time to get used to. You will learn the main navigation and also where to find help in case it is required.

- File management:

  Dealing with files in web-based applications is not always straightforward. You will learn the different options of how to deal with this, which cover:

  - Moodle File Management
  - Web Host File Management
  - File Management via FTP
  - File Management via WebDAV

## Moodle Architecture

We will first look at the overall LAMP architecture on which Moodle is based, before we cover the internal components of the VLE layer.

# The LAMP Architecture

Moodle is developed on the **open-source LAMP framework** consisting of Linux (operating system), Apache (web server), MySQL (database), and PHP (programming language). Due to the portability of these components and the modularity of Moodle itself (that's what the "M" stands for), it can support a wide range of operating systems, database systems, and web servers. A simple overview of the LAMP architecture can be shown as follows:

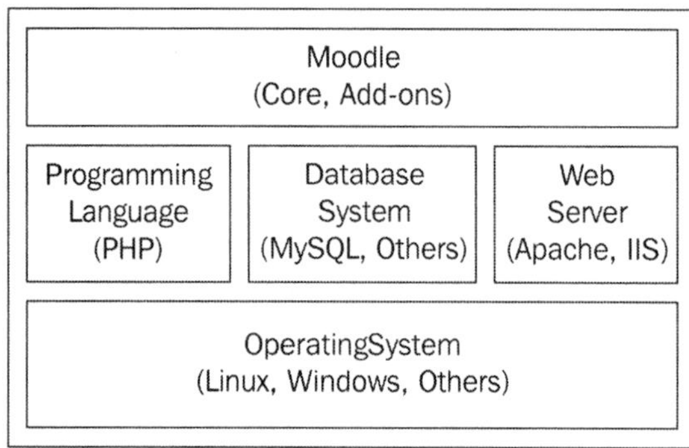


The lowest level is the **Operating System**. While Linux is the preferred platform, other UNIX derivatives such as Solaris and AIX are supported as well, along with Windows and Mac OS X. Certain libraries will have to be installed, a topic we covered in the previous chapter on installation.

**PHP** is the **Programming Language** in which Moodle is developed (accompanied by HTML and CSS files). It is the only component that cannot be replaced with any counterpart.

**MySQL** is the database of choice for most open-source applications, but other database systems such as PostgreSQL, Oracle, and Microsoft SQL Server too work without problems. Again, detailed information has been provided in the chapter on installation.

Apache has become the de-facto standard for the large-scale web applications, closely followed by Microsoft IIS. Both the web servers are supported like any others offering a PHP support.

The interaction of the elements in the Moodle architecture is shown in the following image:

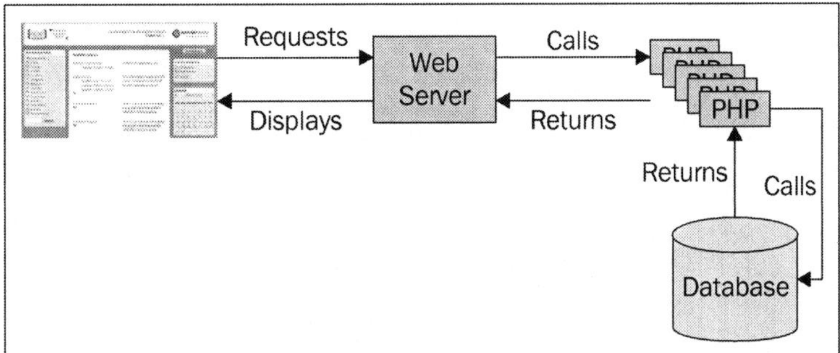


The user makes **Requests** via the web browser interface (for example, display a learning resource). The web browser passes the request on to the **Web Server**, which calls the PHP module that is responsible for the call. The **PHP** module **Calls** the **Database** with an action (query, update, insert, or delete operation) that **Returns** the requested data. Based on this information, the PHP module returns data (usually in the form of HTML code) to the web server, which passes the information to be displayed back to the user's browser.

# The Moodle Layer

Now, let's look at the Moodle layer in more detail. The main building blocks of Moodle are shown in the following image:

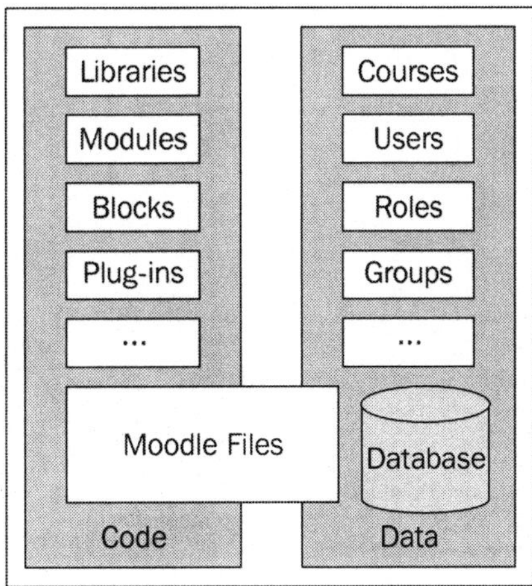

Moodle distinguishes between **Code** (mostly written in PHP, HTML, and CSS) and **Data** (values added in the configuration files via the Moodle interface, or manually).

Moodle **Libraries**, **Modules** (such as resources and activities), **Blocks**, **Plug-ins**, and other units are represented in a code. The code is always stored in files within the Moodle directory structure. The code includes all the elements that deal with the back-end (server) and front-end (user interface) operations.

The data regarding Moodle courses, users, roles, groups, and so on (for example, grades) is mostly stored in the Moodle database. However, certain data, such as user pictures, is stored in specific files or directories.

Now let's have a look at how the Moodle files area, that is, the directory structure is organized.

# Code and Data Locations

Though Moodle takes care of the organization of its code and data, it is good to know where a file is located in your learning system.

All the system files, that is, the files that are required to run Moodle, are located in a number of directories under `$CFG->dirroot` (the root directory of your Moodle installation). These files are potentially replaced when updating Moodle. The structure is as follows (All directories are located on the same level. However, some folders contain sub-directories.):

- `Admin`-code to administrate the server
- `auth`-plug-ins to authenticate the users
- `backup`- code for backup and restore operations
- `blocks`-plug-ins for Moodle blocks
- `blog-code` -for Moodle blogging facility
- `calendar`-code to manage and display calendars
- `course`- code to display and manage courses
- `enroll`-plug-ins to enroll the users
- `error`-code for error-handling
- `files`-code to display and manage the uploaded files
- `filter`-plug-ins for Moodle filters
- `grade`-code to manage the gradebook functionality and reports
- `group`-code to handle groups and groupings
- `install`-code to install Moodle

- `iplookup`-code for looking up IP addresses
- `lang`-localization strings; one directory per language
- `lib`-libraries of the core Moodle code
- `login`-code to handle login and account creation
- `message`-code for the messaging tool
- `mnet`-code to handle the Moodle networking
- `mod`-code of the main Moodle course modules
- `my-code` to handle myMoodle
- `notes`-code to handle notes in the user profiles
- `pix`-generic site graphics
- `question`-code to deal with the question bank
- `rss`-code to handle the RSS feeds
- `search`-code to perform searches
- `sso`-code for single sign-on operations
- `tag`-code for tagging
- `theme`-Moodle themes
- `user`-code to display and manage the users
- `userpix`-code to handle the user pictures (currently not used)

Moodle data that includes everything the users have added to the system such as learning resources by teachers, forum posts, or assignments by students, and system settings by the administrator, is stored in two locations:

1. Data stored in the database
2. Data stored in the `$CFG->dataroot` directory (called "moodledata" by default)

Moodle stores almost all data in the used database, except for the files. Only a link for the files is stored in the database, and the actual files are stored in a directory specified by the `$CFG->dataroot` variable in `config.php`. This is called as moodledata directory and is organized as follows:

```
1             Front page files
2             Files for course number 2
3             Files for course number 3
cache         Caching data
sessions      User session data
temp          Temporary file
upgradelogs   Log file for each Moodle upgrade that has been performed
user          User-related data
```

At creation, each course is allocated a unique number, which is also used as the name for the sub-directory. The exception is the front page, which is treated as a course but is always given the number "one".

> To detect what ID a course has been allocated, take the cursor over the course name and the link will look something like this: `http://.../course/view.php?id=5`. The number that follows the ID is the number of the course, which is five in this case.
>
> When problems occur, or before carrying out a Moodle update, it is sometimes necessary to delete the caching data, user sessions, and any other temporary information Moodle has created. This data is located in the respective directories in the structure shown previously. This is important, since once everybody has logged out, you can safely delete any files in the directories' cache, sessions, and temp, respectively.

# Finding Your Way Around in Moodle

As an administrator, you will be performing most tasks from the Site Administration block on the front page. So we will cover all aspects of the menus and sub-menus in the book.

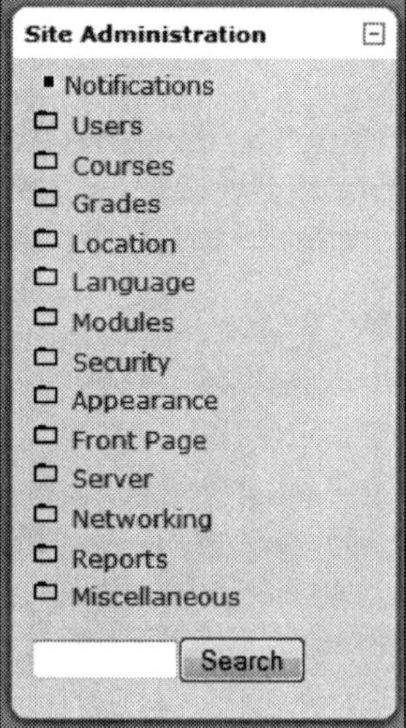


## Breadcrumbs

Moodle uses the so-called breadcrumb trail interface for its navigation; the name is derived from the Hansel and Gretel fairytale! Once you select a menu or sub-menu in the site administration block, Moodle displays the respective crumbs in your navigation bar. These crumbs can be used to jump back to any previous menus. In the menu shown in the figure, the trail consists of five crumbs (**Moodle | Administration | Modules | Activities | Manage activities**):

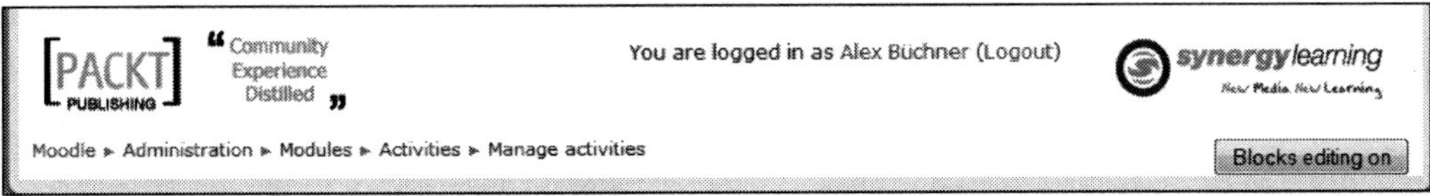


The first crumb is always the name of the site, and represents your Moodle front page. So if you ever get lost, for example, when working on an area in Moodle when the sticky **Site Administration** block is not shown, click on the first crumb and you will be in a familiar territory.

# Administrator Search Facility

A search facility is provided to simplify the identification of any settings in the administration section, which is located below the hierarchical **Administrator** menu.

When searching for any keyword, Moodle displays the result in an expanded form that allows you to change the settings immediately. For example, when searching for the keyword "calendar", four relevant sections appear as the result. The settings can be changed in each section simultaneously, rather than navigating to four separate sections to make changes.

The search facility is also highly beneficial when upgrading from older versions of Moodle, where the configuration settings have been re-organized, and their location is difficult to trace.

# Moodle Bookmarks

Bookmarks are shown in the **Admin Bookmarks** block, which has to be added by turning on editing and selecting the block from the pull-down list. They allow bookmarking any menu in the **Site Administration** for easy access to the pages that cannot be directly referenced via the Site Administration block. Select **bookmark this page** to add a bookmark, and **unbookmark this page** to delete it. Moodle automatically displays the **unbookmark this page** link when you are on the respective page.

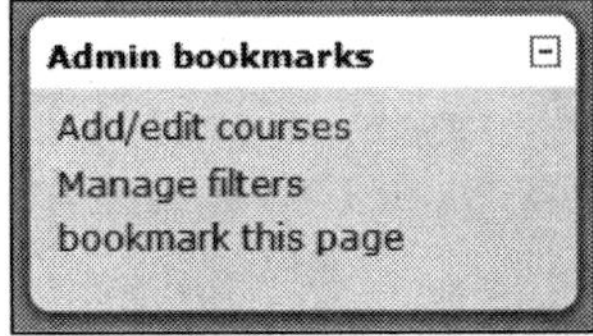

In the previous figure, two pages have already been bookmarked (**Add/edit courses** and **Manage filters**), and the **bookmark this page** link is provided to add more bookmarks.

# Moodle Docs and Help

The entire Moodle documentation is online at `http://docs.moodle.org`. (If you wish to provide your own documentation, modify the `CFG->docroot` value in `config.php`.) A link at the bottom of each page provides a reference to the relevant page in the Moodle Docs. In addition to the actual online documentation, some features provide inline help, which is indicated by a question mark symbol. On clicking, a pop-up window will appear to provide assistance relevant to the respective topic as indicated in the following screenshot:

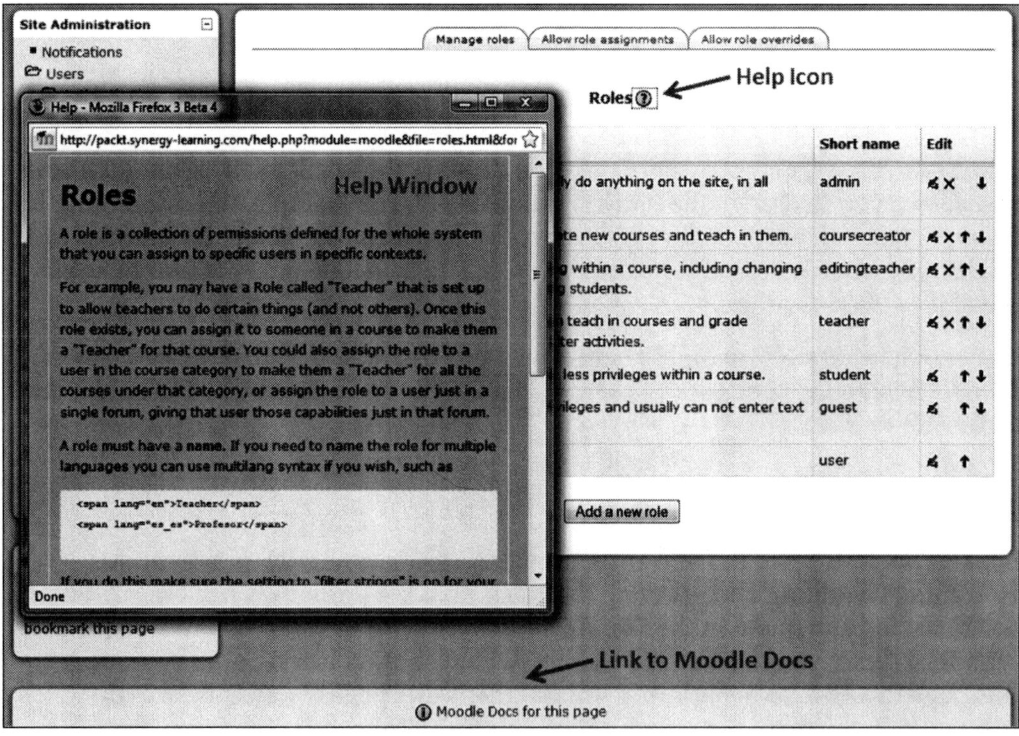

A click on the **Moodle Docs for this page** link in the Assign Roles section opens the following document in your default browser:

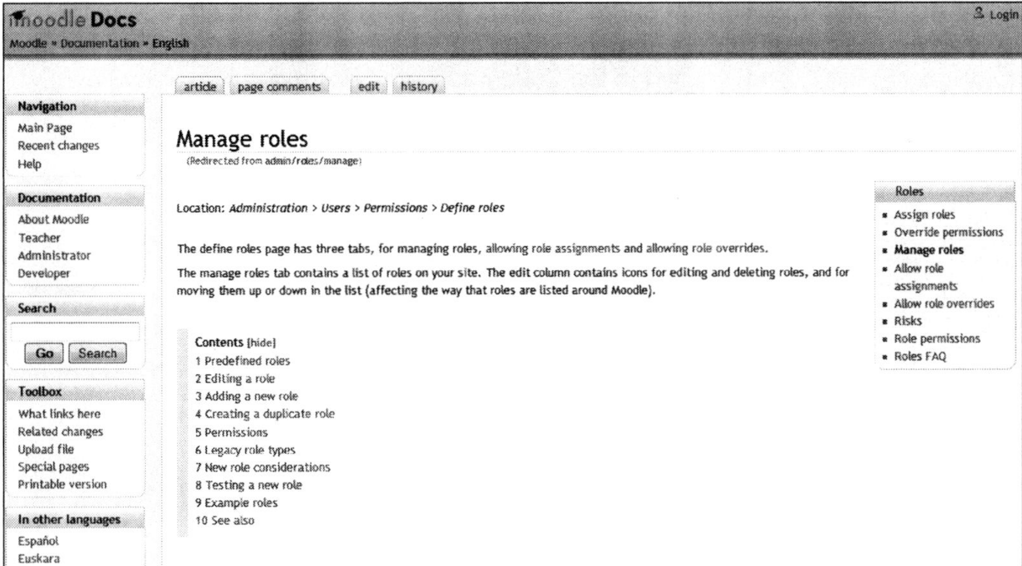


The Moodle community is growing continuously and , at the time of writing, it has well over 400,000 registered users. If you cannot find a solution to any of your Moodle problems, which is relatively rare, go to `http://moodle.org` for help. Moodle will display the results in the order of priority. The search brings forth the already mentioned Moodle Docs, the most active user forums, and the Moodle tracker which keeps track of all issues related to the software (`http://tracker.moodle.org`). A search in the Moodle forums can often result in a large number of links. To narrow down the search space, use the advanced search in the forum search block. A page worth pointing out is `http://docs.moodle.org/en/Category:Administrator`, which is effectively the index for all Moodle administrator topics.

# File Management

Dealing with files in web-based applications is not always straightforward. While Moodle provides a user interface to perform this task, it is sometimes necessary that as the administrator, you will have to bypass this mechanism and use other means.

# Moodle File Management Interface

Moodle offers a (very) basic file management interface that lets you upload, move, delete, and rename files and directories. From the web interface, you only have access the course folders in moodledata (or whatever has been specified in `$CFG->dataroot`). As described in the Code and Data Location section, you have access to the site folder (1) from the front page, and the folders 2, 3, 4, and so on from within the respective courses.

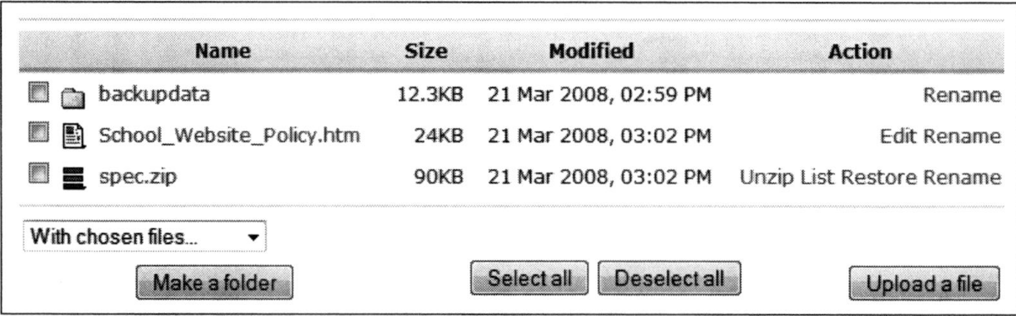


In the previous image , you will see a sample files area containing a directory (**backupdata** - We will deal with this particular location in more detail in Chapter 12) and two files (`School_Website-Policy.htm` and `spec.zip`). In addition to the name, its size, and the last modification timestamp, Moodle also displays context-sensitive actions (on the right) and icons (on the left) for each file and directory.

To select a file or directory, tick the box in the left most column. (Clicking on the name will open the file/directory.). There are buttons such as **Select all** and **Deselect all** for selecting and deselecting files. Once selected, a number of actions can be performed via the **With chosen files...** drop-down menu:

- Move to another folder: You have to select the new destination.
- Delete completely: This irreversible operation has to be confirmed first.
- Create a zip archive: You have to provide a name for the archive.

To create a new folder, press the **Make a folder** button. The name of the folder has to be unique in the directory in which it will be created.

The uploading of files takes place after pressing the **Uploading this file** button:

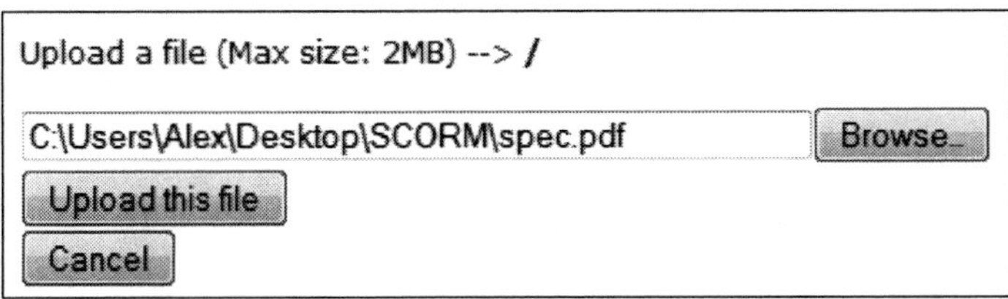


If you position the mouse pointer in the text field, or select the **Browse...** button, the standard file dialog of your local computer will be displayed from which you have to select the file to be uploaded.

Unfortunately, it is possible to upload only one file at a time. However, you can upload a compressed file in ZIP format, and then unzip it using the context-specific link that will appear beside the file. While this is not ideal, it resolves the problem when you have to upload multiple files. If you use this mechanism frequently, make sure the "Path to zip" is set in the System Paths settings (you can find details in Chapter 11 of how to do this). Moodle has its own internal zip and unzip functionality, but using this path allows Moodle to access the native operating system's zip and unzip functionality, which is generally fast and less prone to error.

Each site and course has an upload file limit. It is set to **2MB** for the system referred to in the screenshot. If you have files larger than the limit, you will have to increase the limit.

If you have access to your server's `php.ini` file, modify the following two lines where <value> represents the maximum limit (multiple formats are supported, for example, 20M or 20971520):

```
upload_max_filesize = <value>
post_max_size = <value>
```

If you don't have access to the `php.ini` file, create a `.htaccess` file in your main Moodle directory and add the following two lines:

```
php_value upload_max_filesize = <value>
php_value post_max_size = <value>
```

On some systems you will also have to increase the `LimitRequestBody` parameter, usually found in the Apache configuration file `httpd.conf`.

Alternatively, you can use other file management operations which we will cover next.

# Web Host File Management

Most web hosts (for example, Cpanel and Plesk) offer a web interface that provides a file management facility. These interfaces allow you to upload files and directories in a more flexible way than using the simple Moodle file interface.

The advantages of using a web interface are:

- Ability to upload multiple files
- No upload limit
- More user-friendly interface than its Moodle counterpart, or any shell-based tools

The disadvantages of using a web interface are:

- File management is not very flexible
- Uploading large files will (still) be slow because they are copied over HTTP

# File Management via FTP

When uploading large files via the Moodle interface or any other web browser-based facility, copying takes place over HTTP, which is by its nature very slow. An alternative is to use commands that use more efficient network protocols.

FTP is the best known command for transferring data from one computer to another through a network. This avoids the HTTP overhead and is significantly faster. Alternatively, you can use **secure FTP (sFTP)**, which is more secure, but two to three times slower than the standard FTP. Some popular FTP clients are:

- gFTP (for Linux)
- WinSCP (Windows)
- Cyberduck (Mac OS X)
- FireFTP (Firefox plug-in)
- Built-in FTP clients in web authoring tools such as Adobe Dreamweaver

For very large files, such as high-quality learning resources, it is common to upload a large ZIP archive via FTP and then use the built-in zip link in the files' web interface to uncompress the archived files. Again, make sure the "Path to zip" is set in the System Paths settings to increase the speed. Be aware that you have to copy the files in the correct location. Use the directory structure explained previously as a reference.

# File Management via WebDAV

**WebDAV** stands for **Web-based Distributed Authoring and Versioning**. According to its website (`www.webdav.org`), "It is a set of extensions to the HTTP protocol which allows users to collaboratively edit and manage files on remote web servers."

In the context of Moodle, it allows you to configure the system in a way that the users can access the course files from a web folder. Web folders are similar to network drives and act like local drives on your PC or Mac. There are a number of advantages to using web folders:

- Drag and drop is fully supported to copy files from and to Moodle instead of the cumbersome file upload mechanism
- Multiple files can be copied to and from Moodle in a single operation
- The upload limit is being bypassed using web folders
- Files can be manipulated without opening Moodle in a web browser
- File upload is faster via WebDAV than the existing upload mechanism
- The mechanism works across operating systems

## WebDAV Prerequisites

The DAV module has to be installed on your web server. On Apache it is called mod_dav. Furthermore, magic_quotes_gpc has to be disabled. For more information on setting up WebDAV, check `http://docs.moodle.org/en/WebDAV_Setup`.

The module only allows access to users who previously had access to course files, such as teachers with editing rights, and does not allow access to other users, such as students. Also, access is provided only to the course folders (including the site files folder); no Moodle system folders can be accessed.

## Setting up WebDAV

Once WebDAV has been installed, you have to enable it in Moodle. Go to **Server | WebDAV** to modify its settings. The link only appears if your WebDAV server is working properly.

At the time of print, WebDAV was not yet included in the core of Moodle. To implement this powerful feature, you have to download a special WebDAV-enabled version (search for `webdav-applyto19.patch`), or manually install the module from the contrib path of **CVS (Concurrent Versioning System)** repository.

| Setting | Description |
|---|---|
| **Enable WebDAV access** | Turn on WebDAV access. |
| **Allow WebDAV to file managers** | To grant file managers (that is, users with the capability `moodle/course:managefiles`) access to WebDAV. |
| **WebDAV root URL** | By default, WebDAV uses your Moodle root URL as the mounting point. In some cases, for example, when bypassing a load balancer, or using a secure HTTP connection, you have to provide an alternate URL. |
| **WebDAV subnet** | To restrict WebDAV usage to your local area network, provide the respective subnet address. |
| **WebDAV session TTL** | It is the number of minutes the WebDAV credentials (username and password) are cached for. Default is 60. |

| | |
|---|---|
| Enable WebDAV access<br>*webdavenable* | ☑ Default: No<br>Enables access to Moodledata using the WebDAV protocol. Only users with 'moodle/site:webdav' capabilities will be allowed to use it (only admins by default). |
| Allow WebDAV to file managers<br>*webdavallowfilemanagers* | ☐ Default: No<br>Allows WebDAV access to users that have are allowed file management ('moodle/course:managefiles') *in any course*. 'Editing teacher' roles normally have this, so this is a handy way to allow editing teachers. |
| WebDAV root URL<br>*webdavroot* | Default: Empty<br>Override wwwroot for WebDAV connections -- normally not needed. Useful to bypass load balancers. |
| WebDAV subnet<br>*webdavsubnet* | Default: Empty<br>Only allow WebDAV connections from this subnet. Can be used to only permit WebDAV access from the local LAN. If empty, connections are accepted from any machine. |
| WebDAV session TTL<br>*webdavsessttl* | 60 Default: 60<br>In minutes. Controls how long the WebDAV cached credentials last. Moodle caches access credentials used over WebDAV to avoid innecesary traffic to the authentication backends. |
| | Save Changes |

Now that WebDAV has been enabled in Moodle, let's connect to it from a PC. The procedure is identical on other operating systems, but some are a bit temperamental when it comes to web folders or mount points. You will find further information on setting up WebDAV at `http://www.webdavsystem.com/server/access`.

Moodle controls the usage of WebDAV through the `moodle/site:webdav` capability. By default, only the Course Creator role has this capability (besides you as the administrator, of course), that is, only the course creators are allowed to connect to Moodle via web folders. To permit other user types to use this powerful mechanism, you will have to modify their roles. To know more, please refer Chapter 6.

## Using WebDAV from Windows

To access files from a course, navigate to the course files in a Moodle course. The standard files dialog now displays some WebDAV information at the top. If you use Windows Explorer, a clickable link is provided called **Connect to Web Folder**. If you use any other browser, copy the URL displayed and paste it in the address bar of your file manager:

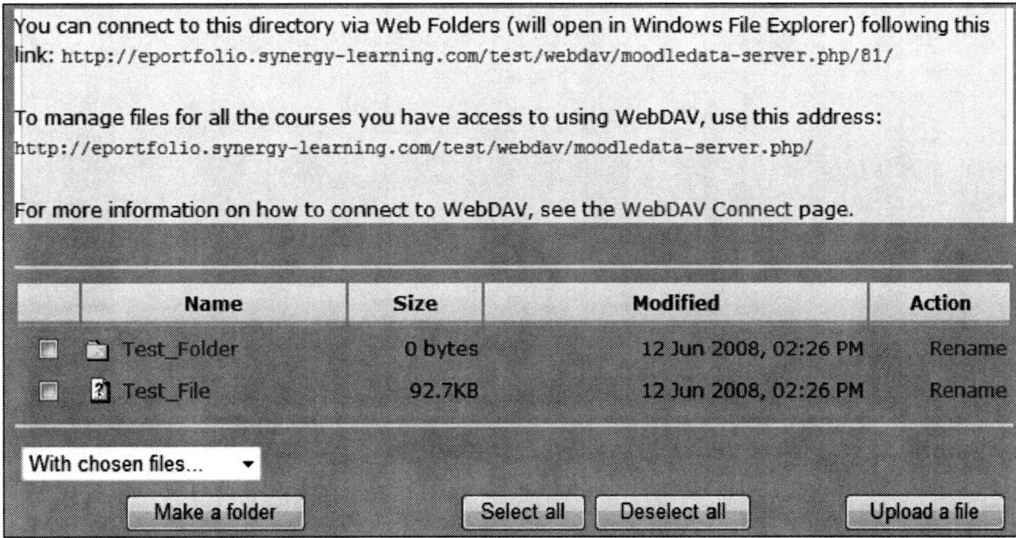

You can connect to this directory via Web Folders (will open in Windows File Explorer) following this link: http://eportfolio.synergy-learning.com/test/webdav/moodledata-server.php/81/
To manage files for all the courses you have access to using WebDAV, use this address:
http://eportfolio.synergy-learning.com/test/webdav/moodledata-server.php/
For more information on how to connect to WebDAV, see the WebDAV Connect page.
Name
Size
Modified
Action
Test_Folder
0 bytes
12 Jun 2008, 02:26 PM
Rename
Test_File
92.7KB
12 Jun 2008, 02:26 PM
Rename
With chosen files...
Make a folder
Select all
Deselect all
Upload a file

The standard Windows dialog will be displayed to connect to network drives. Provide your Moodle user credentials (**Username** and **Password**) and tick the **Remember my password** box if you don't want to re-enter them the next time you connect to Moodle:

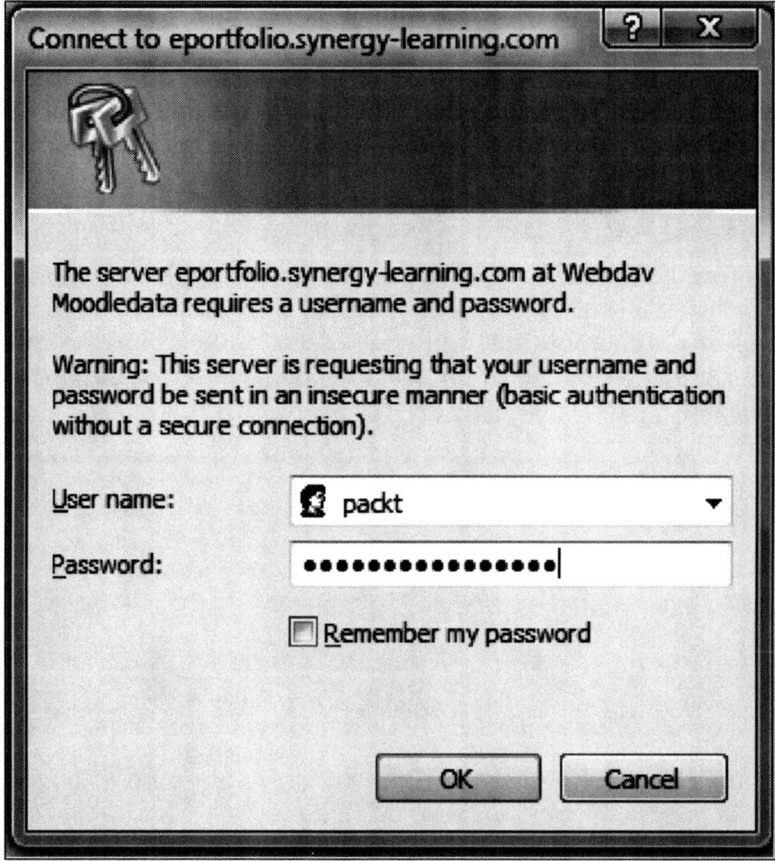


A standard Windows folder will open with your Moodle course files, which you can manipulate as normal. You can now drag and drop files from your PC into the Moodle Web folder. Your teachers will love this feature!

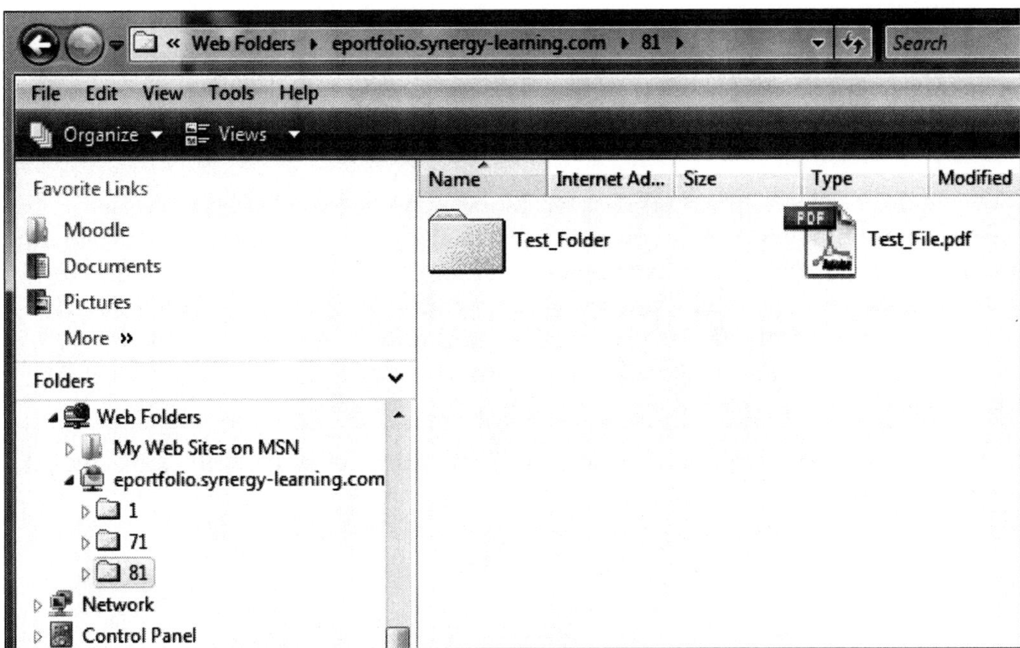


Alternatively, you can connect a Moodle folder as a network drive. This method will allow sharing of files containing all course folders named by their course's short name or ID number (depending on your Windows version) on the network.

When mapping a drive, click **Sign up for online storage** or **connect to a network server** (on Windows XP), and **Connect to a website that you can use to store your documents and Pictures** (on Windows Vista). Then select **Choose another network location** and provide the address given on the Moodle site files screen as well as the username and password.

Your Moodle files will now be mounted as a network drive in **My Network Places**. If even this doesn't work, you may be using a client other than Windows. Have a look at the WebDAV Connect site at `http://docs.moodle.org/en/WebDAV_Connect` for more information.

# Summary

In this chapter, you have learned what the building blocks of Moodle look like and where they are located. Furthermore, we have dealt with a number of options on how to manage files.

As we found out in the previous chapter, Moodle can be installed on multiple operating systems, supports a wide range of database systems, and can be used with different web servers. Due to the openness of Moodle, it should have come across in this chapter that all its components can be accessed without any restrictions. This allows the management of files via a number of channels; we covered Moodle's File Management, Web Host File Management, File Management via FTP and File Management via WebDAV.

Now that your system is up and running and you know what its inside looks like, it is time to add courses and users.

# 4
# Course Management

Moodle stores learning resources in courses, which belong to categories. In this chapter, you will learn how to:

- Organize courses in categories and sub-categories
- Create and manage courses
- Set up meta-courses
- Deal with course requests

In the second part of the chapter, we will cover the different ways to enroll users to courses. The enrolment mechanisms covered are:

- Internal enrolment
- Database-driven enrolment (LDAP, external databases, flat files, and IMS Enterprise files)
- Payment-driven enrolment (PayPal and Authorize.net)

## Course Categories

The role of a Moodle administrator is to manage the categories and courses. It is possible to grant non-administrators rights to deal with categories, but we will deal with this in Chapter 6, when we cover roles. Here, let's start with an overview of the categories.

# Course Categories Overview

Categories act as containers for courses. They can have sub-categories, which can have sub-sub-categories, and so on. This hierarchical structure can be visualized as follows:

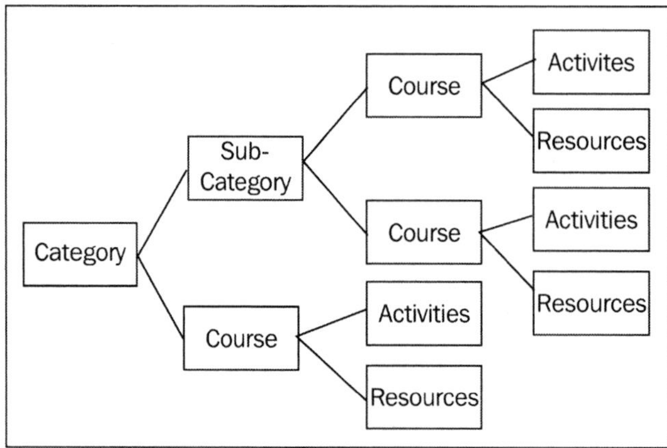


A course always belongs to a single category. It cannot belong to multiple categories and also cannot be without a category. There is one exception to this rule, namely, the front page. Internally, the front page is treated as a course that neither belongs to a category, nor can be deleted.

There are different ways of organizing the courses' and categories' hierarchy, for instance by faculty, by subject area, by intake year, and so on. The following figure shows the positioning of the same course in hierarchies of two different categories representing the same hypothetical organization:

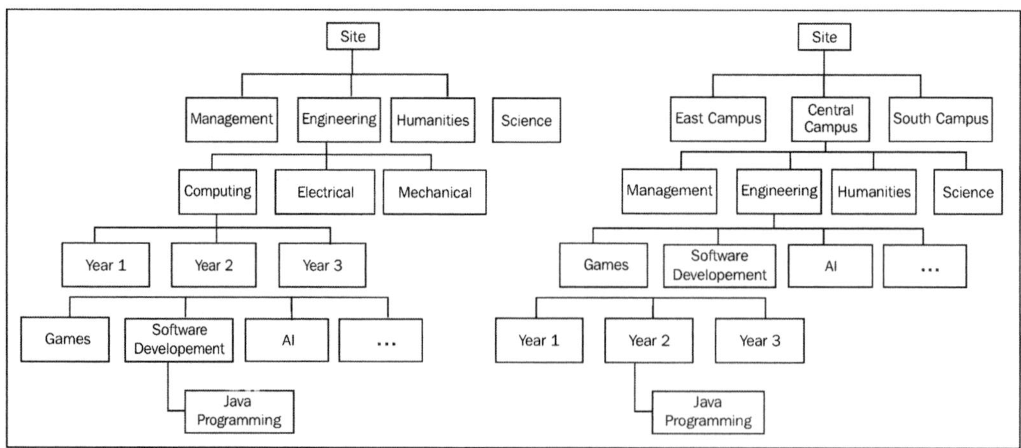

As you can see, each hierarchy represents the same information, but in different forms. There is no right or wrong way when it comes to organizing your courses. The structure entirely depends on:

- The size of your organization
- The number of courses you offer
- The types of courses you run
- The frequency of how often you start courses (once a term, once a year, roll-on-roll-off, and so on)

It is highly advisable to get the right structure the first time around, as changing it is time-consuming and potentially irritating for the users. Also, make a futuristic plan, thinking whether the structure will work in the future, for example, when changing from one academic year to another.

As mentioned before, different organizations apply different categorization approaches. Some examples of the category levels are:

- Campus | Department / School | Year | Subject
- Year of Entry | Topic | Subject
- Customer | Subject | Proficiency Level
- Trainer | Courses

Sometimes the deep levels of categories can be off-putting, since their management is a bit cumbersome. However, bear in mind that only you, as the administrator, will see the entire category structure. The students and teachers will only see the courses they are enrolled or assigned to.

# Managing Course Categories

Once you have planned your category hierarchy structure, it is time to model the organization in Moodle. The categories are administered in the "Courses" section of the administration block (**Courses | Add/edit courses**):

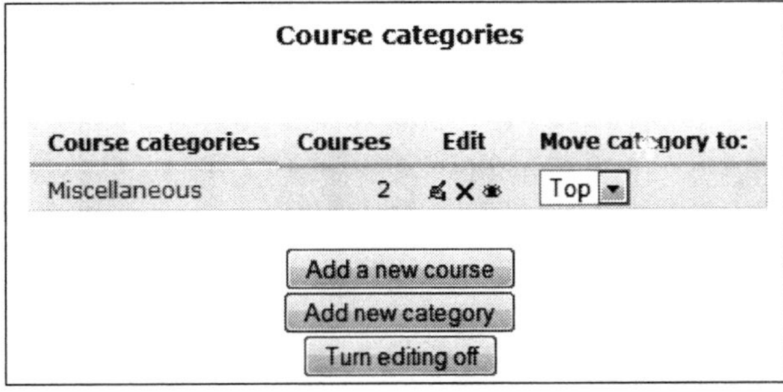

Initially, Moodle comes with a single category called **Miscellaneous**. You can see in the screenshot that **2 courses** already exist in that category in our system.

## Adding Course Categories

To add a new category, click on the **Add new category** option, and enter the new and unique name in the **Category name** field. The Parent category drop-down indicates where in the hierarchy the course is located. To begin with, we select **Top** and come back to it shortly. It is a good practice to provide the optional description.

Once saved, the category will be added at the bottom of the list of the existing categories:

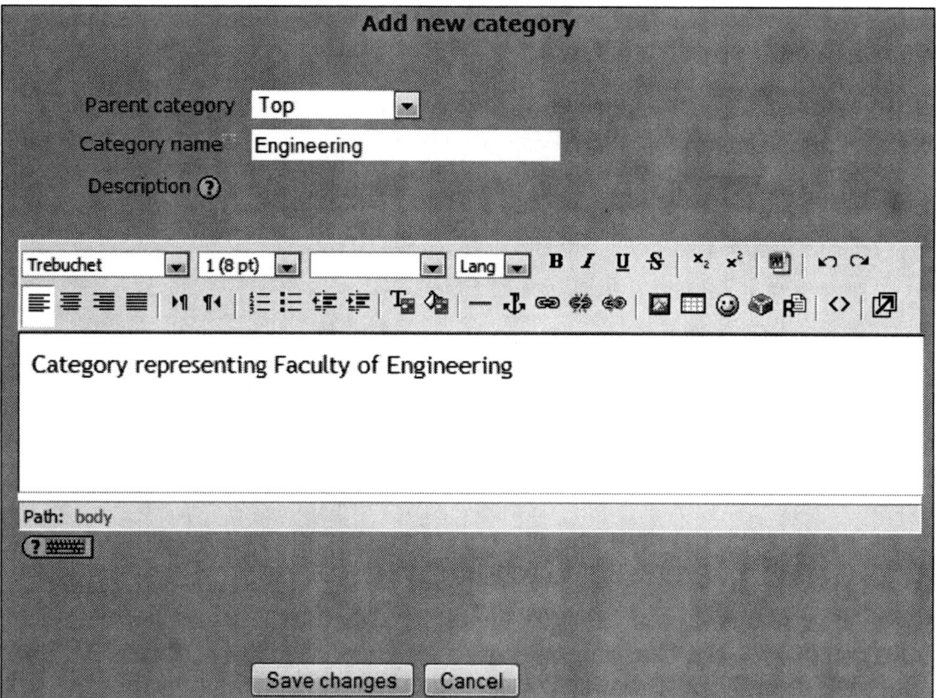


## Course Sub-Categories

As mentioned earlier, to improve the organization of the courses, Moodle allows the creation of sub-categories. You can create a sub-category by choosing an existing category or a new category (as shown in the screenshot), and then moving it into a **Parent Category** using the drop-down menus on the **Course categories** page.

For example, to create sub-categories called **Computing-Year 1**, **Computing-Year 2**, and **Computing-Year 3** in **Computing**, first create the sub-categories and then, one by one, move them into **Computing** using the drop-down menu:

| Course categories | Courses | Edit | Move category to: |
|---|---|---|---|
| Computing | 0 | X ↓ | Top |
| Computing - Year 1 | 0 | X ↓ | Computing |
| Computing - Year 2 | 0 | X ↑ ↓ | Computing |
| Computing - Year 3 | 0 | X ↑ | Computing |

## Deleting Course Categories

When deleting a course category, or using the cross symbol, any courses belonging to the category will be moved to the parent category if one exists, or in the next top-level category. If neither is the case, the courses will be moved to the **Miscellaneous** category.

The **Miscellaneous** category can be deleted as soon as the other categories start to exist. If the last category is deleted from the system, Moodle automatically re-creates this category as it cannot operate without categories.

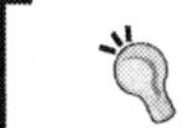

You cannot delete courses by deleting categories. These have to be deleted manually.

## Organizing Courses

Use the up and down arrows to change the position of a course category. When you move a parent category, all the child categories will move with it. Unfortunately, there is no option to automatically arrange categories alphabetically.

You can hide categories using the **eye icon**. This is usually done when the courses within a category are undergoing development, or if you want to create an experimental area (sandpit), which it not seen by anybody but yourself.

On clicking a course category, you are re-directed to the screen that shows all sub-categories and courses belonging to that category. When selecting a sub-category, the same screen is shown with the content of that sub-category. When choosing a course, you are re-redirected to the actual course content.

You also have the option to carry out a number of actions. When you choose the option **Edit this category**, you can rename its title and change its description. Furthermore, the option **Add a sub-category** lets you add a new category, which Moodle automatically positions in the current category:

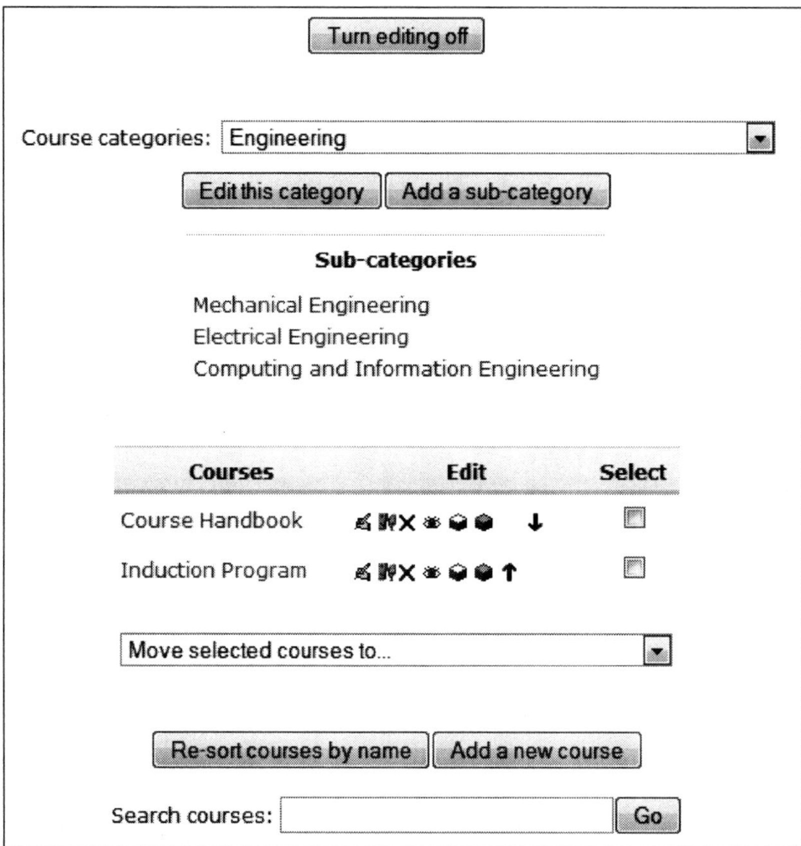


There are a number of icons beside each course, which trigger the following actions:

| | |
|---|---|
| **Settings** | Link to course settings (see the section that follows) |
| **Assign roles** | Link to assigning course roles (see the chapter *Roles Management*) |
| **Delete** | Removal of course and its content |
| **Show/Hide** | Making the course visible/invisible to students |
| **Backup** | Link to course backup facility (see chapter 12) |
| **Restore** | Link to course restore facility (see chapter 12) |
| **Up/Down** | Moving courses up and down. To re-arrange courses alphabetically, press the **Re-sort courses by name** button |

To move a course or a number of courses to another category, first select the course(s), and then the target course location in the **Move selected courses to...** pull-down menu.

In sites with a large number of courses, it is sometimes quicker to search the courses by their names or parts thereof. After clicking **Go**, the found courses, their respective categories, and the same course actions are shown in the previous screenshot.

When you press the **Turn editing off** button, you are directed to a non-editable view of the courses and course categories, which is the one the non-administrators see.

Lastly, you add a new course to the current category by pressing the respective button, which is dealt with in the next section.

# Creating Courses

Once the **Add a new course** button has been selected from within the **Course categories** menu, Moodle directs you to the screen where the course details have to be entered. These details are identical to the course settings that can be edited from within a course by a teacher. The only difference is that, by default, the teacher does not have the right to change the category the course belongs to.

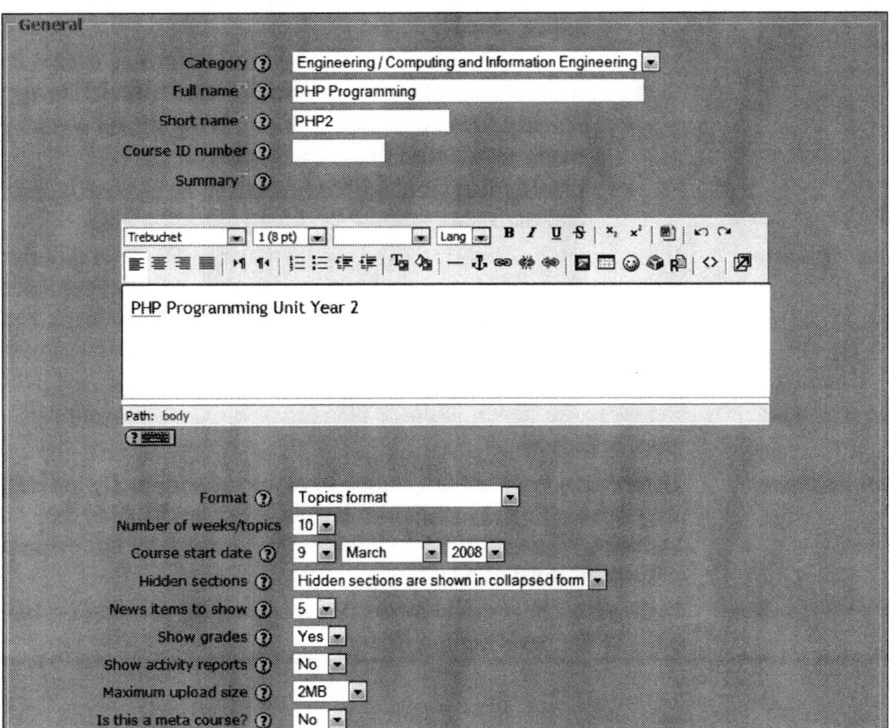

The following settings are available:

| Setting | Description |
|---|---|
| **Category** | Category to which the course belongs. |
| **Full name** | The full name of the course is displayed at the top of the screen and in the course listings. |
| **Short name** | Many organizations have a shorthand way of referring to a course, for example 1CB2. The field is compulsory since it is used in several places where the full name is inappropriate (such as in the breadcrumb trail). |
| **Course ID Number** | Official course code (often used in conjunction with external systems). |
| **Summary** | It is recommended to write a concise paragraph that explains what this course is about. The summary is displayed when a user clicks on the information icon, and when the course appears in a list. |
| **Format** | You can select six formats for a course:<br>• **LAMS course format**: requires a LAMS server<br>• **SCORM format**: shows a SCORM package at the beginning of course<br>• **Social format**: one main (social) forum, which is listed on the main course page, for example a notice board<br>• **Topics format**: similar to the weekly format, except that each week is called a topic and no time-restriction applies<br>• **Weekly format (default)**: course is organized week by week, with a start and a finish date<br>• **Weekly format (CSS/No tables)**: same as weekly, but without using tables (good for screen readers) |
| **Number of weeks/ topics** | In the weekly course format, it is the number of weeks that the course will run for, starting from the course's commencement date. In the topics format, it's the number of topics in the course. Both of these translate to the number of "boxes" in the center column of the course page. |
| **Course start date** | Refers to the starting date of the course; only relevant for weekly formats. |
| **Hidden Sections** | Determines how hidden course sections are shown. By default, they are displayed as small collapsed areas, invisible to the learners. When completely hidden, the learners are not presented with any information. |
| **News items to show** | Determines how many recent items appear on your course home page in the news section (if any). |

| Setting | Description |
|---|---|
| **Show grades** | Determines whether the students are shown the Grades link in their Administration block. You can set this to No and still grade your activities. |
| **Show activity reports** | Determines whether the activity reports of the students and teachers can be seen by other students of the course. |
| **Maximum upload size** | This setting limits the size of a file a user can upload into this course. |
| **Is this a meta course?** | We deal with meta-courses later in this section. |

Enrolment per se is dealt with in the second part of this chapter. Here, we only cover the basic settings as shown in the following screenshot:

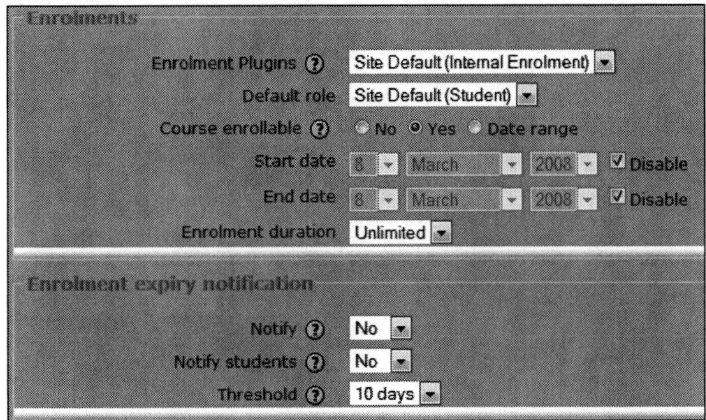


| Setting | Description |
|---|---|
| **Enrolment Plugins** | Select the enrolment plugin that has to be used for this course. See Enrolment section in this chapter. |
| **Default role** | This is the role assigned when assignment is automatic (rather than manual). This value overrides the value of **Default role for users** in a course (**Users \| Permissions \| User policies** in the Site Administration block). |
| **Course enrollable**<br>**Date Range** | During the preparation of a course, it is sometimes necessary to avoid enrolment until it is ready. Also, a date can be specified when the course can be enrolled to. |
| **Enrolment Duration** | The number of days the users are enrolled in the course (starting from the moment they enroll). If set, they are automatically unenrolled after the specified time has elapsed. It's useful for timed courses. |
| **Enrolment expiry notification** | The three fields specify whether the course teachers (**Notify**) and students (**Notify Students**) will be notified. A **Threshold** has to be set indicating how many days prior to expiry the notification will be sent. |

The remaining settings of cover groups, availability, language and roles are shown in the following screenshot:

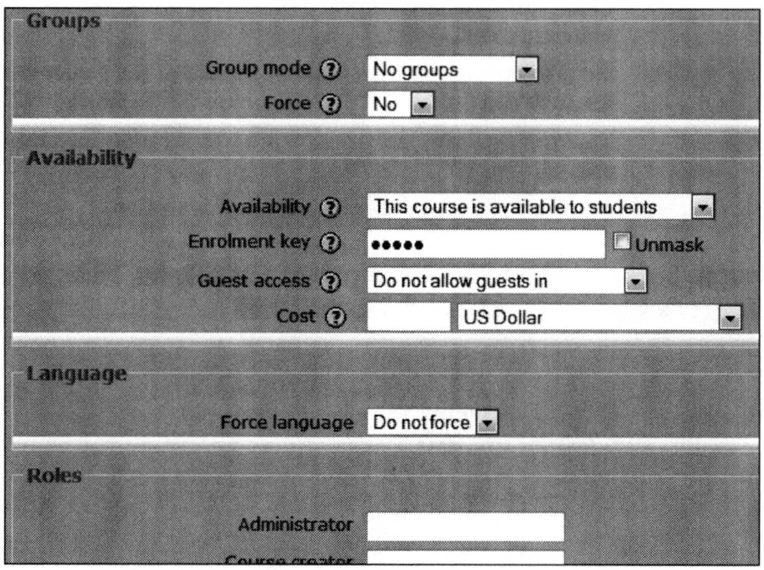


| Setting | Description |
|---|---|
| **Group mode** | Sets group mode of the course to:<br>• **No groups** (default)<br>There are no sub-groups. Everyone is a part of one big community or class.<br>• **Separate groups**<br>Each group can only see their own group, while others are invisible.<br>• **Visible Groups**<br>Each group works in their own group, but can also see other groups. |
| **Force** | If set, the selected group mode is used for every activity and group settings in individual activities are ignored. This is useful when the same course is run multiple times with separate student cohorts. Also, if group mode is forced and set to No groups, no Groups link will be shown in the course administration menu. |
| **Availability** | If set to **not available**, the course is hidden. Except the course teachers and administrators, no one would be able to see it on course listings. |
| **Enrolment key** | This is basically a course password, which is required when self-enrolment is chosen. |

| Setting | Description |
|---|---|
| **Guest Access** | Allows Guest (read-only) access to the course where you can select whether the guests require the enrolment key or not. |
| **Cost** | If your site uses payment-based enrolment (will shortly be discussed), then you can enter a course cost here that overrides the specified default cost. |
| **Force language** | If set, the selected language is used throughout the course and cannot be changed. |

Once a course has been created, you can assign the users to various roles in the course (that is enrolling students and assigning teachers). We have dedicated the entire *Roles Management* section (Chapter 6) to roles and will have to ignore this for now. After this step, which will be covered in the later chapter, the course is ready for the teacher to be constructed.

# Meta Courses—Sharing Enrolment across Courses

Meta courses are courses which take their enrolment from other courses. They populate many courses from one enrolment or one course from many enrolments. This is useful in the following scenarios:

1. Multiple courses want to share information or resources (meta course)
2. A course is part of a qualification where students have to be enrolled in a number of courses; each course is set up as a meta course

Both scenarios are depicted in the following screenshot:

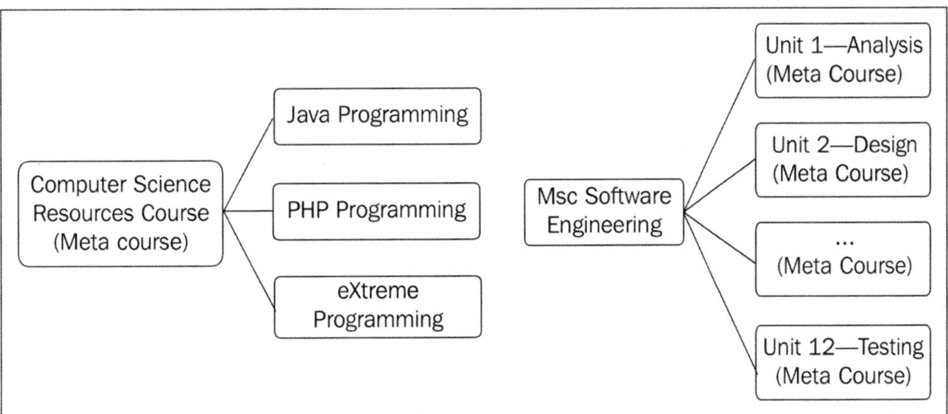

The teachers have the right to set the Meta courses parameter in Course settings and then manage its dependents via the **Child courses** menu in the course administration block. While it is the role of the teacher to manage meta courses, experience has shown that the administrator is frequently asked to set these up on the behalf of others.

To set up the first scenario where the meta course holds shared resources, you have to create all four courses and change the **Meta course** parameter in the course settings of the **Computer Science Resources Course** to **Yes**. This will trigger the display of the **Child courses** link in the course administration block. When you follow it, you will be able to select the three programming courses as shown in the following image:

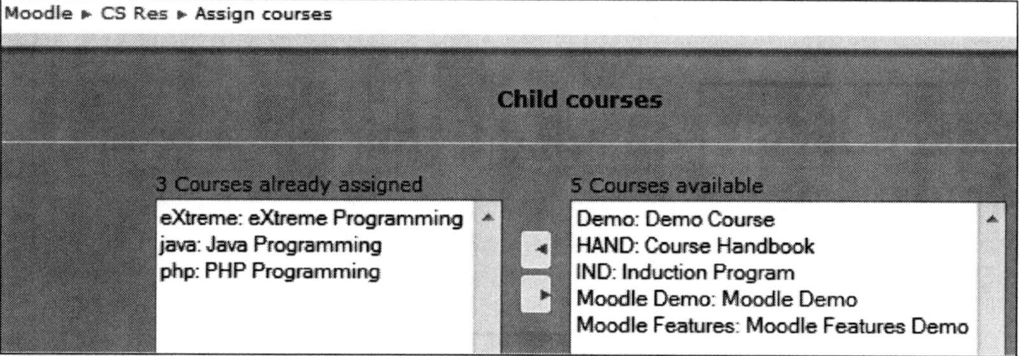


To model the second scenario, you will have to create all 13 courses (one course for MSc Software Engineering and a course for each unit) and set the **Meta course** flag in each unit course to **Yes**. You will then have to go to the **Child courses** link in each unit course and select the MSc course as the dependent.

# Course Requests—Enabling Teachers to Ask for New Courses

Only the administrators or course creators (or any other role with the course creation rights) are allowed to create new courses. In order to streamline the procedure for requesting courses, especially in larger organizations, Moodle offers a course requesting facility. This has to be enabled in **Courses | Course request** in the **Site Administration** block:

**Course request**

Enable course requests
*enablecourserequests*
☑ Default: No
This will allow any user to request a course be created.

Default category for course requests
*defaultrequestcategory*
Computing
Courses requested by users will be automatically placed in this category.

Save Changes

As soon as the feature is enabled, each teacher has the ability to request new courses (via the **Course request** button on the **All courses** screen). The information that has to be provided is:

- Full name
- Short name
- Summary
- Reasons for wanting the course
- Enrolment key (optional)

A new button labeled **Courses pending approval** appears in the familiar Course categories screen (**Courses | Add/edit courses**). When you select it, a list of requested courses is shown, which you can then approve or reject by selecting the appropriate link.

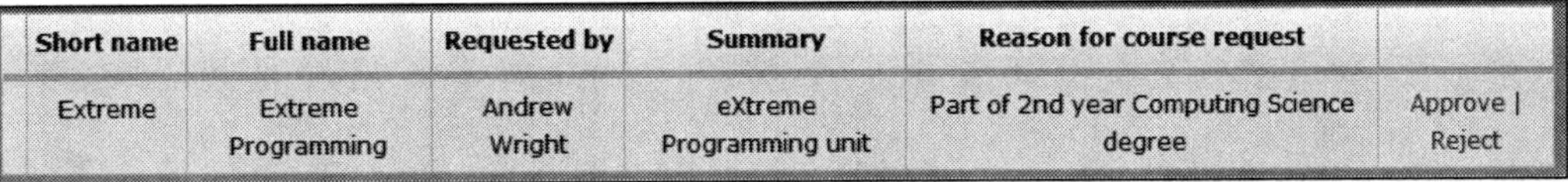

| Short name | Full name | Requested by | Summary | Reason for course request | |
|---|---|---|---|---|---|
| Extreme | Extreme Programming | Andrew Wright | eXtreme Programming unit | Part of 2nd year Computing Science degree | Approve \| Reject |

When you approve a screen, the familiar course settings screen appears, which contains the provided values of the course, and also the default category specified in the system settings.

If you reject a course, a reason has to be given, which is then emailed to the requester.

# Forms of Enrolment

The students need to be given access to a course before they are allowed to use it. The users need to be assigned a role within a course before they are allowed to do anything. They can be assigned the role automatically by self-enrolling, or manually using the **Assign roles** link in the course administration block (see Chapter 6–*Roles Management*).

Granting access is done via the enrolment mechanism. Moodle supports a wide range of enrolment options which are discussed in the remainder of the chapter.

The actual enrolment of students does not require administrator rights, and is a task which should be performed by teachers. The role of the administrator is to set up the available site-wide enrolment mechanisms and they are covered next.

You access the course enrolments configuration page via **Courses | Enrolments** in the **Site Administration** block. Each supported enrolment mechanism is represented by an enrolment plug-in that can be enabled and configured separately.

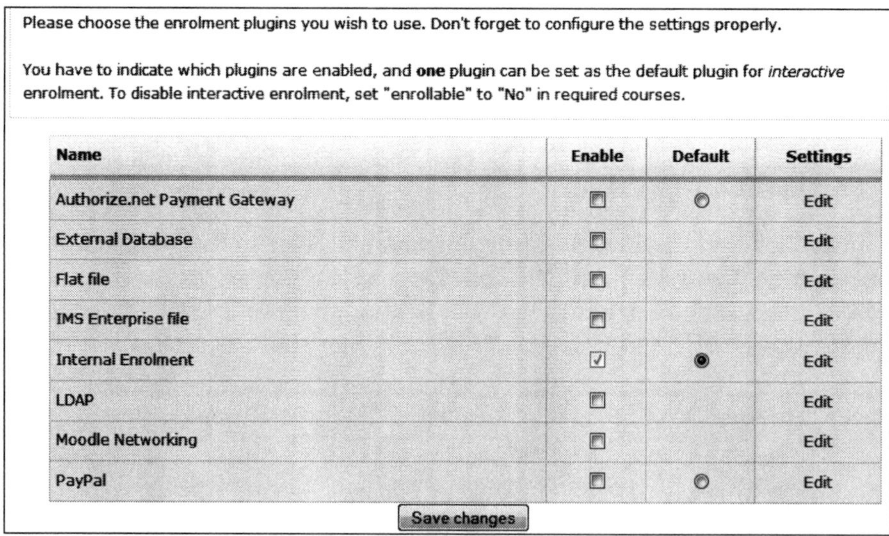

Please choose the enrolment plugins you wish to use. Don't forget to configure the settings properly.
You have to indicate which plugins are enabled, and one plugin can be set as the default plugin for interactive enrolment. To disable interactive enrolment, set "enrollable" to "No" in required courses.
Name
Enable
Default
Settings
Authorize.net Payment Gateway
External Database
Flat file
IMS Enterprise file
Internal Enrolment
LDAP
Moodle Networking
PayPal
Edit
Save changes


Each plug-in can be enabled or disabled separately, and multiple plug-ins can be enabled simultaneously (multi-enrolment). Internal enrolment and the two types of payment enrolments can be used as default mechanisms, while all plug-ins can be or have to be configured.

Students ought to have a user account before they can be enrolled in a course.

Each enrolment type is now covered in some detail except Moodle Networking, to which a separate chapter has been dedicated. The type of enrolment mechanism you choose depends entirely on the infrastructure you have in place, that is, where and in what format your learners' data is stored.

# Internal Enrolment

Internal enrolment is the only plug-in that cannot be de-activated and is the default enrolment mechanism when Moodle is installed.

The teacher, of course, can enrol users **manually** via the **Assign roles** link in the Administration block within the respective course.

Moodle also supports the concept of **self-enrolment**. The concept of self-enrolment is relatively simple: A course contains a password, known as the "enrolment key". Anyone who knows this key is able to add themselves to a course.

The enrolment key is set in course settings, as already discussed. The teacher has to inform the students about the key and ideally limit the enrolment period to an appropriate time frame to avoid any misuse.

Once the enrolment key has been set, learners will have to enter it when they try to access the course for the first time. If the key is entered correctly, access will be granted, otherwise it will be denied.

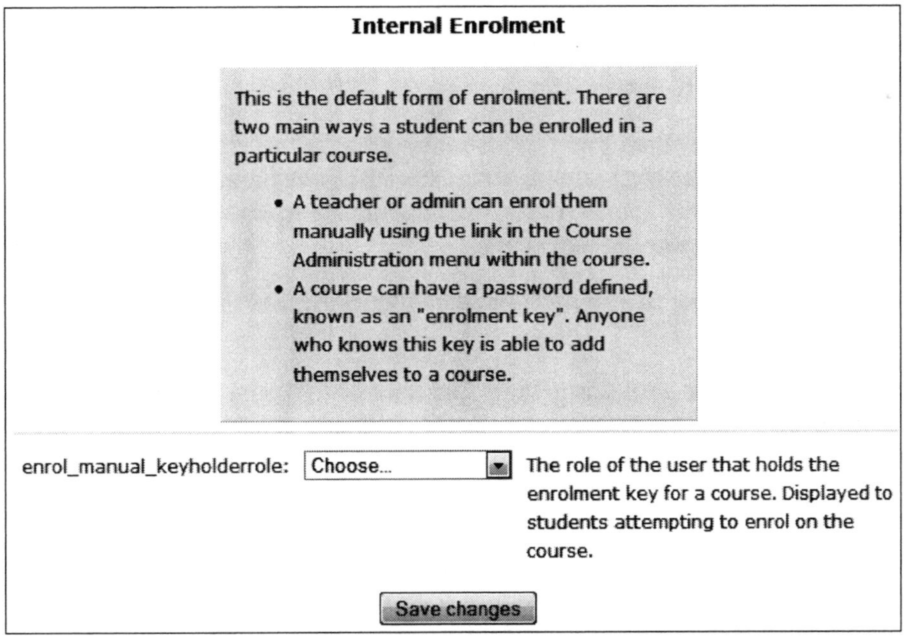

There is only a single setting for the internal enrolment plug-in called **enrol_manual_keyholderrole** that affects the screen the students will see when they attempt to enroll to a course where an enrolment key is required. It will list anybody who is assigned to the specified role as "contacts" to whom we can request the enrolment key. If this is not set (default), the name of the first person with an update privilege for the course is displayed.

# Database-driven Enrolment

In larger organizations, it is common to store certain user-related information on a separate database or directory. If this information contains course-related information, it should be utilized for enrolment. In doing so, you minimize the efforts which are necessary when using manual enrolment.

## LDAP

**LDAP**, the **Lightweight Directory Access Protocol**, is an application standard for querying and modifying the directory services running over TCP or IP. It is used by many organizations to store learner details and is therefore well suited as an enrolment source for Moodle.

It is necessary that the PHP LDAP module is installed on the server for the enrolment to work. If it is not installed, Moodle will display an error message. The module also supports Microsoft's implementation of LDAP, called Active Directory, as well as OpenLDAP, an open-source implementation of the authentication mechanism. Most sites that use LDAP enrolment also use LDAP for authentication. It is discussed in great detail in the next chapter.

The principle of the enrolment method is rather simple, but effective. The information stored in the data source about students, teachers, and courses is mapped onto the Moodle counterparts. Enrolments are updated when a user logs in. All we have to provide are the mappings.

Moodle makes a number of assumptions when working with LDAP enrolment such as:

- Your LDAP tree contains groups that map onto courses.
- Each group has multiple membership entries to map to students.
- Users have a valid ID number field.

The LDAP settings have been annotated on the right-hand side of the screen with detailed explanations that were discussed earlier. I will provide additional information where applicable. If you are not sure where to locate some of the required information, contact your system administrator who should have these values.

There are five sections of parameters which have to be provided.

**LDAP Server Settings**

| | | |
|---|---|---|
| enrol_ldap_host_url: | ldap://123.456.678.90 | Specify LDAP host in URL-form like 'ldap://ldap.myorg.com/' or 'ldaps://ldap.myorg.com/' |
| enrol_ldap_version: | 3 | The version of the LDAP protocol your server is using. |
| enrol_ldap_bind_dn: | oups,dc=ldap,dc=uni,dc=ac,dc=uk | If you want to use bind-user to search users, specify it here. Someting like 'cn=ldapuser,ou=public,o=org' |
| ldap_bind_pw: | ••••• | Password for bind-user. |
| ldap_search_sub: | No | Search group memberships from subcontexts. |

It is important to set the **ldap_search_sub** (that is, the search subcontext) correctly. If it is set to **No**, the subcontexts will not be searched, but the search will be potentially faster and vice- a-versa:

**Role mapping**

| Roles | LDAP contexts | LDAP member attribute |
|---|---|---|
| Administrator | | |
| Course creator | | |
| Teacher | oups,dc=ldap,dc=uni,dc=ac,dc=uk | teacherid |
| Non-editing teacher | | |
| Student | oups,dc=ldap,dc=uni,dc=ac,dc=uk | studentid |
| Guest | | |
| Authenticated user | | |

Role mappings have to be set, which contain a context (usually the same as the one in the server settings) and the member attribute (user IDs).

**Course enrolment settings**

| | | | |
|---|---|---|---|
| enrol_ldap_objectclass: | moodleGroup | | objectClass used to search courses. Usually 'posixGroup'. |
| enrol_ldap_course_idnumber: | uid | Update local data: No<br>Lock value: Yes | Map to the unique identifier in LDAP, usually *cn* or *uid*. It is recommended to lock the value if you are using automatic course creation. |
| enrol_ldap_course_shortname: | | Update local data: No<br>Lock value: No | Optional: LDAP field to get the shortname from. |
| enrol_ldap_course_fullname: | fullname | Update local data: No<br>Lock value: Yes | Optional: LDAP field to get the full name from. |
| enrol_ldap_course_summary: | | Update local data: No<br>Lock value: No | Optional: LDAP field to get the summary from. |

It is recommended to lock fields, especially when the automatic course creation has been activated.

| Automatic course creation settings | | |
|---|---|---|
| enrol_ldap_autocreate: | yes | Courses can be created automatically if there are enrolments to a course that doesn't yet exist in Moodle. |
| enrol_ldap_category: | Computing | The category for auto-created courses. |
| enrol_ldap_template: | | Optional: auto-created courses can copy their settings from a template course. |

Automatic course creation is a potentially time-saving facility. A course is created for each entry on the LDAP server in the category specified. To expedite the process and to guarantee consistency among courses, you should create a course with the preferred settings and use it (course ID) as a template for all newly-created courses.

# External Database

A lot of organizations use a **Management Information System (MIS)**, either proprietary or developed in-house, that holds information about the staff and / or learners, and the courses they are enrolled in. It makes perfect sense to utilize this data for enrolment to Moodle. Since all MISs use a database at its core, all we have to do is to get access to the relevant data.

The bad news is that there is a plethora of database systems out there that have to be supported, from the big players such as Oracle and Microsoft SQL Server to the lesser known systems such as Informix or Sybase. The good news is that there exists a layer ADO, a successor to ODBC, which does all the hard work for us. We only have to talk to the ADO layer and its internals deal with the rest, no matter what database it is talking to.

The database has to contain a course ID and a user ID. These two fields are compared against the fields that you choose in the local course and user tables.

**External Database Server Settings**

| | | |
|---|---|---|
| enrol_dbtype: | oci8po | Database type |
| enrol_dbhost: | localhost | Server IP name or number |
| enrol_dbuser: | MOODLE | Server user |
| enrol_dbpass: | ●●●●● | Server password |
| enrol_dbname: | EBS | Database name |
| enrol_dbtable: | COMP | Database table |

**Enrolment (remote) database fields.**

| | | |
|---|---|---|
| enrol_localcoursefield: | id | The name of the field in the course table that we are using to match entries in the remote database (eg idnumber). |
| enrol_localuserfield: | username | The name of the field in the user table that we are using to match entries in the remote database (eg idnumber). |
| enrol_db_localrolefield: | | The name of the field in the roles table that we are using to match entries in the remote database (eg shortname). |
| enrol_remotecoursefield: | COURSECODE | The name of the field in the remote table that we are using to match entries in the course table. |
| enrol_remoteuserfield: | USERNAME | The name of the field in the remote table that we are using to match entries in the user table. |
| enrol_db_remoterolefield: | | The name of the field in the remote table that we are using to match entries in the roles table. |

**Roles**

| | | |
|---|---|---|
| enrol_db_defaultcourseroleid: | Default | The role that will be assigned by default if no other role is specified. |

**Auto-creation of new courses**

| | | |
|---|---|---|
| enrol_db_autocreate: | No | Courses can be created automatically if there are enrolments to a course that doesn't yet exist in Moodle. |
| enrol_db_category: | Computing | The category for auto-created courses. |
| enrol_db_template: | | Optional: auto-created courses can copy their settings from a template course. Type here the shortname of the template course. |

**General Options**

| | | |
|---|---|---|
| enrol_db_ignorehiddencourse: | No | If set to yes users will not be enroled on courses that are set to be unavailable to students. |
| enrol_db_disableunenrol: | No | If set to yes users previously enrolled by the external database plugin will not be unenrolled by the same plugin regardless of the database contents. |

Save changes

The database connection settings have been annotated on the right-hand side of the screen with good explanations. If you are not sure where to locate some of the required information, contact your database administrator.

Some databases, such as Oracle, are case-sensitive, that is, the field names have to be provided with the correct casing for the database link to work properly.

## Flat File

Moodle provides a flat file enrolment mechanism. The method will repeatedly (via the Moodle cron process) check for and process a specially-formatted, comma-separated text file in the location that you specify. The format of the file is as follows:

```
action, role, userid, courseid, start (optional), finish (optional)
```

| Field | Description |
|---|---|
| action | `add` (to add an enrolment) or `del` (to remove it) |
| role | `student` (Student), `teacher` (non-editing teacher) or `teacheredit` (Teacher) |
| userid | ID number of the user to be enrolled |
| courseid | ID number of course in which the user is to be enrolled |
| start | (Optional) Start time in seconds since epoch (1 Jan 1970) |
| finish | (Optional) End time in seconds since epoch (1 Jan 1970) |

The following is a sample file snippet:

```
add, teacher, 5, Psychology1
add, student, 12, Psychology1
del, student, 17, English2
add, student, 29, English, 1207008000, 1227916800
```

The start time and end time have to be provided together. To generate the numbers since epoch, it is best to use an online converter.

In the text file settings, you have to provide the absolute file location on the server. If no file is specified, Moodle will look for the default file at `moodledata/1/enrolments.txt`. Moodle should be able to read the file and delete it once it has been processed.

You can choose to have a log file sent to the administrator, and a notification to the teachers and students. The default roles can be overridden with other values if needed:

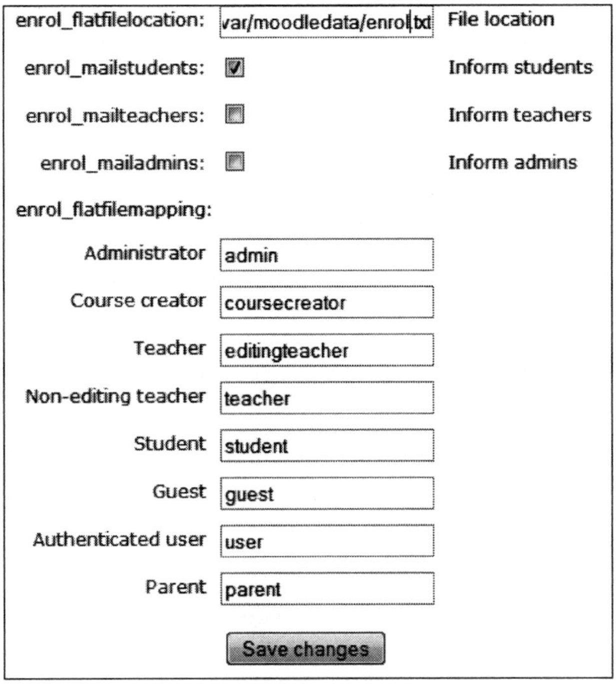

| | | |
|---|---|---|
| enrol_flatfilelocation: | var/moodledata/enrol.txt | File location |
| enrol_mailstudents: | [x] | Inform students |
| enrol_mailteachers: | [ ] | Inform teachers |
| enrol_mailadmins: | [ ] | Inform admins |
| enrol_flatfilemapping: | | |
| Administrator | admin | |
| Course creator | coursecreator | |
| Teacher | editingteacher | |
| Non-editing teacher | teacher | |
| Student | student | |
| Guest | guest | |
| Authenticated user | user | |
| Parent | parent | |
| | Save changes | |

# IMS Enterprise File

The IMS Global Learning Consortium has specified an XML file format that represents the student and course information. Moodle is capable of using any file that conforms to the format as enrolment source. Like the flat file format, Moodle checks regularly for its presence, and if found it will process the file and delete it. You can find details of the basic structure of the format at `http://yoursite/help.php?module=enrol/imsenterprise&file=formatoverview.html` on your Moodle site.

The plug-in is also able to create user accounts if they aren't yet created, or change user details if requested. Furthermore, new courses can also be created if they are not found on Moodle.

All other fields, including role mappings are self-explanatory:

**Basic settings**

File location: /var/moodledata/1/ims.xml

Log file output location (blank for no logging):

Notify admin by email:

**User data options**

Create user accounts for users not yet registered in Moodle:

Delete user accounts when specified in IMS data:

Change usernames to lower case:

Change personal names to Title Case:

Use the "sourcedid" for a person's userid if the "userid" field is not found:

Roles

The IMS Enterprise specification includes 8 distinct role types. Please choose how you want them to be assigned in Moodle, including whether any of them should be ignored.

"Learner" (01): Student

"Instructor" (02): Teacher

"Content Developer" (03): Teacher

"Member" (04): Student

"Manager" (05): Administrator

"Mentor" (06): Non-editing teacher

"Administrator" (07): Administrator

"TeachingAssistant" (08): Non-editing teacher

**Course data options**

Truncate course codes to this length: 0

Create new (hidden) courses if not found in Moodle:

Create new (hidden) course categories if not found in Moodle:

Allow the IMS data to **unenrol** students/teachers:

**Miscellaneous**

Only process data if the following target is specified:

Tick this box if using "Capita" (their XML format is slightly wrong):

*Once you have saved your settings, you may wish to perform an IMS Enterprise import right now.*

Save changes

# Enrolment with Payment

Moodle comes with two enrolment plug-ins that enable you to set up paid courses. There exist other third-party plug-ins fulfilling the same purpose, but they have not been incorporated in the core Moodle system. A popular example is **aMember**, which is a membership and subscription script that supports a wide range of payment systems.

## PayPal

You have to specify the default cost and currency of a course. This amount can be overridden in the course settings. If the amount for any course is zero, then students are not asked to pay for the entry. If you enter an enrolment key in the course settings, then the students will also have the option to enroll using a key. This is useful if you have a mixture of paying and non-paying learners.

You require a valid PayPal account that can be set up at no cost at `www.paypal.com`. The language encoding has to be set to UTF-8 / Unicode in the **More Options** area of your PayPal account:

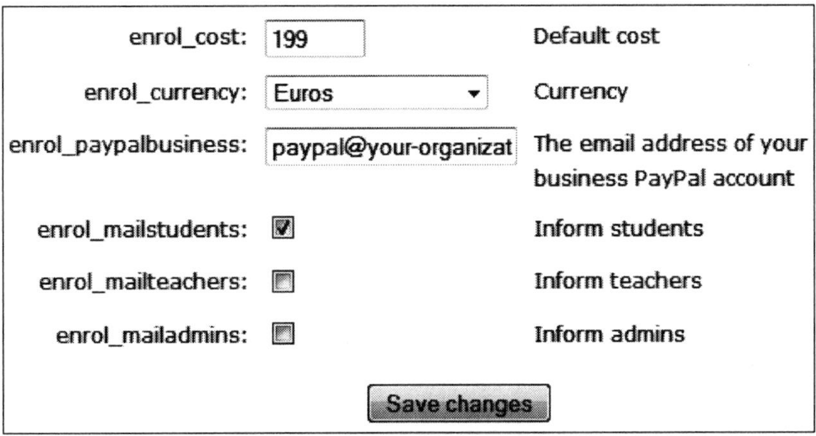


## Authorize.net Payment Gateway

Authorize.net is a payment gateway that supports credit card and electronic check payments. Like PayPal, you require an account to use it. It is also possible to set up a test account for testing purposes. (See `www.authorize.net` for details.)

The payment enrolment plug-in requires a secure login, for which you need to purchase or generate a valid **SSL (Secure Sockets Layer)** certificate. To turn this feature on, go to **Security | HTTP Security** and tick **Use HTTPS for logins**. Once this has been done successfully, you will have to enter a number of settings that follow:

- General Settings (default cost and currency)
- Authorize.net Merchant Account Settings (account details, transaction settings, and supported cards)
- Order Review & Scheduled Capture Settings (requires cron)
- Email Sending Settings

Once the merchant, transaction, and reviewing settings have been entered, the payment method can be used for enrolments. You can still provide a key for self-enrolment and support a mix of paying and non-paying learners. A new Payments link will appear in the administration block at the course level where you manage the received payments. Details are provided for each order as shown in the screenshot (courtesy of Ethem Evlice):

**Order Details** You are logged in as Admin User (Logout)

MAB ▶ MAB100 ▶ MAB100 ▶ Payment Management ▶ OrderID: 1 [Destroy]

| | |
|---|---|
| **Payment Method:** | Credit Card |
| **Name on Card:** | Test User (**Test User**) |
| **CC last four:** | 1111 |
| **Amount:** | USD 100.00 |
| **TransactionID:** | 0 |
| **Time:** | Monday, 14 July 2008, 11:43 AM |
| **Settlement Date:** | Not settled |
| **Status:** | **Tested** |

Moodle Docs for this page

# Summary

In this chapter you have learned everything about courses and categories. As we have discovered, courses are key to Moodle since all content, no matter what type, prepared by teachers and learned by students is situated in courses. Even Moodle's front page is a course, but we will deal with this later when we customize the look and feel of your VLE.

Closely related to courses is the enrolment of students. It is important that you understand the difference between enrolment, which we covered in this chapter, and authentication, which we will discuss in great detail in the following chapter.

# 5

# User Management

In this chapter, you will learn how to manage users in your Moodle system. We will first look at what information is stored for each user and how we can extend their profiles. We will then perform a number of standard user actions that include:

- Browsing users
- Filtering users
- Bulk user actions

A number of mechanisms are covered to manually add new users to Moodle, namely:

- Adding individual users
- Uploading users and their pictures in bulk
- Self-enrolment

We will then deal with a wide range of user authentication types, before concluding the chapter with a best practice section. That is a lot to take in, so we better get going.

## Authentication Versus Enrolment

Before we start, it is important to understand the difference between authentication and enrolment.

Moodle users have to be authenticated in order to establish a personal account. **Authentication** grants users access to the system through login where a username and password have to be given. (This also applies to guest accounts where a username is allotted internally.) Moodle supports a significant number of authentication mechanisms, which are discussed later in detail.

**Enrolment** happens at course level as discussed in the previous chapter. However, a user has to be authenticated to the system before enrolment to a course can take place. So, the workflow is usually as follows (There are exceptions as always, but we will deal with them when we get there.):

1. Create your courses and categories (as dealt with in Chapter 4)
2. Create your users, and make provision for automatic account creation or set up self-registration (dealt with in this chapter)
3. Associate users to courses (covered in this chapter and in Chapter 4) and optionally assign roles (which we will cover in Chapter 6)

# User Profiles

Other than guests, each user has a profile that contains information about him or her. We will first deal with the information that is stored for each user and how it is organized in Moodle.

You can view or change your profile by clicking on your name, which is usually found in the header or footer of your system. Select the **Edit profile** tab to view the most commonly used fields. To see all fields, select the **Show Advanced** button. The button will then toggle to **Hide Advanced**.

# Profile Fields

Moodle's user profiles are divided into a number of categories such as:

- General: Standard user fields
- Picture of: Image of user
- Interests: Tags for social-networking activities
- Optional: Additional user information
- User-defined: Newly created fields

Let's take a look at these one by one. **General**, is the first category as shown in the following screenshot:

# Category "General"

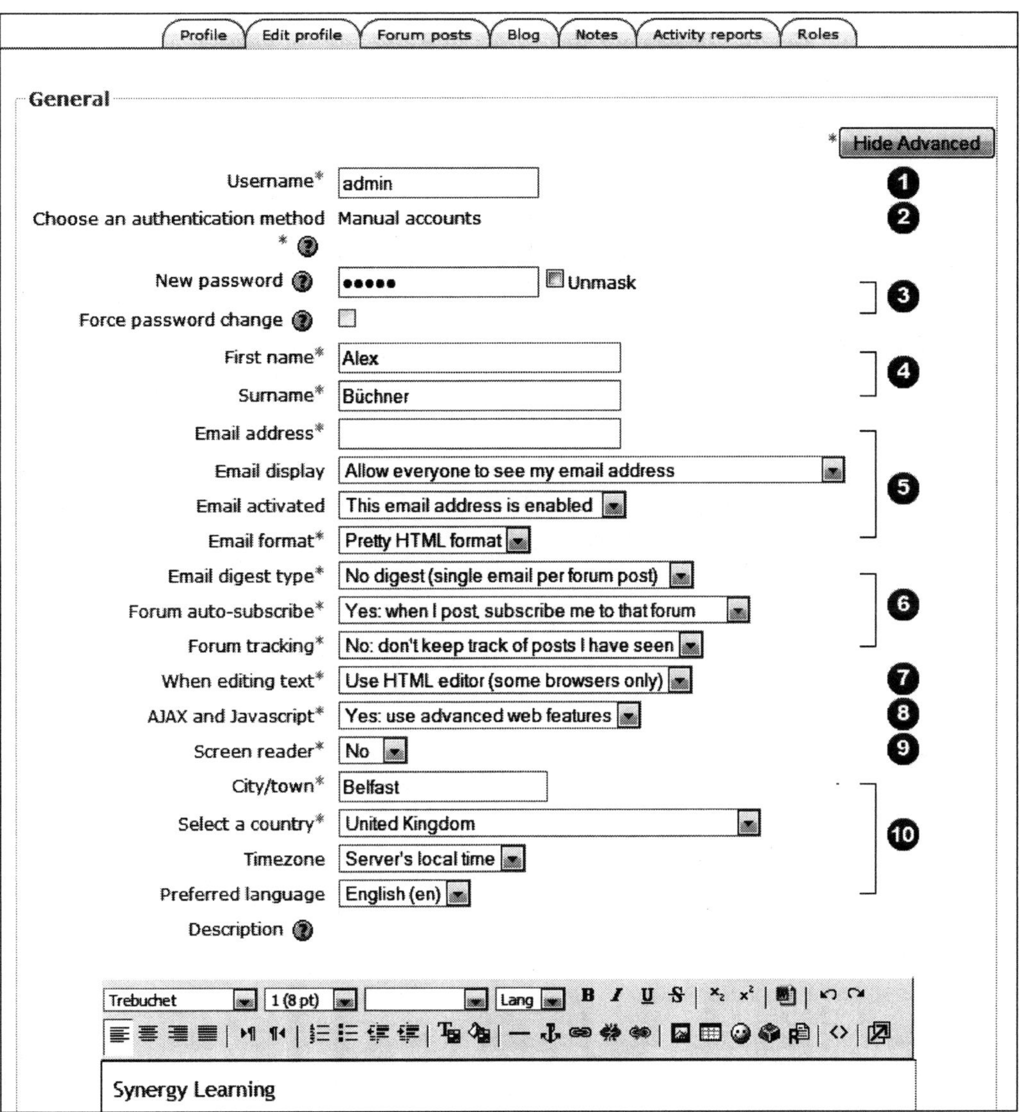
Profile
Edit profile
Forum posts
Blog
Notes
Activity reports
Roles
General
Hide Advanced
Username*
admin
Choose an authentication method *
Manual accounts
New password
Unmask
Force password change
First name*
Alex
Surname*
Büchner
Email address*
Email display
Allow everyone to see my email address
Email activated
This email address is enabled
Email format*
Pretty HTML format
Email digest type*
No digest (single email per forum post)
Forum auto-subscribe*
Yes: when I post, subscribe me to that forum
Forum tracking*
No: don't keep track of posts I have seen
When editing text*
Use HTML editor (some browsers only)
AJAX and Javascript*
Yes: use advanced web features
Screen reader*
No
City/town*
Belfast
Select a country*
United Kingdom
Timezone
Server's local time
Preferred language
English (en)
Description
Trebuchet
1 (8 pt)
Lang
Synergy Learning
1
2
3
4
5
6
7
8
9
10

Most of these items are self-explanatory, but there are a few things you need to know about each of them. Here is a description of each profile element, along with tips to use them effectively:

1. **Username**

   A unique username has to be provided. It is highly recommended to develop a naming scheme to which each username has to conform, for instance, `Firstname.Surname` or `YearOfEntry-Initial.Surname` (different naming schemes are discussed in the *Best Practice* section of this chapter). By default, only alphanumeric characters are allowed. If you want students to use non-alphanumeric characters in their usernames, you have to enable this by turning on **Allow extended characters in usernames** in **Security | Site Policies** in the **Site Administration** block. It is important to remember that *you ought to have administrator rights to change the username.*

2. **Authentication method**

   This menu allows changes to the authentication method for the user, if more than one authentication method has been activated for the site. In the screenshot, only **Manual accounts** have been set up, and therefore no choice is available.

[  Warning: Selecting the incorrect authentication method will prevent the user from logging in or even deleting his or her account completely. ]

3. **Password information**

   A password should be provided for security reasons. If the user has to change the given (default) password on their first login, the **Force password change** option has to be selected. You can unmask or show your own password, but not the password of other users. However, you can override the existing password of a user.

4. **First name** and **Surname**

   These are compulsory fields for users, for which diacritical marks are fully supported.

5. **Email information**

   There are four entries dictating how Moodle and other users can communicate with the current user through emails:

| | |
|---|---|
| **Email address** | Refers to the user's email address. This is a compulsory field and has to be unique in Moodle. It is important that the email address is correct, since Moodle makes regular use of it (for example, when new posts have been added to a forum). |
| **Email display** | Choices can be made as to who exactly can see the user's email address. The choices are: to hide the email address from everyone, allow only the people in the same course to see it (default), or display it for everyone who is logged on to Moodle. Administrators and teachers (with editing rights) will always be able to see email addresses even if they are hidden. |
| **Email activated** | The user's email functionality can be activated (default) or deactivated. Users will not be able to send or receive any emails when the facility is deactivated. This is sometimes necessary in (smaller) schools where students are not being given an email address. |
| **Email format** | This setting dictates whether an email sent by a user from Moodle is formatted using HTML (default) or is sent in plain text. Most modern email clients have the ability to receive and display HTML content. |

6. **Forum information**

   There are three forum-related entries:

| | |
|---|---|
| **Email digest type** | This setting determines how a user receives any posts from forums to which he or she has subscribed. There are three possible choices, which are: **No digest** (individual emails for each post, which is the default), **Complete** (a single list of posts daily), or **Subjects** (a single list daily with only the post topics included). |
| **Forum auto-subscribe** | This setting dictates whether a user is automatically subscribed to forums that he/she posts to. If it is set to subscribe (default), the system will automatically email the copies of new posts in forums the user has subscribed to, unless they manually override it when posting. |
| **Forum tracking** | If enabled, the posts that have not yet been read will be highlighted, which improves forum navigation. Forum tracking is disabled by default. |

7. **When editing text**

   This option determines whether to use plain text or the native HTML text editor of Moodle. This can usually be left on **Use HTML editor (some browsers only)**, which allows for text-formatting options. If a user is experiencing difficulties in editing text, the setting should be changed to **Use standard web forms**. The setting is also useful if you are entering programming code and wish to preserve indentation.

8. **AJAX and JavaScript**

   Moodle has a drag-and-drop interface for arranging items in courses, which requires AJAX and JavaScript. If a web browser does not support these technologies (older versions of Safari on OS X, some Linux browsers, and browsers on handheld devices and gaming consoles have occasional problems with this new technology), the option will be set to **No: use basic web features**.

9. **Screen Reader**

   If selected, pages will be rendered to be accessible via screen readers which are used by visually impaired users.

10. **Location, Timezone, and Language**

    **City/town** and **Country** are used to further identify users by geographical location. They are both compulsory fields.

    **Timezone** is used to convert time-related messages on the system (such as assignment deadlines) from the local time zone (typically, the server's time, but it can be set to anything) to the correct time in whichever zone you have selected. It is necessitated as your users may be geographically spread across a number of time zones.

    The default language of the system is shown and can be changed to the preferred language of the user.

Additionally, a **Description** field is shown that is used to provide additional information about the user. As an administrator, the field can be left empty. However, when a user logs in to his or her profile, the field is compulsory.

## Category "Picture of"

The second category is called **Picture of** and, as the name suggests, deals with the image attached to a user.

To upload a new picture, click the **Browse** button and select the image from your hard disk as shown in the screenshot. The image cannot be larger than the maximum size listed (here **2MB**), or it will not be uploaded. If your image is too large, it is recommended to reduce its size to a minimum of 100x100 pixels. The formats supported are JPG, GIF, and PNG. However, be careful with transparent backgrounds as they are not supported by older browsers.

The **Picture description** is used as an alternate text, which is important for accessibility conformance.

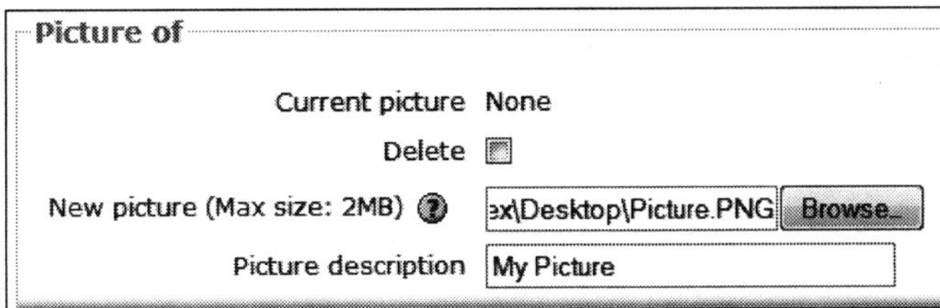


Once a picture has been assigned, it will be shown instead of the **None** label. To delete the picture, select the corresponding checkbox and the picture will be removed when the profile information is updated

Moodle will automatically crop the image to a square and resize it to 100x100 pixels for the larger view, and 35x35 pixels for the smaller view.

> Both these small images are created by Moodle in the upload process, which also reduces the file's size to around 4K. Pictures are stored in the user's sub-folder of the Moodle data folder. The two images are called `f1.jpg` and `f2.jpg`. All uploaded user pictures can be viewed via the URL `<moodle url>/userpix/` (a login is required).

If you suspect that your learners are likely to misuse this feature by uploading unsuitable pictures, you can disallow the functionality. Go to **Security | Site policies** in the **Site Administration** block, and tick the **Disable User Profile Images** box at the bottom of the screen. Bear in mind that once this feature is disabled, pictures cannot be assigned to any user (except the administrator), and nor will it be possible for teachers to represent groups in courses with images:

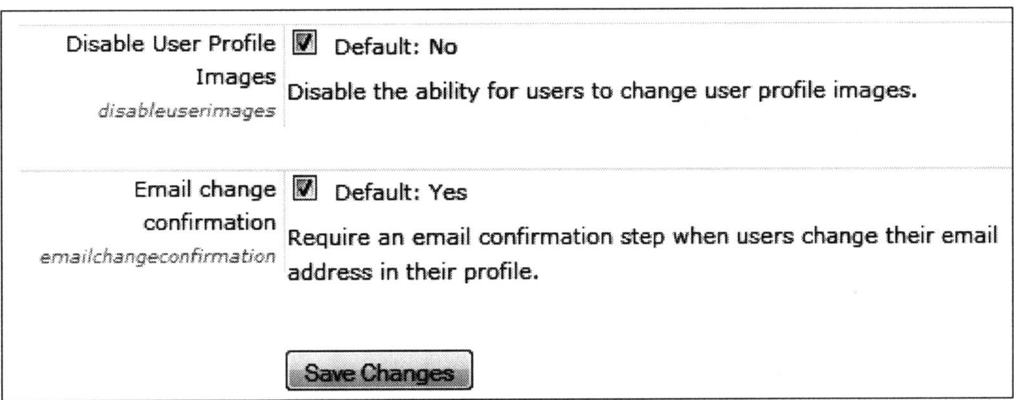

## Category "Interests"

Interests such as hobbies or professional activities have to be entered, separated by commas, as seen in the screenshot. The given **List of interests** is used as a tag, which forms the basis for supported social activities such as the Flickr and YouTube block. You can find more information about Moodle tagging at `http://docs.moodle.org/en/Tags`.

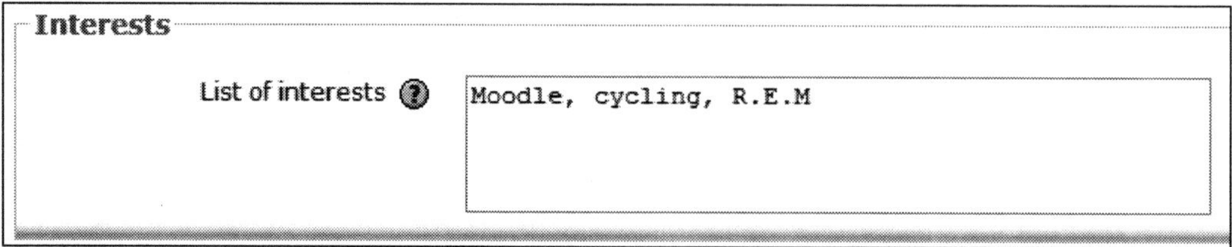


## Category "Optional"

More personal details are grouped into the **Optional** category, the last user category, as shown in the following screenshot:

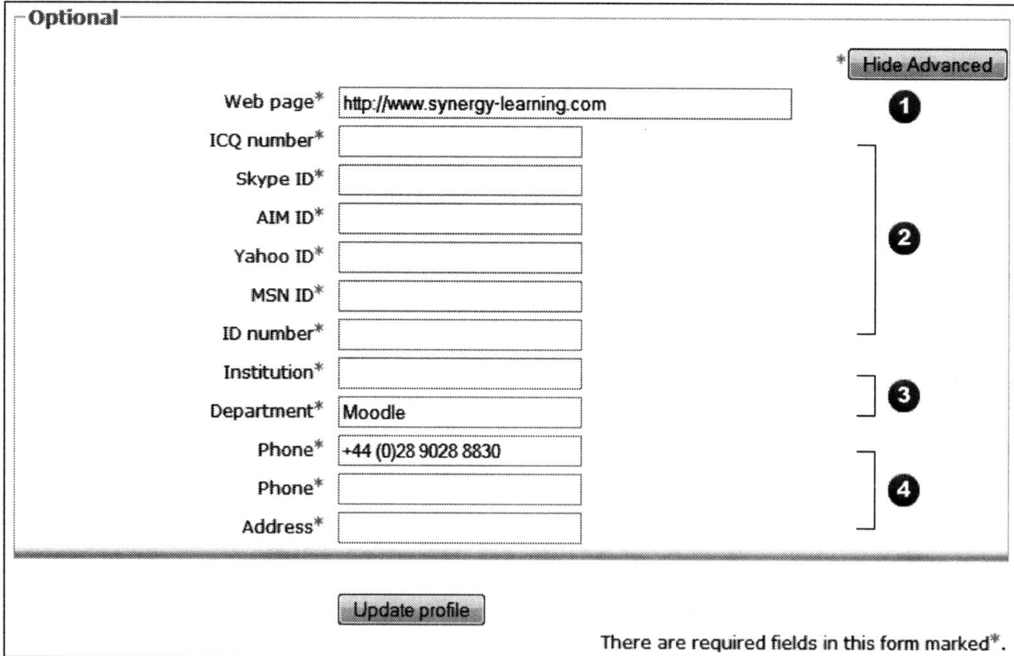

The options could be listed as follows:

1. Web Page

   It is the URL of the user's web or home page.
2. Messenger Information

   Moodle supports a range of popular messenger services. These are ICQ, Skype AIM, Yahoo! Messenger, and Microsoft's MSN. While entering any of the service's IDs, Moodle will make use of that service's functionality (for instance, display Skype's status information in the user's profile).
3. ID number, Institution, and Department

   It will contain IDs of students or staff, and information on school and department.
4. Contact Details

   It has the user's phone numbers and postal address.

Even when the **Update profile** button has been pressed, the image might not appear to have changed. If this is so, use the **Reload** button in your browser. If it still doesn't appear (as it happens in some rare cases), clear the cache of your web browser.

# Creating User-Defined Profile Fields

Moodle allows new arbitrary fields to be added to the user profile. This feature can be found in **Users | Accounts | User profile fields** in the **Site Administration** block as shown in the following screenshot:

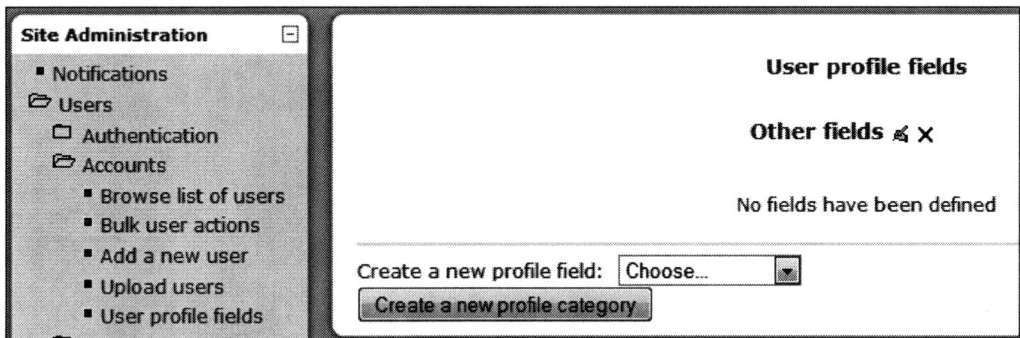

## Profile Categories

The profile fields are organized in categories (General, Picture of, Interests, and Optional). Additional categories can be created, and the user-defined fields can then be placed within those new categories. A default category called **Other fields** is already present, which can be deleted or renamed via the standard Moodle icons. To create a new category, select the **Create a new profile category** button seen in the preceding screenshot.

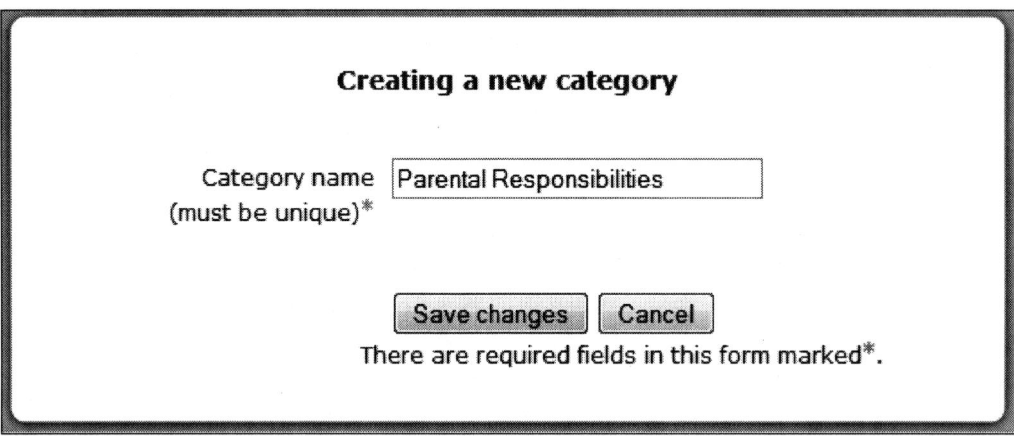


You are asked to provide a unique category name. The category will be displayed at the bottom of the user profile if profile fields have been added to the category.

## Profile Fields

Once a category has been created, four types of profile fields can be added to Moodle via the **Create a new profile field** pull-down menu:

- Checkbox

  This allows setting a value to true or false.
- Menu of choices

  This allows the selection of a value from a predefined list.
- Text area

  This allows entering multiline formatted text.
- Text input

  This allows entering a single line of text or a number.

Once you've chosen your field type, you're taken to the setting screen for that field. This has two sections: **Common settings** deals with settings that apply to all fields. **Specific settings** are settings that apply only to the chosen field type. Let's look at these settings.

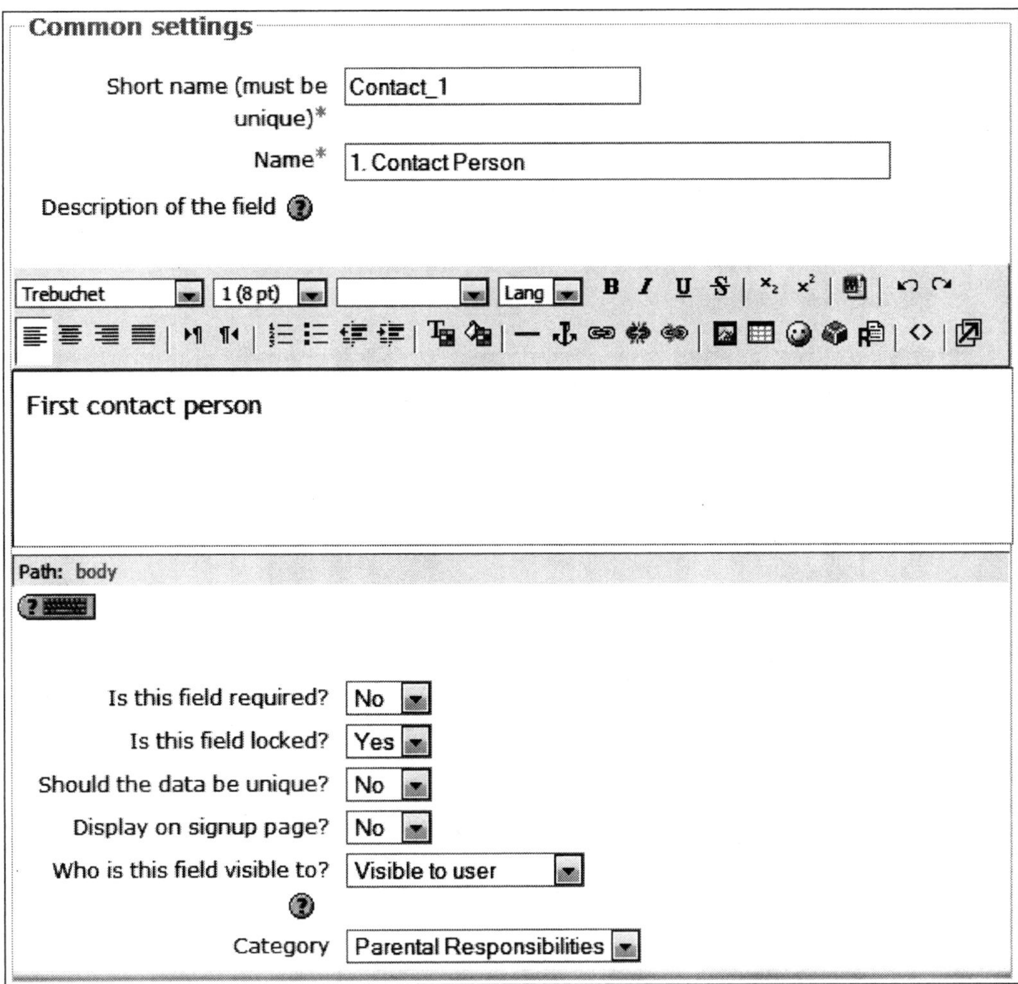


The **Short name** is a unique identifier of the field that is accompanied by the actual **Name**, which is the label displayed in the profile. An optional **Description** of the field can be given.

If the field is compulsory, the **Is this field required?** menu has to be set to **Yes**. The field can be **locked**, that is, the user cannot modify it. If the value entered has to be **unique**, the setting has to be changed accordingly.

When self-registration is enabled, a number of default fields have to be provided at signup. If the new field should also be displayed on the **signup page**, the setting has to be changed to **Yes**. This can be very useful in a commercial training setting, when additional information such as the address of the learner or previous qualifications is required.

The custom field can be given one of three **visibility** settings:

- The **Not visible** setting is typically set by an administrator who wants to hold private data of the users
- The **Visible to user** setting is normally selected for fields that hold sensitive information
- The **Visible to everyone** setting is used for any other type of information (default)

A **Category** has to be selected from a list of created values entered before the specific settings have to be provided for each field type. It is possible to select only the newlycreated categories; default categories can unfortunately not be selected. For example, if you wish to extend the existing address field with a postcode, you will have to do this in a separate category.

In addition to the common field settings, specific settings have to be provided for each profile field type.

## Text Input Field Type

For the text input type, a **Default value**, the **Display size** (size of text box), and the **Maximum length** have to be provided. Additionally, it has to be specified if the field is a password field, which will lead to the masking being turned on:

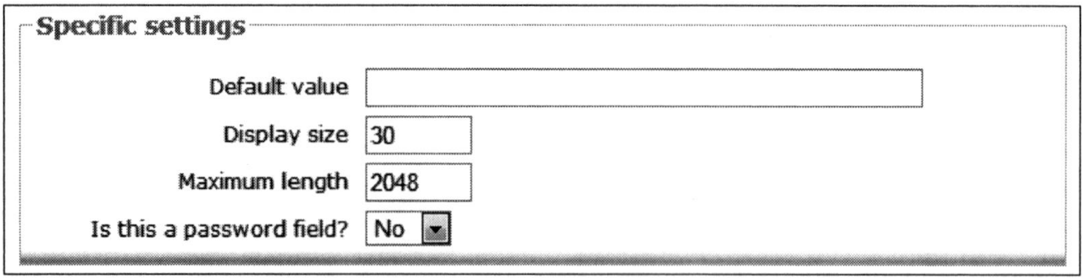

Specific settings

Default value

Display size 30

Maximum length 2048

Is this a password field? No

## Menu of Choices Field Type

For the Menu of choices type, a list of **Menu options** and an optional **Default value** have to be provided. The list consists of a single item per line. In the example shown, three options (**Father, Mother,** and **Carer**) have been entered, with **Mother** being the default value:

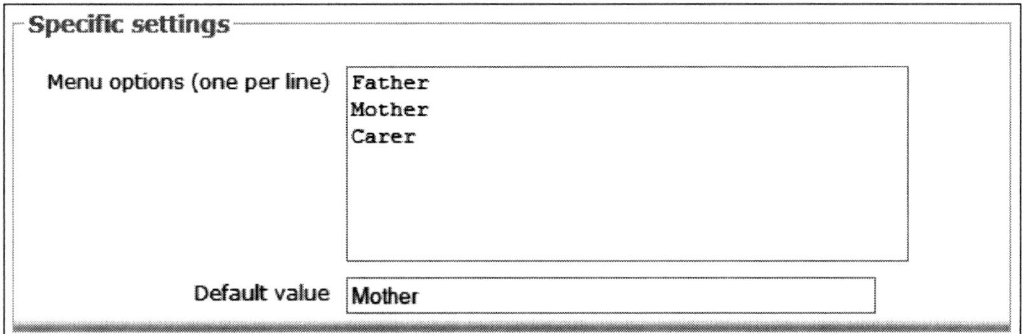


## Text Area Field Type

The text area field type allows users to define a default value on their own along with the dimensions of the displayed field (**Columns** and **Rows**):

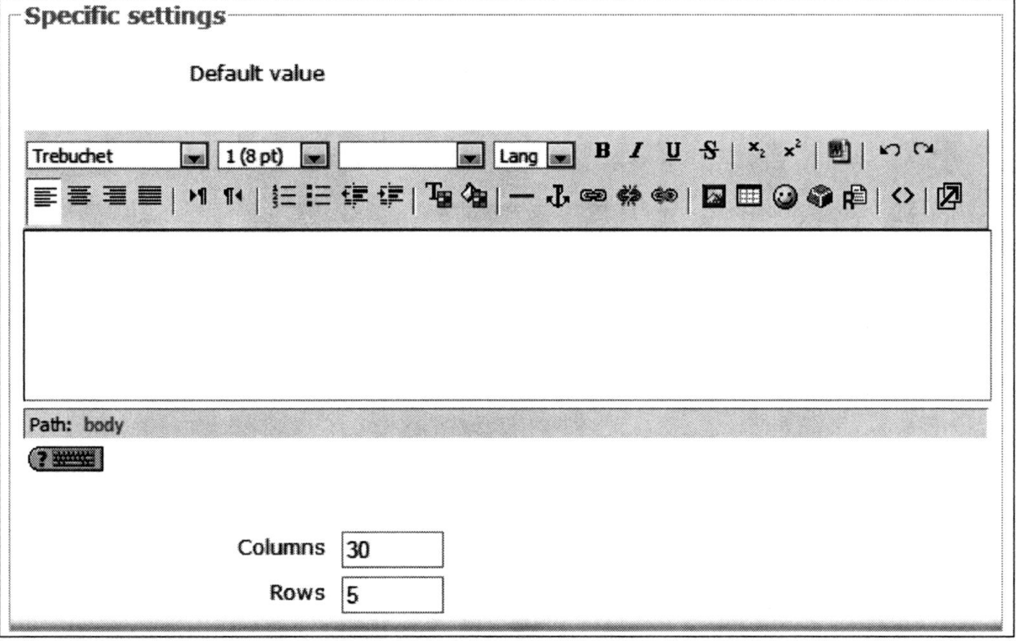

## Display Order of Profile Fields

Once all the required fields have been added, the order in which they will be displayed can be changed by using the up and down arrows:

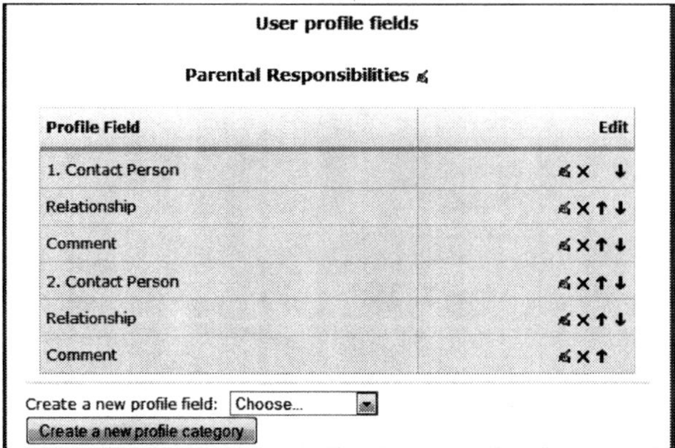


## Using Profile Fields

These fields will be shown in the user profile in the same way as generic Moodle fields:

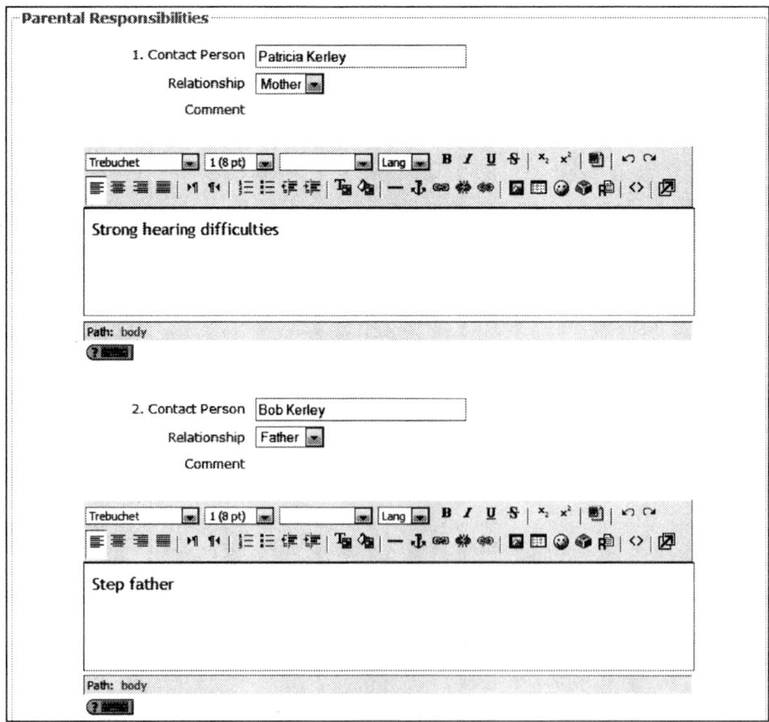

# Standard User Actions

So far, you have learned what user information Moodle is holding and how to extend what is stored in each profile. It is time now to work with the existing users.

# Browsing Users

The quickest way to get access to your Moodle users is via **Users | Accounts | Browse list of users** in the **Site Administration** block. Initially, a list of users is displayed ordered by first name. Thirty users are shown at a time and, if applicable, you can navigate via the **(Next)** and **(Previous)** links or jump directly to another page by selecting a number. Each column can be sorted in ascending or descending order by clicking on the column header:

144 Users
Page: 1 2 3 4 5 (Next)
New filter
Show Advanced
Full name
contains
Add filter
Add a new user
First name / Surname
Email address
City/town
Country
Last access
Adam Stevenson
Adam.Stevenson@yourschool.org.uk
London
United Kingdom
Never
Edit
Delete
Alex Büchner
alex@synergy-learning.com
Belfast
United Kingdom
51 secs
Edit
Alex Newton
Alex.Newton@yourschool.org.uk
London
United Kingdom
10 days 4 hours
Edit
Delete
Amanda Binnington
Amanda.Binnington@yourschool.org.uk
London
United Kingdom
Never
Edit
Delete

You can view an individual's profile information by clicking on a user's name in the first column. Here you are looking at your own (admin) profile, and not the profile of another user. If it were another user, the appearance would be different. You would see the courses they are enrolled into and there would be no **Change password** button among other information.

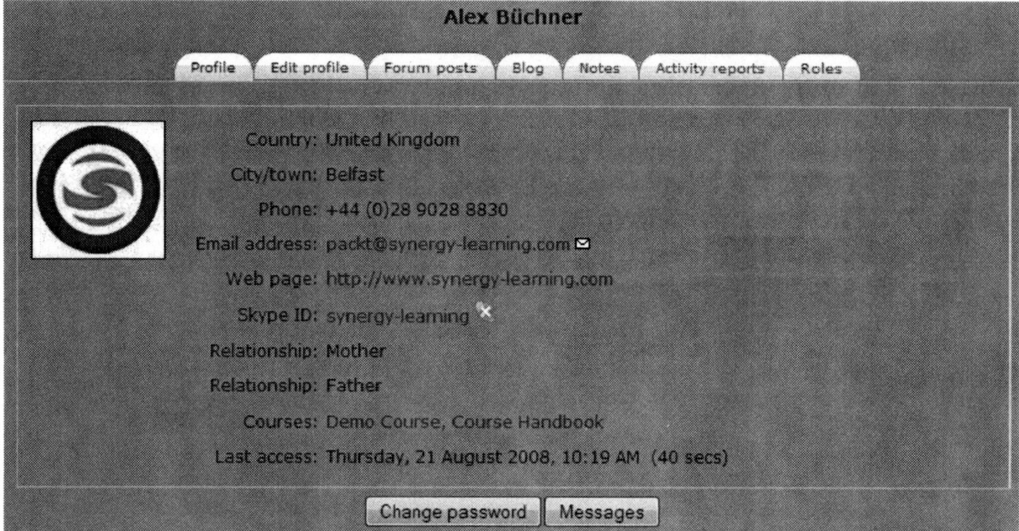


The profile provides detailed information about the user. Hyperlinks are provided to email, web pages, and some messaging services. For instance, in the screenshot a link is provided to initiate Skype, which also shows that the user's status is currently unavailable.

Two regularly used operations can be accessed by the **Change password** and **Messages** buttons. The **Messages** button will not appear if the messaging system has been disabled. For more detailed changes, select the **Edit profile** tab at the top, which will let you make modifications to all user profile fields as discussed earlier.

To delete an individual user, go back to the participants' list and select the **Delete** link in the right-most column. A confirmation screen has to be answered before the user is irreversibly removed from Moodle.

# Filtering Users

Very often, we may be required to search for a particular user or for a number of users. Moodle provides a very powerful and flexible filtering mechanism to narrow down the list of displayed users. In basic mode you can filter by full name, that is, the first name and last name combined.

The following filter operations are available, all of which are case-insensitive:

| Filter Operation | Description |
|---|---|
| contains | The provided text has to be present in the field. |
| doesn't contain | The opposite of "contains". |
| is equal to | The provided text has to be the same as the value of the field. |
| starts with | The field has to start with the provided text. |
| ends with | The field has to finish with the provided text. |
| is empty | The field has to be empty. |

For example, when adding the filter **Full name starts with chr**, all users are displayed whose names begin with "Chr":

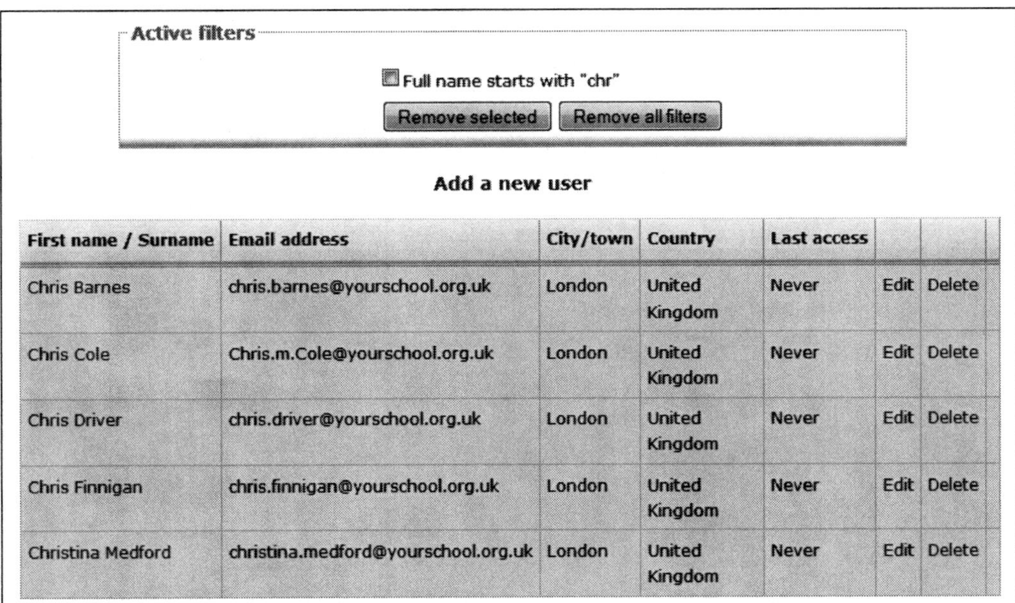


| First name / Surname | Email address | City/town | Country | Last access | | |
|---|---|---|---|---|---|---|
| Chris Barnes | chris.barnes@yourschool.org.uk | London | United Kingdom | Never | Edit | Delete |
| Chris Cole | Chris.m.Cole@yourschool.org.uk | London | United Kingdom | Never | Edit | Delete |
| Chris Driver | chris.driver@yourschool.org.uk | London | United Kingdom | Never | Edit | Delete |
| Chris Finnigan | chris.finnigan@yourschool.org.uk | London | United Kingdom | Never | Edit | Delete |
| Christina Medford | christina.medford@yourschool.org.uk | London | United Kingdom | Never | Edit | Delete |

You can see at the top that the added filter is now active. This becomes more useful once multiple filters have been added, which is done in the advanced mode (switched on via the **Show Advanced** button). Now, we have the ability to apply filters on a wide range of fields:

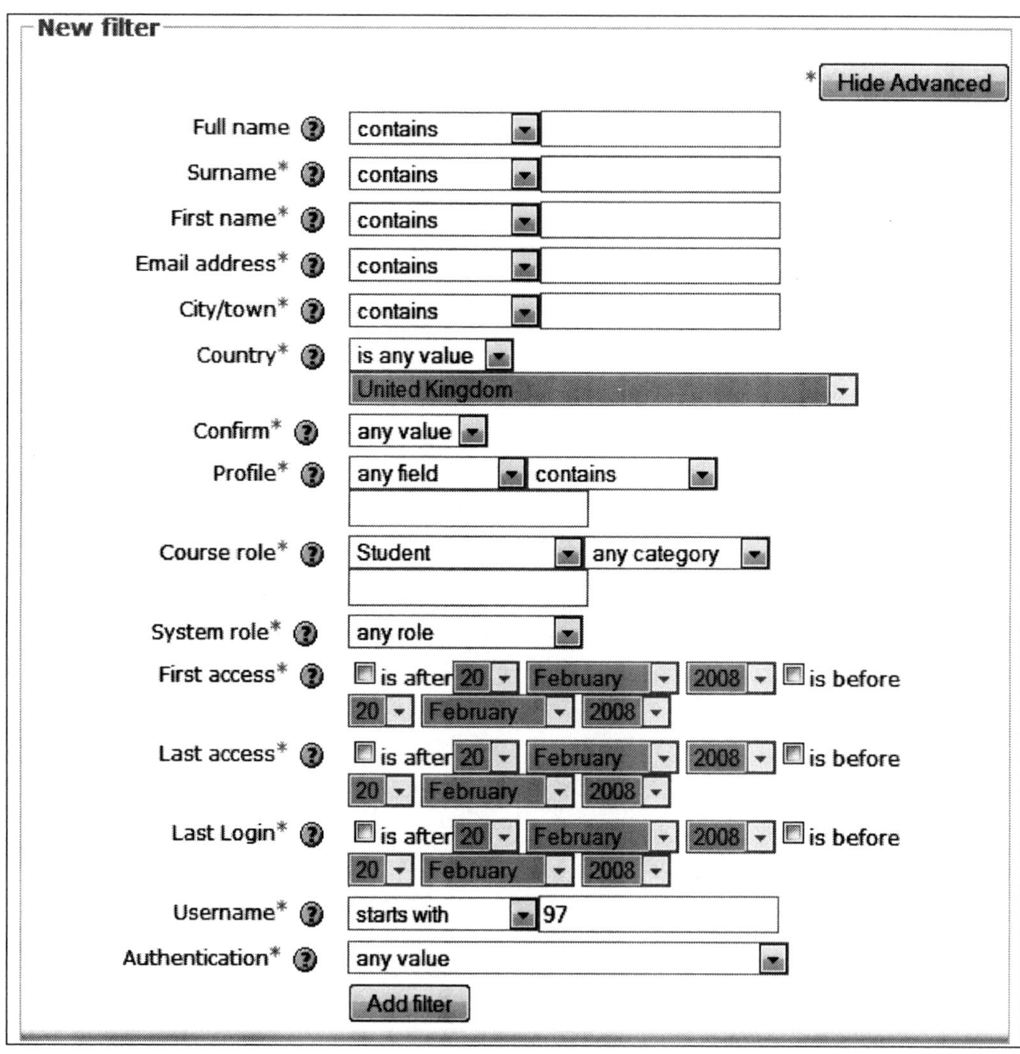


For instance, in the screenshot, we are looking for all users who are students in a course (**Course role = Student**) and whose **username starts with 97** (our naming scheme starts with the year of entry). Using this mechanism, it is possible to add as many filters as required.

Every time a filter is added, it will be shown in the **Active filters** frame and will be applied to the user data in Moodle:

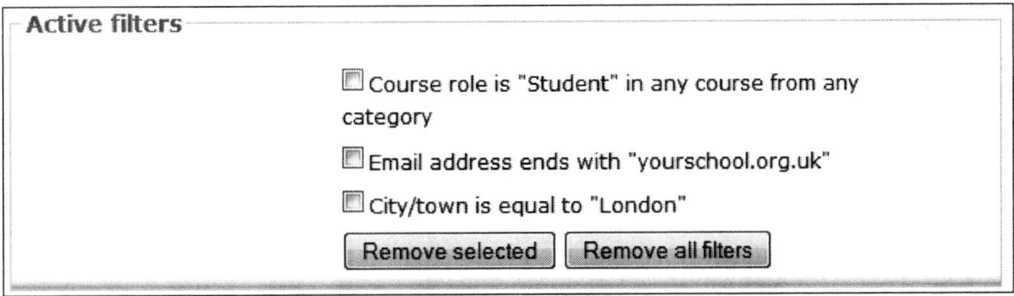


In the example, three self-explanatory filters have been added. It is now possible to either delete individual filters (tick filter and press **Remove selected** button) or remove all filters.

The filter criteria for text fields have been described earlier in this section. Depending on the field type, there are a number of additional operations that can be used.

| Filter Operation | Field Type | Description |
|---|---|---|
| is any value | Lists | All values are acceptable; filter is disabled. |
| is equal to | Lists | List value has to be the same as the one selected. |
| isn't equal to | Lists | Opposite of "is equal to". |
| any value | Yes / No | Value can be either Yes or No; filter is disabled. |
| Yes | Yes / No | Value has to be Yes. |
| No | Yes / No | Value has to be No. |
| is defined | Profile fields | The field has to be defined for the user. |
| isn't defined | Profile fields | Opposite of "is defined". |
| is after | Date | All dates after specified day, month, and year. |
| is before | Date | All dates before specified day, month, and year. |

The profile criterion offers a choice of all user-defined fields (as specified earlier). The authentication criterion offers a selection of all authentication methods supported. We will deal with these later in the chapter.

The current filter settings are saved and can be used next time you log in. Not only that, they are also saved for bulk-uploading, which is covered next.

# Bulk User Actions

There are several actions that Moodle allows you to take on many users at a time. They are:

- Confirm registration
- Send bulk messages
- Delete a user
- Display a summary of their profile
- Download their profile details to a file

As an administrator, you can apply these operations. Moodle calls them bulk user actions, which you access at **Users** | **Accounts** | **Bulk user actions** in the **Site Administration** block:

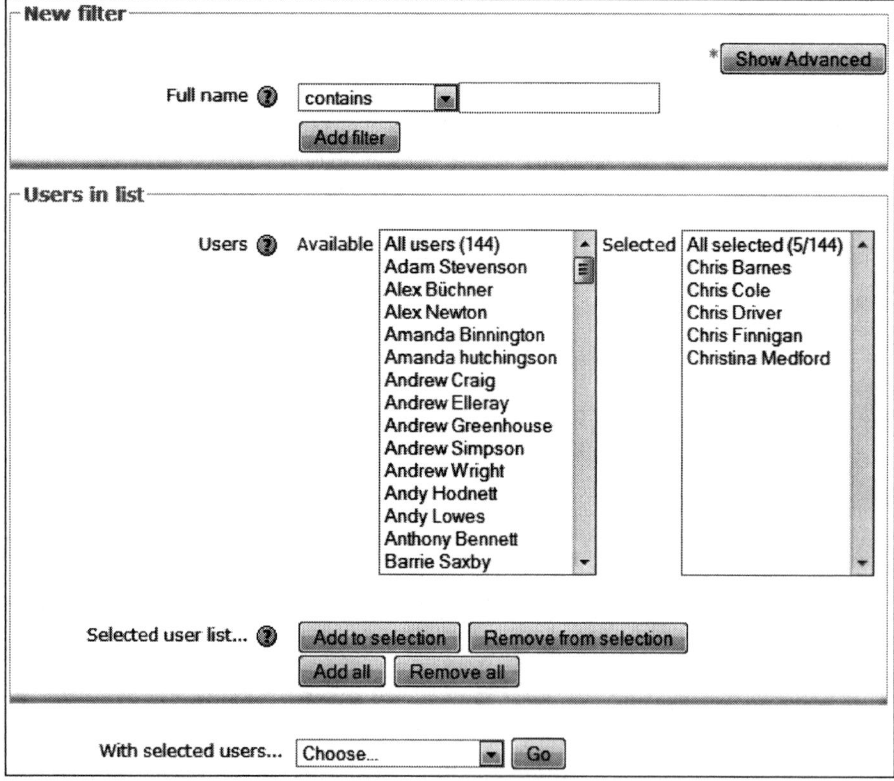


The screen contains two main parts. The first part is the familiar filter and is identical to the one in the **Browse list of users** sub-menu.

The second part displays the users that match the specified filter criteria in the **Available** list. Before you can do anything with the users, you have to move them into the **Selected** list using the **Add to selection** button. In the screenshot shown, five users have been moved across. To move them back to the original list, select the users and press the **Remove from selection** button. Moodle provides you with the two buttons—**Add all** to add all users from the **Available** to the **Selected** list, and **Remove all** to remove all users from the **Selected** list and put them back to the **Available** list.

The advantage of this approach is that you can apply a number of filters in succession and select the respective users. For example, if you wish to select all users from two different entry years, you can create a filter for all usernames starting with 97 and select all users. You can then delete the filter and create another filter for all usernames starting with 98. For the theorists among you, this is the equivalent of a logical **UNION** operator.

When the **Go** button from the **With selected users...** is pressed, the operation selected in this section will be performed on the users from the **Selected** list. The available operations are shown in the table that follows:

| **Action** | **Description** |
|---|---|
| Confirm | After a confirmation screen, pending user accounts will be confirmed. (This is only applicable if self-registration is used.) |
| Add/send message | You are asked to write a message body and specify the format in which the message will be sent. The options are:<br>• Moodle auto-format<br>• HTML format<br>• Plain text format<br>• Markdown text format |
| Delete | After a confirmation screen, users will be irreversibly removed from the system. |
| Display on page | User information is shown on screen. The fields displayed are **Full name, Email address, City/town, Country, and Last access.** |
| Download | You can choose between three download formats:<br>• Text: Comma-separated text file<br>• ODF: Open Document Format<br>• Excel: Microsoft Excel<br><br>The fields that are included are (Moodle's internal user) ID, Username, Email address, First name, Surname, ID number, City/town, and Country. |

# Manual Accounts

There are three manual ways for users to get access to an existing Moodle system and its courses:

- Adding individual users
- Bulk uploading of users
- Self-registration (email authentication)

You will learn how to perform and support each type in the following three sections.

# Adding Individual Users

To add user accounts manually, go to **Users | Accounts | Add a new user** in the **Site Administration** block. You will be confronted with the same screen when you edit a user's profile.

You should avoid adding individual users as much as possible as it is a very time-consuming, cumbersome, and potentially error-prone procedure. However, there are situations when you cannot avoid it, for example, when a pupil joins the school half-way through the term.

If you have more than one user to add, use Moodle's batch-uploading facility that we will look at next.

# Bulk-Uploading of Users and Their Pictures

Uploading users in bulk allows the importing of multiple user accounts from a text file or the updating of user accounts that already exist in your system. The operation is typically carried out once when transferring existing pupil information from an existing system onto Moodle.

Student information is often available in an existing application, for example, a school management system such as **SIMS** (**Student Information Management System**), which can export data to an Excel spreadsheet or directly to a text file. You may also want to import users from another learning management system such as **Blackboard**.

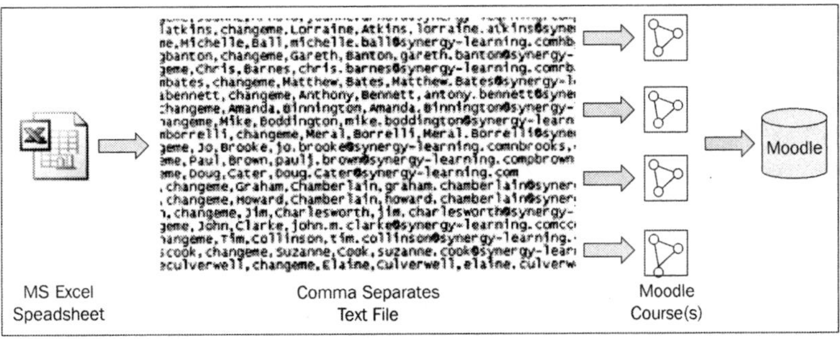


# Text File Format

Before uploading users, you have to generate a text file that has to conform to a certain format. Its general format is called **comma-separated text file** or **CSV** for short, which is a flat text file format. You can create a CSV file like this in Excel or any other spreadsheet application. Use the first row to provide field names, and then fill in each cell with the required data. Then save the file as CSV, making sure that you specify that the top row contains field names.

The format of a text file has to be as follows:

- Each line of the file contains a single record
- Each record is a series of data separated by commas or other delimiters
- The first record of the file contains a list of fieldnames that define the format of the rest of the file

The following is an example of a valid input file:

```
username,password,firstname,lastname,email
galmond,pwd,Graham,Almond,graham.almond@yourschool.ac.uk
earmstrong,pwd,Eleanor,Armstrong,eleanor.armstrong@yourschool.ac.uk
jarnold,pwd,Joanne,Arnold,joanne.arnold@yourschool.ac.uk
```

The first line contains the list of fields that is provided, while the remaining three lines represent individual users to be uploaded.

The upload function in Moodle supports five types of data fields:

- Required: Compulsory fields that have to be included
- Optional: If no value is provided, specified default values will be used
- Custom: User-defined profile fields
- Enrolment: Deals with courses, roles, and groups
- Special: Used for changing or removing users

## Required Fields

When adding new users, only the `firstname` and `lastname` are compulsory. When updating records, only the `username` is required. You might recall that the user profile has a few more compulsory fields, such as the email address. If these fields are not provided, a default value has to be specified. We will deal with this a little later.

The sample file shown in the previous section is an example of a valid input file containing five fields including the required `firstname` and `lastname`.

## Optional fields

As mentioned, the default fields are required, but do not have to be specified. If they are not included in the text file, default values are taken instead.

| Field | Values |
|---|---|
| address | Text |
| ajax | 0-No, 1-Yes |
| auth | Text (from existing list) |
| autosubscribe | 0-No, 1-Yes |
| city | Text |
| country | Text (from existing list) |
| department | Text |
| description | Text |
| emailstop | 0-enabled, 1-disabled |
| htmleditor | 0-standard web forms, 1-HTML Editor |
| icq | Text |
| idnumber | Text |
| institution | Text |
| lang | Text (from existing list) |
| maildisplay | 0-Hide, 1-Allow everyone, 2-Allow course members |
| mailformat | 0-Pretty, 1-Plain |
| passwd | Text |
| phone1 | Text |
| phone2 | Text |
| timezone | Text (from existing list) |
| url | Text |

Let us assume that the default city has been set to Birmingham. In order to override the field for the users who are not living in the default town, the following sample file can be used:

```
username,password,firstname,lastname,city, email
galmond,changeme,Graham,Almond,London,graham.almond@yourschool.ac.uk
earmstrong,changeme,Eleanor,Armstrong,,eleanor.armstrong@yourschool.
ac.uk
jarnold,changeme,Joanne,Arnold,York,joanne.arnold@yourschool.ac.uk
```

In this file, a city field has been added. After uploading the file, Graham Almond's city is set to London and Joanna Arnold's to York. Eleanor Armstrong's city has been left empty and will be set to the default value of Birmingham.

It is important to include empty fields in the data when the default setting has to be used. It must be left empty even if it is the last field in each record. An empty field is represented by two consecutive commas (as shown in the sample file example).

[  If you set the password to `changeme`, the user will be forced to change the password when they log in for the first time. ]

In fields that have numeric values, the options are numbered in the same order as they appear in the Moodle interface; the numbering starts with 0. For instance, **maildisplay** allows the following settings:

1. Hide my email address from everyone.
2. Allow everyone to see my email address.
3. Allow only other course members to see my email address.

For Boolean fields such as **autosubscribe**, use 1 for Yes and 0 for No.

If any fields in your upload file contain commas (for example in the description), you have to encode them as `,` the upload function will automatically convert these back to commas.

## Custom Fields

Any user-defined fields that you have specified (in our case, the ones for parental responsibilities) can also be used as part of the batch-upload process. Each field has to be preceded by `profile_field_`. For instance, the field number one representing the **Contact Person** would be called `profile_field_Contact1`.

Custom fields are treated in the same way as optional fields. If they are specified, the values are taken; otherwise default values will be used instead.

## Enrolment Fields

Enrolment fields allow you to assign roles to users, that is, you can enroll them into courses and also groups. Groups are created by teachers in courses. Roles, which we have just touched upon, will be covered in great detail in Chapter 6.

Each course has to be specified separately by course1, course2, course3, and so on. The course name is the short name of the course. Each corresponding type, role, and group has to have the same postfix, that is, role1 and group1 have to correspond to course1.

It is further possible to set the role of a user in a course. One option to achieve this is the usage of the legacy mechanism of types that are used to tell Moodle whether the user is a **Student** (1), an **Editing Teacher** (2), or a **Non-Editing teacher** (3) in a corresponding course. If the type is left blank, or if no course is specified, the user will be enrolled as **Student**.

The second option is the usage of roles in a corresponding course. Each role has a short name and a role ID, either of which can be specified.

If you want to assign users to groups in a course (group1 in course1, group2 in course2, and so on) you have to specify the group name or ID.

The following is an example demonstrating some of the enrolment features:

```
firstname, lastname, course1, role1, course2
Graham, Almond, Advanced, Teacher, Staff
Eva, Armstrong, Advanced, Examiner, Staff
Jonny, Arnold, Basic, Teacher, Staff
```

As before, the first line specifies the fields in the file. course1 and its corresponding role2 as well as course2 are optional enrolment fields. `Graham Almond` will be assigned the `Teacher` role in the `Advanced` course and a `Student` role in the `Staff` course (no role has been specified and hence the default is set). Similarly, `Eva Armstrong` will be assigned the `Examiner` role in the `Advanced` course and a `Student` role in the `Staff` course. And `Jonny Arnold` will be a `Teacher` in the `Basic` course, and a `Student` in the course labeled `Staff`.

## Special Fields

Two special fields are supported that allow you to change usernames or delete users. The former is represented with the field name `oldusername`, while the latter is called `deleted`.

# Uploading Users

In order to upload users, go to **Users | Accounts | Upload users** in the **Site Administration** block:

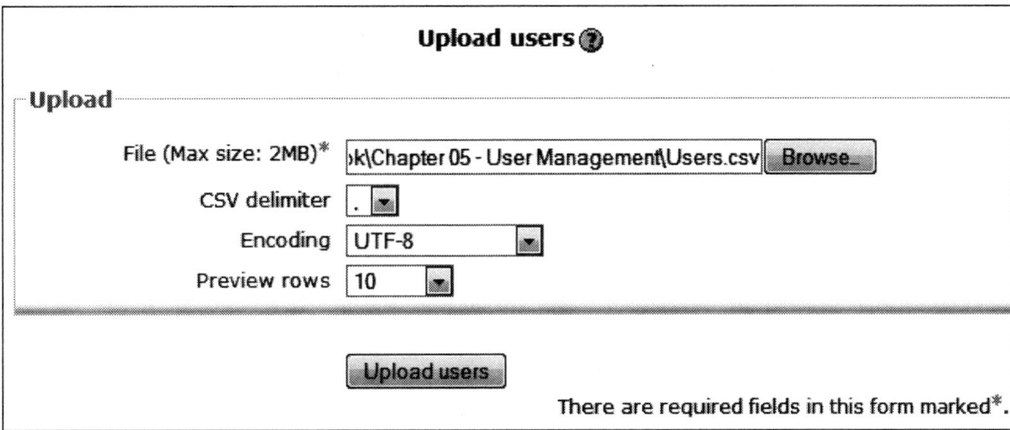


The following settings are available:

| Setting | Description |
|---|---|
| **File** | The location of the comma-delimited text file on your local computer. |
| **CSV Delimiter** | Specify whether the delimiter is a comma (default), semicolon, colon, or tab. |
| **Encoding** | Encoding the scheme of your upload file, which specifies the locale in which it has been saved (default is UTF-8). |
| **Preview rows** | The number of rows that will be displayed on the preview screen. (default is 10) |

Once this screen has been confirmed, you will see the preview followed by a number of settings, followed by all user fields for which default values can be set. Look at the following screenshot:

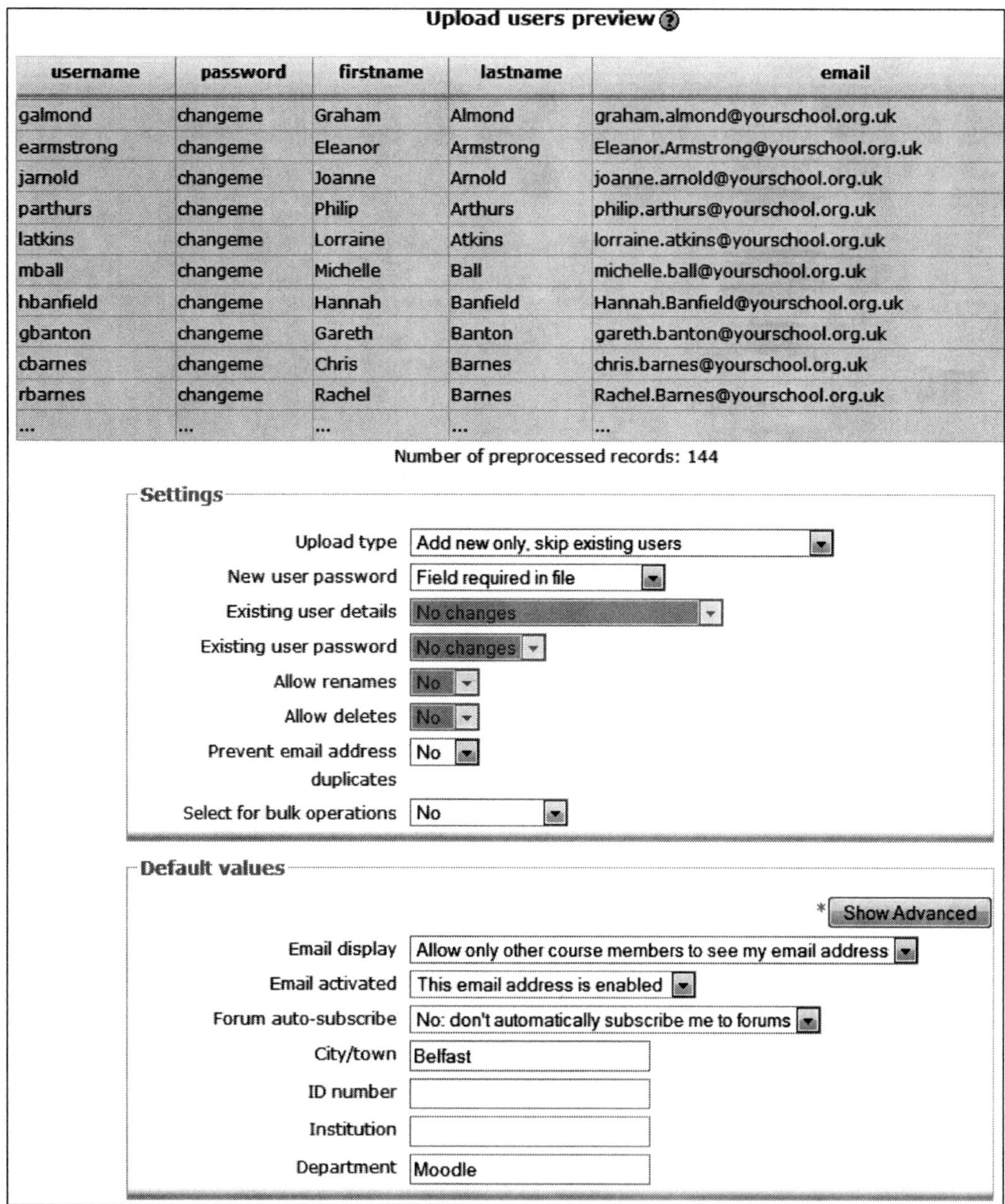

**Upload users preview**

| username | password | firstname | lastname | email |
|---|---|---|---|---|
| galmond | changeme | Graham | Almond | graham.almond@yourschool.org.uk |
| earmstrong | changeme | Eleanor | Armstrong | Eleanor.Armstrong@yourschool.org.uk |
| jarnold | changeme | Joanne | Arnold | joanne.arnold@yourschool.org.uk |
| parthurs | changeme | Philip | Arthurs | philip.arthurs@yourschool.org.uk |
| latkins | changeme | Lorraine | Atkins | lorraine.atkins@yourschool.org.uk |
| mball | changeme | Michelle | Ball | michelle.ball@yourschool.org.uk |
| hbanfield | changeme | Hannah | Banfield | Hannah.Banfield@yourschool.org.uk |
| gbanton | changeme | Gareth | Banton | gareth.banton@yourschool.org.uk |
| cbarnes | changeme | Chris | Barnes | chris.barnes@yourschool.org.uk |
| rbarnes | changeme | Rachel | Barnes | Rachel.Barnes@yourschool.org.uk |
| ... | ... | ... | ... | ... |

Number of preprocessed records: 144

**Settings**

Upload type: Add new only, skip existing users
New user password: Field required in file
Existing user details: No changes
Existing user password: No changes
Allow renames: No
Allow deletes: No
Prevent email address duplicates: No
Select for bulk operations: No

**Default values**

* Show Advanced

Email display: Allow only other course members to see my email address
Email activated: This email address is enabled
Forum auto-subscribe: No: don't automatically subscribe me to forums
City/town: Belfast
ID number:
Institution:
Department: Moodle

The following settings have to be applied:

| Setting | Description |
|---|---|
| **Upload Type** | There are four self-explanatory upload types:<br>• Add new only, skip existing users<br>• Add all, append counter to usernames if needed<br>• Add new and update existing users<br>• Update existing users only |
| **New user password** | Moodle either requires a password to be in the file (**Field required in file**) or it will generate a password automatically if none is specified. (**Create password if needed.**) This has to be changed by the user via the lost password mechanism or manually by the administrator if no email is provided. (not available for **Update existing users only** type) |
| **Existing user details** | Specifies what is done with the existing user details when a user is updated. The options are:<br>• No changes<br>• Override with file<br>• Override with file and defaults<br>• Fill in missing (fields) from file and defaults |
| **Existing user password** | Specifies what is done with users' passwords when a user is updated. It can either be left unchanged (No changes) or be overridden (Update). |
| **Allow renames** | Specifies whether renaming of users (that is, first name and/or last name) is allowed. This only applies to the special field `oldusername`, which has to be present in the text file. |
| **Allow deletes** | Specifies whether removing of users is allowed. This only applies to the special field `deleted`, which has to be present in the text file. |
| **Prevent email address duplicates** | Specifies whether the same email address is allowed for multiple users. This should be set to Yes to avoid any conflicts. |
| **Select for bulk operations** | You can specify if new users, updated users, or all users should be selected for bulk operations. You will see the respective names in the **Selected** list of **Bulk user actions**. |

# Setting Default Values and Templates

As mentioned earlier, the Moodle batch upload function supports default values that are used instead of optional fields, if no value has been set. This includes all the values in the user profile that can be uploaded and also any user-defined custom fields.

Each text-based field can be populated using a **template**. This is useful for some fields, for instance the URL of students' websites, and is compulsory for required fields if not specified in the text file, for example the username and email address. Moodle will warn you if latter is the case. For example, in the screenshot shown the **Username** has not been provided, which is indicated by a red warning message:

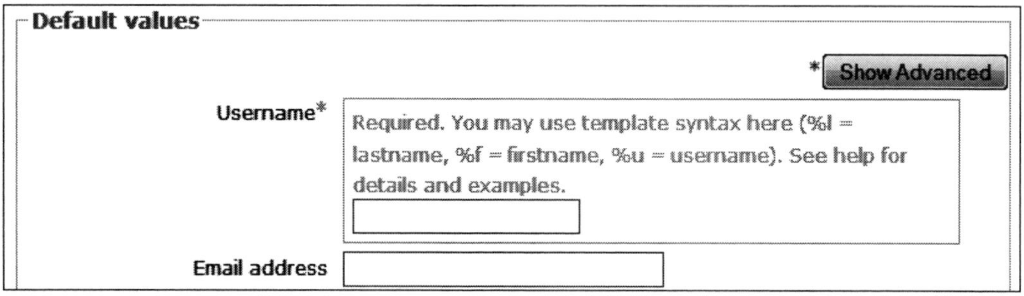

Default values

Show Advanced

Username* Required. You may use template syntax here (%l = lastname, %f = firstname, %u = username). See help for details and examples.

Email address

The template (or pattern) will create a value based on the values of other fields and the standard characters you specify. For example, if the username should be the first name of a user, followed by a full stop, and then the surname, the template you have to specify would look like this: `%f.%l`

These four replacement values can be used:

- `%f` will be replaced by the `firstname`
- `%l` will be replaced by the `lastname`
- `%u` will be replaced by the `username`
- `%%` will be replaced by the % (required if you need a percentage sign in the generated text)

Between the percent sign and any of the three code letters (l, f, and u), the following modifiers are allowed:

- \- value will be converted to lowercase
- \+ value will be converted to UPPERCASE
- ~ value will be converted to Title Case
- # (where the hash represents a decimal number) value will be truncated to those many characters

For instance, if `firstname` (`%f`) is Caroline and `lastname` (`%l`) is Gordon, the following values will be generated as shown in the following table:

| Pattern | Value |
|---|---|
| `%f%l` | `CarolineGordon` |
| `%l%f` | `GordonCaroline` |
| `%l%1f` | `GordonC` |
| `%-f_%-l` | `caroline_gordon` |

```
http://www.youruni.edu/~%-1f%-l/-http://www.youruni.edu/~cgordon/
```

The last template is an example of how to embed the replacement values inside other text, in this case a URL that represents a user's homepage.

## Loading of Data

Once all settings have been specified, all the default values have been set, and the **Upload Users** button has been pressed, Moodle will finally start the actual importing process.

Moodle displays a large table that contains all the user fields that have been added and/or changed. It also displays a status for each field, including any problems or errors that have occurred.

At the end of the user upload process, a short message is displayed summarizing the upload. It contains the number of users created, the number of users skipped, and the number of errors occurred:

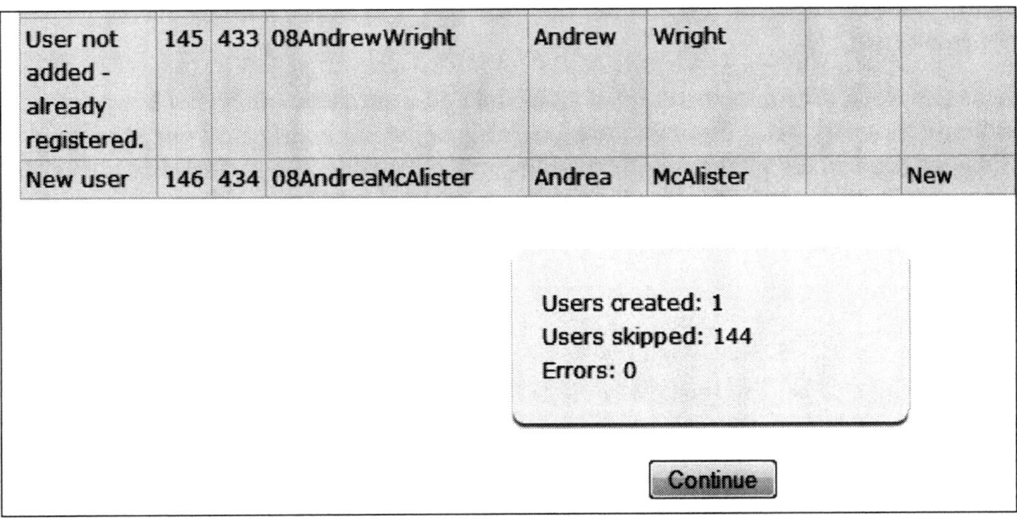

User not added - already registered.
145
433
08AndrewWright
Andrew
Wright
New user
146
434
08AndreaMcAlister
Andrea
McAlister
New
Users created: 1
Users skipped: 144
Errors: 0
Continue

If errors occurred, you would see them flagged in the listing. It is recommended that you identify the respective users immediately and modify their user settings manually.

## Uploading User Pictures

The process to upload users, described so far, does not support user profile pictures. These have to be uploaded separately at **Users | Accounts | Upload user pictures** in the **Site Administration** block:

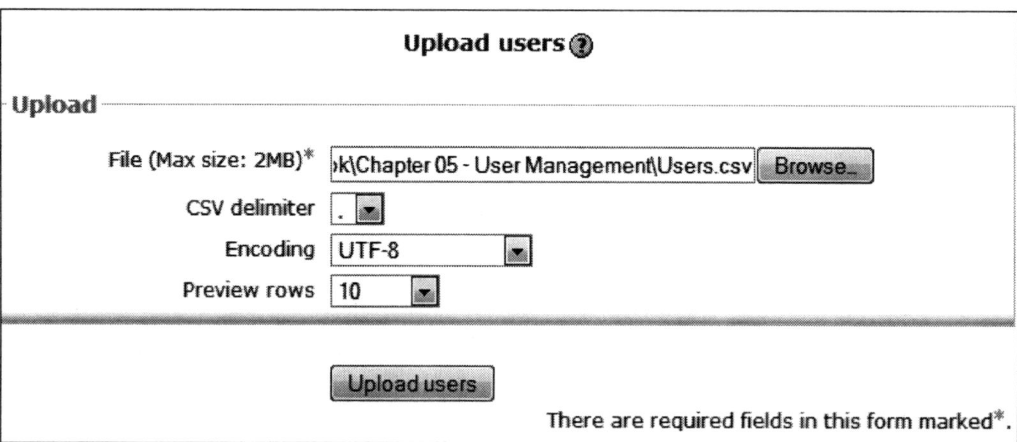


The pictures to be uploaded have to be archived in a ZIP file. Each image filename has to conform to the `user-attribute.extension` format. The user attribute is the `username`, `idnumber`, or the `ID` of the user. This attribute is used to match the picture to an existing user, and you have to select the attribute in the respective pull-down menu. The extension is the filename extension (jpg, gif, or png). Image filenames are not case-sensitive.

For example, if username consists of an initial and a surname (or %1f%l if expressed in template style), valid filenames are `asmith.png`, `ejones.png`, and `mstripe.png`. If the users exist, the pictures will be added to their profile. If a picture already exists for a user, it will only be replaced if you have selected the **Overwrite existing user pictures** option.

# Self-Registration

Email-based self-registration is the default authentication method. When a new user signs up with Moodle via the **Create my new account** button, she or he can choose her or his own new username and password. Once this step has been completed, a confirmation mail is sent to the user's email address, which contains a secure link to a page where the user has to confirm the account. The sign-up screen looks as follows:

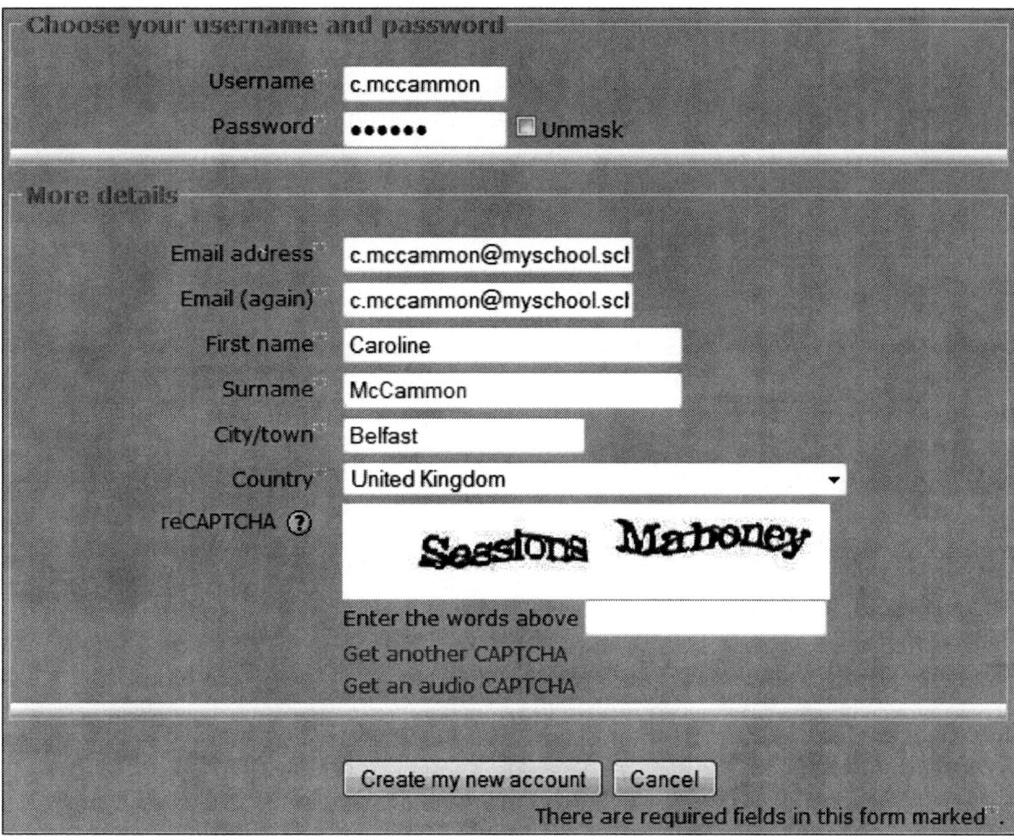


We saw earlier how to add more fields to the sign-up screen (tick **display on signup page** option). This is often invaluable in a commercial training setting when additional information such as the address of the learner has to be gathered.

Moodle supports a **CAPTCHA** mechanism that has been activated on the signup screen shown in the previous screenshot. The mechanism is used to avoid automated signups by bots. In order to activate this facility, you have to sign up for a free account at `www.recaptcha.net`, add the public and private key provided in the common authentication settings (shown next), and enable the **reCAPTCHA** element setting in **Users | Authentication | Email-based self registration** in the **Site Administration** block.

# User Authentication

Now that you know everything about users and the content that is stored about them, let's look at how to authenticate them with Moodle. So far we have dealt with two different authentication mechanisms, namely, manual accounts and email-based self-registration. These are activated by default after the installation of Moodle and can be configured.

Moodle supports a number of additional authentication types that have to be activated first. Furthermore, Moodle supports **multi-authentication**, that is, authentication from disparate authentication sources. For example, your organization might use an LDAP server containing user information for all your full-time students and staff, but wishes to manage part-time users manually.

## Common Authentication Settings

Whatever your preferred authentication system(s), there are a number of common settings that apply across the mechanisms. You can access these at **Users | Authentication| Manage authentication** in the **Site Administration** block.

You can see a list of authentication plug-ins on this page. Each plug-in can be activated by clicking on the closed-eye icon. If you click on the open-eye icon, it will be deactivated again. Settings for each type, which are discussed in this section, are accessed by the respective link or directly through the **Site Administration** menu once they are active. First of all, let us have a look at the common authentication settings (**Users | Authentication | Manage authentication** in the **Site Administration** block).

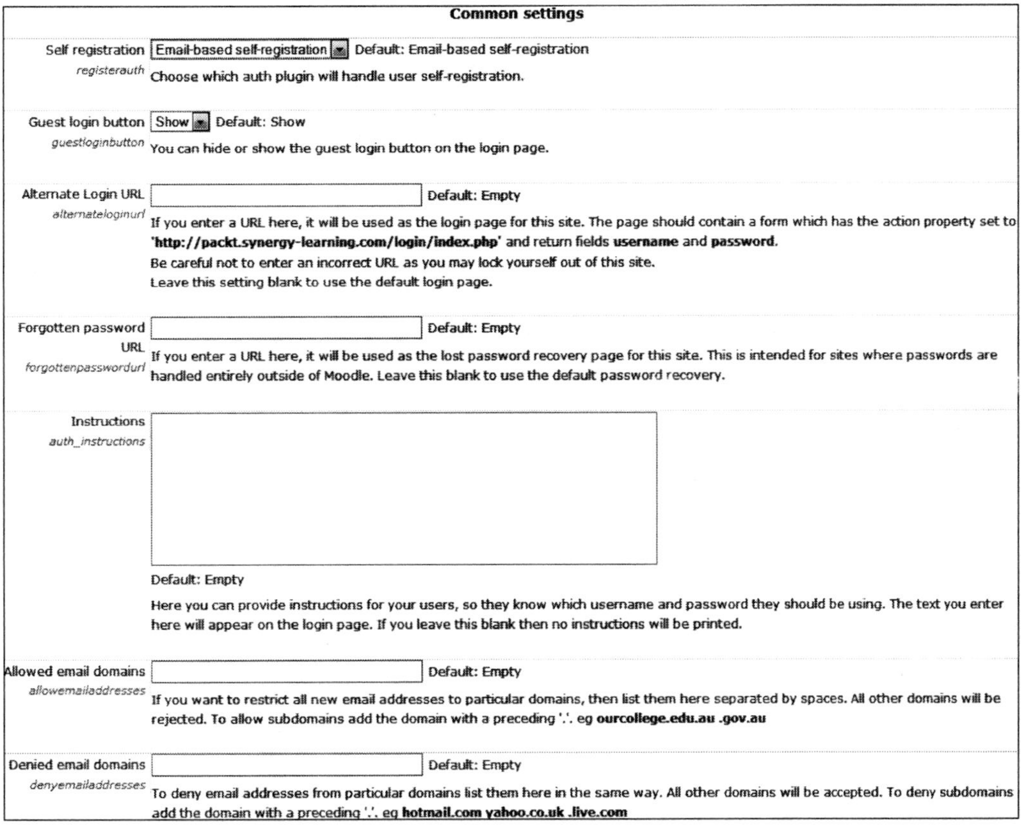

**Common settings**

Self registration [Email-based self-registration] Default: Email-based self-registration
*registerauth* Choose which auth plugin will handle user self-registration.

Guest login button [Show] Default: Show
*guestloginbutton* You can hide or show the guest login button on the login page.

Alternate Login URL [ ] Default: Empty
*alternateloginurl* If you enter a URL here, it will be used as the login page for this site. The page should contain a form which has the action property set to **'http://packt.synergy-learning.com/login/index.php'** and return fields **username** and **password**.
Be careful not to enter an incorrect URL as you may lock yourself out of this site.
Leave this setting blank to use the default login page.

Forgotten password URL [ ] Default: Empty
*forgottenpasswordurl* If you enter a URL here, it will be used as the lost password recovery page for this site. This is intended for sites where passwords are handled entirely outside of Moodle. Leave this blank to use the default password recovery.

Instructions
*auth_instructions*
Default: Empty
Here you can provide instructions for your users, so they know which username and password they should be using. The text you enter here will appear on the login page. If you leave this blank then no instructions will be printed.

Allowed email domains [ ] Default: Empty
*allowemailaddresses* If you want to restrict all new email addresses to particular domains, then list them here separated by spaces. All other domains will be rejected. To allow subdomains add the domain with a preceding '.'. eg **ourcollege.edu.au .gov.au**

Denied email domains [ ] Default: Empty
*denyemailaddresses* To deny email addresses from particular domains list them here in the same way. All other domains will be accepted. To deny subdomains add the domain with a preceding '.'. eg **hotmail.com yahoo.co.uk .live.com**

| Setting | Description |
|---|---|
| **Self-registration** | Here you specify which plug-in is used for self-registration. You can disable this mechanism, or if a third-party custom plug-in is present that provides an alternative to the built-in email-based modules, it can be selected. |
| **Guest login button** | By default, guest access is allowed to your Moodle system. If you disable this, which is recommended for most educational and commercial sites, the guest login button will not be shown on the login screen. |
| **Alternate Login URL** | By default, users have to log on to Moodle via the standard login screen. However, to change the source of the login information (that is, username and password), enter the correct URL here. This is necessary when you wish to have a login block on a separate web page, such as your homepage. Details of this mechanism are shown in Chapter 7. |

| Setting | Description |
| --- | --- |
| **Forgotten password URL** | Moodle has a built-in mechanism to deal with lost or forgotten passwords. If you use an authentication method that has its own system to do this, you have to enter its URL here. |
| **Instructions** | It is good practice to provide information on how to sign up for the system and what format the usernames should have. |
| **Allowed email domains** | You can restrict the email domains that are allowed on your system, for example, yourschool.co.uk or college.edu, and such others. |
| **Denied email domains** | Similarly, you can specify which email domains are not allowed on your system, for instance hotmail.com or gmail.com. |
| **ReCAPTCHA public key** | This is the key for displaying reCAPTCHA element on sign-up form (see self-registration section). |
| **ReCAPTCHA private key** | This is the key for communicating with reCAPTCHA server (see self-registration section). |

# Manual Account Settings

You have the ability to lock fields for accounts that are manually created or uploaded via batch files. If a field is **Locked**, the user will not be able to change its value. This is useful for fields such as first name and surname.

If you lock any compulsory fields, you either have to guarantee that they are populated correctly or you set its lock state to **Unlocked**, if empty. This will force the user to fill the value and then it would be locked. In the following screenshot, this has been done for the email address field. If a required field is locked and not populated, Moodle will not operate correctly.

Unfortunately, the locking mechanism is only available for the user fields that you can see in the screenshot:

Manual accounts
This method removes any way for users to create their own accounts.
All accounts must be manually created by the admin user.
None
Lock user fields
First name
Locked
Surname
Locked
Email address
Unlocked if empty
Phone 1
Unlocked
Phone 2
Unlocked
Department
Unlocked
Address
Unlocked
City/town
Unlocked
Country
Unlocked
Description
Unlocked
ID number
Unlocked
Language
Unlocked
You can lock user data fields. This is useful for sites where the user data is maintained by the administrators manually by editing user records or uploading using the 'Upload users' facility. If you are locking fields that are required by Moodle, make sure that you provide that data when creating user accounts or the accounts will be unusable.
Consider setting the lock mode to 'Unlocked if empty' to avoid this problem.
Save changes

# Self-Registration Settings

Email-based self-registration is the default authentication method in Moodle, where users create their own usernames and provide initial registration information. This process is followed up by an email that has to be confirmed.

The same locking settings can be set for self-registration as for manual accounts. Also, the same restrictions apply as described earlier.

# LDAP Server Settings

We have already seen a basic introduction to LDAP in the previous chapter. Now let's look at how it can be utilized for authentication. We will only cover the basic LDAP settings and exclude advanced setups such as multiple LDAP servers or secure LDAP. These are discussed in great detail in the Moodle Docs at `docs.moodle.org/en/LDAP_authentication`.

The principle of the authentication method is rather simple, but effective: If the entered username and password are valid, Moodle creates a new user account in its database if it doesn't already exist. If it does exist, the username and password are checked against LDAP for validity.

There are a number of parameters that you have to set to communicate with an LDAP server. The settings have been amended with detailed explanations (which I will not repeat). I will now provide additional information where applicable. If you are not sure where to locate some of the required information, contact your system administrator who should have these values.

## LDAP Server and Bind Settings

In the bind settings, if you have multiple contexts, it is recommended to put them in order of importance as Moodle stops searching once it has found an entry. For example, if you have ***`ou=Students`*** and ***`ou=Staff`*** and your students make up 90% of the logins, it is recommended to put them before their lecturers, unless staff is given priority.

**LDAP server settings**

| | | |
|---|---|---|
| Host URL | ldaps://123.456.789.001 | Specify LDAP host in URL-form like 'ldap://ldap.myorg.com/' or 'ldaps://ldap.myorg.com/' Separate multipleservers with ';' to get failover support. |
| Version | 3 | The version of the LDAP protocol your server is using. |
| LDAP encoding | utf-8 | Specify encoding used by LDAP server. Most probably utf-8, MS AD v2 uses default platform encoding such as cp1252, cp1250, etc. |

**Bind settings**

| | | |
|---|---|---|
| Hide passwords | Yes | Select yes to prevent passwords from being stored in Moodle's DB. |
| Distinguished Name | cn=LDAP,ou=CS,o=RESTRICTED | If you want to use bind-user to search users, specify it here. Something like 'cn=ldapuser,ou=public,o=org' |
| Password | ●●●●● | Password for bind-user. |

# User Lookup Settings

For multiple contexts, the same applies as for the distinguished name in the bind settings. It is important to set the **Search subcontexts** correctly. If it is set to **No**, subcontexts will not be searched, but the search is potentially faster and vice-a-versa.

**User lookup settings**

| Setting | Value | Description |
|---|---|---|
| User type | Novell Edirectory | Select how users are stored in LDAP. This setting also specifies how login expiration, grace logins and user creation will work. |
| Contexts | NT;ou=STUDENTS,o=STUDENT | List of contexts where users are located. Separate different contexts with ';'. For example: 'ou=users,o=org; ou=others,o=org' |
| Search subcontexts | Yes | Search users from subcontexts. |
| Dereference aliases | No | Determines how aliases are handled during search. Select one of the following values: "No" (LDAP_DEREF_NEVER) or "Yes" (LDAP_DEREF_ALWAYS) |
| User attribute | cn | Optional: Overrides the attribute used to name/search users. Usually 'cn'. |
| Member attribute | member | Optional: Overrides user member attribute, when users belongs to a group. Usually 'member' |
| Member attribute uses dn | | Optional: Overrides handling of member attribute values, either 0 or 1 |
| Object class | | Optional: Overrides objectClass used to name/search users on ldap_user_type. Usually you dont need to chage this. |

# Password-Related Settings

Changing LDAP passwords from Moodle usually requires a secure LDAP (for example, when using Active Directory).

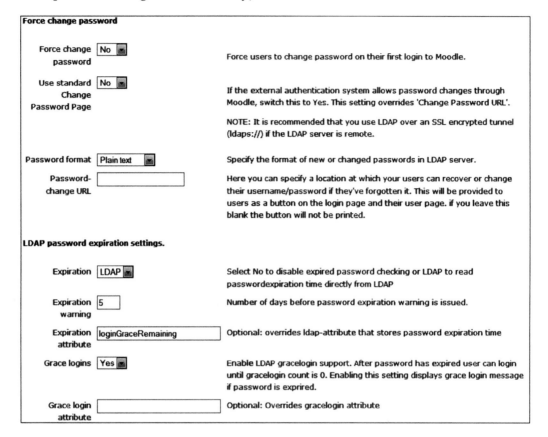

**Force change password**

| Setting | Value | Description |
|---|---|---|
| Force change password | No | Force users to change password on their first login to Moodle. |
| Use standard Change Password Page | No | If the external authentication system allows password changes through Moodle, switch this to Yes. This setting overrides 'Change Password URL'.<br>NOTE: It is recommended that you use LDAP over an SSL encrypted tunnel (ldaps://) if the LDAP server is remote. |
| Password format | Plain text | Specify the format of new or changed passwords in LDAP server. |
| Password-change URL | | Here you can specify a location at which your users can recover or change their username/password if they've forgotten it. This will be provided to users as a button on the login page and their user page. if you leave this blank the button will not be printed. |

**LDAP password expiration settings.**

| Setting | Value | Description |
|---|---|---|
| Expiration | LDAP | Select No to disable expired password checking or LDAP to read passwordexpiration time directly from LDAP |
| Expiration warning | 5 | Number of days before password expiration warning is issued. |
| Expiration attribute | loginGraceRemaining | Optional: overrides ldap-attribute that stores password expiration time |
| Grace logins | Yes | Enable LDAP gracelogin support. After password has expired user can login until gracelogin count is 0. Enabling this setting displays grace login message if password is exprired. |
| Grace login attribute | | Optional: Overrides gracelogin attribute |

# Miscellaneous LDAP Settings

Apart from the settings we have seen till now, there are certain miscellaneous settings that are explained using the following screenshot:

**Enable user creation**

| | | |
|---|---|---|
| Create users externally | No | New (anonymous) users can create user accounts on the external authentication source and confirmed via email. If you enable this , remember to also configure module-specific options for user creation. |
| Context for new users | | If you enable user creation with email confirmation, specify the context where users are created. This context should be different from other users to prevent security issues. You don't need to add this context to ldap_context-variable, Moodle will search for users from this context automatically. **Note!** You have to modify the method user_create() in file auth/ldap /auth.php to make user creation work |

**Course creator**

| | | |
|---|---|---|
| Creators | | List of groups or contexts whose members are allowed to create new courses. Separate multiple groups with ';'. Usually something like 'cn=teachers,ou=staff,o=myorg' |

**Cron synchronization script**

| | | |
|---|---|---|
| Removed ext user | Keep internal | Specify what to do with internal user account during mass synchronization when user was removed from external source. Only suspended users are automatically revived if they reappear in ext source. |

**NTLM SSO**

| | | |
|---|---|---|
| Enable | No | Set to yes to attempt Single Sign On with the NTLM domain. **Note:** this requires additional setup on the webserver to work, see http://docs.moodle.org/en/NTLM_authentication |
| Subnet | | If set, it will only attempt SSO with clients in this subnet. Format: xxx.xxx.xxx.xxx/bitmask |

## Data Field Mappings

User profile information is stored in the LDAP server. In order to connect the two, a mapping has to be provided where, for each field in Moodle, the counterpart in the server has to be provided. All fields are optional. Default values are used if you leave any of the fields blank:

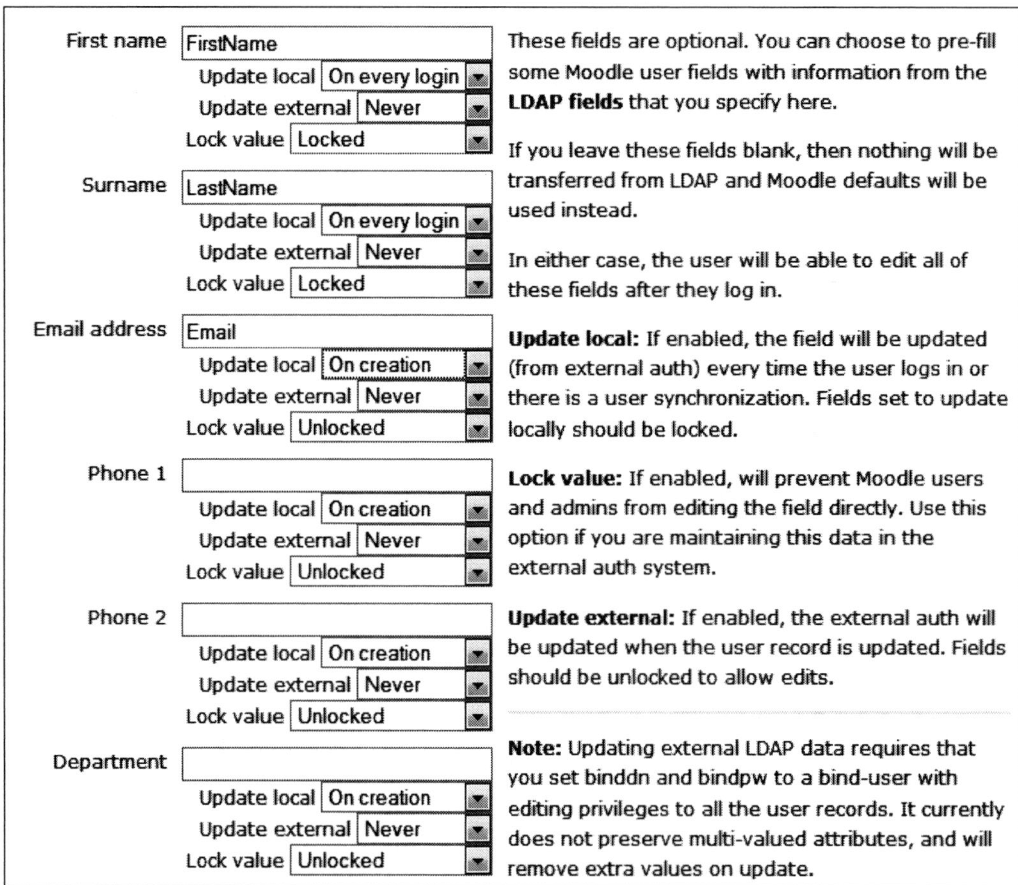


## External Database Settings

Now that we have a basic idea about the external database, let's have a look at its authentication method. The authentication method contains two types of parameters that you have to provide, namely, connection settings and data field mappings.

## Connection Settings

The database connection settings have been amended with good explanations (which I will not repeat). If you are not sure where to locate some of the required information, contact your database administrator who should have these values.

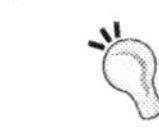

Some databases such as Oracle are case-sensitive, that is, field names have to be provided with the correct casing for the database link to work properly.

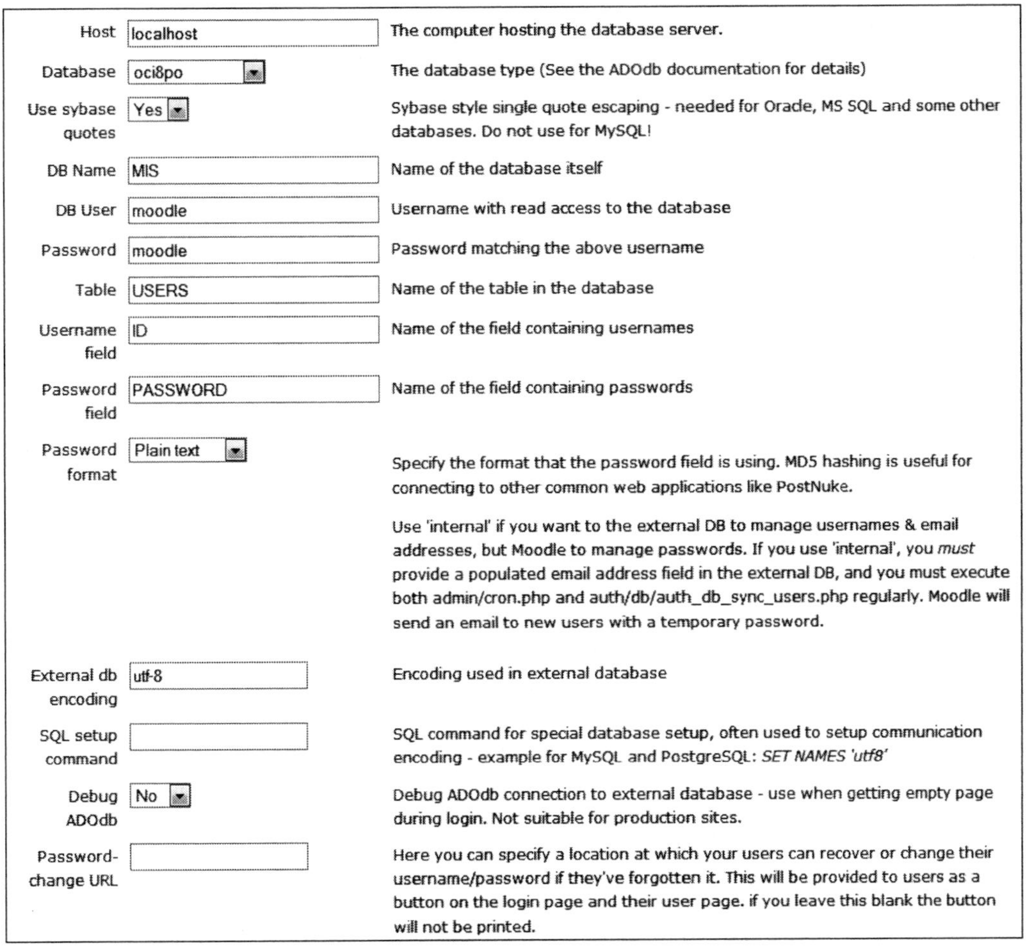

| Setting | Value | Description |
|---|---|---|
| Host | localhost | The computer hosting the database server. |
| Database | oci8po | The database type (See the ADOdb documentation for details) |
| Use sybase quotes | Yes | Sybase style single quote escaping - needed for Oracle, MS SQL and some other databases. Do not use for MySQL! |
| DB Name | MIS | Name of the database itself |
| DB User | moodle | Username with read access to the database |
| Password | moodle | Password matching the above username |
| Table | USERS | Name of the table in the database |
| Username field | ID | Name of the field containing usernames |
| Password field | PASSWORD | Name of the field containing passwords |
| Password format | Plain text | Specify the format that the password field is using. MD5 hashing is useful for connecting to other common web applications like PostNuke.<br>Use 'internal' if you want to the external DB to manage usernames & email addresses, but Moodle to manage passwords. If you use 'internal', you *must* provide a populated email address field in the external DB, and you must execute both admin/cron.php and auth/db/auth_db_sync_users.php regularly. Moodle will send an email to new users with a temporary password. |
| External db encoding | utf-8 | Encoding used in external database |
| SQL setup command | | SQL command for special database setup, often used to setup communication encoding - example for MySQL and PostgreSQL: *SET NAMES 'utf8'* |
| Debug ADOdb | No | Debug ADOdb connection to external database - use when getting empty page during login. Not suitable for production sites. |
| Password-change URL | | Here you can specify a location at which your users can recover or change their username/password if they've forgotten it. This will be provided to users as a button on the login page and their user page. if you leave this blank the button will not be printed. |

In the example shown, the MIS is hosted on the same server as Moodle (localhost). This can be beneficial if the server is powerful enough to run both applications in parallel, but can be detrimental to the performance if the hardware specification is sub-optimal. We will cover more of this in Chapter 11.

If you experience problems establishing a connection between Moodle and the external database, use the debug mode (**Debug ADOdb**), which will display information that is useful in locating the source of the problem.

## Data Field Mappings

User profile information is stored in the external database. In order to connect the two, a mapping has to be provided where, for each field in Moodle, the counterpart in the MIS has to be provided. All fields are optional. Default values are used if you leave any of the fields blank:

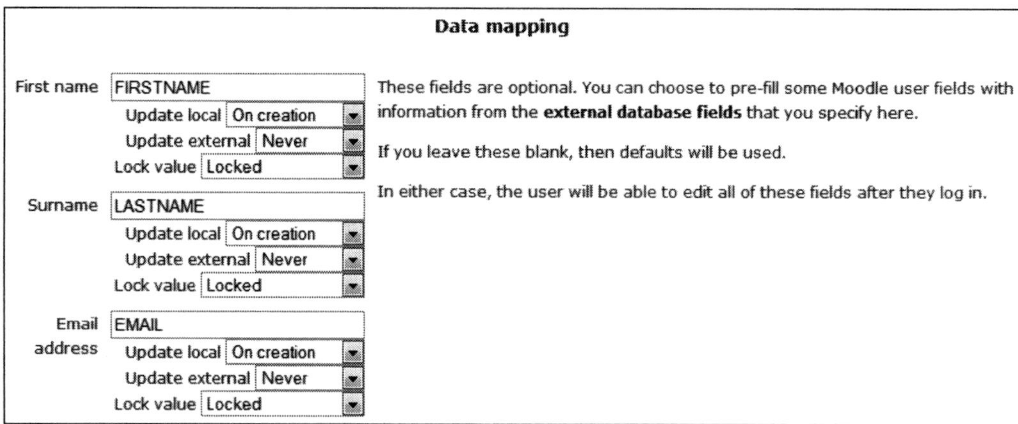


If you provide field information, you have to set four parameters for each data field:

| Setting | Description |
|---|---|
| **Field name** | Field name in the external database representing the value in Moodle. |
| **Update local** | For each external user, information is stored locally. You can update this information **on creation** (faster, but potentially not up-to-date) or **every login** (a bit slower, but always up-to-date). |
| **Update external** | If a user updates the value of the data field in Moodle, you can decide if you want to write that information back to the external database (**on update**) or not (**never**). Often, the external database is a read-only view that will not let you write to it. |
| **Lock value** | You can specify if the value can be changed by the user. The setting is identical to the lock field, explained earlier in the chapter. |

# Other Authentication Mechanisms

In addition to the popular authentication mechanisms that we have dealt with so far, Moodle supports a number of less popular external authentication methods as well as some internal ones, which we will cover next.

## External Moodle Authentication Methods

Due to the fact that these external authentication methods are less popular than LDAP and external databases, we will only cover them in some brevity. I will also provide some pointers to websites for further information.

- CAS Server (SSO)

  **CAS (Central Authentication Service)** is an open-source authentication server that supports Single sign-on (SSO) in a web environment. It utilizes LDAP and therefore requires the PHP LDAP modules to be installed.

  More information on CAS can be found on the JA-SIG website at `www.ja-sig.org/products/cas/overview/cas2_architecture/index.html`.

- FirstClass Server

  FirstClass, by Open Text Corporation, is a commercial client/server groupware, email, online conferencing, voice/fax services, and bulletin-board system for Windows, Macintosh, and Linux. The product is used for authentication of pupil accounts.

  In addition to some FirstClass specific settings, user fields can be locked in the same way as described earlier.

- IMAP Server

  **IMAP (Internet Message Access Protocol)** is a standard used by many email servers such as Microsoft Exchange. The user contact information in the server is used for Moodle authentication.

  In addition to some IMAP specific settings, user fields can be locked in the same way as described earlier.

  The IMAP consortium has a dedicated website that can be found at `www.imap.org`.

- NNTP Server

  **NNTP (Network News Transfer Protocol)** is mainly used for transferring news articles and usenet messages between news servers. Its user details are used for Moodle authentication.

- PAM

  **PAM** or **Pluggable Authentication Module** is yet another authentication scheme that maps user information onto a higher level of application interface. PAM is open-source and has been adopted as the authentication framework of the **Common Desktop Environment** (**CDE**) and is currently supported by all main Linux derivatives. The PHP PAM Authentication module has to be installed on the Moodle server.

- POP3 Server

  **POP3** (**Post Office Protocol version 3**) is a standard used by many email servers. The user contact information in the server is used for Moodle authentication.

  In addition to some POP3-specific settings, user fields can be locked in the same way as were described earlier.

- RADIUS Server

  **RADIUS** (**Remote Authentication Dial In User Service**) is a protocol for controlling access to various network resources. It supports authentication, authorization, accounting, and is used by Internet service providers.

  It is necessary to install Auth_RADIUS module on the server.

- Shibboleth

  Shibboleth is an open-source middleware that provides Internet single sign-on across organizational boundaries. Privacy and security are at the heart of Shibboleth, which is the main reason for its growing popularity. However, the price to pay is a complicated setup process that is detailed in the README ***file*** at `auth/shibboleth/README.txt` of your Moodle site.

  More information on Shibboleth can be found at `shibboleth.internet2.edu`.

## Internal Moodle Authentication Methods

Moodle provides three authentication methods that are used for a number of internal operations:

- No login

  This plug-in has no settings and cannot be disabled. Its purpose is to suspend a user from logging in to your Moodle system. This is done in the user's profile where you have to select the authentication method in the **Choose an authentication method** drop-down list.

- No authentication

  When this method is enabled, users can create accounts without any kind of authentication and email-based confirmation. It is highly recommended not to use this method since it creates a very insecure Moodle site, and should only be used for testing purposes.

  Only user fields can be locked in the same way as described earlier.

  This authentication method is the default role for logged-in users (**Users | Permissions | User Policies**). It is assigned to every logged-in user in addition to any other roles. The role has been created to grant users access to certain functionalities, even if they are not enrolled in a course, for instance posting blog entries, managing personal calendar entries, changing profile, and so on.

- Moodle network authentication

  Moodle networking allows the connection of multiple Moodle sites in a peer-to-peer or hub style. Chapter 14 has been dedicated to the details of this powerful feature.

# Username–Best Practices

User management in an organization is a critical subject for a range of reasons:

- Once implemented, it is difficult to change (sustainability).
- A system that is too simple is potentially unsafe and not future-proof.
- A system that is too complicated is unlikely to be accepted by pupils and is likely to cause administrative difficulties.

There is no ideal user management scheme, since the preference in every organization is different. However, there are a number of issues that are considered to be best practice.

Usernames have to be unique. The simplest way to implement this is to give each user a unique number, which is never reused even after students have finished a course. However, such a number-based system will be very difficult for learners to remember, especially younger pupils. It is therefore necessary to come up with a more user-friendly scheme considering the following potential issues:

- `firstname.lastname` causes difficulties when the same name exists twice in a course.
- `class.firstname.lastname` causes difficulties when the same name exists twice in a class. Also, when learners transfer from one class to another, there is a potential conflict.

- `startyear.firstname.lastname` causes difficulties when the same name exists more than once in a year. Furthermore, students who have to repeat a class or join a school at a later stage will be out of sync with the rest of the pupils in the same class. The same holds for the naming scheme `endyear.firstname.lastname`.

A system-compliant naming scheme would therefore be `startyear.firstname.lastname`, with an optional number added in case there is an overlap. Students who repeat or join the school at a later stage would then be changed manually to be in sync with the rest of their peers in the year. Examples are 04.caroline.killen, 05.jim.smith.1, 05.jim.smith.2 and 06.sarabjot.anand.

For smaller learning organizations, a system which uses `firstname.lastname` as a scheme with an added number (in case of name duplication) is usually sufficient. The same applies to training providers who have rolling start dates of users.

Irrespective of the scheme chosen, it is recommended to provide this information on the login page as a reminder. The text can be changed in **Users | Authentication | Manage Authentication** in the **Site Administration** block as described earlier:

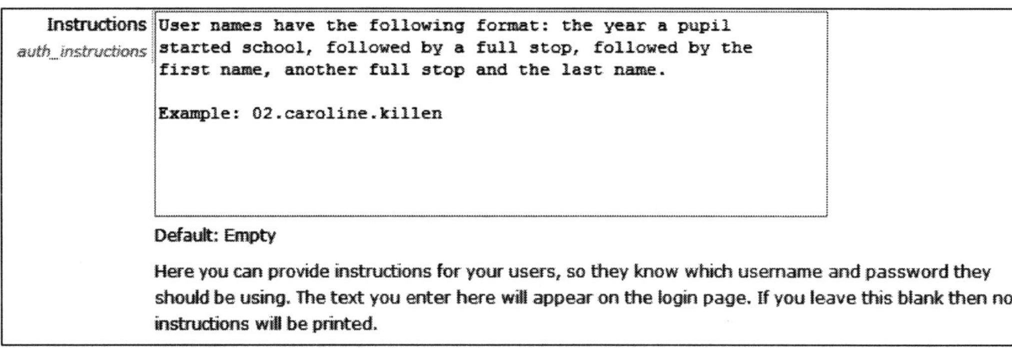

Instructions
auth_instructions
User names have the following format: the year a pupil started school, followed by a full stop, followed by the first name, another full stop and the last name.
Example: 02.caroline.killen
Default: Empty
Here you can provide instructions for your users, so they know which username and password they should be using. The text you enter here will appear on the login page. If you leave this blank then no instructions will be printed.

Some schools still do not make use of email addresses. As it is a compulsory field in Moodle, it is necessary to work around this issue. You will have to come up with a unique "dummy" email address scheme or void email addresses that have to be used for identification purposes. In order to avoid the usage of the actual email address, it is necessary that you deactivate it in the user's profile.

# Summary

Phew! That was a lot to take in for one chapter. This chapter demonstrated the many different ways Moodle provides to manage users. We first looked at what information is stored for each user and how their profiles can be extended. We then performed a number of standard user actions which included:

- Browsing users
- Filtering users
- Bulk user actions

A number of mechanisms were covered to manually add new users to Moodle, namely:

- Adding individual users
- Uploading users and their pictures in bulk
- Self-enrolment

We finally dealt with a wide range of user authentication types, before concluding the chapter with a best practice section. The next step is to grant users roles, that is, the rights as to what they are allowed to do and what they are not. This will be dealt with in the next chapter.

# 6
# Roles and Permissions

In the last chapter, we dealt with the management of users. Now we will introduce roles, a complex but powerful subject. Roles define what users can or cannot see and perform in your Moodle system.

In this chapter you will:

- Understand how roles work, and how they fit into different contexts.
- Assign roles to different users in different contexts.
- Modify roles and create new ones, including a role for parents or mentors.
- Manage a range of administrative role-related settings.

## Moodle's PreDefined Roles

Moodle comes with a number of predefined roles. These standard roles are suitable for some educational setups, but most institutions require modifications to the roles' system in order to tailor Moodle to their specific needs.

Each role has permissions for a number of actions that can be carried out in Moodle. For example, an administrator and a course creator are able to create new courses, whereas all other roles are denied this right. Likewise, a teacher is allowed to moderate forums, whereas students are only allowed to contribute to them.

The description of each standard role and the short names (that are used internally and in operations such as user batch upload, covered in the previous chapter) given by Moodle are listed in the table that follows:

| Role | Description | Short Name |
|---|---|---|
| Administrator | Administrators have full access to the entire site and all courses. | admin |
| Course creator | Course creators can create new courses and also teach them. | coursecreator |
| Teacher | Teachers can do anything within a course, including changing activities and grading students. | editingteacher |
| Non-editing Teacher | Non-editing teachers can teach courses and grade students, but not alter any activities. | teacher |
| Student | Students are able to perform allocated tasks that include resources and activities, among others. | student |
| Guest | Guests have minimal privileges and usually cannot enter text anywhere. | guest |
| Authenticated User | This additional role is given once user logs in. It is an exception role and is mostly used by Moodle internally. | user |

Before we can actually do anything with roles, we need to understand the concept of contexts, which is dealt with next.

# Contexts

Contexts are the areas in Moodle where roles can be assigned to users. A role can be assigned within different contexts. A user has a role in any given context, where a context can be a course, an activity module, a user, a block, or Moodle itself. Moodle comes with the following seven contexts that you will come across a lot in this chapter.

| Role | Coverage |
|---|---|
| System | Entire Moodle system (also known as core or global context) |
| Category | Categories and sub-categories |
| Course | Courses |
| Activity | Course activities and resources |
| Block | Moodle blocks |
| User | Users |
| Front Page | Front Page and files that can accessed outside courses |

Each context is like a ring-fenced area in which certain actions can be carried out. It is sometimes referred to as **scope**. You can compare this to a large company with multiple divisions and departments. A manager in the Finance division has certain rights and shoulders responsibilities of every department in his division, but these do not apply to departments in other divisions of the organization.

To implement such a structure, it is important that role assignments to users be made at the correct context level. For example, a teacher's role should be assigned at **Course context** level, a forum moderator for a particular forum should be assigned at **Activity** level, an administrator should be assigned at **System** level, and so on. While it is possible to assign any role in any context, some roles just don't make any sense. Unfortunately, Moodle doesn't warn you about this, since it cannot distinguish between intentional and unintentional assignments.

Contexts are hierarchical, that is, permissions are inherited from higher to lower contexts. Rights in higher context are more general, whereas the ones at a lower context are more specific. The same applies in the company structure mentioned: A sales manager at country level would have the same rights at regional level, whereas the opposite is not true.

The following figure shows the contexts that exist in Moodle and how they are arranged hierarchically.

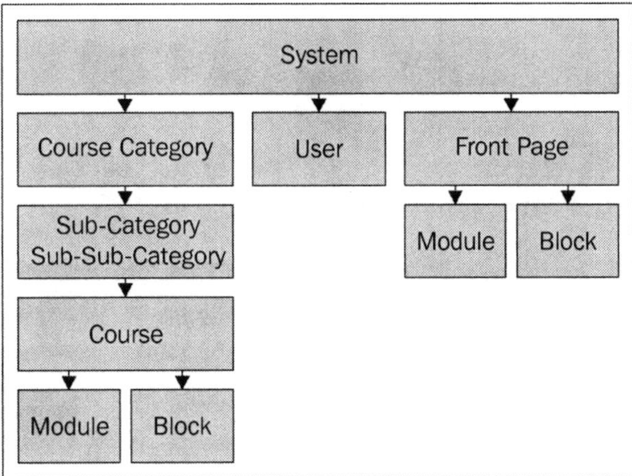

The System context is the root node of the hierarchy, that is, every role assigned in this context will apply to any other context below it. The **Course Category** context on the next level acts as a parent to the Course context. If sub-categories and sub-sub-categories, and so on have been created, respective contexts will exist. On the lowest level, you can see the **Module** and the **Block** contexts, respectively. Like Course, the **Front Page** context has a Module and Block sub-context (the front page is internally treated as a course). The **User** context is a standalone entity that does not have any children in the hierarchy.

For example, Jim is a teacher for a course. Therefore, he has a teacher's role in the relevant context (that is, the class he is teaching). He will have this role in all areas of the course, including blocks and modules (that is, activities and resources).

The advantage of organizing contexts in this way is its potential extensibility. New contexts might be added in future versions of Moodle, when and if required, without changing any of the exiting roles system.

# Assignment of Roles

As mentioned before, assigning roles to users is done for and in a particular context. The process of the actual role assignment is identical for each context. What is different is the location of each context and the method of its access. The process of assigning roles to users is described first, before outlining how and where to assign them in individual contexts.

# Time for some action: Assigning Roles

1. Navigate to the **Assign roles** screen for the required context (I will explain how to find the 'Assign roles' screen for each context shown). You will see a screen like this:

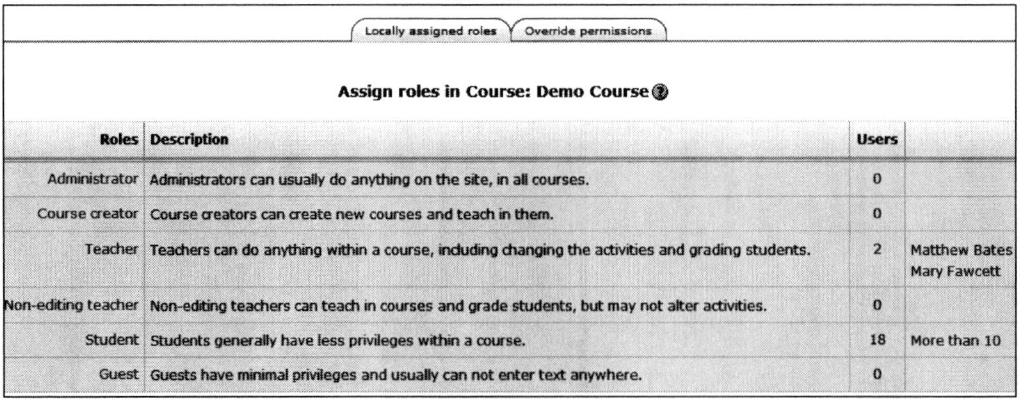

Locally assigned roles | Override permissions

**Assign roles in Course: Demo Course**

| Roles | Description | Users | |
|---|---|---|---|
| Administrator | Administrators can usually do anything on the site, in all courses. | 0 | |
| Course creator | Course creators can create new courses and teach in them. | 0 | |
| Teacher | Teachers can do anything within a course, including changing the activities and grading students. | 2 | Matthew Bates<br>Mary Fawcett |
| Non-editing teacher | Non-editing teachers can teach in courses and grade students, but may not alter activities. | 0 | |
| Student | Students generally have less privileges within a course. | 18 | More than 10 |
| Guest | Guests have minimal privileges and usually can not enter text anywhere. | 0 | |

   ◦ In the screenshot, you can see that there are currently two teachers assigned (**Matthew Bates** and **Mary Fawcett**) and eighteen Students (only up to ten names are displayed).

2. Select the role you wish to assign to a user by clicking on the role name. If there are more than ten assignees, follow the link **More than 10**. For example, if you wish to allocate more **Student** roles, you will be directed to the following screen:

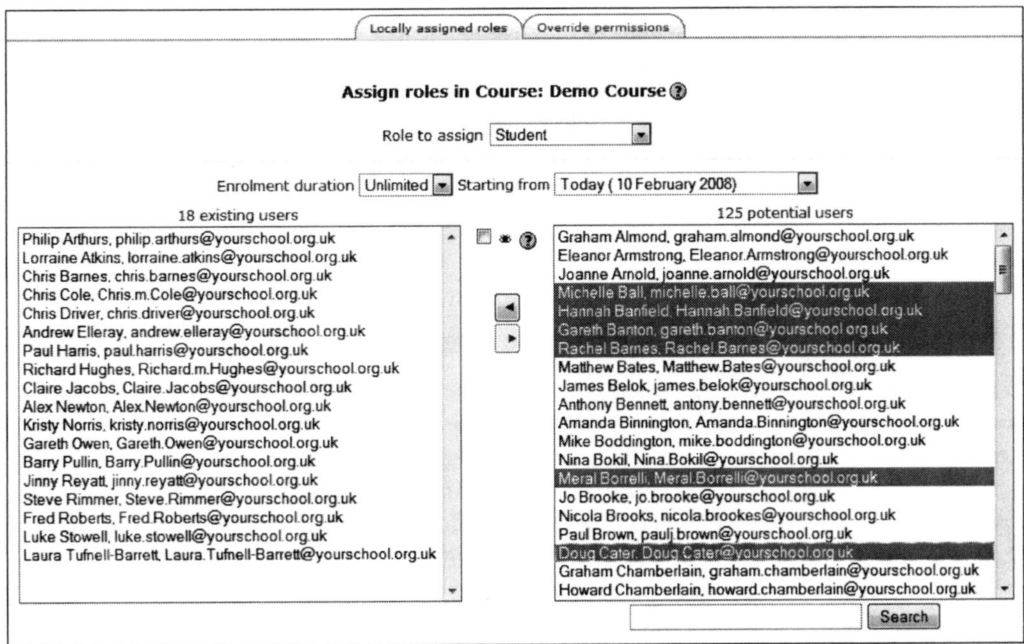


   ◦ Assign the role to users by selecting their names from the **potential users** list and moving them to the category with the left arrow button. Hold down the *SHIFT* key to select a range of users, and the *CTRL* key (*Apple* key on a Mac) to select multiple users. To revoke users' role assignments, select the person in the **existing users** list, and move them with the right arrow button back to the **potential users** group.

> Once a user has been assigned a role, permissions will be granted immediately. There is no need to save any changes.

# Hiding Role Assignments

The fact that a user has been assigned a role in any given context will be visible to other users. To hide which role is assigned to a user, select the **Hide** box (represented by the eye symbol) between the two columns of existing and potential users before you assign the respective role:

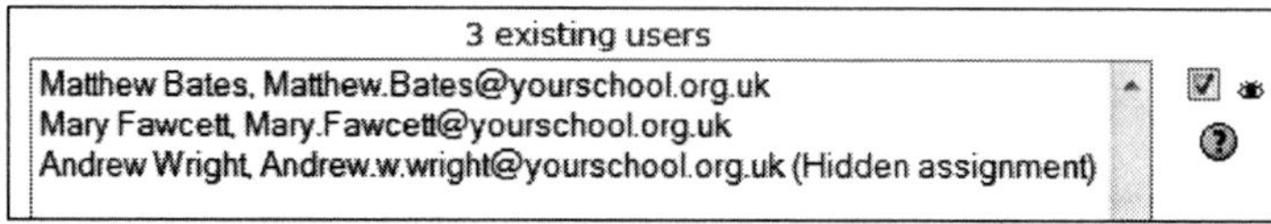


This is necessary if (for example) you have an observer in a course with a Teacher role who wishes not to be identified. Once the assignment has taken place, **Hidden assignment** will appear in parenthesis behind the name, as seen in the screenshot. Bear in mind that role assignments are not hidden from Administrators and Teachers.

# Time-Limited Role Assignments

It is possible to time-limit how long a user is assigned a role. Moodle (slightly confusingly) calls this **Enrolment duration** as the concept originally applied only in the course context, but has now been adopted throughout the system for consistency. After the specified time has elapsed, the role is automatically removed from the specified user. This feature is very useful if you have rolling roles without specific start and end times. It also simplifies the administration of roles, since Moodle will automatically do the removal of role assignment for you. The start of the **Enrolment duration** option is from today; the only exception is when you are in a course where the course's start date (the option **Starting from** in the figure) is also provided as a further option:

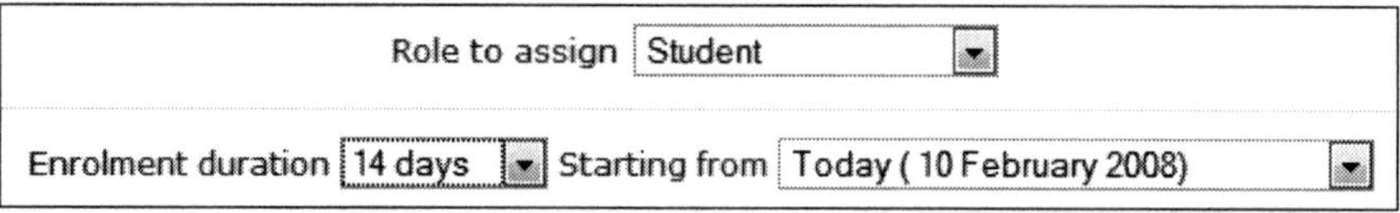


At the top of each role assignment screen, the current context in which the assignments take place is shown. To change the role, select another entry from the pull-down menu:

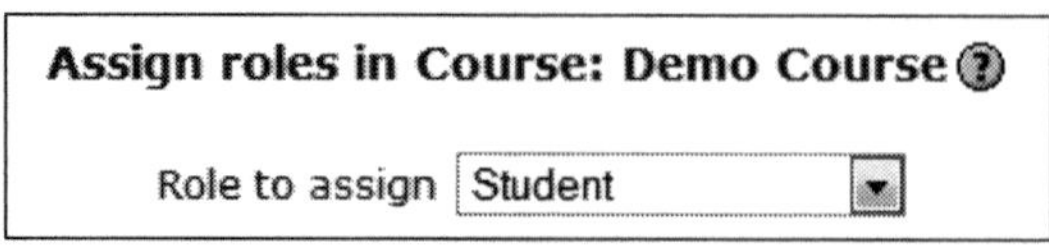

In the example, roles are assigned to users in the Course context. The particular instance is called **Demo Course** and the role that is currently being dealt with is **Student**.

Assigning roles in the incorrect context is a common source of problems. It is highly recommended to check the current context regularly to make sure that no unintended rights are granted.

So far we have dealt with the general concept of contexts, and looked at how to assign roles to users within a context. We now deal with each individual context, as shown in the screenshot at the beginning of the chapter depicting context hierarchy of Moodle.

# System Context

The System context covers the entire Moodle system. Assignment takes place from the **Site Administration** block in **Users | Permissions | Assign system roles**:

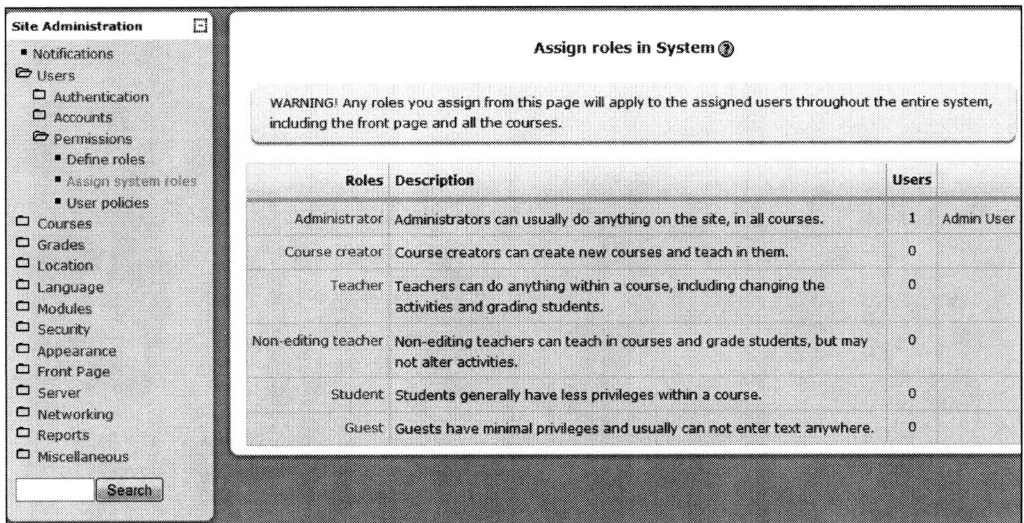


You see the familiar screen, which allows the assignment of roles to users. The only difference to the outlined generic screen is the absence of the **Roles** tab at the top of the screen that does not apply on the top-level context. Instead, a warning is displayed, as seen in the screenshot.

In most Moodle systems with predefined roles, only the Administrator role should be granted at this level. For example, if a Teacher role is granted in the Site context, it means that the individual would not only be allowed to access every single course in the site, but would also have the rights to mark assignments, contribute to discussion forums, delete learning resources, and so on.

There are scenarios when global roles are justified, for instance in very small organizations or if Moodle hosts only a very small number of courses that are attended by all users. Also, some new user-defined roles, such as a School Inspector, are designed to be assigned at global level.

## Course Category Context

The Course category context covers all courses within a category and all of its sub-categories. The role assignment takes place in the **Site Administration** block in **Courses | Add/edit course**, where you have to select the category you wish to deal with (If editing has been turned off, it has to be turned on first.):

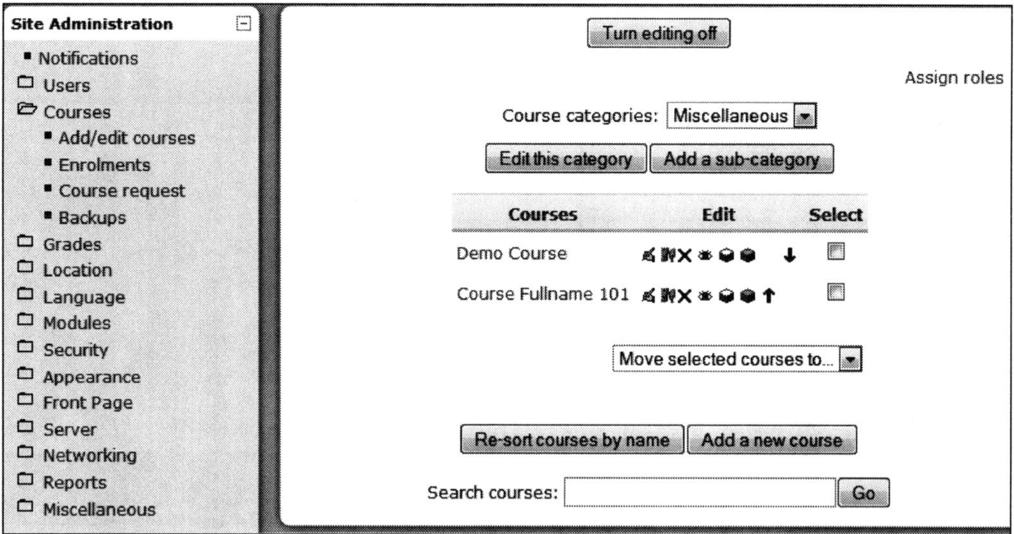


The **Assign roles** link at the top right will direct you to the familiar roles assignment screen. In the screenshot, the selected category is called **Miscellaneous**. The same mechanism applies to sub-categories and sub-sub-categories, and so on.

A typical role that is assigned in the Category context is Course creator. It will allow a dedicated user to create new courses within the specified category, which is very often a department or division. In smaller organizations, it is possible to assign the Teacher role access to all courses within the category.

# Course Context

As the name suggests, in this context all assignments that cover a course are granted. The assignment takes place in the actual course. You must select the **Assign roles** link in the menu in the **Site Administration** block. This will direct you to the familiar Assign roles screen.

Alternatively, you can get to the same screen by selecting **Courses | Add/edit course** in the **Site Administration** block, where you have to select the category in which your course is located. (If editing has been turned off, it has to be turned on first.) Beside each course, you will find the **Assign roles** icon that has to be selected:

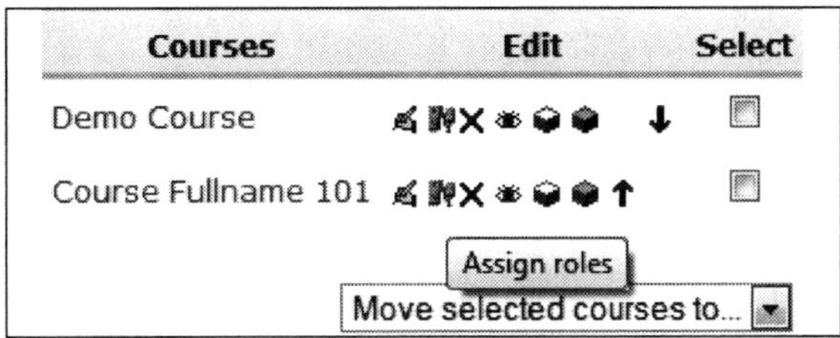


The course context is most frequently used for assigning roles since, in most cases, a course has a teacher and a number of students where everybody has the same rights. The example used to explain the assignment of roles earlier is from a Course context.

When a student is enrolled to a course, either by self-enrolment or any other enrolment mechanism, Moodle will automatically assign that student a role in the relevant course (context). This also applies if you upload users in batch mode and provide a course a user has to be enrolled to.

# Module Context

Once you are within a course, it is possible to assign roles to users within individual modules, that is, resources and activities. When editing module properties, you will see two roles tabs at the top of the screen. The one labeled **Locally assigned roles** will lead to the familiar "Assign roles" screen, and the **Override permissions** tab lets you change inherited roles. We will deal with this later in the chapter.

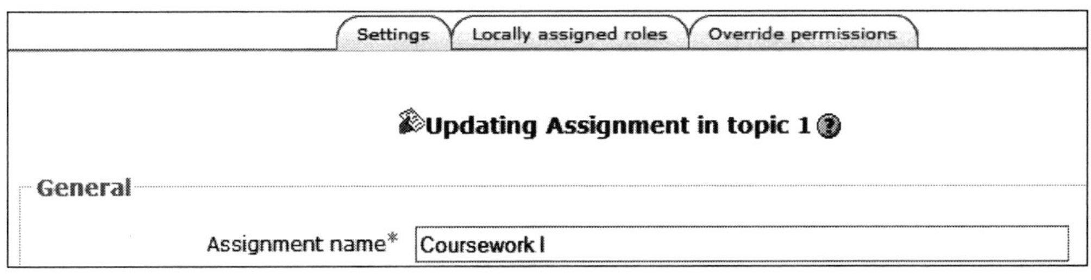

The Module context is often used by teachers to assign new capabilities to their students. A regularly cited example is that of a forum moderator. If you wish to put a student in charge of a forum so that she or he learns how to moderate discussions, she or he requires the rights to edit and delete posts (among others). These rights are provided by the Teacher role, and it is perfectly feasible to make a student a teacher in a single activity. It is further possible, and often recommended, to time the assignment via the enrolment duration option.

The Course context is the parent of the Module context. From Moodle 1.8 onwards, the Module context can also be a child of the Site context, which applies if an activity or resource is placed on the front page.

Users with a Teacher role have the rights to assign roles in the Module context. However, it is often up to the Moodle administrator to carry out the task on their behalf, due to the complexity of the roles system. The same applies to the Block context, which is covered next.

# Block Context

Similar to the Module context, the Block context allows the assignment of rights on block level within a course. You will see a roles icon in the top left corner of each block, which will lead to the **Assign roles** screen (Editing has to be turned on.):

Like the Module context, the Course context is the parent of the Block context. From Moodle 1.8 onwards, the Block context can also be a child of the Site context, which applies to any blocks that are placed on the front page.

Sticky blocks, whether in My Moodle or in the Course pages, are an exception to the rule and roles cannot be assigned in them. The roles icon is not displayed as it is in other blocks.

## User Context

The User context is a standalone context, which has only the System context as parent. It deals with all issues relating a user outside a course. They include the user's profile, forum posts, blog entries, notes and reports, logs, and grades.

The assignment of roles takes place in the **Roles** tab in the user profile page, as seen in the following screenshot:

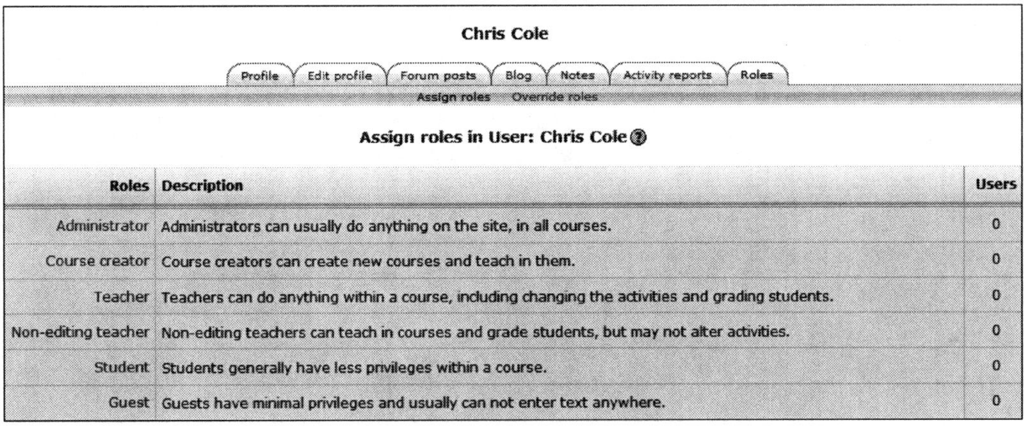

**Chris Cole**

Profile | Edit profile | Forum posts | Blog | Notes | Activity reports | Roles

Assign roles | Override roles

**Assign roles in User: Chris Cole**

| Roles | Description | Users |
|---|---|---|
| Administrator | Administrators can usually do anything on the site, in all courses. | 0 |
| Course creator | Course creators can create new courses and teach in them. | 0 |
| Teacher | Teachers can do anything within a course, including changing the activities and grading students. | 0 |
| Non-editing teacher | Non-editing teachers can teach in courses and grade students, but may not alter activities. | 0 |
| Student | Students generally have less privileges within a course. | 0 |
| Guest | Guests have minimal privileges and usually can not enter text anywhere. | 0 |

Roles assigned in the User context will only have access to information accessible from this user screen. Examples of custom roles are the Parent or Mentor role (which we will deal with in the example section of this chapter) and a Human Resources role.

# Front Page Context

The Front Page context has the System context as parent, and like the Course context, Module and Block subcontexts. It is accessed via **Front Page | Front Page roles** in the **Site Administration** block:

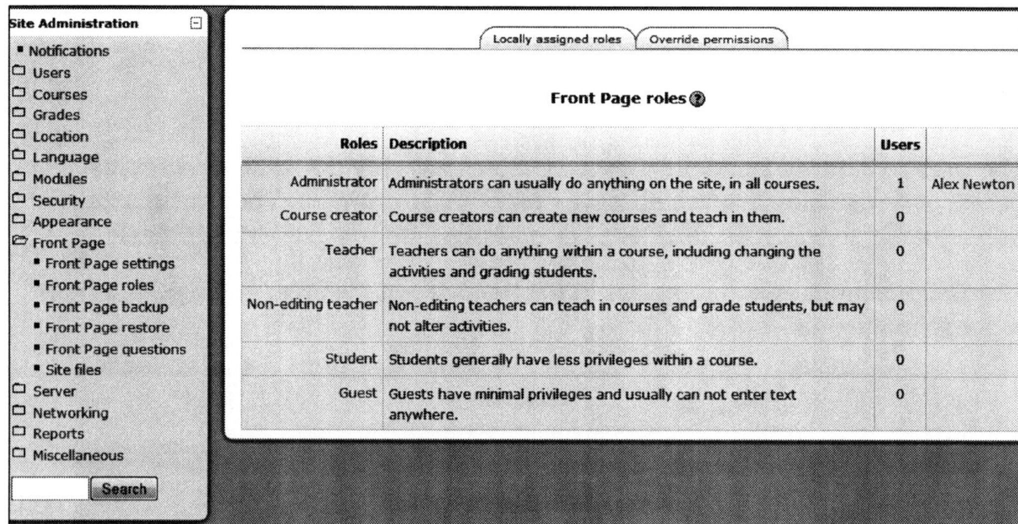


The naming of the context is sometimes a little confusing. Front page files are generally accessed only via the front page. However, sometimes (for example) when storing a school policy file, files stored in the Front Page area are also accessed elsewhere in Moodle. This is the reason why the Site file sub-menu is positioned in the **Front Page** menu in the **Site Administration** block, as shown in the screenshot that follows.

A typical user in the Front Page context is a designer who is responsible for the layout and content of the front page of the Moodle system. When assigned, only the **Front Page** menu and its sub-menus are accessible:

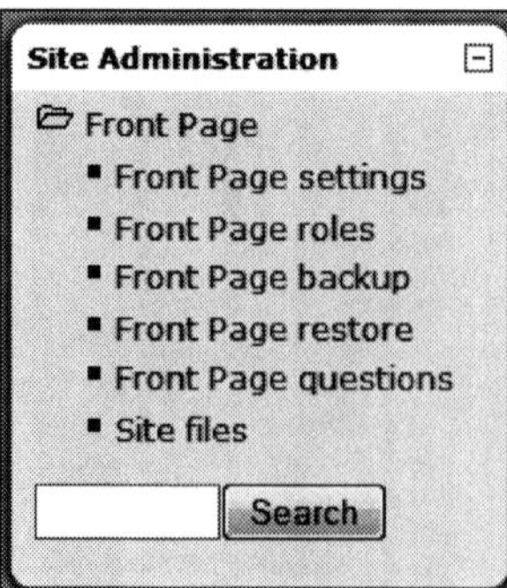

You can either assign the designer (user) an Administrator or a Teacher role. The administrator has the ability to assign other administrators, whereas the teacher does not have this permission. Either way, assigning a standard role in the context allows read-only access to user profiles and courses. If this is not acceptable, a separate Designer role has to be created.

## Multiple Roles

It is not uncommon for a user to be assigned more than a single role. For example, a class teacher who is also made course creator is responsible for the Moodle administration, or acts as a support teacher in a different class. In fact, every logged in user is assigned the "Authenticated user" role in the System context. (We will deal with this later in the chapter.)

In addition to the user's main role, the user can also fulfill one or more additional roles in other contexts. A significant part of the roles infrastructure in Moodle is the ability to assign multiple roles to a user at the same time. The equivalent in our initial company example is a member of staff who is in charge of the marketing department, but is also temporarily put in charge of the sales division.

To specify an additional role, the actual context has to be selected as shown in the previous sub-sections. You will then be able to assign additional roles as necessary.

It is technically possible to assign two or more roles to the same user in the same context. Having said this, it is hard to think of situations where such a setup would actually make sense, especially when you only use predefined roles. The real problem is the potential of conflicts, which Moodle has to resolve. For example, if one role has the ability to delete a forum post and another does not, but a user has been assigned both the roles in the same context, which right applies? While Moodle has a built-in resolution mechanism for these scenarios, it is best to completely avoid such scenarios.

# Capabilities and Permissions

So far, we have given users existing roles in different Moodle contexts. In the following few pages, we want to have a look at the inside of a role that is called **capabilities** and **permissions**. Once we have understood them, we will be able to modify existing roles and create entirely new custom ones.

# Role Definitions

Existing roles are accessed via **Users** | **Permissions** | **Define Roles** in the **Site Administration** block. The screen that will be shown is similar to the familiar roles assignment screen, but has a very different purpose:

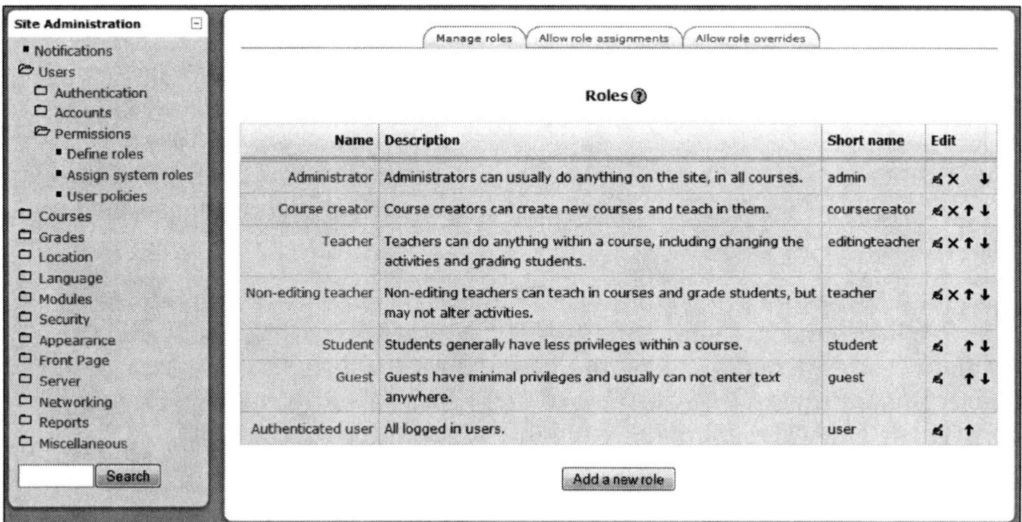


When you click on a role name, its composition is shown. Each role contains a unique **Name**, a unique **Short name** (used when uploading users), and an optional **Description**.

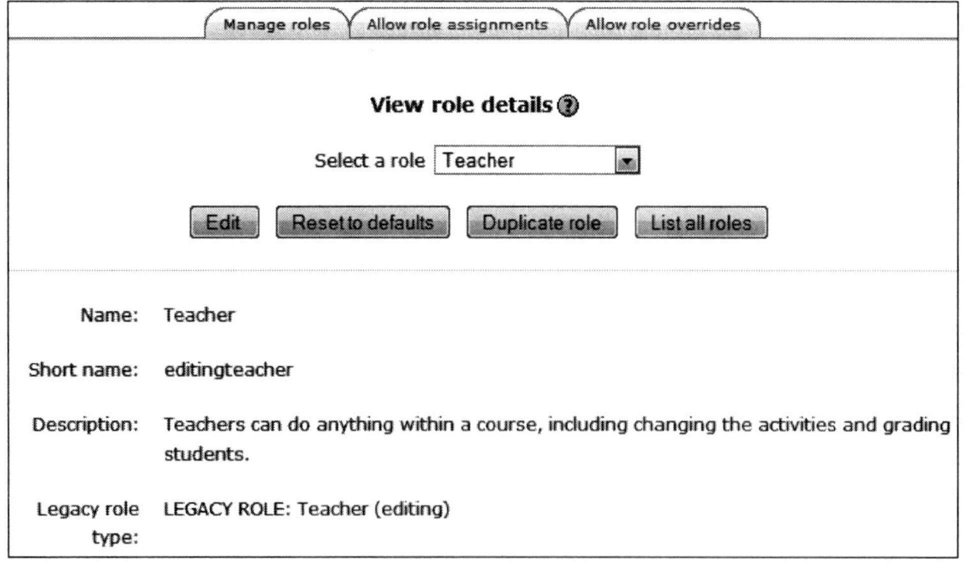

The **Legacy role type** has been introduced for backward compatibility, to allow old legacy code that has not been fully ported to work with the new system comprising new roles and capabilities. It is expected that this facility will disappear in the future (this might be for some time since a lot of core code depends on it), and should be ignored in due course unless you are working with legacy code or third-party add-ons.

In addition to these four fields, each role consists of a large number of capabilities. Currently, Moodle's roles system contains approximately 200 capabilities. A **capability** is a description of a particular Moodle feature (for example) to grade assignments or to edit a Wiki page. Each capability represents a permissible Moodle action:

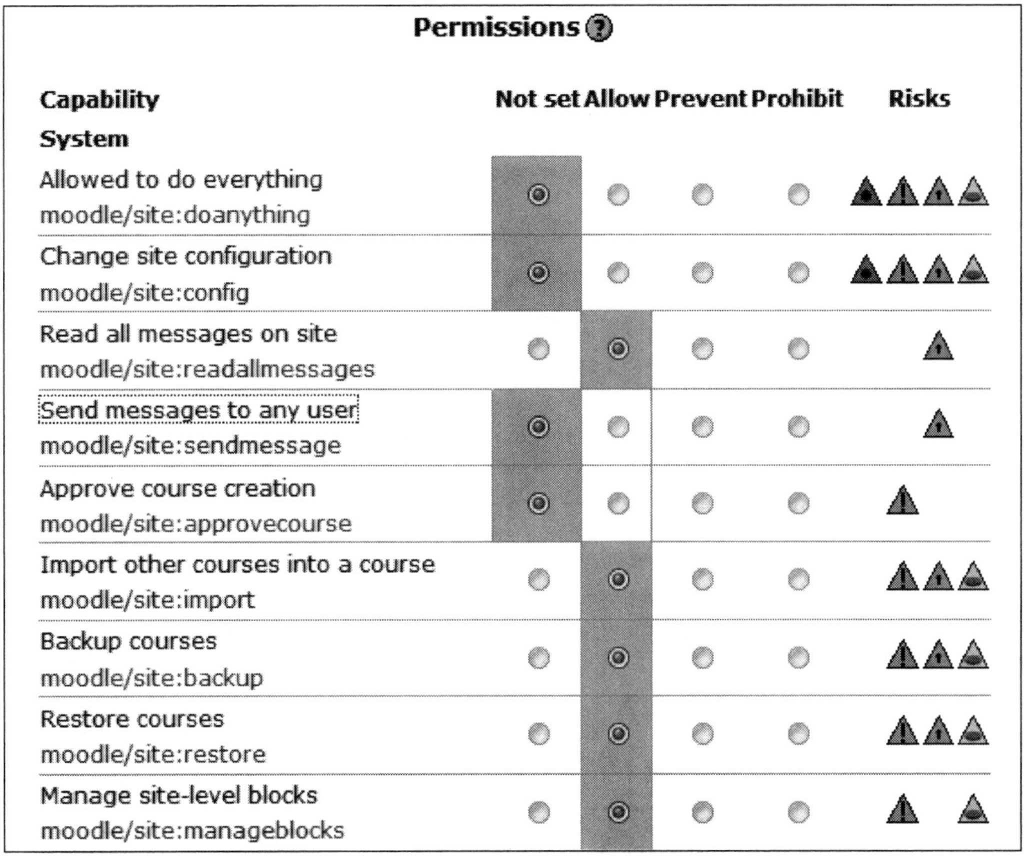

**Permissions**

| Capability | Not set | Allow | Prevent | Prohibit | Risks |
|---|---|---|---|---|---|
| **System** | | | | | |
| Allowed to do everything<br>moodle/site:doanything | ◉ | ○ | ○ | ○ | |
| Change site configuration<br>moodle/site:config | ◉ | ○ | ○ | ○ | |
| Read all messages on site<br>moodle/site:readallmessages | ○ | ◉ | ○ | ○ | |
| Send messages to any user<br>moodle/site:sendmessage | ◉ | ○ | ○ | ○ | |
| Approve course creation<br>moodle/site:approvecourse | ◉ | ○ | ○ | ○ | |
| Import other courses into a course<br>moodle/site:import | ○ | ◉ | ○ | ○ | |
| Backup courses<br>moodle/site:backup | ○ | ◉ | ○ | ○ | |
| Restore courses<br>moodle/site:restore | ○ | ◉ | ○ | ○ | |
| Manage site-level blocks<br>moodle/site:manageblocks | ○ | ◉ | ○ | ○ | |

A **permission** is a capability and its value, taken together. So each row of the table in the screenshot represents a permission. The left column is the capability name and the radio buttons specify the value. So, each permission has a description, a unique name, a value, and up to four associated risks.

The description, for example, **Approve course creation** provides a short explanation of the capability. On clicking, the description or the online Moodle documentation is opened in a separate browser. The name, for instance **moodle/site:approvecourse**, follows a strict naming convention that identifies the capability in the overall role system: `level/type:function`. The level states to which part of Moodle the capability belongs (such as moodle, mod, block, gradereport, or enroll). The type is the class of the capability and the function identifies the actual functionality.

The permission of each capability has to have one of the four values:

| Permission | Description |
|---|---|
| **Not Set** | By default, all permissions for a new role are set to this value. The value, in the context where it will be assigned, will be inherited from the parent context. To determine what this value is, Moodle searches upward through each context, until it finds an explicit value (**Allow, Prevent**, or **Prohibit**) for this capability, that is, the search terminates when an explicit permission is found. For example, if a role is assigned to a user in a Course context and a capability has a value of "Not set", then the actual permission will be whatever the user has at the category level, or failing to find an explicit permission at the category level, at the site level. If no explicit permission is found, then the value in the current context becomes "Prevent". |
| **Allow** | To grant permission for a capability choose "Allow". It applies in the context in which the role will be assigned and all contexts that are below it (children, grandchildren, and so forth). For example, when assigned in the course context, students will be able to start new discussions in all forums in that course, unless some forum contains an override or a new assignment with a "Prevent" or "Prohibit" value for this capability. |
| **Prevent** | To remove permission for a capability, choose "Prevent". If it has been granted in a higher context (no matter at what level), it will be overridden. The value can be overridden again in a lower context. |
| **Prohibit** | This is the same as "Prevent", but the value cannot be overridden again in a lower context. The value is rarely needed, but useful when an admin wants to prohibit a user from certain functionality throughout the entire site, in which case the capability is set to "Prohibit", and then assigned in the site context. |

Principally, permissions at lower contexts override permissions at higher contexts. The exception is "Prohibit", which by definition cannot be overridden at lower levels.

# Resolving Permission Conflicts

There is a possibility of conflict if two users are assigned the same role in the same context, where one role allows a capability and the other prevents it. In this case, Moodle will look upwards in higher contexts for a decider. This does not apply to Guest accounts, where "Prevent" will be used by default.

For example, a user has two roles in the Course context, one that allows functionality and one that prevents it. In this case, Moodle checks the Category and the System contexts respectively, looking for another defined permission. If none is found, then the permission is set to "Prevent".

## Permission Risks

Additionally, Moodle displays the risks associated with each capability, that is, the risks that each capability can potentially raise. They can be any combination of the following four risk types:

| Risk | Icon | Description |
|---|---|---|
| Configuration | | Users can change site configuration and behavior. |
| XSS | | Users can add files and texts that allow cross-site scripting (potentially malicious scripts that are embedded in web pages and executed on the user's computer). |
| Privacy | | Users can gain access to private information about other users |
| Spam | | Users can send spam to site users or others. |

Risks are only displayed. It is not possible to change these settings, since they only act as warnings. When you click on a risk icon, the "Risks" documentation page is opened in a separate browser window.

Moodle's default roles have been designed with the following capability risks in mind:

| Role | Allowed Risks |
|---|---|
| Administrator | All capabilities |
| Teacher | Certain capabilities with XSS and privacy risks, mainly adding and updating content |
| Student | Certain capabilities with spam risks |
| Guest | Only capabilities with no risks |

# Modifying Roles

To edit a role, either click on the **Edit** button at the top of the **View role details** screen or select the **Edit** icon in the **Edit** column on the screen listing the main roles:

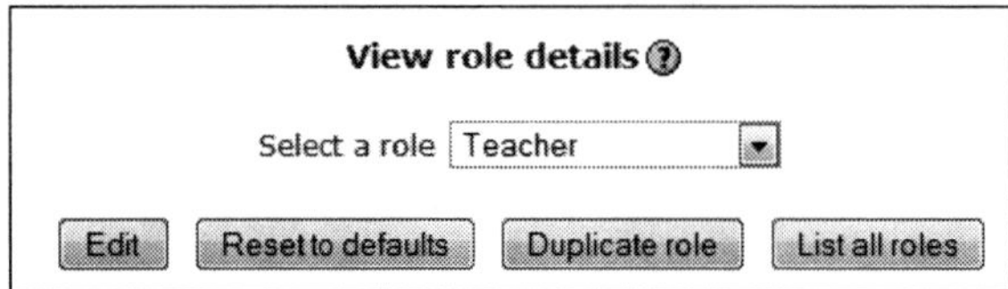


When editing a role, you can change the standard fields as well as their permissions. For example, some schools change the role name "Student" to "Pupil", while some training organizations change the role name "Teacher" to "Instructor" (see the following screenshot). Bear in mind that these are only changes to the name of the role, and not the corresponding labels used throughout Moodle.

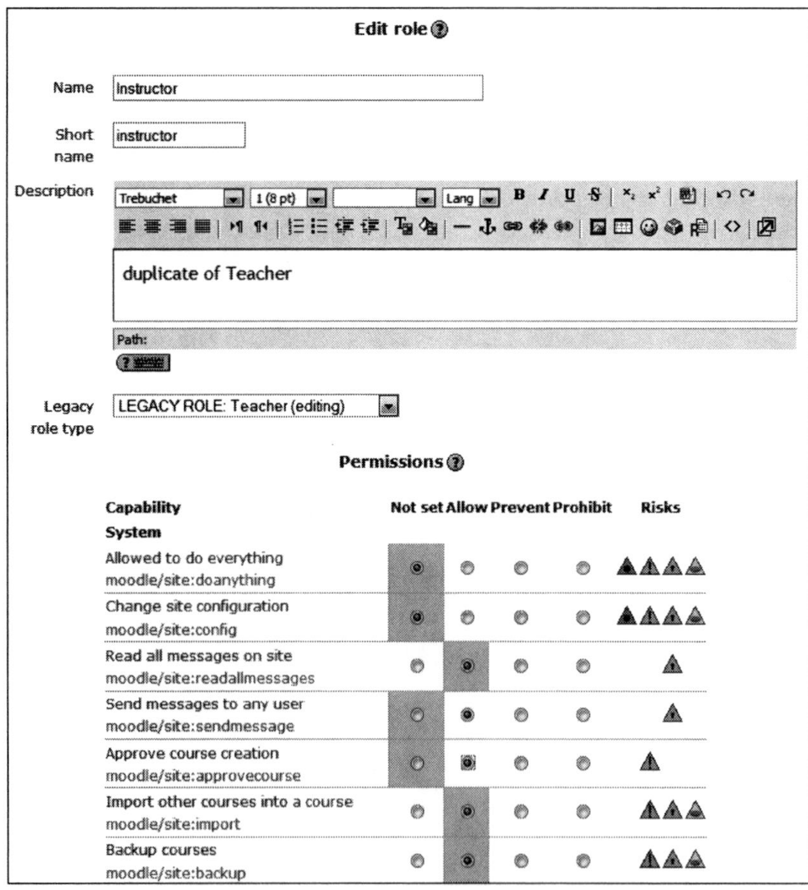

When you change capabilities in a role that has been copied from a legacy role, its original values are highlighted. For example, in the preceding screenshot **Send messages to any user** and **Approve course creation** have been set to **Allow**, but the **Not set** value remains highlighted. Do not forget to save your role changes once applied.

Unless you are confident with your role modifications, it is recommended to duplicate a role first (using the **Duplicate role** button) and then edit it. Keeping the default roles untouched also makes maintenance easier in case multiple administrators work on the same system or a third party is providing support.

For example, if for reasons of privacy or otherwise, your organization decides not to allow users to see the profiles of other users, you would edit the Student role and search for the **moodle/user:viewdetails** capability and change it from "Allow" to "Not set".

# Overriding Roles

It is possible to override permissions of a role in a given context using the **Override permissions** tab in the roles assignment screen. Overrides are specific permissions designed to change a role in a specific context, allowing you to tweak your permissions as required. Tweaking involves granting additional rights or revoking existing rights.

For example, if pupils with the role of Student in a course are usually allowed to start new discussions in forums, but there is one particular forum for which you want to restrict that capability. You can then set an override that prevents the capability of students to start new discussions in this forum (namely `mod/ forum: startdiscussion`).

Overrides can also be used to open up areas of your site and courses to grant users extra permissions. For example, you may want to experiment giving students the ability to grade some assignments (see the following screenshot) or to peer rate forum posts:

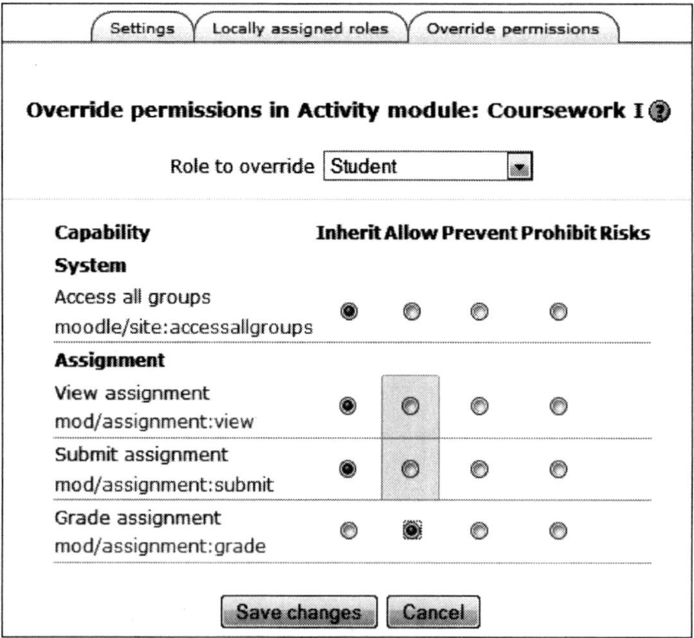


Depending on the context in which permissions are being overridden, only relevant capabilities are shown. For example, in the preceding example, only four capabilities are displayed. The underlying gray boxes show permissions that have been copied. The highlighted value is the value of this permission in this role in the parent context. In the screenshot, it would therefore make no difference whether the capability values **View assignment** and **Submit assignment** are set to **Allow** or left at **Inherit**.

It is possible to control the users who can view blocks. For example, you might have a block that you don't want guest users to see. To hide the block from guests on the front page, access the roles page of the block (editing has to be turned on), go to the **Override permissions** tab, select the guest role, set the capability **moodle/block:view** to prevent, and then save the changes made.

# Creating Custom Roles

As mentioned, Moodle allows the creation of new roles. Examples of such custom roles are Parent, Teaching Assistant, Secretary, Inspector, and Librarian. New roles are defined at **Users | Permissions | Define Roles** in the **Site Administration** block using the **Add a new role** button:

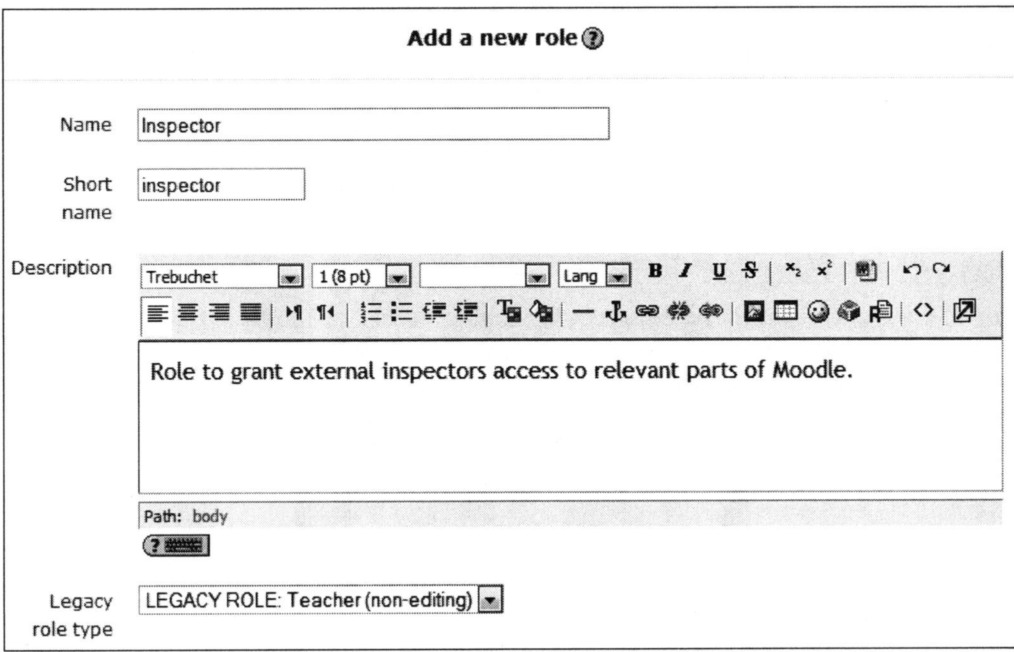


Duplicating a role is a commonly-used way of creating a new role. It not only minimizes the amount of work required, but also reduces mistakes in new roles.

# Example Roles

MoodleDocs has provided a number of sample roles that might be relevant to your organization. If not, they offer a good starting point to create other roles:

- **Inspector** (`http://docs.moodle.org/en/Inspector_role`)

  The role is used to provide external inspectors or verifiers the permission to view all courses in Moodle without having to enroll.

- **Demo teacher** (`http://docs.moodle.org/en/Demo_teacher_role`)

  The role is used to provide a demonstration teacher with an account that has a password and profile that cannot be changed.

- **Forum moderator** (`http://docs.moodle.org/en/Forum_moderator_role`)

  The role is used in a particular forum and provides a user with the ability to edit or delete forum posts, split discussions, and move discussions to other forums.
- **Calendar editor** (`http://docs.moodle.org/en/Calendar_editor_role`)

  The role is used to enable a person to add site events to the calendar.
- **Question creator** (`http://docs.moodle.org/en/ Question_creator_role`)

  The role is used to enable students to create questions for use in quizzes.
- **Blogger** (`http://docs.moodle.org/en/ Blogger_role`)

  The role is used to limit blogging to specific users.

## Parent or Mentor Role

One of the most popular and sought after custom roles in Moodle is the one of a parent, guardian, or mentor. The idea is to grant permission to users to view certain profile information, such as activity reports, grades, blog entries, and forum posts of their children, guardees, or mentees. This can be achieved with the creation of a new role. Furthermore, the specially-introduced Mentees block has to be placed on the front page to give users, who have been assigned the role, access the user context.

1. Create new role
   a. Go to **Users** | **Permissions** | **Define roles** in the **Site Administration** block.
   b. Add a new role and name it Parent or Mentor. Provide an appropriate short name and a description.
   c. Leave the Legacy role type set to **None**.
   d. Change the capability **moodle/user:viewdetails** to **Allow**. This grants access to the user profile page.
   e. Change the following capabilities in the User section to **Allow**, which grants access to individual tabs on the user profile page:
      - **moodle/user:readuserposts**: To read the child's forum posts
      - **moodle/user:readuserblogs**: To read the child's blog entries
      - **moodle/user:viewuseractivitiesreport**: To view the child's activity reports and grades

2. **Create user account for parent**

   Each parent requires a separate user account, which is set up as explained in the previous chapter (Go to **Users | Add a new user** in the **Site Administration** and add details for the parent or use Moodle's bulk upload facility). In our example, the father is called Roy Harris and his children are called Frank Harris and Paul Harris:

| First name / Surname | Email address | City/town | Country | Last access | | |
|---|---|---|---|---|---|---|
| Frank Harris | Frank.Harris@yourschool.org.uk | London | United Kingdom | Never | Edit | Delete |
| Paul Harris | paul.harris@yourschool.org.uk | London | United Kingdom | Never | Edit | Delete |
| Roy Harris | roy.harries@yourschool.sch.uk | London | United Kingdom | Never | Edit | Delete |

3. **Link parent to pupil**

   Each parent has to be linked to each child. Unlike the creation of users, this process cannot be automated via batch files and is a potentially time-consuming process.

   a. Access the first child's profile page and click on the **Roles** tab (Frank Harris).
   b. Choose **Parent** as the role to assign.
   c. Select the parent (Roy Harris) in the **potential users** list and add it to the **existing users** list.
   d. Repeat the steps (a) to (c) for the second child, Paul Harris.

4. **Add mentee block**

   A special **Mentees block** has been introduced to facilitate access to user information.

   a. Go to your front page and turn on editing.
   b. Add the Mentees block to the front page (it can also be added as a sticky block in My Moodle) and change its title via the **configuration** icon to "Parent Access".

c. Log in as Roy Harris and you should see the following block:

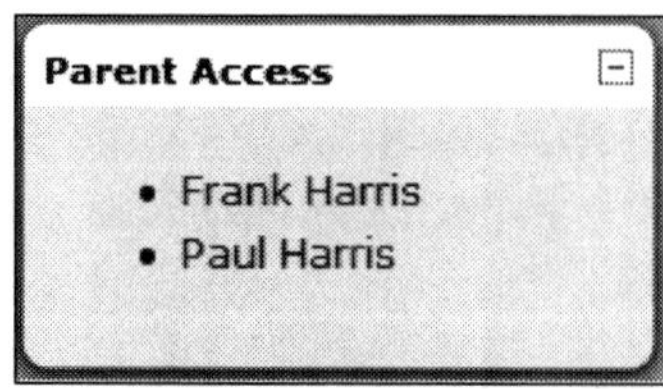


When selecting a name, the respective user profile will be shown, which includes any posts sent to forums, blog entries and activity reports, including logs and grades.

## Testing New Roles

After creating a new role, it is recommended to test it thoroughly before it is assigned to any users. To do this, create a test account and assign the new role to it. Log out as administrator and login as newly created user to test the new role. Alternatively, use a different browser (not a new window in the same browser) to test out the role without logging out as administrator.

If you have modified a predefined role and would like to roll back to its factory settings, go to **Users | Permissions | Define roles** in the **Site Administration** block, select a role, and press the **Reset to defaults** button. This will replace its existing values with the one from the built-in legacy capabilities.

# Roles Management

We have now dealt with all important issues of how to use, modify, and create roles. Moodle offers a number of system settings that are important while working extensively with roles.

# Allowing Roles Assignments and Overrides

By default, some roles have the right to allow other roles to assign roles. For instance, a teacher is only allowed to assign Non-editing teacher, Student, and Guest roles, whereas the administrator is allowed to assign all roles except Authenticated user (because this is automatically assigned when a user signs in for the first time). There are instances when you either wish to change the default settings, for example, a teacher assigns roles to other teachers, or when newly created roles have to be managed. To achieve this, go to the **Allow roles assignments** tab in **Users | Permissions | Define Roles** in the **Site Administration** block:

Manage roles | Allow role assignments | Allow role overrides

You can allow people who have the roles on the left side to assign some of the column roles to other people

| | Administrator | Course creator | Teacher | Non-editing teacher | Student | Guest | Authenticated user | Parent |
|---|---|---|---|---|---|---|---|---|
| Administrator | ☑ | ☑ | ☑ | ☑ | ☑ | ☑ | ☐ | ☑ |
| Course creator | ☐ | ☐ | ☑ | ☑ | ☑ | ☑ | ☐ | ☑ |
| Teacher | ☐ | ☐ | ☑ | ☑ | ☑ | ☑ | ☐ | ☑ |
| Non-editing teacher | ☐ | ☐ | ☐ | ☐ | ☐ | ☐ | ☐ | ☐ |
| Student | ☐ | ☐ | ☐ | ☐ | ☐ | ☐ | ☐ | ☐ |
| Guest | ☐ | ☐ | ☐ | ☐ | ☐ | ☐ | ☐ | ☐ |
| Authenticated user | ☐ | ☐ | ☐ | ☐ | ☐ | ☐ | ☐ | ☐ |
| Parent | ☐ | ☐ | ☐ | ☐ | ☐ | ☐ | ☐ | ☐ |

Save changes

In the screenshot, the modified allowances have been highlighted. Teachers are allowed to assign Teacher roles, and both Course creators and Teachers are allowed to assign the new Parent role.

The identical mechanism exists for role overrides. It is accessed via the **Allow role overrides** tab on the same screen.

# Assignment of Default Roles

When adding a user to Moodle, a standard role is assigned. This can be specified in **Users | Permissions | User Policies** in the **Site Administration** block:

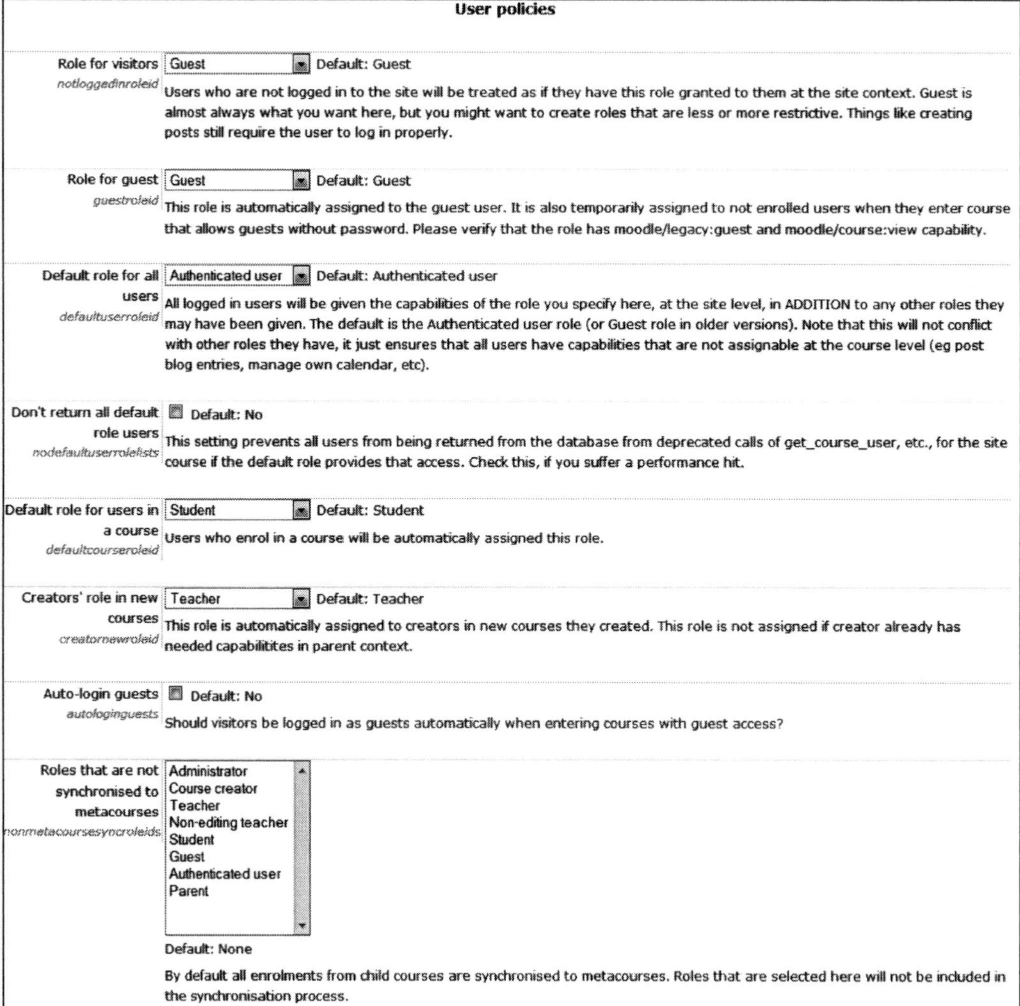

User policies
Role for visitors
notloggedinroleid
Guest
Default: Guest
Users who are not logged in to the site will be treated as if they have this role granted to them at the site context. Guest is almost always what you want here, but you might want to create roles that are less or more restrictive. Things like creating posts still require the user to log in properly.
Role for guest
guestroleid
Guest
Default: Guest
This role is automatically assigned to the guest user. It is also temporarily assigned to not enrolled users when they enter course that allows guests without password. Please verify that the role has moodle/legacy:guest and moodle/course:view capability.
Default role for all users
defaultuserroleid
Authenticated user
Default: Authenticated user
All logged in users will be given the capabilities of the role you specify here, at the site level, in ADDITION to any other roles they may have been given. The default is the Authenticated user role (or Guest role in older versions). Note that this will not conflict with other roles they have, it just ensures that all users have capabilities that are not assignable at the course level (eg post blog entries, manage own calendar, etc).
Don't return all default role users
nodefaultuserrolelists
Default: No
This setting prevents all users from being returned from the database from deprecated calls of get_course_user, etc., for the site course if the default role provides that access. Check this, if you suffer a performance hit.
Default role for users in a course
defaultcourseroleid
Student
Default: Student
Users who enrol in a course will be automatically assigned this role.
Creators' role in new courses
creatornewroleid
Teacher
Default: Teacher
This role is automatically assigned to creators in new courses they created. This role is not assigned if creator already has needed capabilitites in parent context.
Auto-login guests
autologinguests
Default: No
Should visitors be logged in as guests automatically when entering courses with guest access?
Roles that are not synchronised to metacourses
nonmetacoursesyncroleids
Administrator
Course creator
Teacher
Non-editing teacher
Student
Guest
Authenticated user
Parent
Default: None
By default all enrolments from child courses are synchronised to metacourses. Roles that are selected here will not be included in the synchronisation process.

This screen assigns default roles for visitors (users who are not logged in) and guests.

Moodle comes with a predefined role called **Authenticated user**, which is the default role for all logged-in users. It is assigned to every logged-in user in addition to any other roles. The role has been created to grant users access to certain functionality even if they are not enrolled in a course, for instance posting blog entries, managing personal calendar entries, changing profile, and so on.

The **Don't return all default role users** setting can be ignored at the moment. We will deal with this in Chapter 11.

You can further specify the roles that are given automatically to users in courses and the users who have created a course.

Metacourses combine enrolments from multiple courses and by default, users have the same role in a metacourse as in the normal courses. If this is not required, the roles that should not be synchronized have to be selected accordingly.

Changing settings in User policies can have major impact on what new users are allowed to do to your Moodle system, even locking out the administrator!

## Assigning Front Page Roles

In addition to the default roles in the User policies section, it is also possible to specify a default front page role. This can be accessed in **Front Page | Front Page settings** in the **Site Administration** block. To enable logged-in users to participate in activities positioned on the front page, a default front page role, usually Student or Teacher, can be set. It is also possible to allow logged-in users to participate in these activities by setting an authenticated user role override.

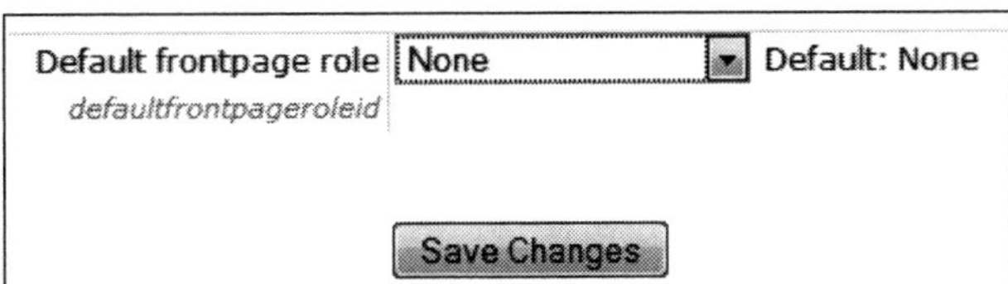


## Roles—Best Practice

Roles sometimes cause problems in Moodle sites, and it is therefore advised to follow some recommendations regarding roles:

- Touch the roles only when you have understood them thoroughly.
- Never grant a user a role that is beyond their competence.
- Avoid assigning multiple predefined roles to users whenever possible.
- Avoid System roles for teachers and pupils.
- Avoid role assignments that don't make sense.
- Keep track of role assignments to ensure maintainability in the future.
- Do not change the permissions of predefined roles.

# Summary

In this chapter, you have learned what roles are and how they are applied in different contexts. We then covered the modification of existing roles before creating our own custom roles, such as Parent, Inspector, or Librarian. Finally, we looked at the management of administrative role-related settings.

Getting your head around the roles concept in Moodle is vital if you wish to add/remove functionality for a distinct group of users. As always, there is a trade-off between the complexity of such a system and its flexibility. While you can argue about the user-friendliness of the roles system, it has certainly proven to be one of the most powerful additions to Moodle when it was introduced back in version 1.7.

The interconnection among courses, users, and roles is crucial. Once this has been set up and configured properly, your Moodle is technically ready to go. However, before that, you probably want to first change the look and feel. This is what the next chapter is all about.

# 7

# Moodle: Look and Feel

Your system is now fully operational with users, courses, and roles in place. It is time now to change its look and feel. Out goes the standard orange Moodle theme and in comes a site that is in line with the corporate branding of your organization.

After providing a general overview of Moodle's look and feel elements, we will cover the following subjects:

- Front page customization

  This includes front page settings, block arrangement, front page roles, backup, restore, questions, and site files. You will also learn how to support personalization via the My Moodle feature, and how to make blocks sticky.
- Moodle themes

  This includes theme selection, theme types, and theme settings. We then look at theme creation, which covers theme design and development, and theme styles.
- Look and feel good practice

  The key elements that we will deal with are consistency, browser support, and accessibility.

## Look and Feel: An Overview

Moodle can be fully customized in terms of layout and branding. It has to be stressed that certain aspects of changing the look and feel require some design skills. While you as an administrator will be able to make most of the relevant adjustments, it might be necessary to get a professional designer involved, especially when it comes to styling.

The two relevant components for customization are the Moodle front page and Moodle themes. Before we cover both of these areas in detail, let's try to understand which part is responsible for which element of the look and feel of your site.

In the following screenshot, have a look at the front page of the Moodle site after we have logged in as administrator. It is not obvious which parts are driven by the Moodle theme and by the front page settings. The following table, which looks at the page's elements from top to bottom, sheds some light on this:

| Element | Settings | Theme | Other |
|---|---|---|---|
| Logos | | X | |
| Logged-in information (location and font) | | X | |
| Language Drop Down | | | X |
| Site Administration block (position) | X | | |
| Available Courses block (position) | X | | |
| Available Courses block (content) | | | X |
| Course categories and Calendar block (position) | X | | |
| Course categories and Calendar block (icons, fonts, colors) | | X | |
| Footer text | | X | |
| Footer logo | | X | |
| Copyright statement | | X | |

While this list is by no means complete, it hopefully gives you an idea that the look and feel of your site is driven by a number of different elements.

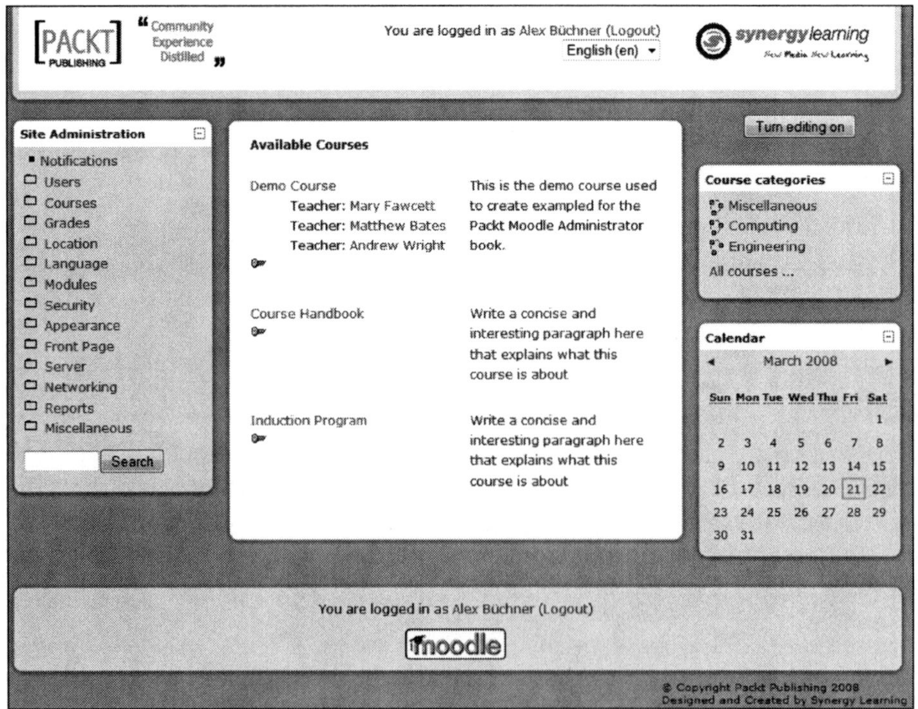

In short, the settings (mostly front page settings as well as a few related parameters) dictate what content users will see before and after they log on. The theme is responsible for the design scheme or branding, that is, the header and footer as well as colors, fonts, icons, and so on used throughout the site.

We will now cover both components in some detail.

# Customizing Your Front Page

The appearance of Moodle's front page changes after a user has logged in. The content and layout of the page before and after login can be customized to represent the identity of your organization.

Look at the following screenshot. It is the same site that the preceding screenshot was taken from, but before a user has logged in. In this particular example, a **Login** block is shown on the left and the **Course categories** are displayed in the center, as opposed to the list of available courses:

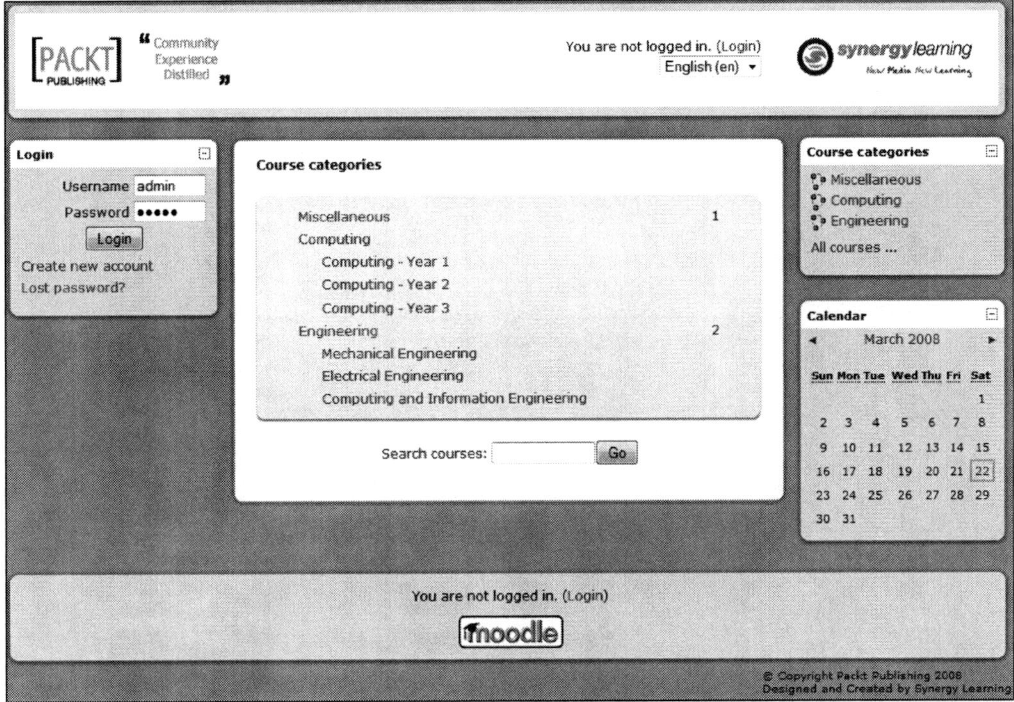

# Front Page Settings

To customize the front page, you either have to be logged in as Moodle administrator, or have front-page-related permissions in the **Front Page** context. From the **Site Administration** block, select **Front Page | Front Page Settings**. The screen showing all available parameters will be loaded displaying your current settings that are changeable:

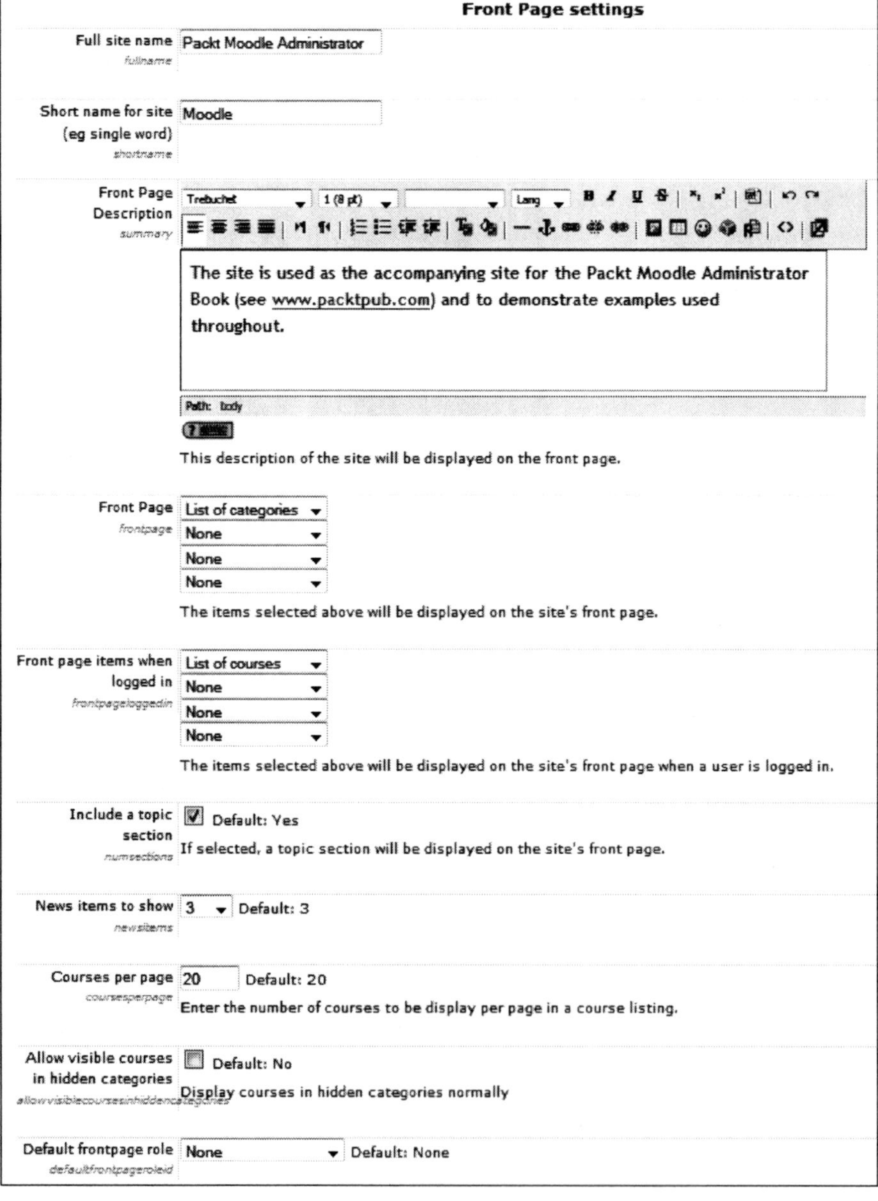

Front Page settings
Full site name
fullname
Packt Moodle Administrator
Short name for site (eg single word)
shortname
Moodle
Front Page Description
summary
The site is used as the accompanying site for the Packt Moodle Administrator Book (see www.packtpub.com) and to demonstrate examples used throughout.
This description of the site will be displayed on the front page.
Front Page
frontpage
List of categories
None
None
None
The items selected above will be displayed on the site's front page.
Front page items when logged in
frontpageloggedin
List of courses
None
None
None
The items selected above will be displayed on the site's front page when a user is logged in.
Include a topic section
numsections
Default: Yes
If selected, a topic section will be displayed on the site's front page.
News items to show
newsitems
3
Default: 3
Courses per page
coursesperpage
20
Default: 20
Enter the number of courses to be display per page in a course listing.
Allow visible courses in hidden categories
allowvisiblecoursesinhiddencategories
Default: No
Display courses in hidden categories normally
Default frontpage role
defaultfrontpageroleid
None
Default: None

| *Setting* | *Description* |
|---|---|
| **Full site name** | This is the name that appears in the browser's title bar. It is usually the full name of your organization, or the name of the dedicated course, or qualification the site is used for. |
| **Short name for site** | This is the name that appears as the first item in the breadcrumb trail. |
| **Front Page Description** | This description of the site will be displayed on the front page via the **Site Description** block. It can, therefore, only be displayed in the left or right column, never in the center of the front page. The description text is also picked up by the Google search engine spider, if allowed. |
| **Front Page** | Moodle can display up to four elements in the center column of the front page when not logged in.<br>• List of courses<br>• List of categories<br>• News items<br>• Combo list (categories and courses)<br>The order of the elements is the same as the one chosen in the pull-down menus. |
| **Front page items when logged in** | Same as "Front Page", but used when logged in. |
| **Include a topic section** | If ticked, an additional topic section (just like the topic blocks in the center column of a topics-format course) appears on top of the front page's center column. It can contain any mix of resources or activities available in Moodle. It is very often used to provide information about the site. |
| **News items to show** | Number of news items that are displayed. |
| **Courses per page** | This is a threshold setting that is used when displaying courses within categories. If there are more courses in a category than specified, page navigation will be displayed at the top of the page. Also, when a combo list is used, course names are only displayed if the number is less than the specified threshold. For all other categories, only the number of courses is shown after the category name. |
| **Allow visible courses in hidden categories** | By default, courses in hidden categories are not shown unless the said setting is applied. |
| **Default frontpage role** | If logged-in users should be allowed to participate in front page activities, a default front page role should be set. The default is **None**. |

The front page settings mainly dictate what is displayed at the center of the page. Now let's have a look at the blocks on the left and right.

It is possible to rearrange the column order, but the feature is rarely used in Moodle.

# Arranging Front Page Blocks

To configure the left and right column areas with blocks, you have to turn on editing (using the **Blocks editing on** button). The menu includes blocks that are not available in courses such as **Course/Site description** and **Main menu**:

Blocks are added to the front page in exactly the same way as in courses. To change their position, use the standard arrows.

The **Main Menu** block allows you to add any installed Moodle resource or activity inside the block. For example, using labels and links to (internal or external) websites, you are able to create a menu-like structure on your front page.

If the **Include a topic section** parameter has been selected in the **Front Page settings**, you have to edit the part and add any installed Moodle activity or resource. This topic section is usually used by organizations to add a welcome message to visitors, often accompanied by a picture or other multimedia content.

# Login From a Different Website

The purpose of the **Login** block is for users to authenticate themselves by entering their username and password. It is possible to log into Moodle from a different website, maybe your organization's homepage, effectively avoiding the **Login** block. To implement this, you will have to add some HTML code on that page:

```
<form class="loginform" name="login" method="post" action="http://www.
mysite.com/login/index.php">
    <p>Username :
      <input size="10" name="username" />
    </p>
    <p>Password :
      <input size="10" name="password" type="password" />
    </p>
    <p>
      <input name="Submit" value="Login" type="submit" />
    </p>
</form>
```

The form will pass the username and password to your Moodle system. You will have to replace `www.mysite.com` with your URL. This address has to be entered in the **Alternate Login URL** field at **Users | Authentication | Manage authentication** in the **Site Administration** block.

# Other Front Page Items

The Moodle front page is treated as a standalone component in Moodle, and therefore has a top-level menu with a number of features that can all be accessed via the **Front Page** item in the **Site Administration** menu:

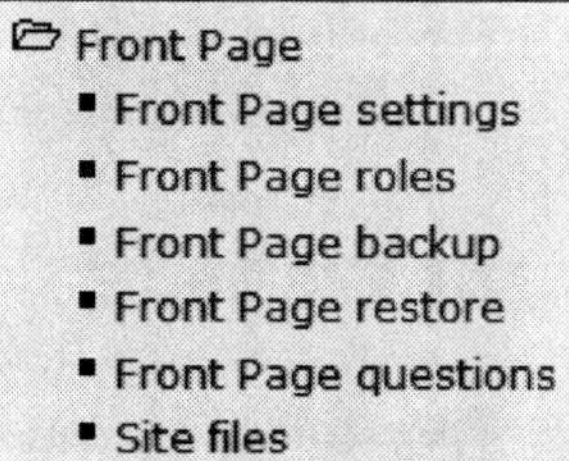


Having now looked in detail at the Front Page settings, let's turn to examining the other available options.

## Front Page Roles

The front page has its own context in which roles can be assigned to users. This allows a separate user to develop and maintain the front page without having access to any other elements in Moodle. Since the front page is treated as a course, a Teacher role is usually sufficient for this.

This feature has been discussed in great detail in the previous chapter, which dealt with the management of roles.

## Front Page Backup and Restore

The front page has its own backup and restore facilities to back up and restore all elements of the front page including any content. The mechanism of performing backup and restore is the same as for course backups, which is dealt with in Chapter 12.

Front page backups are stored in the `backupdata` folder in the **Site Files** area, and can be accessed by anybody who is aware of the URL. It is therefore best to move the created ZIP files to a more secure location.

## Front Page Questions

Since the Moodle front page is treated in the same way as a course, it also has its own question bank, which is used to store any questions used on front-page quizzes. For more information on quizzes and the question bank, go to the MoodleDocs at `http://docs.moodle.org/en/Quiz`.

## Site Files

The files areas of all courses are separate from each other, that is, files in Moodle belong to a course and can only be accessed by users who have been granted appropriate rights. The difference between Site files and the files area of any other course is that files in Site files can be accessed without logging in.

Files placed in this location are meant for the front page, but can be accessed from anywhere in the system. In fact, if the location is known, files can be even be accessed from outside Moodle.

Make sure that in the Site files area, you only place files that are acceptable to be seen by users who are not authenticated on your Moodle system.

Typical files to be placed in this area are any images you want to show on the front page (such as the logo of your organization) or any document that you want to be accessed (for example, the curriculum). However, it is also used for other files that to be accessible without access to a course, such as the Site Policy Agreement, which has to be accepted before starting Moodle (see Chapter 10, where the site policy is dealt with). To access these publicly available Site files elsewhere (for example, as a resource within other courses), you have to copy the link location that has the format: `http://mysite.com/file.php/1/file.doc`.

## Allow Personalization via My Moodle

By default, the same front page is displayed for all users on your Moodle system. To relax this restriction and to allow users to personalize their own front page, you have to activate the My Moodle feature via the **Force users to use My Moodle** setting in **Appearance | My Moodle** in the **Site Administration** block.

Once enabled, Moodle creates a **/my** directory for each user (except administrators) at their first login, which is displayed instead of the main Moodle front page. It is a very flexible feature that is similar to a customizable dashboard, but requires some more disk space on your server. Once logged in, users will have the ability to edit their page by adding blocks to their My Moodle area. The center of the page will be populated by the main front page, for instance displaying a list of courses, that users cannot modify.

## Making Blocks Sticky

There might be some blocks that you wish to "stick", that is, display on each My Moodle page, making them effectively compulsory blocks. For example, you might want to pin the **Calendar** block on the top right corner of each user's My Moodle page. To do this, go to **Modules | Blocks | Sticky blocks** in the **Site Administration** block and select **My Moodle** from the pull-down menu:

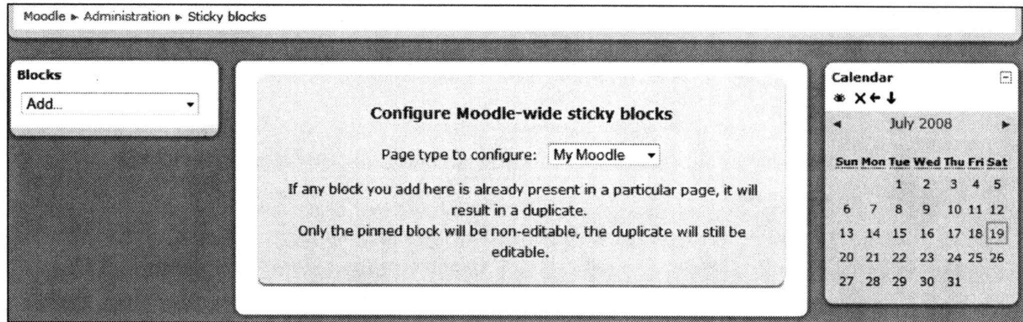


You can now add any item from the pull-down menu in the **Blocks** block. If the block is single instance (that is, only one occurrence is allowed per page), the block will not be available for the user to choose from. If the user has already selected a particular block, a duplicate will appear on their site, which can be edited and deleted.

To prevent users from editing their My Moodle pages, change the **moodle/my:managebIocks** capability in the **Authenticated user** role from **Allow** to **Not set**.

The sticky block feature is also available for course pages. A course creator has the ability to add and position blocks inside a course unless they have been made sticky. Select the **Course page** item from the same menu to configure the sticky blocks for courses, as shown in the preceding screenshot.

# Moodle Themes

Moodle provides a flexible skinning mechanism to brand your site according to existing guidelines. Before we create our own theme, we first have to cover a number of basics.

## Selecting a Moodle Theme

Moodle comes with a number of standard themes, which are chosen via **Appearance | Themes | Theme Selector** in the **Site Administration** block:

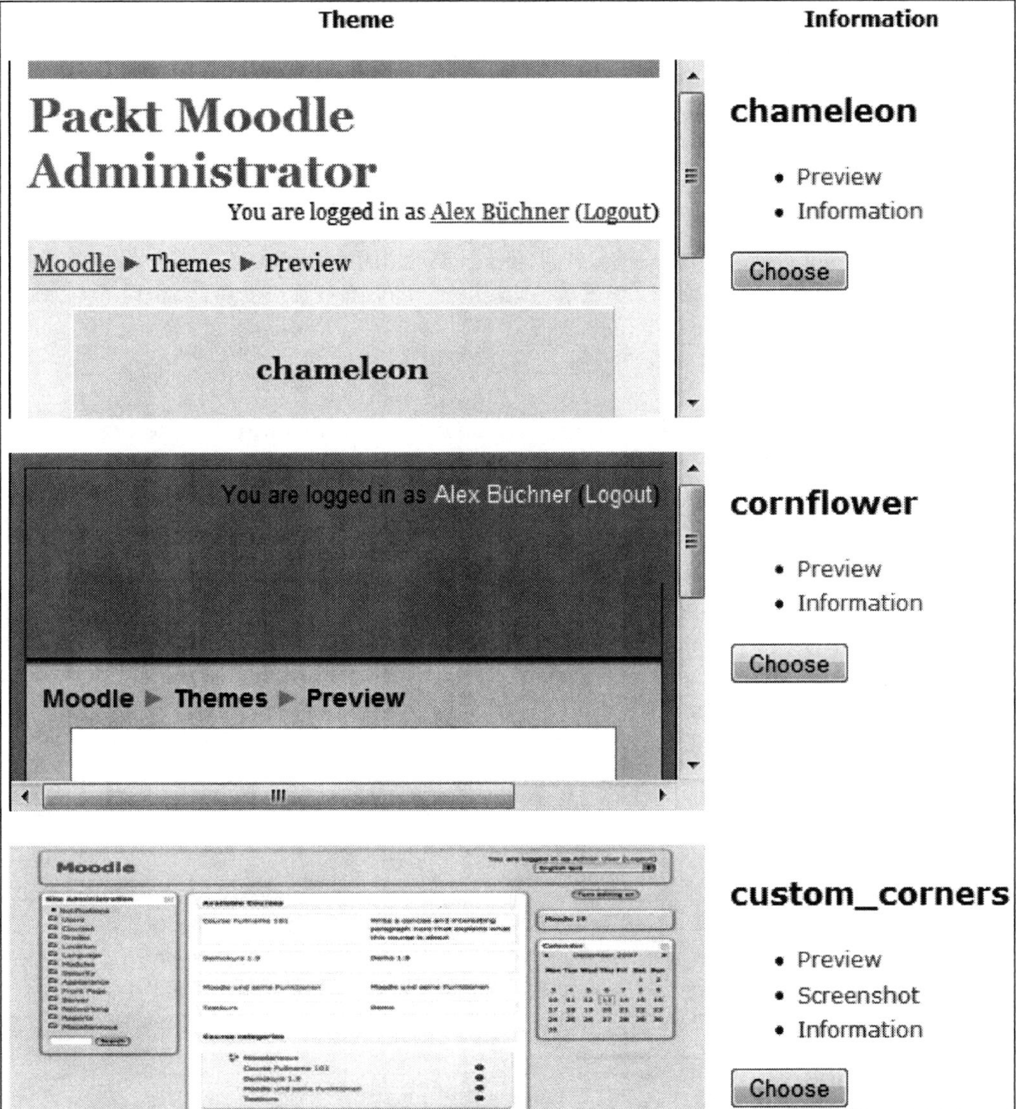

There are 15 themes in the standard Moodle distribution. Additional user-created themes also appear in this list. There is a database of public Moodle themes, which you access via the **Themes** link in the main menu of `http://moodle.org`. Alternatively, you can also commission a **Moodle Partner** to develop a professional theme for your site.

To select a theme, press the **Choose** button, which activates the skin straightaway. Most themes provide a **Preview** and some textual **Information**, with some also offering a **Screenshot**.

# Theme Types

Like roles, themes are assigned in different contexts, namely Site (System), User, Course, and Category. However, two additional areas, that is, Session and Page are supported by Moodle. These theme types are explained in the following list:

- Site Theme

  If no other theme is selected, this theme is applied throughout the site. This is the default, when you first install Moodle.
- User Theme

  If enabled, users are allowed to select their personal theme as a part of their profile.
- Course Theme

  If enabled, each editing teacher can specify a course theme in the course settings (**Force theme** parameter under **Edit course settings**).
- Category Theme

  A theme can be set for each category (**Force theme** parameter when editing course settings).
- Session Theme

  If you need to apply a theme temporarily (that is until you log out), you add the theme parameter to the URL of a course. For example, on our site we would replace `http://.../course/view.php?id=5` with `http://.../course/view.php?id=5&theme=packttheme`.

There are a number of scenarios where this feature is useful:

- Theme testing
- Provision of themes via links instead of Moodle settings (theme gallery)
- Provision of themes for different devices, for example PDAs, mobile phones, or game consoles

You have to activate session themes by setting the `$CFG->allowthemechangeonurl` parameter in config.php to `true`.

- Page Theme

  Page themes are set in code and have only been added for completeness.

The following table shows theme priority: where it is displayed, and where the setting is changed. To change the precedence order, modify the `$CFG->themeorder` parameter in `config.php`. The default is set to `array('page', 'course', 'category', 'session', 'user', 'site')`.

| Type | Overrides | Displays | Setting Location |
|---|---|---|---|
| Site | None | All pages, except course and category (if set) | Theme Selector |
| User | Site | All pages, except course and category (if set) | User profile |
| Course | Site/User/Category Session | Course | Course settings |
| Category | Site/User/Session | All courses in category, except course (if set) | Category editing |
| Session | Site/User | All pages, except course and category (if set) | `config.php` |
| Page | All | Depends on code | In code |

There is some trade-off when allowing theme types other than the site theme: While applying themes such as user, course, category, and so on, additional processing is required that will make Moodle slower. However, not allowing them may amount to limited customization. The site theme is used throughout the system, which sometimes is a required feature.

# Theme Settings

Armed with all the information provided to this point, the theme settings (**Appearance | Themes | Theme settings** in the **Site Administration** block) are almost self-explanatory:

**Theme settings**

| | |
|---|---|
| Theme list<br>*themelist* | [ ] Default: Empty<br>Leave this blank to allow any valid theme to be used. If you want to shorten the theme menu, you can specify a comma-separated list of names here (Don't use spaces!). For example: standard,orangewhite. |
| Allow user themes<br>*allowuserthemes* | ☐ Default: No<br>If you enable this, then users will be allowed to set their own themes. User themes override site themes (but not course themes) |
| Allow course themes<br>*allowcoursethemes* | ☐ Default: No<br>If you enable this, then courses will be allowed to set their own themes. Course themes override all other theme choices (site, user, or session themes) |
| Allow category themes<br>*allowcategorythemes* | ☐ Default: No<br>If you enable this, then themes can be set at the category level. This will affect all child categories and courses unless they have specifically set their own theme. WARNING: Enabling category themes may affect performance. |
| Allow users to hide blocks<br>*allowuserblockhiding* | ☑ Default: Yes<br>Do you want to allow users to hide/show side blocks throughout this site? This feature uses Javascript and cookies to remember the state of each collapsible block, and only affects the user's own view. |
| Show blocks on module pages<br>*showblocksonmodpages* | ☐ Default: No<br>Some activity modules support blocks on their pages. If you turn this on, then teachers will be able to add side blocks on those pages, otherwise the interface does not show this feature. |
| Hide activity type navigation<br>*hideactivitytypenavlink* | Hide from nobody ▾ Default: Hide from nobody<br>Select from whom to hide the activity type (e.g. Quizzes) link in the navigation displayed for activity modules. |

| Setting | Description |
|---|---|
| **Theme list** | To limit the number of available themes, name them in the text box separated by commas and no spaces. |
| **Allow user themes** | Users will be able to set their own themes. |
| **Allow course themes** | Editing teachers can set course themes. |
| **Allow category themes** | Enables category themes. |
| **Allow users to hide blocks** | By default, users are allowed to show and hide blocks via the icon at the top right of each block, which toggles between a plus and minus symbol. This can be turned off if the functionality is not desired. |
| **Show blocks on module pages** | Some Moodle activities allow side blocks. If enabled, the blocks' pull-down menu will be shown to editing teachers. |
| **Hide activity type navigation** | The activity type (for example, Quizzes) crumb in the navigation bar can be hidden from nobody (default), students or all users. |

There is one additional theme-related setting that is still in an experimental stage, and should be avoided in a production environment. It is the **Smart pix search** parameter in **Miscellaneous | Experimental** in the **Site Administration** block. When enabled, icons that are used across themes do not have to be a part of every single theme. Instead, if an icon is missing for the current theme, Moodle will search the parent themes and then the Moodle **/pix** folder. This minimizes the number of icon files you have to maintain, but comes at a slight performance cost.

Now that we have the skill set to work with existing themes, it is time to create our own themes.

# Creating Your Own Theme

As an administrator, you are unlikely to be involved in the creation of a full-blown custom theme as this task requires strong designing skills. However, you will be able to make basic modifications to existing themes and create simple new ones.

## Theme Creation Basics

Moodle uses **Cascading Style Sheets (CSS)** to describe the presentation of each element that is displayed. CSS is used to define different aspects of HTML and XHTML presentation including colors, fonts, layout, and so on. You will find more information about the specification of CSS at `http://www.w3.org/Style/CSS`.

Themes are located in the theme folder. Each theme is stored in a separate folder, where each folder typically contains the following files:

`config.php`: Theme settings (described next)

`favicon.ico`: Icon shown in browser URL locator and tabs

`footer.html`: Contains all elements in the footer (for example, copyright information)

`header.html`: Contains all elements in the header (for example, logo and navigation)

`meta.php`: Used to add IE-specific CSS files to page headers

`pix/`: Pictures and icons used in the theme

`README.html`: Information displayed after theme has been selected (optional)

`screenshot.jpg`: Screenshot of theme for preview (optional)

`styles.php`: Called from header.html to bridge to CSS files (don't change)

`styles_color.css`: Representation of colors

`styles_fonts.css`: Representation of fonts

`styles_layout.css`: Representation of layout

`styles_ie6.css`: Microsoft IE6 specific styles

`styles_ie7.css`: Microsoft IE7 specific styles

`styles_moz.css`: Browser styles

The `config.php` file contains a number of variables that control how Moodle uses theme:

| Theme Variable | Type | Description |
|---|---|---|
| `sheets` | array | Order in which included style sheet files are used in the theme. |
| `standardsheets` | array | List of styles used from the standard theme. |
| `parent` | theme | Name of parent theme (see Parent Themes section). |
| `parentsheets` | array | List of styles used from the parent theme. |
| `modsheets` | true/false | If set to "true" (which is default setting), `styles.php` will be used for all activity modules. Disable this only if needed. |

| Theme Variable | Type | Description |
|---|---|---|
| `blocksheets` | true/false | If set to "true" (which is default setting), `styles.php` will be used for all block modules. Disable this only if needed. |
| `langsheets` | true/false | If changed to "true", `styles.php` will be used for each language. That way, different styles can be used for different languages. |
| `navmenuwidth` | number | Number of characters displayed in the **Jump to...** menu inside modules (default is 50). |
| • `makenavmenulist` | true/false | If changed to "true", a variable called `$navmenulist` will be available in `header.html`, which is used for creating pop-up navigation menus such as the **Jump to...** menu. |
| • `resource_mp3_player_colors` | Settings | Settings of the built-in Moodle MP3 player:<br>• Colors (bgColour, btnColour, btnBorderColour, iconColour, iconOverColour, trackColour, handleColour, loaderColour)<br>• Fonts (font and fontColour)<br>• Player (buffer, waitForPlay, and autoPlay) |
| • `filter_mediaplugin_colors` | Settings | Settings of the built-in Moodle media player:<br>• Colors (same as previous)<br>• Player (waitForPlay) |
| • `custompix` | true/false | If changed to "true", a **pix** directory is required containing copies of `moodle/pix` and `pix/mod` containing custom icons for activities. |

To read more on theme basics, go to `http://docs.moodle.org/en/Theme_basics` where you will find a very well documented **Help** section.

# Moodle Theme Styles

At the heart of CSS are the styles. Moodle uses consistent plain English for the naming of styles. For the forum elements displayed in the following screenshot, a few sample styles have been labeled:

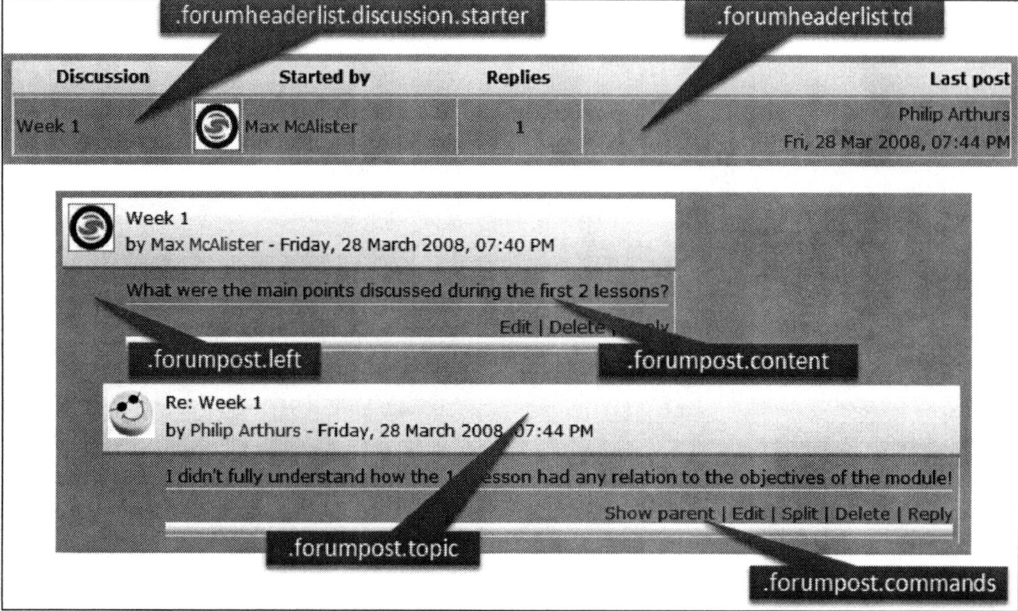


You can see that each element of Moodle is represented by a style. In total, there are well over 2,000 styles in Moodle (!), which gives designer a high degree of freedom. Due to the large number of styles, it is best to use a CSS tool such as the **Web Developer** add-on for Firefox or **CSSEdit** on Mac OS X. They allow you to point at a web page element, and the tool then displays the relevant style information. Alternatively, you can use the so-called Chameleon theme, which we will discuss in the next section.

# Theme Design and Development

## Logo Replacement

The simplest form of theme customization is to choose the standard theme **formal_white** and replace the image files with the ones of your organization. While this won't win any design competitions, it creates a very basic branding of your site.

All you have to do is to replace the files **logo.jpg** and **logo_small.jpg** with your own images. The former logo is used on the front page and the latter on all other pages.

## The Chameleon Theme

Chameleon is an interactive Moodle theme that is used to change styles on the fly. To activate the Chameleon theme, you have to perform the following actions:

1. Select the Chameleon theme using the theme selector.
2. Set `$THEME->chameleonenabled = true;` in your `config.php`.
3. <*Shift*><*Click*> on any element to open the floating CSS window displaying all elements under the mouse.

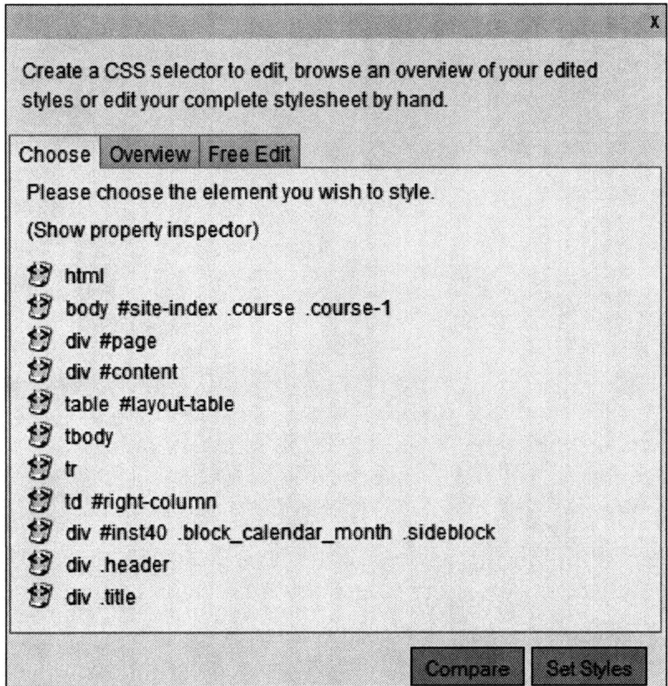

The preceding screenshot was taken from the Calendar block. To display the property inspector, select the **Show property inspector** link or click directly on an element you wish to change. Each element is described in more detail in the **Overview** tab where you have full editing capability:

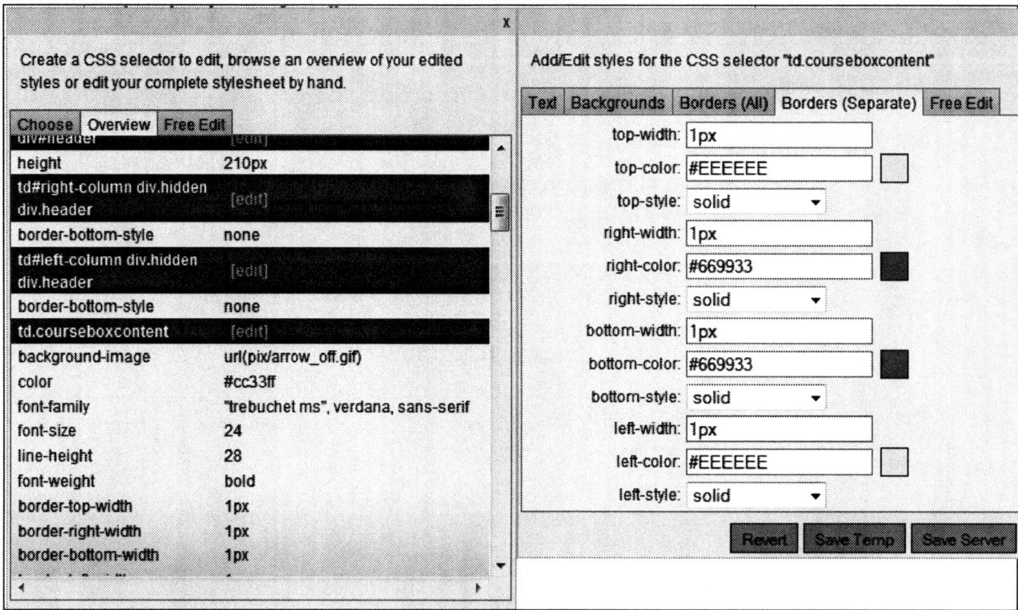


Once the settings have been saved, the changes apply immediately, which is a great way to experiment with settings. There is also a **Free Edit** tab for more advanced users who are familiar with editing CSS in code.

## Parent Themes

A powerful mechanism of CSS is the ability to re-use parts of a theme (the parent theme), and create a new derivative (the child theme). This inheritance mechanism is known as **cascading**. There are a number of situations where this approach is beneficial:

- A general look and feel for the site (parent) and different color schemes for different departments and faculties (children).
- Support for different types of visual impairment and color blindness. The same theme can be provided in variations that suit different users.
- If you need to provide the same theme for different organizations, you only have to modify the brand-specific items, such as the logo in `header.html`.

In order to use parent themes, you will have to modify the `$THEME->parent` and `$THEME->parentsheets` variables in `config.php` (see *Appendix II* for syntax).

## Rounded Corners

Moodle supports a feature that lets you display rounded corners at the bottom side of blocks. The following is a sample CSS style to facilitate this (the greater the radius value, the larger the curve):

```
.sideblock .content {
  -moz-border-radius-bottomleft:20px;
  -moz-border-radius-bottomright:20px;
}
```

Unfortunately, the feature is only supported in Firefox. If you wish to be browser agnostic, it is better to create your own corner images and display them as a background, which will show the picture at the bottom of each block. For example:

```
.sideblock.content {
  background:url(graphics/sideblock_curved_corner.jpg) bottom;
}
```

Moodle also supports themes containing custom corner (for more details see `http://docs.moodle.org/en/Custom_corners_theme`). The feature has to be enabled by setting the `$THEME->customcorners` in `config.php` to true. However, it is still in an experimental stage and should not be used in production settings.

## Custom Themes

Creating a full-blown Moodle theme requires the expertise of a web designer who is familiar with HTML, CSS, and the relevant PHP coding. This is beyond the scope of an administrator's responsibilities as well as this book. Most organizations would revert to a professional design agency that is able to design and develop Moodle themes.

The following is a mockup example of a professional custom theme (courtesy of and designed by Synergy Learning):

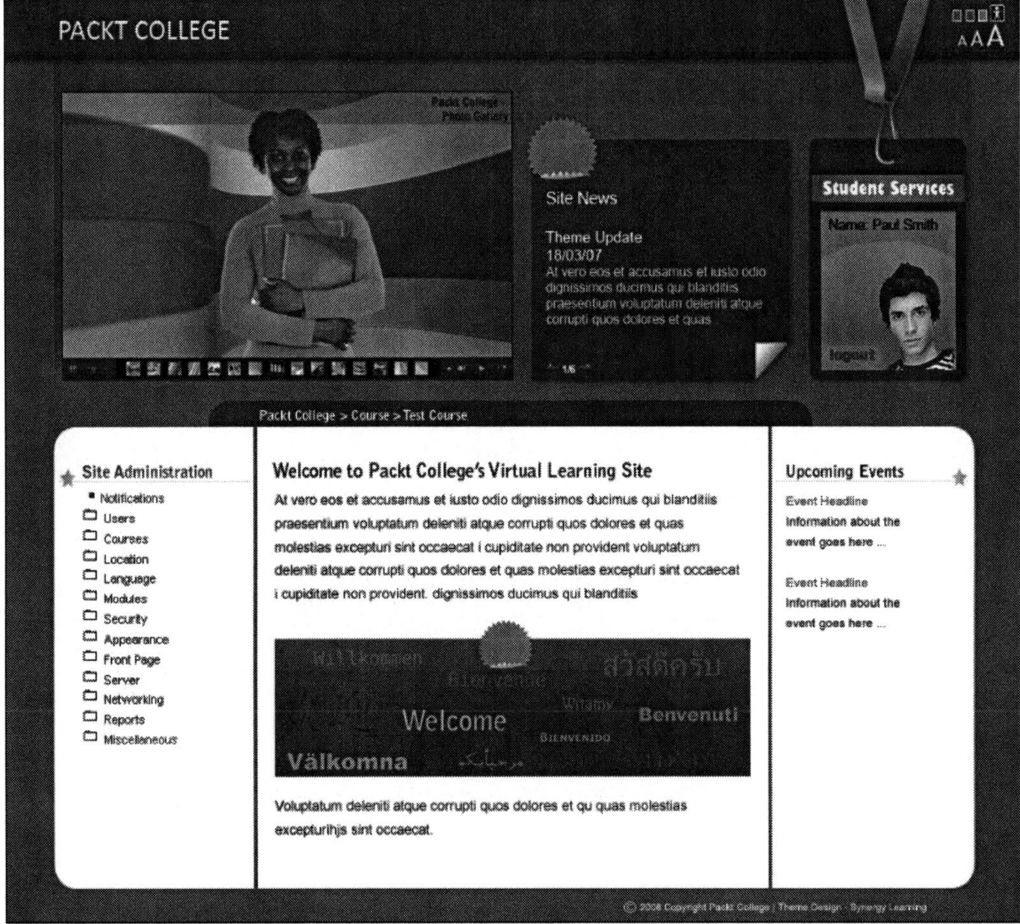


# Look and Feel: Good Practice

Nothing is right or wrong when it comes to VLE design and layout. But there are a number of good practice guidelines, which should help you to produce a professional look and feel that represents the corporate identity of your organization.

# Consistency

The key to theme development is consistency. In order to guarantee a good learning experience, it is important that the look and feel is coherent throughout the site. Links should all look identical, blocks should be arranged consistently, and so on.

While it is tempting to be very creative with styles in Moodle themes and the arrangement of blocks, bear in mind that good design principles still apply!

# Supporting Different Browsers

Make sure you test your styles in multiple browsers on different operating systems. Unfortunately, Moodle themes are notorious for displaying correctly in one browser, but not in another. The introduction of the **Internet Explorer specific style sheets** has improved matters, but there is still a need to check the following minimum browsers:

- Internet Explorer 6 (Windows and OS X)
- Internet Explorer 7 (Windows only)
- Firefox (Windows, OS X, and Linux)
- Safari (Windows and OS X)

# Guaranteeing Accessibility

In most educational settings, accessibility, that is, the ability to access Moodle's functionality by users with certain disabilities is now a legal requirement. So, it is important to make sure that your system complies with the respective standards. CSS is Moodle's representation layer that is independent from the content layer, which is represented in XHTML. Thus, accessibility can be achieved directly via the theme.

To create a very basic accessibility style sheet, duplicate an existing theme folder (for example, `standardwhite`). Within that folder, create a new style sheet file (for example, `access.css`) and add the various style IDs and classes that need to be overwritten.

The following is a sample code that changes the body background to black with yellow text, and increases the font size:

```
body { background-color: #000000; background-image: none;
                  color:#FFFF00}
p { font-size:16px;}
```

Once all customization is finalized, you have to add the new style sheet to the style's configuration file `config.php`. Now add your theme to the `$THEME->sheets` parameter.

Moodle provides links to three external sites that check the current page for standard compliance. To activate these, go to **Server | Debugging** in the **Site Administration** block and change the **Debug messages** drop-down to **Normal**. After saving the changes, links to **Validate HTML**, **Section 508 Check**, and **WCAG 1 (2, 3) Check** will be displayed at the bottom of your page (if supported by your theme).

# Summary

After providing a general overview of look and feel elements in Moodle, the chapter covered front page customization, Moodle themes, and some good practices.

As mentioned before, the front page in Moodle is a course. This has advantages (you can do everything you can do in a course and a little bit more), but it also has drawbacks (you can only do what you can do in a course and might feel limited by this). However, some organizations are now using the Moodle front page as their homepage. Again, this might or might not work for you.

Also, there has been some criticism about the non-state-of-the-art look and feel of Moodle. The latest additions to Moodle themes, however, have proven to allow the creation of sites with a professional look and feel. Here we presented few of them. A competent designer should be able to get into more detail using CSS.

Now that your Moodle hopefully looks the way you want it to, it is time to enable all the functionalities that you wish to offer your users. These configuration settings are dealt with in the next chapter.

# 8
# Moodle Configuration

Your system is now fully operational and has the look and feel to reflect the branding of your site. As with all complex software, there are a significant number of configuration activities that can be carried out to bring Moodle in line with your organization's needs and requirements.

Moodle comes with a multitude of configuration options. In this chapter we will cover the most important settings, some of which might not be relevant to your organization:

- Accessibility

  We are looking at Moodle supporting users with different types of accessibility problems such as visual impairment and motoric difficulties.
- Localization

  Moodle is used throughout the world, and is therefore required to support different locales, including different languages, dates, times, and time zones. We will be dealing with the configuration of all four localization elements.
- Module configuration

  Moodle comes with a number of modules such as activities, resources, blocks, and filters as part of its core installation. We will be dealing with the configuration of these modules.
- Grades and gradebook settings

  The gradebook is one of the most important constructs of a virtual learning environment. There are a significant number of settings at administration level that are briefly covered.
- Miscellaneous settings

  These settings will cover the setup of the Moodle editor, site-wide tags, and the experimental section where upcoming features are already available.

There are a number of additional configuration topics, which are covered in dedicated chapters dealing with security, optimization, and networking.

# Accessibility

We have touched upon accessibility in the previous chapter when we dealt with the creation of themes. We will now look at all other settings in Moodle that impact accessibility.

An area has been dedicated to Moodle accessibility in the MoodleDocs, which you can access at `http://docs.moodle.org/en/accessibility`. It provides useful links to standards, guidelines, legislation, and also subject-related tools and resources.

We know from the previous chapter that Moodle provides links to three external sites that check the current page for standard compliance. We have also seen how to activate them. Alternatively, you can install the **Compliance block,** which you can find in the **Modules and plugins** section on `www.moodle.org`. The installation of third-party modules is covered in detail in Chapter 13.

# Accessibility Supported by the Moodle Editor

Moodle is fully compliant with all major accessibility standards. This has been achieved by implementing **XHTML 1.0 Strict**, which only allows the usage of compliant HTML constructs and the implementation of the Moodle forms library. This guarantees consistency across forms, and also supports standard screen readers.

The compliance is only guaranteed for Moodle pages, but not for newly created and uploaded content or any third-party learning resources. It is therefore recommended to encourage the creation of XHTML Strict content if new web content is developed. A key part of this restricted standard is the non-support for tables. It is possible to hide the table button in the Moodle editor, which is used throughout the system (see Editing Options later in this chapter):

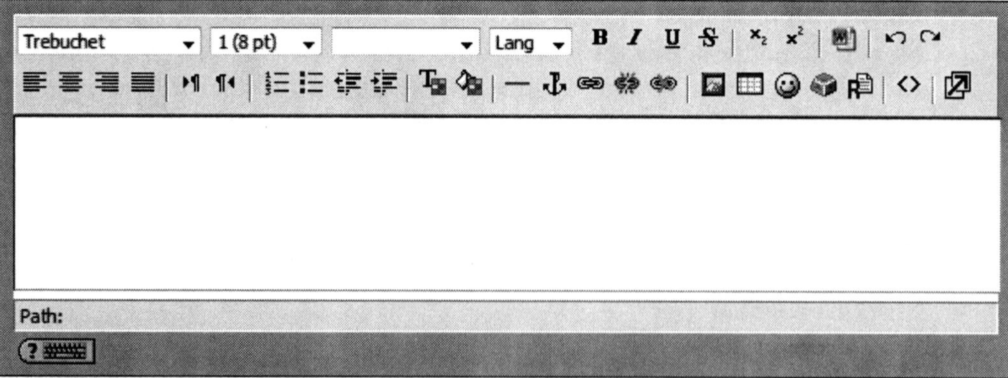

The Moodle interface can be accessed via keyboard only. The *TAB* key is used to jump from field to field. When using the Moodle editor a **Help** link is provided underneath the editor in the shape of a **yellow keyboard** icon, which opens a window listing all editor shortcuts. Tables cannot be accessed using the shortcut keys:

**HTML Editor Shortcut Keys**

The following features are accessible through shortcut keys:

| | |
|---|---|
| Ctrl-O | Change the font |
| Ctrl-P | Change the font size |
| Ctrl-H | Change text format (headings etc.) |
| Ctrl-1 to Ctrl-6 | Change heading level |
| Ctrl-= | Change text language for screen readers, or specify language for the Multilang filter (these appear after the 'Multi' option in the dropdown). |
| Ctrl-B | Make text bold |
| Ctrl-I | Make text italic |
| Ctrl-U | Underline text |
| Ctrl-S | Strikethrough text |

There is also a useful third-party **Accessibility Options** block, which lets the user change the font size and background color of his or her Moodle site. You can find it in the **Modules and plugins section** on `www.moodle.org`. The installation of third-party modules is covered in detail in Chapter 13.

# Screen Reader Support

A **screen reader** is a form of assistive technology used by blind and partially-sighted users to interpret what is displayed on the screen. Once the information has been located, it can be vocalized using speech synthesis software and audio hardware.

Moodle supports screen-reading devices. The setting has to be enabled separately for each user requiring the assistive mode. This is done in the user's profile, where the **Screen reader** setting in advanced mode has to be changed to **Yes**.

Screen readers can only read text and the ALT tag in images. It is therefore highly recommended that you provide these tags in any images used.

# Localization

Localization is concerned with the adaptation of software so it can be used in different locales. A **locale** is linked to a region where certain cultural aspects apply such as language, formatting of dates and times, calendaric representation, and so on.

Since Moodle is used throughout the world and given the fact that many educational establishments spawn across continents, it is important that localization is fully supported. The key areas in which Moodle can be configured are language-related settings and calendaric information.

## Languages

Moodle supports over 75 languages, including Latin! To represent the character sets of multiple languages, a standard called Unicode has been adopted. It covers most modern scripts used throughout the world. Moodle also fully supports right-to-left writing systems, such as Arabic:

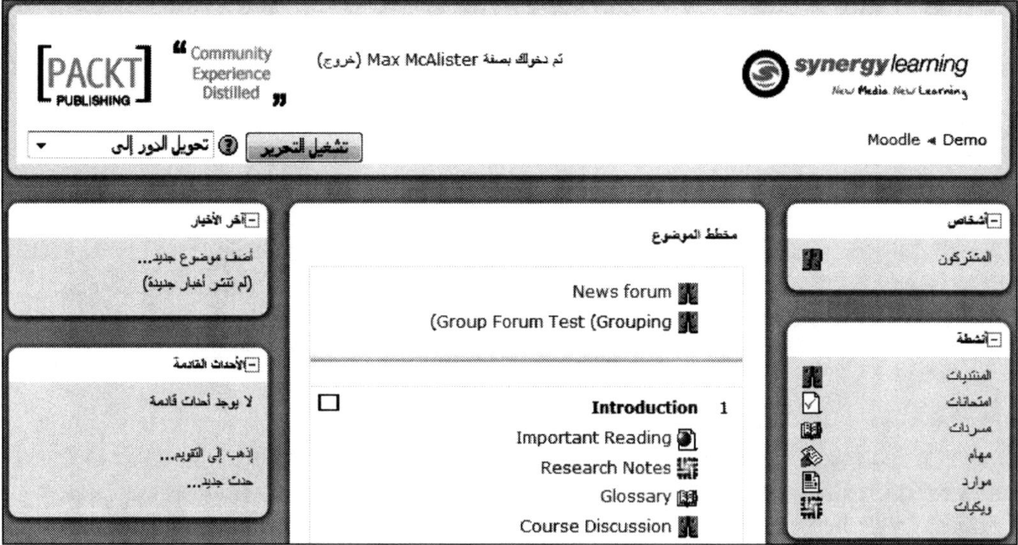


## Language Packs

Locales are characterized by standardized two-letter region code representing a language and optional letters. For example, **pt** represents **Portuguese** as spoken in Portugal, whereas **pt_br** represents **Brazilian Portuguese**.

Moodle uses the same representation. In order to support a language, you have to install its language pack that contains all the terms used in Moodle. Go to **Language | Language Packs** in the **Site Administration** block to include new language packs:

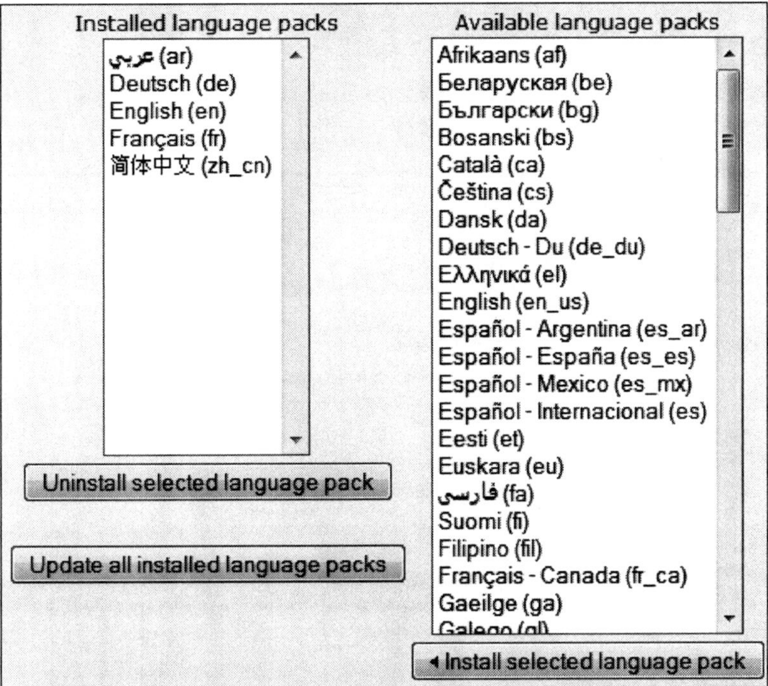


In the preceding screenshot, five language packs, consisting of Arabic, German, English, French, and Simplified Chinese have been installed that you can see in the list on the left. To add more language packs, select the locale on the right and select **Install selected language pack**. To reverse the operation, select a language pack in the list on the left and then click on **Uninstall selected language pack**.

Once installed, the user can choose a language (if configured) from the language menu, which is usually located in the header, or from within their profile. Bear in mind that only terms and phrases that are a part of Moodle will change, whereas any content created will not be translated.

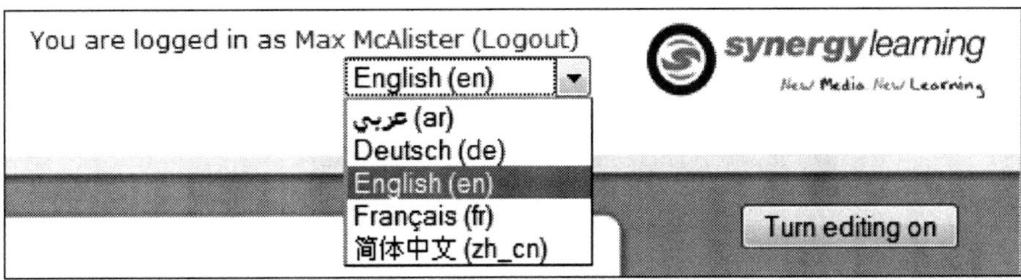

Language packs are kept and maintained at `http://download.moodle.org/lang16`. Some packs are updated more frequently than others. The **Update all installed language packs** copies the latest versions to your server.

# Language Settings

Moodle offers a number of language settings that you find at **Language | Language settings** in the **Site Administration** block:

**Language settings**

| | |
|---|---|
| Language autodetect<br>*autolang* | ☑ Default: Yes<br>Detect default language from browser setting, if disabled site default is used. |
| Default language<br>*lang* | English (en) ▾ Default: English (en)<br>Choose a default language for the whole site. Users can override this setting later. |
| Display language menu<br>*langmenu* | ☑ Default: Yes<br>Choose whether or not you want to display the general-purpose language menu on the home page, login page etc. This does not affect the user's ability to set the preferred language in their own profile. |
| Languages on language menu<br>*langlist* | en,fr,de Default: Empty<br>Leave this blank to allow users to choose from any language you have in this installation of Moodle. However, you can shorten the language menu by entering a comma-separated list of language codes that you want. For example: en,es_es,fr,it |
| Cache language menu<br>*langcache* | ☑ Default: Yes<br>Cache the language menu. Saves a lot of memory and processing power. If you enable this, the menu takes a few minutes to update after you have added or removed languages. |
| Sitewide locale<br>*locale* | Default: Empty<br>Choose a sitewide locale - this will override the format and language of dates for all language packs (though names of days in calendar are not affected). You need to have this locale data installed on your operating system (eg for linux en_US.UTF-8 or es_ES.UTF-8). In most cases this field should be left blank. |
| Excel encoding<br>*latinexcelexport* | Unicode ▾ Default: Unicode<br>Choose the encoding for Excel exports. |

| Settings | Description |
|---|---|
| **Language autodetect** | By default, Moodle detects the language from the used web browser. If you wish to override this and use the default site language instead, uncheck the box. |
| **Default language** | Select the language that will be used throughout the site, unless overridden by individual users via the language menu or in their profiles. Only those languages appear for which a language pack has been installed. |
| **Display language menu** | Specify whether the language menu is displayed on the front page header. The user will always have the ability to change the language in the profile, no matter what the setting is. |
| **Languages on language menu** | If left empty, all installed languages appear in the language menu. To narrow down this list, specify a comma-separated list of locale codes. |
| **Cache language menu** | Unless you are modifying a language pack, it is recommended to leave this setting at Yes. It caches all language strings rather than loading them dynamically. |
| **Sitewide locale** | The localization operations are internally driven by system locales that are selected based on the chosen language pack. If you wish to change this (which is hardly required), select the site-wide locale in its operating system format, such as en_US.UTF-8. The file has to be installed as a part of the operating system. |
| **Excel encoding** | When downloading data in Microsoft Excel format (such as in gradebook reports or log files), Moodle uses the Unicode format. Older versions of Excel only support Latin encoding. |

There are two additional language-related settings, which are both placed in **Security | Site Policies** in the Administration block:

- The **Full name format** option allows you choose the **Language** setting from its pull-down menu. If this is selected, the decision about how names are displayed is made by the respective current language pack. That way, you can cater for local sensitivities with regard to first names.
- The **Allow extended characters in usernames** parameter removes the limitation of only using alphanumeric characters in usernames.

# Language Editing

Each phrase, term, and string used in Moodle is represented in language files, which are tied to certain modules in Moodle (located in the `lang` directory). There are two scenarios when you want to edit language files:

- A particular phrase is not translated yet and you want to rectify this situation. This happens frequently in languages other than English when a new version of Moodle is released.
- You want to change certain words or phrases, for example "grades" to "marks".

To edit a language file go to **Language | Language editing** in the **Site Administration** block, where for each selectable language you have three options (seen as three tabs), which are listed next.

## Checking for Untranslated Words or Phrases

For any language other than English, some phrases might not have been translated. To check out which ones these are, select the first option that tells you how many phrases there are in total and how many are missing. It further lists all the missing phrases and the corresponding files:

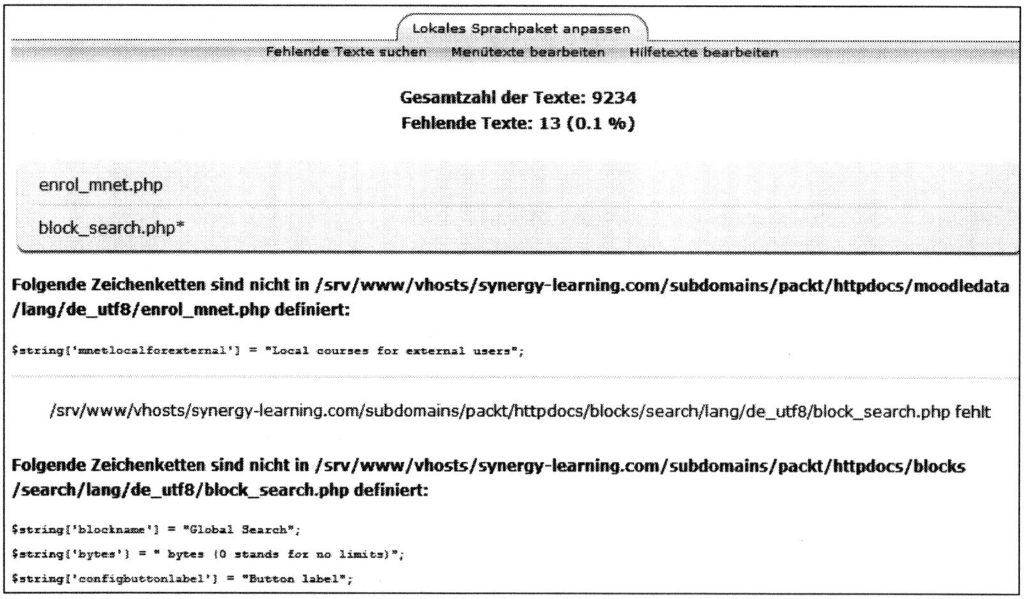

Lokales Sprachpaket anpassen

Fehlende Texte suchen Menütexte bearbeiten Hilfetexte bearbeiten

**Gesamtzahl der Texte: 9234**
**Fehlende Texte: 13 (0.1 %)**

enrol_mnet.php

block_search.php*

**Folgende Zeichenketten sind nicht in /srv/www/vhosts/synergy-learning.com/subdomains/packt/httpdocs/moodledata/lang/de_utf8/enrol_mnet.php definiert:**

```
$string['mnetlocalforexternal'] = "Local courses for external users";
```

/srv/www/vhosts/synergy-learning.com/subdomains/packt/httpdocs/blocks/search/lang/de_utf8/block_search.php fehlt

**Folgende Zeichenketten sind nicht in /srv/www/vhosts/synergy-learning.com/subdomains/packt/httpdocs/blocks/search/lang/de_utf8/block_search.php definiert:**

```
$string['blockname'] = "Global Search";
$string['bytes'] = " bytes (0 stands for no limits)";
$string['configbuttonlabel'] = "Button label";
```

The preceding is a sample screenshot from the German translation, which contains 9,234 phrases of which 13 (0.1%) are missing. The next step is to edit phrases.

[ Moodle creates a local directory located somewhere inside `$CFG->dataroot` where it stores your edited phrases. Make sure that you have write access to the `lang` directory to avoid any error messages. ]

## Editing Words or Phrases

As mentioned earlier, Moodle keeps a separate language file for each module. This separation is beneficial as it frees the underlying code (developed by programmers) from the localization (worked on by translators). However, it has the disadvantage that you have to know where the respective strings are located. In most cases, this is quite straightforward, but sometimes you will have to search in a number of places. Once you have selected the module, the English phrases (along with the localization string only relevant to developers) appear on the left and the localized phrases on the right side of the screen, which are editable.

In the following sample, the `calendar.php` module has been chosen:

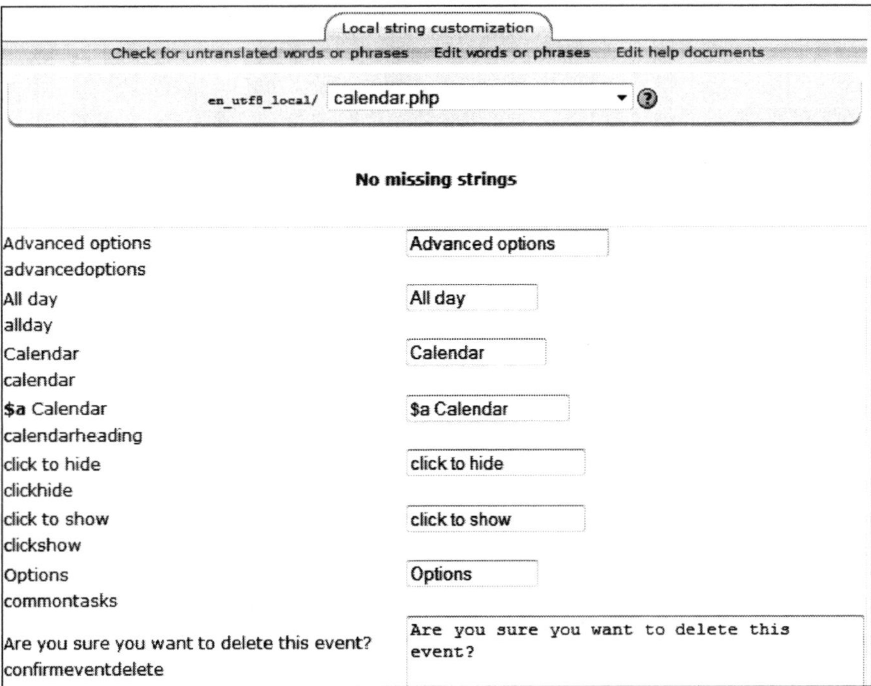


To modify a phrase, simply edit the string on the right and press one of the **Save changes: calendar.php** buttons that are displayed throughout the page. You might have spotted the **$a** parameter in the fourth phrase from the top. This is a so-called placeholder, which is substituted on the fly, for instance with today's date or a username.

## Editing Help Documents

Every time you click on a question mark icon a help text is shown. These texts can also be modified. In the following example, the `langedit.html` file has been selected. The top field gives you space to replace the master language pack with your own version:

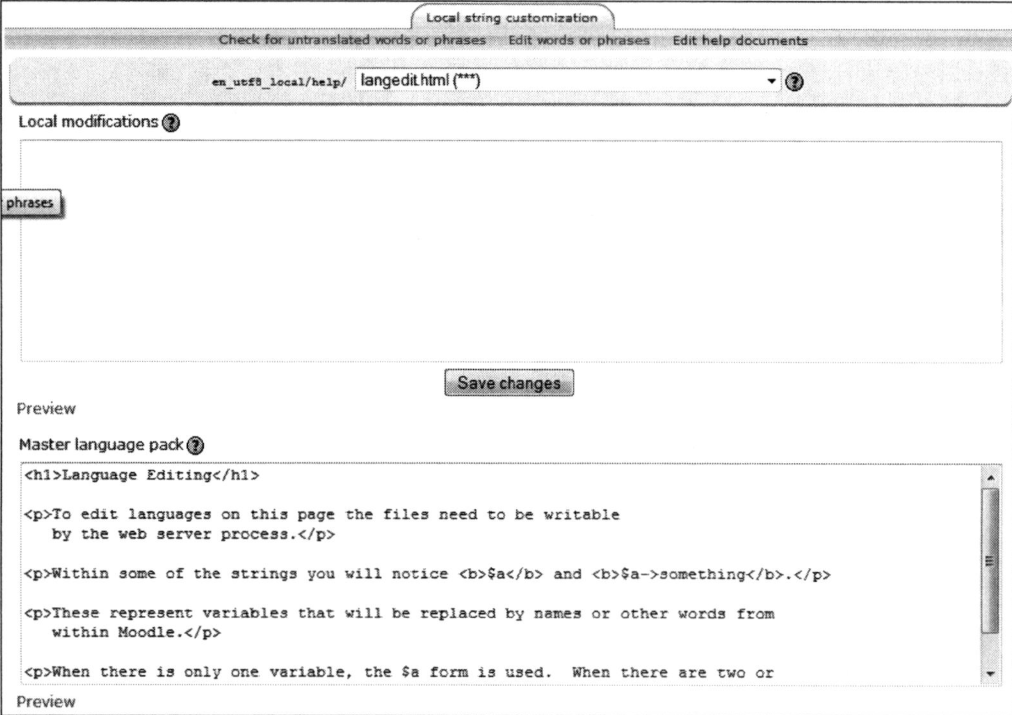


## Maintaining Language Packs

If you are involved in translating a language pack or creating a new one, the language pack maintenance is represented by the `moodle/site:langeditmaster` capability. For clarity, it is recommended to create a Translator role.

Once allowed, an additional tab will appear in the language editing menu with the same three tabs that could be seen in all screenshots shown under "Language Editing". The difference is that the modifications are stored in the master file and not a local copy. Make sure you take backup of all your language-related data before upgrading to a newer version of Moodle as all translated phrases in the master files will be overridden!

## Miscellaneous Language Settings

If you wish to give a non-admin user the right to edit local files, you have to allow the `moodle/site:langeditlocal` capability and assign it in the System context.

If you have users who deal with multi-language content, it is recommended to turn on the **Multi language content** filter in **Modules | Filters | Manage filters** and enable the **Filter all strings** setting in the **Common settings** (both options are explained in more detail in the filter configuration section ahead). The multi-language filter supports the `<span lang="xx" class="multilang">` tag by default; the older `<lang>` tag can be enabled as well.

# Calendaric Information

Different cultures represent calendaric information—date, times and time zones—in different formats.

## Calendars

Moodle formats date and time according to the set locale for Gregorian calendars (others are currently not supported). A few additional settings are changeable at **Appearance | Calendar** in the **Site Administration** block (only the relevant fields are shown):

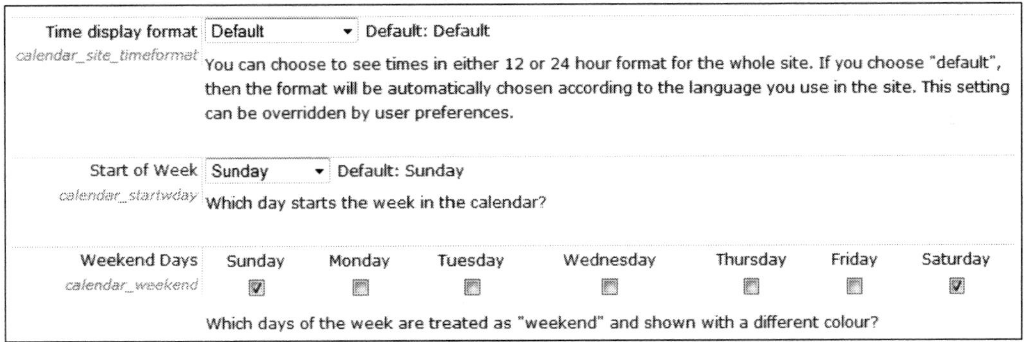
Time display format
calendar_site_timeformat
Default
Default: Default
You can choose to see times in either 12 or 24 hour format for the whole site. If you choose "default", then the format will be automatically chosen according to the language you use in the site. This setting can be overridden by user preferences.
Start of Week
calendar_startwday
Sunday
Default: Sunday
Which day starts the week in the calendar?
Weekend Days
calendar_weekend
Sunday
Monday
Tuesday
Wednesday
Thursday
Friday
Saturday
Which days of the week are treated as "weekend" and shown with a different colour?

Timings are displayed according to the selected locale, which can be overridden by a 12-hour and 24-hour clock, respectively.

Different countries have a different start of the week. For instance, in the North America the week starts on Sunday whereas in Europe it starts on Monday.

Not all countries use the default values of Saturday and Sunday as the weekend. For example, in Islamic countries, the weekend is on Friday and Saturday whereas Sunday is a normal working day. This can be specified in the **Weekend days** section.

# Time Zones

Moodle supports systems that spawn across time zones. This happens in three scenarios:

- In countries that cover more than a single time zone.
- Sites that have learners from multiple countries or time zones.
- Where the server is hosted outside the time zone of the organization, for example with an Internet service provider.

To modify the default time zone parameters, go to **Location | Location settings** in the **Site Administration** block:

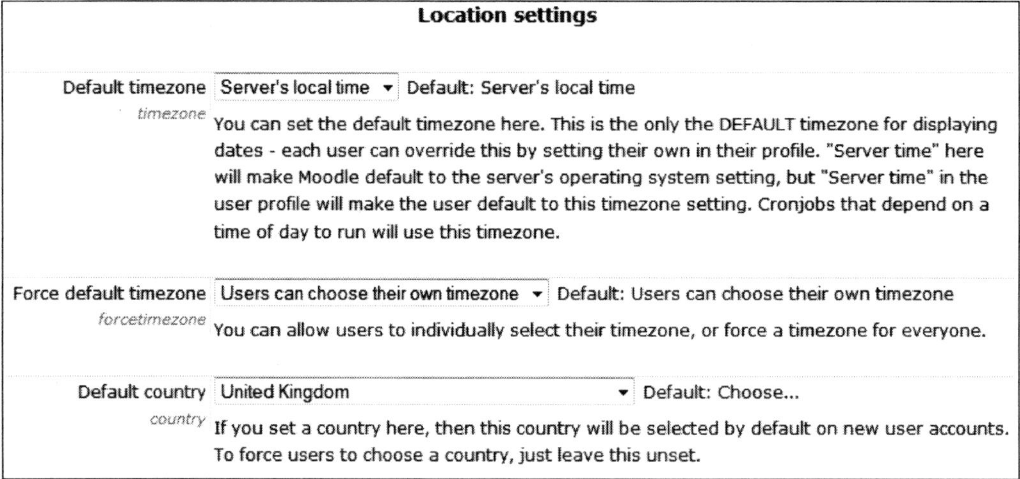

Location settings
Default timezone
timezone
Server's local time
Default: Server's local time
You can set the default timezone here. This is the only the DEFAULT timezone for displaying dates - each user can override this by setting their own in their profile. "Server time" here will make Moodle default to the server's operating system setting, but "Server time" in the user profile will make the user default to this timezone setting. Cronjobs that depend on a time of day to run will use this timezone.
Force default timezone
forcetimezone
Users can choose their own timezone
Default: Users can choose their own timezone
You can allow users to individually select their timezone, or force a timezone for everyone.
Default country
country
United Kingdom
Default: Choose...
If you set a country here, then this country will be selected by default on new user accounts. To force users to choose a country, just leave this unset.

The **Default timezone** is used throughout the system. The initial value is the server's system time, which might not reflect your local time. Each learner can change this setting in his or her user profile unless it is forced to be set to a particular time. Displayed times, for example, for an assignment deadline are adjusted to the selected time zone. If specified, the **Default country** is used for new user accounts.

Often, rules in certain time zones (there are over 2,000 separate ones!) change, for instance the adjustment of daylight saving time. If this is the case, you should update these settings via **Location | Update timezones** in the **Site Administration** block. New versions of Moodle always contain the latest version of the time zone rules.

# Module Configuration

Moodle distinguishes between three types of modules that are used in courses and the front page (which is treated as a course):

- Activities (which also covers resources)
- Blocks
- Filters

Most modules are enabled by default and are set to their default values. You get access to these settings in the **Modules** menu in the **Site Administration** block.

Be careful when modifying settings in activities, blocks, and filters. Inappropriate values can cause problems inside courses.

# Configuration of Activities

Selecting **Modules | Activities | Manage activities** in the **Site Administration** block displays the following screen:

**Activities**

| Activity module | Activities | Version | Hide/Show | Delete | Settings |
|---|---|---|---|---|---|
| Assignment | 3 | 2007101511 | | Delete | Settings |
| Chat | 0 | 2007101509 | | Delete | Settings |
| Choice | 0 | 2007101509 | | Delete | |
| Database | 0 | 2007101509 | | Delete | Settings |
| Forum | 5 | 2007101511 | | | Settings |
| Glossary | 1 | 2007101509 | | Delete | Settings |
| Hot Potatoes Quiz | 0 | 2007101511 | | Delete | Settings |
| Journal | 0 | 2007101509 | | Delete | |
| LAMS | 0 | 2007101509 | | Delete | Settings |
| Label | 0 | 2007101509 | | Delete | |
| Lesson | 0 | 2007101509 | | Delete | |
| Quiz | 1 | 2007101509 | | Delete | Settings |
| Resource | 1 | 2007101509 | | Delete | Settings |
| SCORM/AICC | 0 | 2007110500 | | Delete | Settings |
| Survey | 0 | 2007101509 | | Delete | |
| Wiki | 1 | 2007101509 | | Delete | |
| Workshop | 0 | 2007101509 | | Delete | |

The table displays the following information:

| Column | Description |
|---|---|
| **Activity module** | Icon and name of the activity/resource as they appear in courses. |
| **Activities** | The number of times the activity/resource is used in Moodle. When you click on the number a table is shown, which displays the courses in which the activity/resource has been used as well as the standard course operations. |
| **Version** | Version of the activity/resource (format YYYYMMDDHH). |
| **Hide / Show** | The open eye indicates that the activity/resource is shown, that is available for use, where the closed eye indicates that it is hidden (unavailable). |
| **Delete** | Delete action, except forum activity. |
| **Settings** | Link to activity/resource settings (not available for all items). |

Clicking on the show or hide icon toggles its state; if it is hidden it will change to shown and vice versa. If an activity/resource is hidden, it will not appear in the Activities or Resources drop-down in any Moodle course. Hidden activities and resources that are already present in courses are hidden, but are still in the system. It means that once the activity/resource is visible again, the items will also show in the courses.

You can delete any Moodle activity resource (apart from the forum activity). If you delete an activity or resource that has been used anywhere in Moodle, all the already created activities/resources will also be deleted and so will any associated user data! Deleting an activity/resource cannot be undone; it has to be installed from scratch.

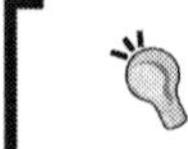

[ It is highly recommended not to delete any activities unless you are 100% sure that you will never need them. If you wish to prevent usage of an activity or resource type, it is better to hide it instead. ]

Some activities and resources, for instance **Hot Potatoes Quiz** and **LAMS**, are hidden by default because they link to third-party software. Others, such as **Journal**, are not maintained anymore and have been included because plenty of sites still have courses that use these activities.

The settings are different for each activity/resource. For example, the **Assignment** settings only contain three variables (to set maximum default size for assignment uploads, to count number of words or letters, and to allow/disallow showing recent submissions). But the **Quiz** settings allow the modification of a wide range of variables.

The parameters of all standard Moodle activities and resources are explained in the respective Module Docs pages.

## Configuration of Blocks

Selecting **Modules | Blocks | Manage blocks** in the **Site Administration** block displays the table shown in the next screenshot.

The table displays the same information as for **Activities**, but with an additional **Multiple** column. The **Multiple** flag indicates whether a block can be used more than once in a course. For example, you can only have one Ca**lendar**, but you can have as many **Remote RSS Feeds** as you wish.

You can delete any Moodle block. If you delete a block that is used anywhere in Moodle, all the content that was already created will also be deleted! Deleting a block cannot be undone; it has to be installed from scratch.

Do NOT delete or hide the **Site Administration** block as you will not be able to access any system settings anymore.

All blocks are shown by default. Some blocks require additional settings to be set elsewhere for the block to function. For example, RSS feeds have to be enabled (**Server | RSS**) or **Global Search** has to be activated (**Miscellaneous | Experimental**).

The parameters of all standard Moodle blocks are explained in the respective Module Docs pages.

**Blocks**

| Name | Instances | Version | Hide/Show | Multiple | Delete | Settings |
|---|---|---|---|---|---|---|
| Activities | 3 | 2007101509 | | | Delete | |
| Admin bookmarks | 1 | 2007101509 | | | Delete | |
| Administration | 3 | 2007101509 | | | Delete | |
| Blog Menu | 3 | 2007101509 | | | Delete | |
| Blog Tags | 3 | 2007101509 | | Yes (change) | Delete | |
| Calendar | 2 | 2007101509 | | | Delete | |
| Course/Site Description | 0 | 2007101509 | | | Delete | |
| Courses | 4 | 2007101509 | | | Delete | Settings |
| Flickr | 0 | 2007101509 | | Yes (change) | Delete | |
| Global Search | 0 | 2007112700 | | | Delete | Settings |
| HTML | 0 | 2007101509 | | Yes (change) | Delete | |
| Latest News | 3 | 2007101509 | | | Delete | |
| Loan calculator | 0 | 2007101509 | | | Delete | |
| Login | 1 | 2007101509 | | | Delete | |
| Main Menu | 1 | 2007101509 | | | Delete | |
| Mentees | 0 | 2007101509 | | Yes (change) | Delete | |
| Messages | 0 | 2007101509 | | | Delete | |
| Network Servers | 0 | 2007101509 | | | Delete | |
| Online Users | 0 | 2007101509 | | | Delete | Settings |
| People | 3 | 2007101509 | | | Delete | |
| Quiz Results | 0 | 2007101509 | | Yes (change) | Delete | |
| Random Glossary Entry | 0 | 2007101509 | | Yes (change) | Delete | |
| Recent Activity | 3 | 2007101509 | | | Delete | |
| Remote RSS Feeds | 0 | 2007101509 | | Yes (change) | Delete | Settings |
| Search Forums | 3 | 2007101509 | | | Delete | |
| Section Links | 0 | 2007101509 | | | Delete | |
| Site Administration | 2 | 2007101509 | | | Delete | |
| Social Activities | 0 | 2007101509 | | | Delete | |
| Tags | 0 | 2007101509 | | Yes (change) | Delete | |
| Upcoming Events | 3 | 2007101509 | | | Delete | |
| Youtube | 0 | 2007101509 | | Yes (change) | Delete | |

# Configuration of Filters

Filters scan any text that has been entered via the Moodle editor and automatically transform it into different, often more complex forms. For example, entries or concepts in glossaries are automatically hyperlinked in text, URLs pointing to MP3 or other audio files become embedded Flash-based controls that offer pause and rewind functionality, and so on.

Moodle comes with a number of standard filters that can be accessed via **Modules | Filters | Manage filters** in the **Site Administration** block:

| Name | Disable/Enable | Up/Down | Settings |
|---|---|---|---|
| Multimedia Plugins | | ↓ | Settings |
| TeX Notation | | ↑ ↓ | Settings |
| Algebra Notation | | ↑ | |
| Database Auto-linking | | | |
| Glossary Auto-linking | | | |
| Resource Names Auto-linking | | | |
| Wiki Page Auto-linking | | | |
| Activity Names Auto-linking | | | |
| Word Censorship | | | Settings |
| Email Protection | | | |
| Multi-Language Content | | | Settings |
| Tidy | | | |

Changes in table above are saved automatically.

By default all filters are disabled. You enable them by toggling the eye symbol. Additionally, you can change the order in which the filters are applied to text, using the up and down arrows. The filtering mechanism operates on a first come basis, that is, if a filter detects a text element that has to be transformed it will do so before the next filter is applied.

Filters cannot be removed via the Moodle admin interface; the only way to delete a filter is by removing the respective files from the `filter` directory. As with activities and blocks it is recommended to hide filters if you don't require them on your site.

The parameters of all standard Moodle filters are explained in the respective Module Docs pages. In addition to the filter-specific settings, Moodle provides a number of **Common settings** that are shared among all filters:

| Common settings | |
|---|---|
| Text cache lifetime *cachetext* | 1 minutes ▾ Default: 1 minutes<br>For larger sites or sites that use text filters, this setting can really speed things up. Copies of texts will be retained in their processed form for the time specified here. Setting this too small may actually slow things down slightly, but setting it too large may mean texts take too long to refresh (with new links, for example). |
| Filter uploaded files *filteruploadedfiles* | None ▾ Default: None<br>Process all uploaded HTML and text files with the filters before displaying them, only uploaded HTML files or none at all. |
| Filter match once per page *filtermatchoneperpage* | Default: No<br>Automatic linking filters will only generate a single link for the first matching text instance found on the complete page. All others are ignored. |
| Filter match once per text *filtermatchonepertext* | Default: No<br>Automatic linking filters will only generate a single link for the first matching text instance found in each item of text (e.g., resource, block) on the page. All others are ignored. This setting is ignored if the one per page setting is *yes*. |
| Filter all strings *filterall* | Default: No<br>Filter all strings, including headings, titles, navigation bar and so on. This is mostly useful when using the multilang filter, otherwise it will just create extra load on your site for little gain. |

| Setting | Description |
|---|---|
| Text cache lifetime | It's the time for which Moodle keeps text to be filtered in a dedicated cache (also see Chapter 11). |
| Filter uploaded files | By default only text entered via the Moodle editor is filtered. If you wish to include uploaded files, you have the choice of HTML files only and All files. |
| Filter match once per page | Enable this setting if the filter stops analyzing text after it finds a match, that is, only the first occurrence will be transformed. |
| Filter match once per text | Enable this setting if the filter only generates a single link for the first matching text instance found in each item of text on a page. This setting is ignored if the Filter match once per page parameter is enabled. |
| Filter all strings | By default only text inside a resource is filtered. Enable this setting if all strings including headings, titles, and breadcrumbs should be filtered as well. |

# Grades and Gradebook Settings

The gradebook is one of the most important constructs of any virtual learning environment, and Moodle is no exception. The gradebook is a container holding grades for all learners in Moodle. The flexibility and customizability of any gradebook has a very high degree of complexity. As a consequence, there are a huge number of administrator settings at your disposal that affect the way teachers use grades throughout the system.

The majority of settings are tightly linked to the gradebook, and the related reports that are dealt with by teachers at course level. A site-wide agreement on default values and global settings for grades should be in place for your organization.

Additionally, the inline help for each setting is very comprehensive, as is the accompanying area in the MoodleDocs at `http://docs.moodle.org/en/Gradebook`, which contains a number of pages dedicated to administrators. We describe each section (sub-menu) in general within the **Grades** area in the **Site Administration** block and highlight some key parameters.

- **General settings**

  These are parameters that influence the gradebook and grades in general. The two settings that are turned off by default and are regularly required are **Outcomes** (also known as competencies) and **Enable publishing** (the ability to publish results via external URLs).

- **Grade category settings**

  Grades are organized categories and here you set the relevant settings.

- **Grade item settings**

  These are the parameters that impact individual grades.

- **Scales**

  Here, you specify site-wide scales that are used for grading and rating. The global scales are often linked to qualifications that are offered by your organization. Some sites remove the provided scale **Separate and Connected ways of knowing** if it doesn't map onto their learning environment.

  Each scale comprises of a name, the scale itself (a list of comma-separated items) and an optional description. Scales can be uploaded implicitly via the Outcomes menu.

- **Outcomes**

  Outcomes are used by most vocational and some academic curricula to specify the expected competencies or goals of the subject being taught. You can either add global (standard) outcomes one-by-one or create a CSV file, and upload in batch mode.

  Each outcome comprises of a full name, a short name, a scale, and an optional description. The import file supports the following values in its header: `outcome_name`, `outcome_shortname`, `outcome_description`, `scale_name`, `scale_items`, and `scale_description`.

- **Letters**

  Education systems in Anglo-Saxon countries often use a system of letters (A, A-, B+, ..., F) to grade items. Here, you specify which percentage range correspond to which grading letter.

- **Report Settings**

  Moodle comes with a number of predefined gradebook reports. The respective settings determine appearance and content of the reports. If additional user-defined reports (plug-ins) are installed on your system, this list is likely to have a separate configuration page for each report type. (A good tutorial on how to create your own custom reports can be found at `http://docs.moodle.org/en/Development:Gradebook_Report_Tutorial`.) The different types of report are:

  - **Grader Report**

  These parameters include whether to show calculations, show or hide icons, column averages, and so on. Teachers can override most settings in their personal report preferences tab.

  - **Overview Report**

  Only a single setting to determine whether ranking information is shown is reported.

  - **User Report**

  It shows the settings that determine whether ranking information is shown and how to deal with hidden items.

# Miscellaneous Settings

There are a number of configuration settings that do not fit into any of the above categories. Such settings are covered in the following sub-sections.

# Editing Options

When changing content, Moodle's actions are triggered by icons. For instance, by moving a block to the right, pages are reloaded automatically after each action. A significantly more intuitive and time-efficient mode has been implemented that allows the same operations to be performed via a drag-and-drop mechanism, which requires support for AJAX and Javascript. To activate this mode go to **Appearance | AJAX and Javascript** in the **Site Administration** block and enable AJAX. You can also limit this interactive mode to non-courses only by selecting the second option.

Bear in mind that only some areas of Moodle support AJAX, others use the static approach. Also, not all web browsers fully support AJAX, especially older browsers and browsers tailored for specific hardware such as mobile devices and games consoles.

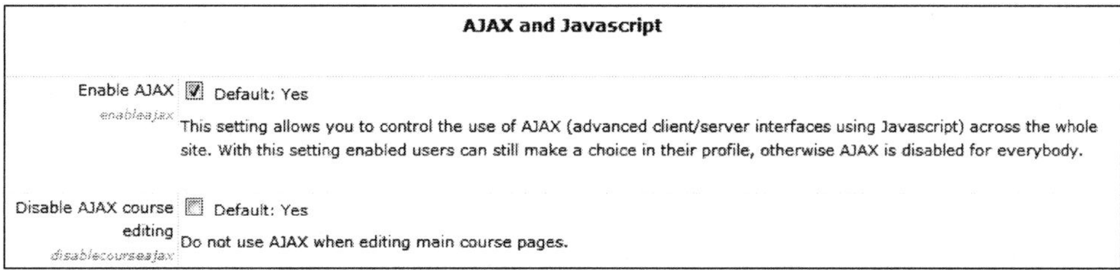


The Moodle editor is used throughout the system for entering formatted text. Writing text works pretty much the way you would expect, but you also have the ability to include smilies, URLs, images, tables, HTML tags, and the like. Moodle allows full configuration of the **Editor,** which applies to all text editors throughout. The configuration takes place at **Appearance | HTML Editor** in the **Site Administration** block:

**HTML editor**

Use HTML editor *htmleditor* — Default: Yes
Choose whether or not to allow use of the embedded HTML text editor. Even if you choose allow, this editor will only appear when the user is using a compatible web browser. Users can also choose not to use it.

Background color *editorbackgroundcolor* — #ffffff — Default: #ffffff
Define the edit area's background color.
Valid values are, for example: #FFFFFF or white

Font family *editorfontfamily* — Trebuchet MS,Verdana,Arial,He — Default: Trebuchet MS,Verdana,Arial,Helvetica,sans-serif
The font-family property is a list of font family names and/or generic family names. Family names must be seperated with comma.

Font size *editorfontsize* — Default: Empty
The default font-size sets the size of a font.
Valid values are for example: medium, large, smaller, larger, 10pt, 11px.

Font list *editorfontlist*

| | |
|---|---|
| Trebuchet | Trebuchet MS,Verdan |
| Arial | arial,helvetica,sans-se |
| Courier New | courier new,courier,m |
| Georgia | georgia,times new ron |
| Tahoma | tahoma,arial,helvetica |
| Times New Roman | times new roman,time |
| Verdana | verdana,arial,helvetica |
| Impact | impact |
| Wingdings | wingdings |

Select the fonts that should appear in the editor's drop-down list.

Word format filter *editorkillword* — Default: Yes
This setting enables or disables Word-specific format filtering.

| Setting | Description |
|---|---|
| **Use HTML editor** | The HTML editor is used if the box is ticked and the browser is not incompatible (some older browsers and some browsers on mobile devices will not display). Alternatively, the **text only** editor is used. |
| **Background color** | Background color of the editor in web color format is specified as an RGB triplet (`#000000` is black and `#FFFFFF` is white). You will find more details on web colors at `http://en.wikipedia.org/wiki/Web_colors`. |
| **Font family** | Sets the editor's default font family (default is Trebuchet MS). The property is a list of font family names separated by commas. Font family details are shown at http://en.wikipedia.org/wiki/Font_family_(HTML). |
| **Font size** | Sets the default font size for the editor. Valid values are, for example, **medium, large, smaller, larger, 10pt, 11px**. If left empty, 8pt is used. |
| **Font list** | The fonts that appear in the editor's font drop-down list are listed in the left column. The right column states which font family is used for the particular font. |
| **Word format filter** | This setting enables or disables Word-specific format filtering, for example the multimedia filter. Filters are configured in the **Modules** section in the **Site Administration** block. |
| **Hide buttons** | Any button that is selected will be hidden in the HTML editor and cannot be used. To find out the purpose of each button, take the mouse pointer to each icon. It is recommended not to hide the **Enlarge Editor** icon as it allows editing in full screen mode and provides additional table functions. |
| **Emoticons** | The Moodle editor comes with a number of icons that are entered via the corresponding emoticons. For example, (martin) is replaced with a beardy face!<br>To add new emoticons, add a code and a name, then add an image as `name.gif` in `/pix/s`. |

The Moodle editor supports EMBED and OBJECT tags that allow the incorporation of multimedia content (for example, streaming videos from YouTube). If you want to allow this operation, go to **Security | Site Policies** in the **Site Administration** block and enable **Allow EMBED and OBJECT tags**.

The editor uses a mechanism called **KSES** to remove any unwanted HTML elements and attributes. A more secure version (called **HTML Purifier**) is currently under development (see the Experimental section that follows), but has the drawback that it doesn't support EMBED and OBJECT tags, MathML tags, or the `<lang>` tags.

# Tags

Social networking is the latest buzz on the Internet that conforms with Moodle's pedagogical philosophy of social constructivism. One activity in this Web 2.0 environment is that of tagging, that is, describing artefacts or users using keywords or tags. These tags are then harnessed for searching, sharing, and other collaborative activities to match interests.

Users create their own tags that represent their private or educational interests, and depending on the size of their social network (in our case Moodle and any Internet services that can be incorporated) matching will take place. However, as an educational institution you might want to create a number of site-wide tags that can be used in addition to the user-defined tags. To do this, go to **Appearance | Manage tags** in the **Site Administration** block:

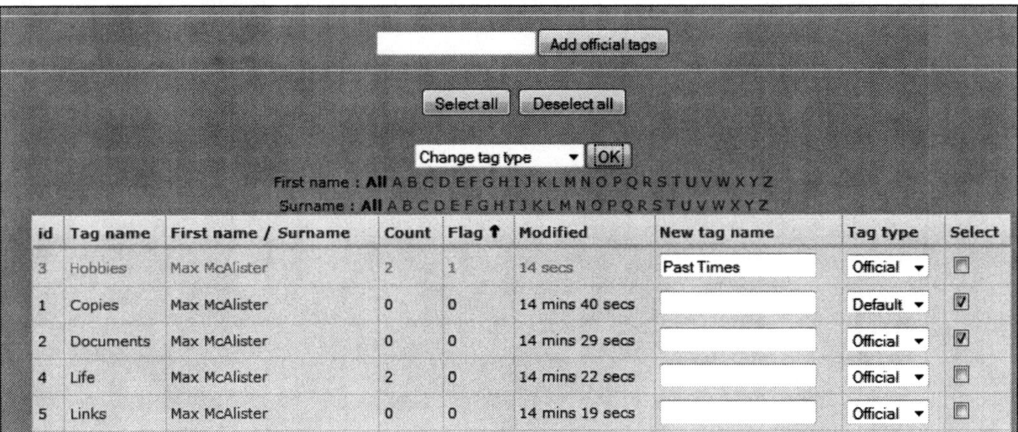


Add a site-wide tag by entering its name in the text field and press the **Add official tags** button. All global tags are shown in the list underneath, where for each tag the name, creator, usage counter, number tags that have been flagged as inappropriate, and time since last modified is listed. Tags can further be renamed and their type can be changed (**official** and **default**). Additionally, operations that are available for selected tags are **Reset flag**, **Delete**, **Change tag type**, and **Change tag name**.

It might also be necessary to block a user from certain tagging activities. The two relevant capabilities, which can only be applied in the System context, are `moodle/tag:create` and `moodle/tag:edit`.

# Experimental

Moodle is a very dynamic software that evolves and improves constantly. Some functionality is still in an experimental stage, but sufficiently mature to be included in a shipped version. These features are located at **Miscellaneous | Experimental** in the **Site Administration** block.

The list changes over time: Some features passed quality assurance and moved to the set of core features (for instance, AJAX support mentioned under "Editing Options" resided in the experimental section for almost two full versions), while others will be included over time. At the moment, the following four settings are available:

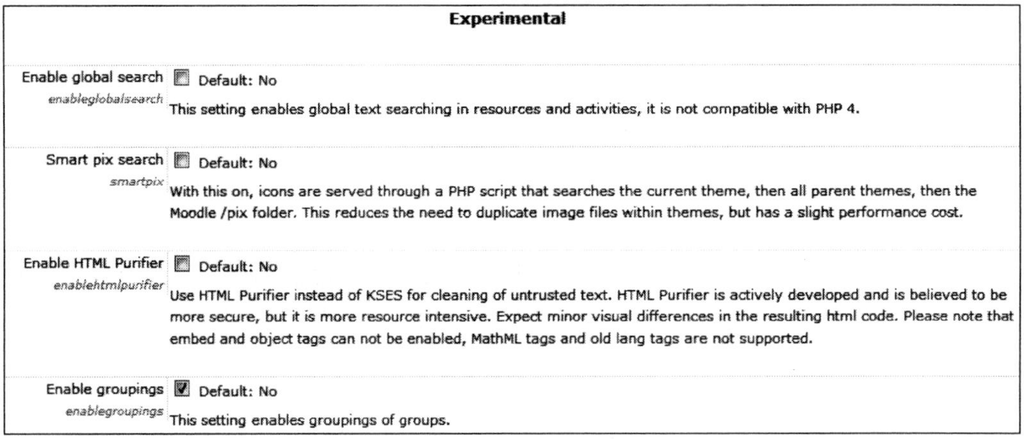

**Experimental**

Enable global search *enableglobalsearch* — Default: No
This setting enables global text searching in resources and activities, it is not compatible with PHP 4.

Smart pix search *smartpix* — Default: No
With this on, icons are served through a PHP script that searches the current theme, then all parent themes, then the Moodle /pix folder. This reduces the need to duplicate image files within themes, but has a slight performance cost.

Enable HTML Purifier *enablehtmlpurifier* — Default: No
Use HTML Purifier instead of KSES for cleaning of untrusted text. HTML Purifier is actively developed and is believed to be more secure, but it is more resource intensive. Expect minor visual differences in the resulting html code. Please note that embed and object tags can not be enabled, MathML tags and old lang tags are not supported.

Enable groupings *enablegroupings* — Default: No
This setting enables groupings of groups.

| Setting | Description |
|---|---|
| **Enable global search** | The default search functionality is restricted to a course. To enable global search that takes into account set permissions of the user carrying out the search, tick this box. PHP 5 is required to run this functionality. |
| **Smart pix search** | This theme-related setting has been covered in Chapter 7. |
| **Enable HTML Purifier** | See Moodle editor configuration described before this section. |
| **Enable Groupings** | Tick this box to enable groupings (groups of groups) within courses |

It is needless to say that any functionality in the experimental section should be used with caution as potential problems can be encountered.

# Summary

In this chapter you have learned how to configure all relevant system settings that don't have a dedicated chapter alloted to them. We covered topics across the field, from accessibility and localization to configuring Moodle modules, the gradebook, and the editor among a few other things.

The abundance of features available via the **Site Administration** block can initially be overwhelming, but you will get to terms with them relatively fast. Also, expect this number to increase with every new version of Moodle!

This concludes Part II of the book that dealt with Moodle configuration, and we are now ready to move on to all aspects of Moodle maintenance.

# 9
# Monitoring User Activity

Moodle collects usage data of all activities taking place from the time a user logs in until he/she logs out. This data can be utilized for a range of monitoring activities that will be examined in this chapter. After providing an overview of monitoring, the chapter deals with two types of techniques:

- Monitoring provided by Moodle

  This includes activity reporting and user tracking as well as some basic statistics.
- Monitoring provided by third parties

  This includes web log analyzers and live data trackers such as Google Analytics.

Given the nature of the tasks involved, we will finish the chapter with some information on privacy and data protection concerns.

## Monitoring Overview

Moodle maintains a detailed log of each action performed by a user. Each record contains data about:

- Who (user) did
- What (action)
- When (date and time)
- Where (IP address)

Given this trail of information, it is possible to perform two major monitoring tasks:

- Reporting
- Tracking

**Reporting** is mainly concerned with summary information of user activities. An example is the number of views of a learning resource in a particular course.

**Tracking** is mainly concerned with finding details about a subset of the data, such as an individual, an activity, or a course. An example is a pupil who insists he/she has submitted an assignment, which cannot be located. The tracking log will be able to shed light on this.

Moodle further offers **Statistics** mode, which provides a graphical summary about the number of hits in courses and the entire site.

If these monitoring facilities do not satisfy your hunger for usage data, you might consider using **external web analysis tools** such as web log analyzers. You can also utilize a **live data tracking system**, such as Google Analytics, that can be embedded in your Moodle site.

Bear in mind that most information you retrieve as part of data reporting and tracking is also available to teachers on course level. While teachers use this information mainly in a pedagogical context (to monitor progress and to measure performance), your role as administrator is to view this data in a site-wide context. Furthermore, you are the one who will be approached if any problems occur, for example a student claiming to have submitted an assignment that is not on the system, or a teacher not being able to log in from home. Additionally, the local course view provides activity reports that are more targeted at a teacher's perspective and, if activated, some basic statistics.

# Reporting

A report presents the content of the Moodle log in some sort of uniform format. Different reports can use the same log. Site-wide reporting can be accessed via **Reports | Logs** in the **Site Administration** block. On top of the page you filter out information about all activities:

**Choose which logs you want to see:**

Packt Moodle Administrator (Site) | All participants | Today, 23 March 2008
All activities | All actions | Display on page | Get these logs

**Or watch current activity:**

**Live logs from the past hour**

The following seven filters are available:

| Field | Description |
|---|---|
| **Courses** | Select a specific course or the entire Moodle site. |
| **Groups** | Select a specific group or all groups (only displayed if group mode is enabled in the selected filtered course). |
| **Participants** | Select a specific user or all participants. |
| **Date** | Specify a particular day or all days of activity. Unfortunately, it is not possible to specify ranges of dates. |
| **Activities** | Select whether you wish to run a report of activities, news, or site errors. |
| **Actions** | You can choose between all actions: view, add, update, delete, and all changes. |
| **Display** | Specify whether you wish to display the report on page (in your web browser), in an Excel spreadsheet, in ODS format, or in a text file. |

Once you have selected a course and pressed **Get these logs** button, the content in each pull-down menu changes context-sensitively. For example, the participants' menu contains the names of all users who have a role in the course, and the activities' menu is populated with all activities and resources. If you watch the breadcrumb trail, you can see what happens internally: Moodle temporarily redirects the reporting tool inside the selected course where the local log viewer is called, which is similar in appearance.

Once you have selected your filtering criteria, a report is displayed that has the following shape:

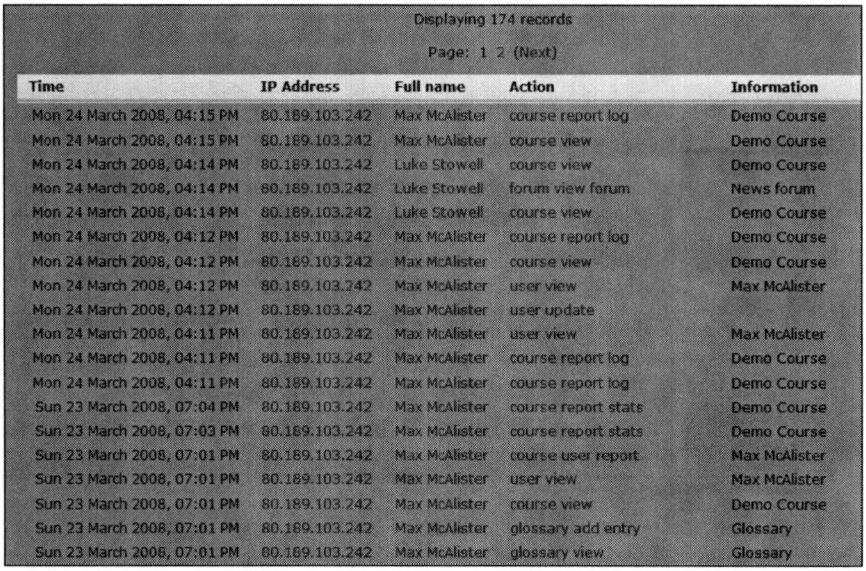

Displaying 174 records

Page: 1 2 (Next)

| Time | IP Address | Full name | Action | Information |
|---|---|---|---|---|
| Mon 24 March 2008, 04:15 PM | 80.189.103.242 | Max McAlister | course report log | Demo Course |
| Mon 24 March 2008, 04:15 PM | 80.189.103.242 | Max McAlister | course view | Demo Course |
| Mon 24 March 2008, 04:14 PM | 80.189.103.242 | Luke Stowell | course view | Demo Course |
| Mon 24 March 2008, 04:14 PM | 80.189.103.242 | Luke Stowell | forum view forum | News forum |
| Mon 24 March 2008, 04:14 PM | 80.189.103.242 | Luke Stowell | course view | Demo Course |
| Mon 24 March 2008, 04:12 PM | 80.189.103.242 | Max McAlister | course report log | Demo Course |
| Mon 24 March 2008, 04:12 PM | 80.189.103.242 | Max McAlister | course view | Demo Course |
| Mon 24 March 2008, 04:12 PM | 80.189.103.242 | Max McAlister | user view | Max McAlister |
| Mon 24 March 2008, 04:12 PM | 80.189.103.242 | Max McAlister | user update | |
| Mon 24 March 2008, 04:11 PM | 80.189.103.242 | Max McAlister | user view | Max McAlister |
| Mon 24 March 2008, 04:11 PM | 80.189.103.242 | Max McAlister | course report log | Demo Course |
| Mon 24 March 2008, 04:11 PM | 80.189.103.242 | Max McAlister | course report log | Demo Course |
| Sun 23 March 2008, 07:04 PM | 80.189.103.242 | Max McAlister | course report stats | Demo Course |
| Sun 23 March 2008, 07:03 PM | 80.189.103.242 | Max McAlister | course report stats | Demo Course |
| Sun 23 March 2008, 07:01 PM | 80.189.103.242 | Max McAlister | course user report | Max McAlister |
| Sun 23 March 2008, 07:01 PM | 80.189.103.242 | Max McAlister | user view | Max McAlister |
| Sun 23 March 2008, 07:01 PM | 80.189.103.242 | Max McAlister | course view | Demo Course |
| Sun 23 March 2008, 07:01 PM | 80.189.103.242 | Max McAlister | glossary add entry | Glossary |
| Sun 23 March 2008, 07:01 PM | 80.189.103.242 | Max McAlister | glossary view | Glossary |

The header shows the number of records that are being displayed. In this case, all usage data from the **Demo Course** has been selected, which returned **174** hits. This tabular information is displayed in reverse order of user's access date and time, that is, the last hit is displayed first. The columns of the table represent the following information:

| Field | Description |
|---|---|
| **Time** | Date and time of the hit. |
| **IP Address** | The (unresolved) IP address; this is useful to see from where the user accessed the page (for example, from home or within the organization). |
| **Full Name** | Name of the user; if a particular user is selected, the same value will be displayed in each row. |
| **Action** | Short description of what the user has been doing; this is very useful to see what resources are being used, or to check whether an individual has viewed the resource he or she claims to have read. |
| **Information** | More details on the action. |

When you click on the IP address in the log, a new window will open displaying the location of user as a pin on the world map. The default database being used is NetGeo. But it is no longer maintained, resulting in it providing incorrect positions.

You can improve this shortcoming by either installing the GeoIP City binary data file (both commercial and free versions are available) or by specifying a Google Maps API key. Both settings are found in the **IP address lookup** section at **Location | Location settings** in the **Site Administration** block.

# Live Logs

Moodle provides a live watcher of activities in the last hour. It is a prepared report that shows the activities that took place in the previous 60 minutes, and is updated automatically every 60 seconds. It can be accessed from the **Live logs from the past hour** link found at the **Reports | Logs** page.

This is useful if you have changed the configuration, for instance a supported authentication or enrolment mechanism, and want to monitor whether it is working properly. Alternatively, you can just sit back and watch what is happening on your site.

Note, the first entry in the live log is the one for you looking at the live log!

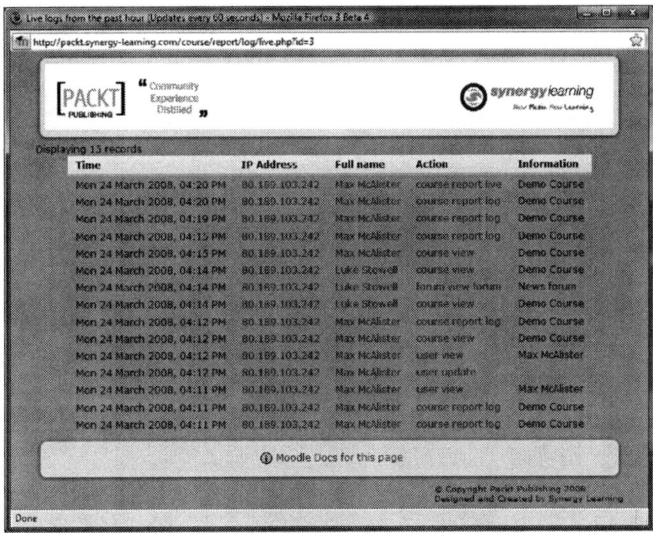


| Time | IP Address | Full name | Action | Information |
|---|---|---|---|---|
| Mon 24 March 2008, 04:20 PM | 80.189.103.242 | Max McAlister | course report live | Demo Course |
| Mon 24 March 2008, 04:20 PM | 80.189.103.242 | Max McAlister | course report log | Demo Course |
| Mon 24 March 2008, 04:19 PM | 80.189.103.242 | Max McAlister | course report log | Demo Course |
| Mon 24 March 2008, 04:15 PM | 80.189.103.242 | Max McAlister | course report log | Demo Course |
| Mon 24 March 2008, 04:15 PM | 80.189.103.242 | Max McAlister | course view | Demo Course |
| Mon 24 March 2008, 04:14 PM | 80.189.103.242 | Luke Stowell | course view | Demo Course |
| Mon 24 March 2008, 04:14 PM | 80.189.103.242 | Luke Stowell | forum view forum | News forum |
| Mon 24 March 2008, 04:14 PM | 80.189.103.242 | Luke Stowell | course view | Demo Course |
| Mon 24 March 2008, 04:12 PM | 80.189.103.242 | Max McAlister | course report log | Demo Course |
| Mon 24 March 2008, 04:12 PM | 80.189.103.242 | Max McAlister | course view | Demo Course |
| Mon 24 March 2008, 04:12 PM | 80.189.103.242 | Max McAlister | user view | Max McAlister |
| Mon 24 March 2008, 04:12 PM | 80.189.103.242 | Max McAlister | user update | |
| Mon 24 March 2008, 04:11 PM | 80.189.103.242 | Max McAlister | user view | Max McAlister |
| Mon 24 March 2008, 04:11 PM | 80.189.103.242 | Max McAlister | course report log | Demo Course |
| Mon 24 March 2008, 04:11 PM | 80.189.103.242 | Max McAlister | course report log | Demo Course |

# Error Reports

When you select **Site Errors** from the activities drop-down, all errors (mainly failed logins that have occurred) are displayed. For example, the following report shows all invalid logins in February and March (Yes, I did provoke the three most recent entries for demonstration purposes.):

| Course | Time | IP Address | Full name | Action | Information |
|---|---|---|---|---|---|
| Site | Sun 23 March 2008, 06:45 PM | 81.129.27.38 | | login error | jonny |
| Site | Sun 23 March 2008, 06:42 PM | 84.13.251.134 | | login error | mark |
| Site | Sun 23 March 2008, 06:33 PM | 80.189.103.242 | | login error | hacker |
| Site | Tue 5 February 2008, 04:16 PM | 80.189.103.242 | | login error | admin |
| Site | Tue 5 February 2008, 04:16 PM | 80.189.103.242 | | login error | admin |

It is good practice to check the error logs on a regular basis to identify problems on your site and potential unauthorized access attempts. These reports can also be set up to arrive by email to the Site Administrator (see the following chapter where we deal with Moodle security issues).

# Exporting of Logs

Unlike other applications (such as web servers), Moodle does not store its log information in text files, but stores it in the Moodle database (in the `mdl_log` table). This allows the exporting of data (via Moodle or phpMyAdmin) for more detailed analysis in third-party applications.

To make further use of information, export the data in either a comma-separated text file or an Excel or ODS spreadsheet by selecting the **Display filter** accordingly. This will show the same information as was shown in Moodle, but it will be possible to manipulate and analyze the data further or run any valid spreadsheet operation against it:

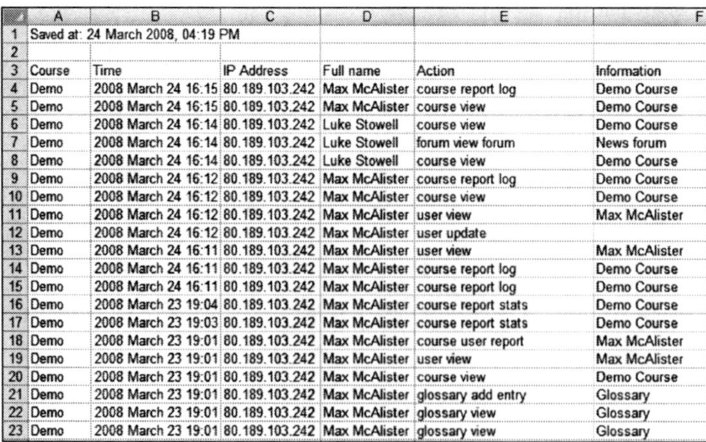

| | A | B | C | D | E | F |
|---|---|---|---|---|---|---|
| 1 | Saved at: 24 March 2008, 04:19 PM | | | | | |
| 2 | | | | | | |
| 3 | Course | Time | IP Address | Full name | Action | Information |
| 4 | Demo | 2008 March 24 16:15 | 80.189.103.242 | Max McAlister | course report log | Demo Course |
| 5 | Demo | 2008 March 24 16:15 | 80.189.103.242 | Max McAlister | course view | Demo Course |
| 6 | Demo | 2008 March 24 16:14 | 80.189.103.242 | Luke Stowell | course view | Demo Course |
| 7 | Demo | 2008 March 24 16:14 | 80.189.103.242 | Luke Stowell | forum view forum | News forum |
| 8 | Demo | 2008 March 24 16:14 | 80.189.103.242 | Luke Stowell | course view | Demo Course |
| 9 | Demo | 2008 March 24 16:12 | 80.189.103.242 | Max McAlister | course report log | Demo Course |
| 10 | Demo | 2008 March 24 16:12 | 80.189.103.242 | Max McAlister | course view | Demo Course |
| 11 | Demo | 2008 March 24 16:12 | 80.189.103.242 | Max McAlister | user view | Max McAlister |
| 12 | Demo | 2008 March 24 16:12 | 80.189.103.242 | Max McAlister | user update | |
| 13 | Demo | 2008 March 24 16:11 | 80.189.103.242 | Max McAlister | user view | Max McAlister |
| 14 | Demo | 2008 March 24 16:11 | 80.189.103.242 | Max McAlister | course report log | Demo Course |
| 15 | Demo | 2008 March 24 16:11 | 80.189.103.242 | Max McAlister | course report log | Demo Course |
| 16 | Demo | 2008 March 23 19:04 | 80.189.103.242 | Max McAlister | course report stats | Demo Course |
| 17 | Demo | 2008 March 23 19:03 | 80.189.103.242 | Max McAlister | course report stats | Demo Course |
| 18 | Demo | 2008 March 23 19:01 | 80.189.103.242 | Max McAlister | course user report | Max McAlister |
| 19 | Demo | 2008 March 23 19:01 | 80.189.103.242 | Max McAlister | user view | Max McAlister |
| 20 | Demo | 2008 March 23 19:01 | 80.189.103.242 | Max McAlister | course view | Demo Course |
| 21 | Demo | 2008 March 23 19:01 | 80.189.103.242 | Max McAlister | glossary add entry | Glossary |
| 22 | Demo | 2008 March 23 19:01 | 80.189.103.242 | Max McAlister | glossary view | Glossary |
| 23 | Demo | 2008 March 23 19:01 | 80.189.103.242 | Max McAlister | glossary view | Glossary |

An example use of this data in a spreadsheet is the introduction of an additional column where you calculate how much time a user has spent on a particular activity.

# Tracking

Tracking of individual user activity takes place in user's profile. You get to the individual's details either via **Users | Accounts | Browse list of users** or by clicking on the user's name whenever it is displayed. To access the tracking information of a user, select the user and then **Activity Reports | All Logs** in the Profile tab:

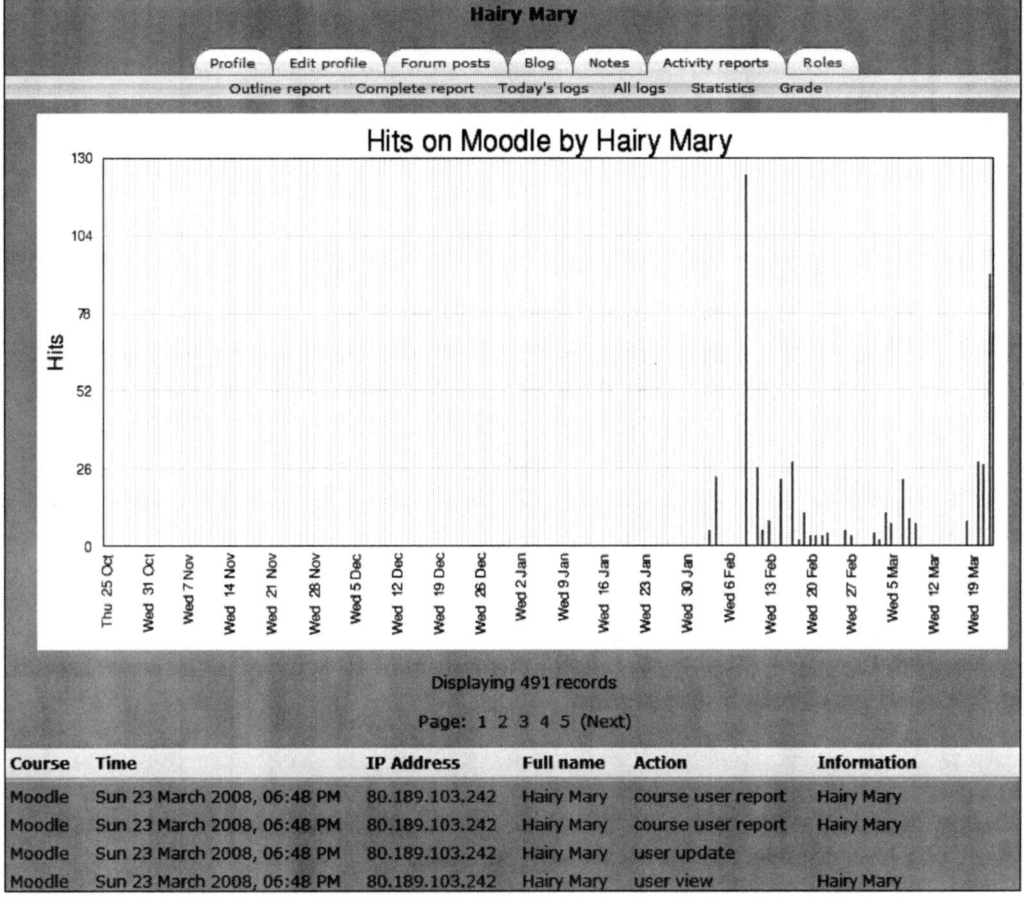


The top part of the screen shows a graph of the number of hits by users in the last few weeks. The bottom part lists detailed information about each individual hit of the user. The columns of the table are the same as the one for reports.

Moodle provides a separate tab to list log information of a particular day The tab (**Today's logs**) is located to the left of the **All logs** tabs in the **Profile** section. The information that you see is identical to the one you are shown when selecting a specific user in the log, as described in the preceding screenshot.

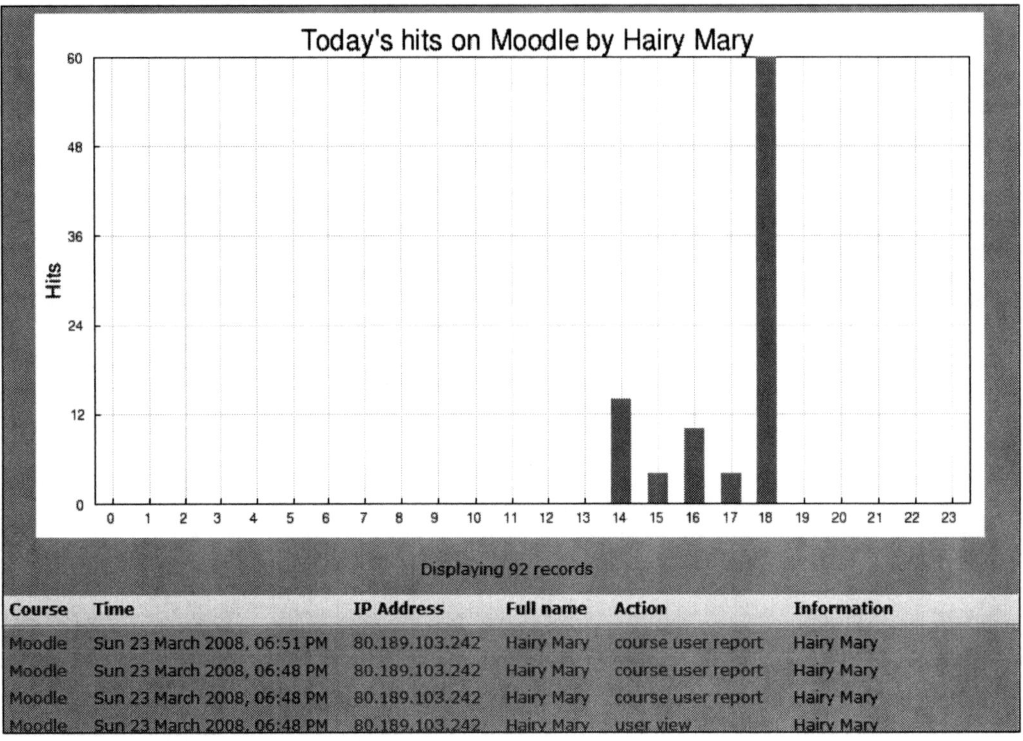


The graph displays an hour-by-hour account of Moodle usage. This view is useful if you want to see what time of the day a user is active on your site. The table underneath the graph displays detailed information of all activity in the same format as described previously in this section.

As mentioned earlier, teachers in a course have full access to the same information to monitor progress and track performance. However, you as the administrator are often approached with claims, problems, or any other anomalies. To shed light on these, you have to revert to the above logging data.

Moodle further provides detailed reports on user's activities within a course:

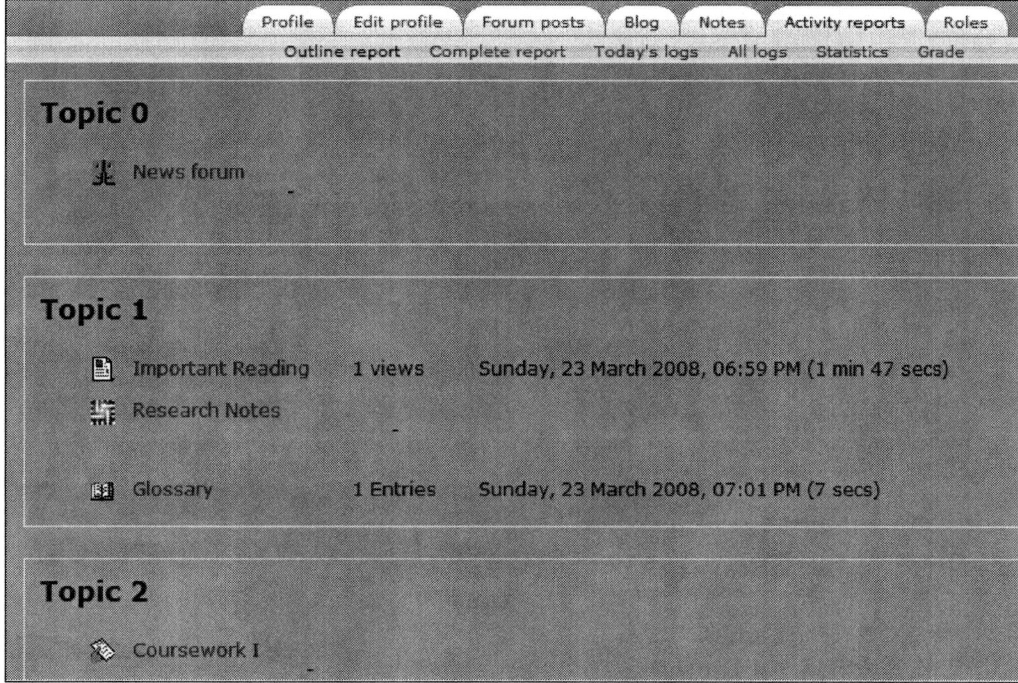


The **Outline report** lists each topic or week, and displays a summary of activities for each item. It displays the title of the resource (hyperlinked), the number of views, the last access, and the time since the last access. It would be expected that the **Complete report** section in the next tab would provide more detailed information about the user's activities. Unfortunately, it only provides the same information in a different format.

The remaining two links on the **Activity reports** tab include **Grade** (which displays the gradebook of the user) and **Statistics,** if it has been activated. The **Statistics** information is in the same format as the site-wide statistics, which we will cover next.

# Statistics

Moodle has a built-in statistics module, which you can reach via **Reports | Statistics** in the **Site Administration** block. By default the component is disabled and has to be changed first alongside some settings.

# Statistics Settings

The **Statistics** module is deactivated by default due to the fact that the component is very resource-hungry, both in terms of disk space usage and, more importantly, memory usage.

Use the **Statistics** module only if you really require the information and can accept some potentially significant performance reduction.

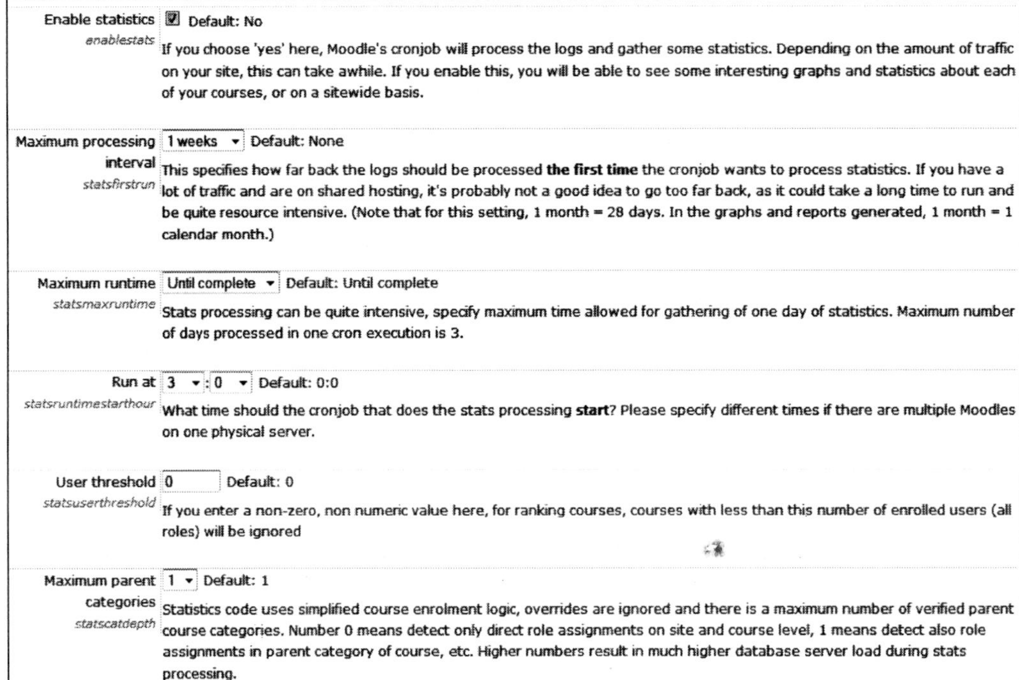

Enable statistics
enablestats
Default: No
If you choose 'yes' here, Moodle's cronjob will process the logs and gather some statistics. Depending on the amount of traffic on your site, this can take awhile. If you enable this, you will be able to see some interesting graphs and statistics about each of your courses, or on a sitewide basis.
Maximum processing interval
statsfirstrun
1 weeks
Default: None
This specifies how far back the logs should be processed the first time the cronjob wants to process statistics. If you have a lot of traffic and are on shared hosting, it's probably not a good idea to go too far back, as it could take a long time to run and be quite resource intensive. (Note that for this setting, 1 month = 28 days. In the graphs and reports generated, 1 month = 1 calendar month.)
Maximum runtime
statsmaxruntime
Until complete
Default: Until complete
Stats processing can be quite intensive, specify maximum time allowed for gathering of one day of statistics. Maximum number of days processed in one cron execution is 3.
Run at
statsruntimestarthour
3 : 0
Default: 0:0
What time should the cronjob that does the stats processing start? Please specify different times if there are multiple Moodles on one physical server.
User threshold
statsuserthreshold
0
Default: 0
If you enter a non-zero, non numeric value here, for ranking courses, courses with less than this number of enrolled users (all roles) will be ignored
Maximum parent categories
statscatdepth
1
Default: 1
Statistics code uses simplified course enrolment logic, overrides are ignored and there is a maximum number of verified parent course categories. Number 0 means detect only direct role assignments on site and course level, 1 means detect also role assignments in parent category of course, etc. Higher numbers result in much higher database server load during stats processing.

The **Statistics** settings shown in the preceding screenshot are located at **Server | Statistics**. The following parameters are available:

| Setting | Description |
|---|---|
| **Enable statistics** | Turn statistics module on and off. |
| **Maximum processing interval** | After enabling the module, Moodle utilizes the logs described here to derive information about statistics. You specify the time this should go back to gather statistics. Beware that this is quite a resource-intensive operation. |
| **Maximum runtime** | You can limit the time for which the statistics gathering process is allowed to run; another mechanism to avoid too much burden on the system. |
| **Run at** | The time at which statistics processing should start. It is highly recommended that this does not clash with the site backup as both operations are potentially very resource-intensive. |
| **User threshold** | Here, the statistics module can be instructed to ignore courses with less than a certain number of enrolled users. |
| **Maximum parent categories** | The statistics module looks up roles in a context hierarchy (see Chapter 6 for more details) and also ignores overrides. The higher the number, the slower the statistics processing. It is recommended to leave this at **1**, that is, including only that category in statistics to which the course belongs. If the parameter is set to **2**, the current course (0), the parent category (1), and the Site context (2) are included (assuming there are no sub-categories specified). |

Now let us have a look at what **Statistics** actually looks like.

# Statistics View

Once you have selected the course (or all courses), the report type (views, post, logins, or all), the time period, the graph (as shown in the previous section), and some tabular information is displayed. Basically, the data shown represents the number of "hits" on a certain day broken down by roles:

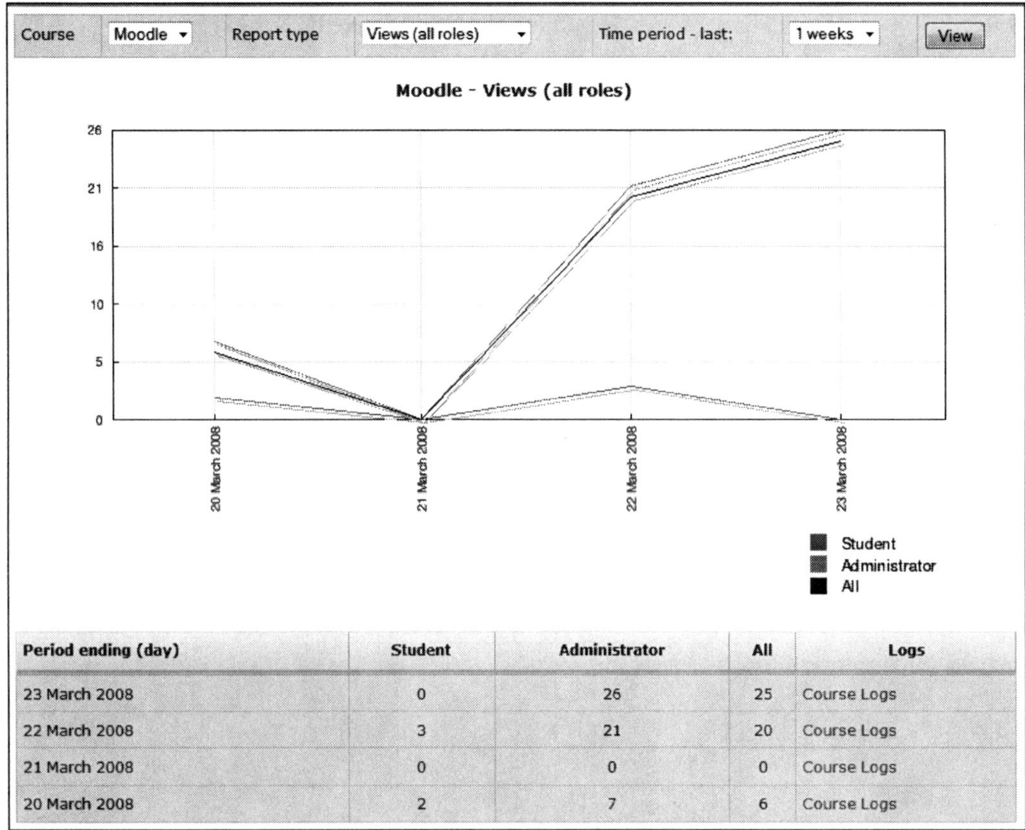


| Period ending (day) | Student | Administrator | All | Logs |
|---|---|---|---|---|
| 23 March 2008 | 0 | 26 | 25 | Course Logs |
| 22 March 2008 | 3 | 21 | 20 | Course Logs |
| 21 March 2008 | 0 | 0 | 0 | Course Logs |
| 20 March 2008 | 2 | 7 | 6 | Course Logs |

You may find this information unsatisfactory. Given the burden the module has on our system and the amount of data available, this seems to be a very simplistic way to display statistics.

To rectify the situation, let us look at two alternative techniques that make use of third-party data analysis tools.

# Web Log Analyzers

Web servers such as Apache and Microsoft IIS maintain textual log files that keep track of every hit on a website. The fields and their formats can be customized so that each log file will potentially look different. The following are two lines from our Moodle test site (IP addresses have been replaced and server directories shortened):

```
123.456.789.0 - - [24/Mar/2008:09:15:30 +0000] "GET .../synergy-
learning/packt/httpdocs/course/view.php?id=3 HTTP/1.0" 404 1045 "-"
"-"

123.456.789.0 - - [24/Mar/2008:09:15:30 +0000] "GET .../synergy-
learning/packt/httpdocs/mod/quiz/view.php?id=12 HTTP/1.0" 404 2180 "-"
"-"
```

As you can see, these files are not meant to be read by human beings. Instead, a number of tools exist such as **web log analysis software**, which read and interpret these files. Open source examples of this tool are AWStats, Webalizer, and Munin; a popular commercial product is WebTrends.

These tools produce detailed statistics that look at the log files from every possible angle. The problem when using web log analyzers with Moodle is that it is database-driven, which requires parameterized URLs (the `?id=12` part). You will have to configure the software you use to reflect these parameters, for example on course level.

# Google Analytics

Google Analytics is a free service (`http://analytics.google.com`), which tracks any traffic to your site. You have to sign up for an account before using the service that offers an abundance of statistics about visitors, traffic sources, content, and user-defined goals. You can find a detailed list of features at `http://www.google.com/analytics/features.html`.

Once set up, you will be able to see powerful analytics of your Moodle site like this:

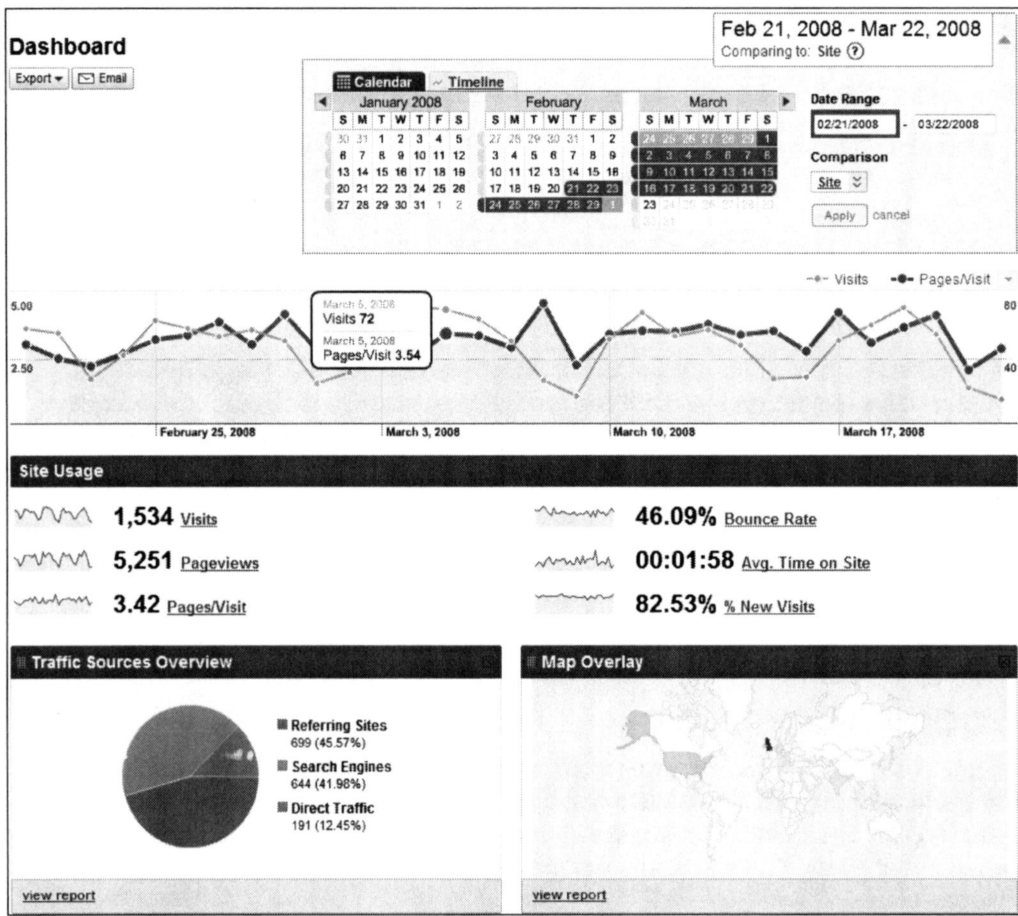


All you have to do is add the following piece of code into your `footer.html` file:

```
<script type="text/javascript">
var gaJsHost = (("https:" == document.location.protocol) ? "https://
ssl." : "http://www.");
document.write(unescape("%3Cscript src='" + gaJsHost + "google-
analytics.com/ga.js' type='text/javascript'%3E%3C/script%3E"));
</script>
<script type="text/javascript">
var pageTracker = _gat._getTracker("UA-XXXXXX-X");
pageTracker._initData();
pageTracker._trackPageview();
</script>
```

You need to update the "xxxxxx-x" in the preceding sample with your own Google Analytics account number. While it is possible to add the code in the `header.html` file, it is recommended not to do so as it has an impact on the performance of your system.

# Privacy and Data Protection Issues

Some of the mechanisms outlined in this chapter might infringe with legislative regulations in either the country you operate Moodle in, or with the rules of the organization for which the VLE is run.

The key issue is the storage of personal data in conjunction with usage information. Moodle stores such data that is potentially not conformant with some privacy laws.

While web log analyzers and tools such as Google Analytics do not store personal data per se, it is potentially possible to derive such information from IP addresses.

Before implementing any of the mentioned tools, make sure that you do not infringe any data protection legislation.

# Summary

In this chapter you have learned how to monitor user activities using Moodle's internal reporting and tracking facilities, as well as third-party tools.

Earlier we mentioned a student who insists that he or she has submitted an assignment that cannot be located. The student will approach the teacher who will then use the course logs to identify the file. If this remains unsuccessful, the teacher will contact you as the administrator to shed some more light on the issue. You can then use the site-wide logs for the user, in case the file has been uploaded in a different course. This escalation is typical in scenarios where problems arise that cannot be resolved at course level.

We concluded the chapter with some information on privacy and data protection concerns, which is a potential issue given the nature of Moodle monitoring. Related to these issues is security, which will be dealt with in the next chapter.

# 10

# Moodle Security

Moodle, like any other web application, has the potential to be misused. Moodle has dedicated an entire administration section to security settings, using which you can fine-tune Moodle's safety. After providing an overview of Moodle security, you will learn about the following topics:

- Notifications

  We are setting up a number of notification mechanisms that warn about potential security issues.
- User security

  We are looking at access to Moodle (self-registration, guest access, protection of user details, and course managers), Moodle passwords, and security in roles.
- Data and content security

  We will be dealing with potential issues in content created within Moodle and visibility of that content. You will learn how to set up a site policy and how to configure the antivirus scanner.
- System security

  We are discussing configuration settings (location of the dataroot directory and the cron process), HTTPS, and module security.

## Security Overview

Moodle takes security extremely seriously and any potential issues are given highest priority. Fixed vulnerabilities often trigger the release of minor versions, for example Moodle 1.8.5, which emphasize the importance of the subject.

The security of a system is as good as its weakest link. Moodle relies on significant software, hardware, and network infrastructure, and security can potentially be compromised in a number of areas. As the focus of this book is on Moodle and the administration thereof, we only cover security elements of Moodle per se. The following areas are **not** dealt with, and it is necessary to consult the respective documentation on security issues:

- Software

  As described in Chapter 3, Moodle's key components comprise of a web server (usually Apache or Microsoft IIS), a database server (for example, MySQL), and a programming language (PHP). Additional PHP and operating system extensions are required, for instance, to support networking.
- Hardware

  Moodle runs on servers that have to be physically hosted. There is an ongoing debate about the safety and security of such systems, which is reflected by the ever-extending precautions by data centers.
- Network

  Any system that is part of a network is potentially vulnerable. Configuration of firewalls, proxy servers, and routers as well as general network security is a key aspect to protect your system from any attacks.

One rule that applies to all elements is that the latest software updates should be installed regularly. Moodle updates were covered in Chapter 2.

It has to be stressed that so far Moodle has not had any major security flaws. But with increasing complexity of the system, it is imperative that you make sure all possible measures are taken to prevent any issues.

# Security Notifications

Moodle has set up a dedicated site dealing with security issues that you can find at `security.moodle.org`. If you register your Moodle site via the **Moodle Registration** button in the **Notifications** area at the top of the **Site Administration** block, your email address will automatically be added to the security alerts' mailing list. It is worth pointing out that the registration needs to be updated after any upgrades or significant changes.

The page also displays any potential problems in other information. We shall deal with the warnings later on, but some sample messages are displayed in the screenshot that follows:

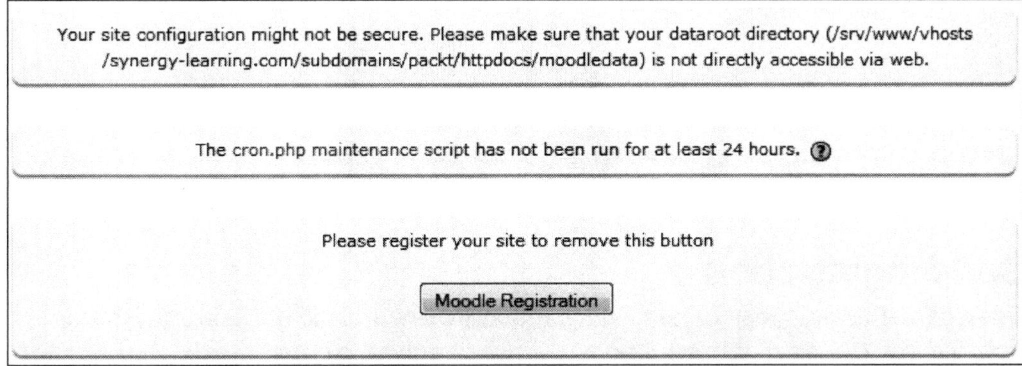

Your site configuration might not be secure. Please make sure that your dataroot directory (/srv/www/vhosts /synergy-learning.com/subdomains/packt/httpdocs/moodledata) is not directly accessible via web.
The cron.php maintenance script has not been run for at least 24 hours.
Please register your site to remove this button
Moodle Registration

Moodle monitors failed login attempts in its log file, as described in Chapter 9. Repeated login failures can indicate that unauthorized users are trying to get access to your system. In addition to checking your log files regularly, you should also consider monitoring these activities by configuring the settings at **Security | Notifications** in the **System Administration** menu:

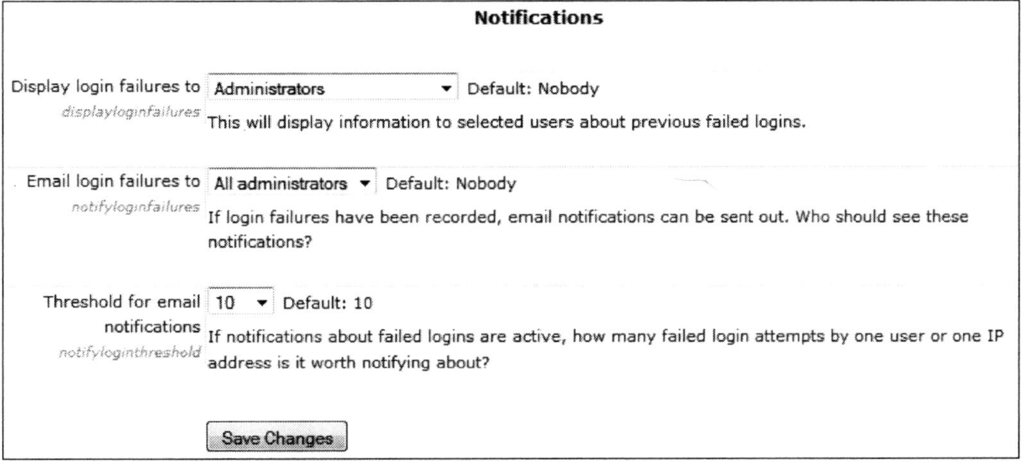


While this is no fool-proof system, it can potentially highlight some problems on your system, and it is recommended that you activate it. Another benefit of getting these notifications emailed to you is the "customer care" aspect of being able to get back to users who got frustrated when trying to get into your site.

# User Security

The key to the security of your system lies in making sure that users only have access to their privileged areas. In this section we will be dealing with access to Moodle, passwords and security in roles.

# Access to Moodle

Users can access Moodle in different ways and it is important to configure access mechanisms correctly.

## Self-Registration

Self-registration is a great feature, which reduces the workload of the administrator significantly. However, it poses a potential risk of unwanted users creating an account either manually or automatically. To reduce this risk, two pairs of settings are located in the **Common settings** of **Users | Authentication | Manage Authentication**.

- Allowed and Denied email domains
- ReCAPTCHA private-and public-keys

The settings have been described in detail in Chapter 5.

## Guest Access

Moodle provides a feature called guest access to users who do not wish to register with the site. While this is very useful for some public sites (such as `moodle.org`), it is unwanted in most educational and commercial settings. To deactivate guest access, go to the **Common settings** of **Users | Authentication | Manage Authentication** and change the **Guest login button** from **Show** to **Hide**.

A second setting that relates to guest access is located in **Users | Permissions | User Policies**, where you will find the **Auto-login guests** checkbox. Turn this on only if you want to log in visitors automatically when they enter a course with guest access.

## Protection of User Details

Identity theft is a common problem on the Internet, and Moodle is no exception. To avoid the possibility of fraudsters gathering details about authenticated users, a number of settings are located in **Security | Site Policies**:

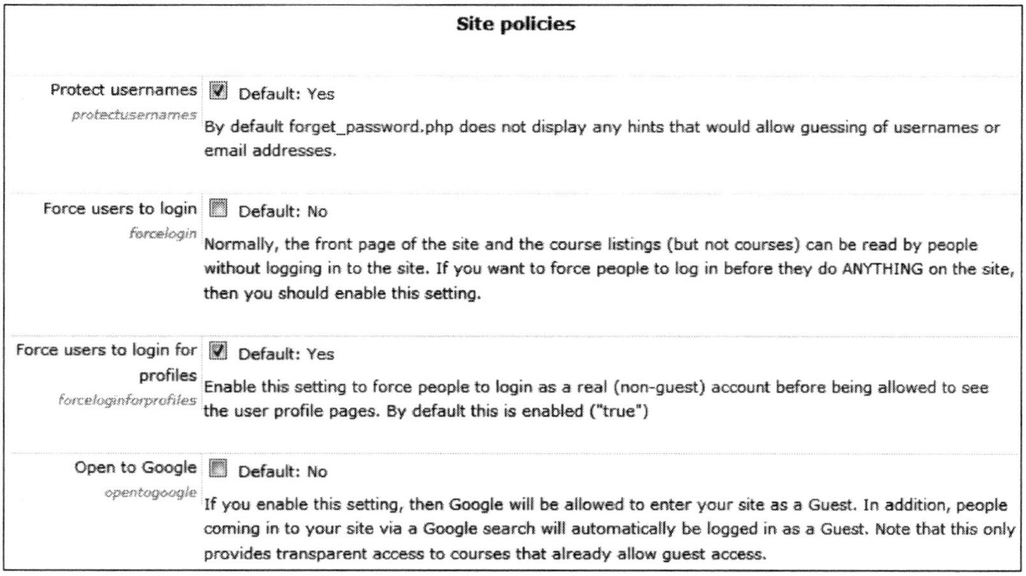

**Site policies**

Protect usernames
*protectusernames*
☑ Default: Yes
By default forget_password.php does not display any hints that would allow guessing of usernames or email addresses.

Force users to login
*forcelogin*
☐ Default: No
Normally, the front page of the site and the course listings (but not courses) can be read by people without logging in to the site. If you want to force people to log in before they do ANYTHING on the site, then you should enable this setting.

Force users to login for profiles
*forceloginforprofiles*
☑ Default: Yes
Enable this setting to force people to login as a real (non-guest) account before being allowed to see the user profile pages. By default this is enabled ("true")

Open to Google
*opentogoogle*
☐ Default: No
If you enable this setting, then Google will be allowed to enter your site as a Guest. In addition, people coming in to your site via a Google search will automatically be logged in as a Guest. Note that this only provides transparent access to courses that already allow guest access.

| Setting | Description |
|---|---|
| **Protect usernames** | If a user cannot remember his/her username or password, Moodle provides a "Forgotten password" screen. By default the message displayed reads: **If you supplied a correct username or email address then an email should have been sent to you**. But if the protection is turned off, the message reads: **An email should have been sent to your address at ******@<domain name>**, which could allow guessing of a username. |
| **Force users to log in** | By default the front page of Moodle is visible to everyone, even if he/she is not logged into the site. If you wish to force users to log in before they see the front page, change this parameter. |
| **Force users to log in for profiles** | When set to **Yes** (default setting) users will have to log in as a real account before they can access the profile pages of other users. |
| **Open to Google** | Moodle can be configured to allow Google to crawl through courses with guest access and add the content to its search engine database. The functionality is turned off by default. |

At the bottom of the **Site policies** screen, you have the ability to activate **Email change confirmation**. If set to **Yes**, users will be sent an email to confirm that their change of email address in their profile is genuine.

## Course Managers

When courses are displayed on the front page, users who are not logged on to the system can see a description and the names of the course managers of each course by clicking on it. By default these are the teachers of the course. To change the names that are displayed for each course, go to **Appearance | Course managers** and select the roles to be displayed:

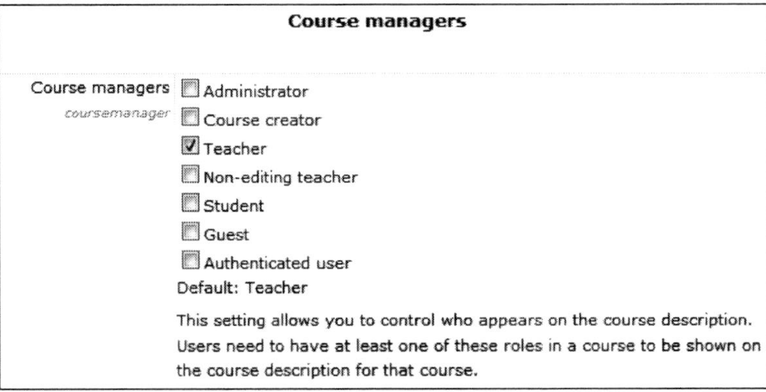


To hide names completely, de-select all roles. As a result, no names will appear when course descriptions are shown.

# Moodle Passwords

Moodle offers a password policy feature, which you have to activate in **Security | Site Policies**:

| | |
|---|---|
| Password Policy *passwordpolicy* | ☑ Default: No<br>Turning this on will make Moodle check user passwords against a valid password policy. Use the settings below to specify your policy (they will be ignored if you set this to 'No'). |
| Password Length *minpasswordlength* | 8 Default: 8<br>Passwords must be at least these many characters long. |
| Digits *minpassworddigits* | 1 Default: 1<br>Passwords must have at least these many digits. |
| Lowercase letters *minpasswordlower* | 1 Default: 1<br>Passwords must have at least these many lower case letters. |
| Uppercase letters *minpasswordupper* | 1 Default: 1<br>Passwords must have at least these many upper case letters. |
| Non-alphanumeric characters *minpasswordnonalphanum* | 1 Default: 1<br>Passwords must have at least these many non-alphanumeric characters. |

The following self-explanatory constraints for passwords are available:

- Minimum password length
- Minimum number of digits (0...9)
- Minimum number of lowercase letters (a...z)
- Minimum number of uppercase letters (A...Z)
- Minimum number of non-alphanumeric characters (such as $%&*)

Moodle's site policy does not provide a parameter for password expiry.

[  It is highly recommended to use a strong password (long, complex, and random) for the Moodle Administrator account even if the password policy is deactivated. ]

# Security in Roles

Moodle allows creation of custom roles such as Parent, Teaching assistant, Secretary, Inspector, and Librarian. However, the flexibility of this powerful mechanism comes with a price in the form of a potential security risk.

## Role Definitions

Moodle displays the risks associated with each capability, that is, the risks that each capability can potentially raise. To recapitulate from Chapter 6, the four risk types are explained in the table that follows:

| **Risk** | **Icon** | **Description** |
|---|---|---|
| Configuration | | Users can change site configuration and behavior. |
| XSS | | Users can add files and texts that allow cross-site scripting (potentially malicious scripts that are embedded in web pages and executed on the user's computer). |
| Privacy | | Users can gain access to the private information of other users, for example, their profile data and grades. |
| Spam | | Users can send spam to site users or others, for instance via the forum notification mechanism. |

Because risks are only displayed to indicate what potential damage a capability can cause, you are responsible for the role definitions and contexts in which the roles are applied.

It is highly recommended to minimize the number of global role assignments as they apply throughout the site, including the front page and all courses.

## Default Roles

Default roles for different user types are assigned in **Users | Permissions | User Policies** in the **Site Administration** block. We dealt with these settings in detail in Chapter 6. Make sure that these are set correctly, especially the guest-and visitor-related roles.

# Data and Content Security

Content can potentially contain malicious elements. It further needs to be protected from unauthorized access. In this section, we shall deal with the security of data and content.

# Content Created Within Moodle

Users are able to create content in Moodle either by using the resource editor or by uploading files. A number of settings are available to prevent misuse.

HTML allows the embedding of code that uses explicit EMBED and OBJECT tags. This mechanism has recently gained popularity with sites such as YouTube and Google Maps providing code to be embedded for their users. Potentially malicious code can be put in the embedded script, which is why its support is deactivated by default. To activate it, go to **Security | Site policies** and locate **Allow EMBED and OBJECT tags** parameter:

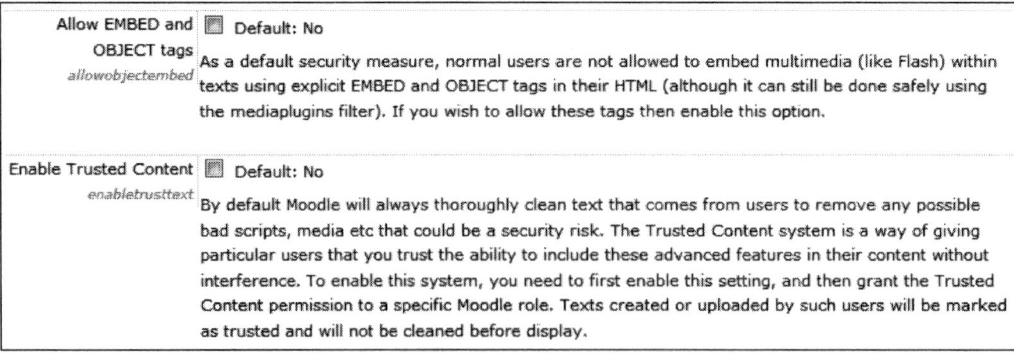

| | |
|---|---|
| Allow EMBED and OBJECT tags<br>*allowobjectembed* | Default: No<br>As a default security measure, normal users are not allowed to embed multimedia (like Flash) within texts using explicit EMBED and OBJECT tags in their HTML (although it can still be done safely using the mediaplugins filter). If you wish to allow these tags then enable this option. |
| Enable Trusted Content<br>*enabletrusttext* | Default: No<br>By default Moodle will always thoroughly clean text that comes from users to remove any possible bad scripts, media etc that could be a security risk. The Trusted Content system is a way of giving particular users that you trust the ability to include these advanced features in their content without interference. To enable this system, you need to first enable this setting, and then grant the Trusted Content permission to a specific Moodle role. Texts created or uploaded by such users will be marked as trusted and will not be cleaned before display. |

The Moodle editor uses a mechanism called KSES to remove any unwanted HTML elements and attributes. A more secure version called HTML Purifier is currently under development, and can be activated in the **Miscellaneous | Experimental** section. It is possible to turn this filter off for users you trust. First, you have to set the **Enable Trusted Content** parameter as shown in the preceding screenshot. Second, you have to allow the `moodle/site:trustcontent` capability for each user you are trusting to submit Javascript and other potentially malicious code.

The multimedia plug-in supports a number of audio and video formats. Shockwave files can contain code that could cause problems on users' local machines. To avoid the usage of SWF files, it is recommended that the **Enable .swf filter** in **Modules | Filters | Multimedia Plugins** remains off.

# Visibility of Content

Blogging and tagging are two social networking tools that are popular in Web 2.0 environments. Tags and blog entries are harnessed for searching, sharing, and other collaborative activities in order to match interests. The potential issue is that the content is visible to users who should not be able to share or view entries. Moodle has tackled this by providing two settings in **Security | Site policies**:

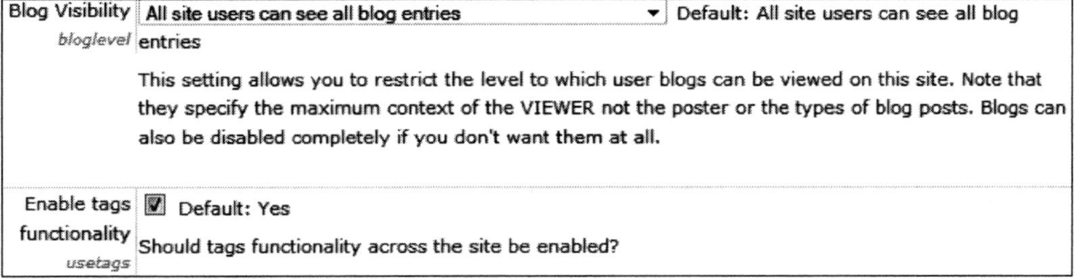


To specify who can view blog entries, set the **Blog Visibility** parameter to any of the following self-explanatory options:

- The world can read entries set to be world-accessible.
- All site users can see all blog entries (default).
- Users can only see blogs for people who share a course.
- Users can only see blogs for people who share a group.
- Users can only see their own blog.
- Disable blog system completely.

You might also consider creating a blogger role on your system allowing the `moodle/blog:create` capability. This will limit blogging to specific users only who have been assigned the new role. You will find more details on a blogger role in the MoodleDocs at `http://docs.moodle.org/en/Blogger_role`.

The tagging functionality can only be turned on and off. If you deactivate the mechanism, tags that are already on the system are kept, and will reappear when the functionality is turned on again.

# Site Policy

Users who have access to Moodle are sometimes as much a threat as unauthorized users. If you have a site policy that all users (not just learners) must see and agree to before using Moodle for the first time, you will have some ammunition when taking action against a user who misuses your system. You specify this text in **Security | Site policies**, which includes a **Site policy URL** entry.

| Site policy URL<br>*sitepolicy* | p/1/School_Website_Policy.htm Default: Empty<br>If you have a site policy that all users must see and agree to before using this site, then specify the URL to it here, otherwise leave this field blank. The URL can point to anywhere - one convenient place would be a file in the site files. eg http://yoursite/file.php/1/policy.html |
|---|---|

You have to specify a URL that contains the policy text, which must be an HTML document. It is good practice to keep the site policy file in the Site files area (**Front Page | Site files**).

[ Do not specify a PDF or Word file as site policy. It will prevent users from logging in to Moodle. ]

Once the site policy has been uploaded and specified, it has to be conformed to by each user the first time he or she logs into Moodle:

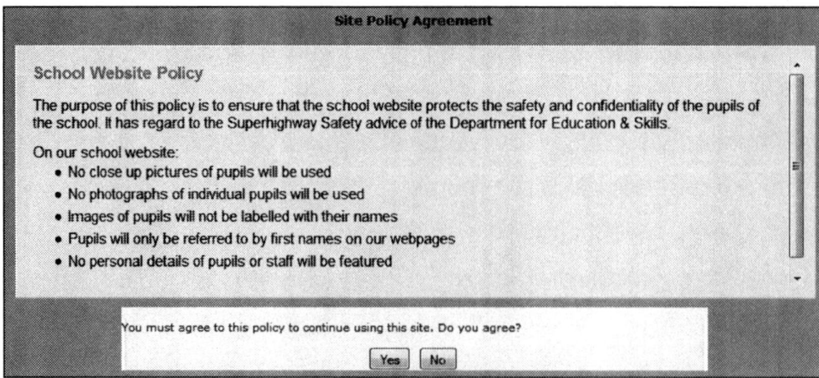

While the site policy does not prevent any misuse, it introduces a psychological barrier and also protects your organization if an issue has to be taken further.

# Antivirus

Moodle supports scanning of uploaded files for viruses using **Clam AntiVirus** (**clamAV**), which is an open-source antivirus toolkit for UNIX, designed especially for systems such as Moodle. See `www.clamav.org` for details, downloads for different operating systems, and to know how to keep the virus definition database up-to-date. You need to install clamAV on your system. Once installed, the scanner is configured at **Security | Anti-Virus** in the **Site Administration** block:

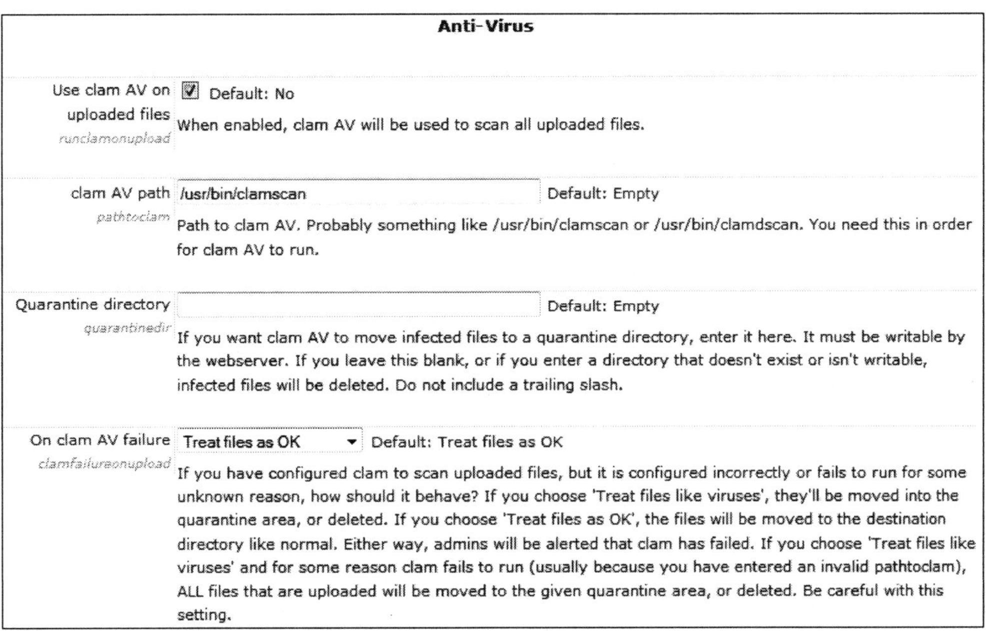


| Setting | Description |
|---|---|
| Use clam AV on uploaded files | Turn clamAV on or off. |
| clam AV path | Location of clamAV on your system. Typical default paths are provided. |
| Quarantine directory | By default, any infected files are deleted. If you wish to keep them, specify a writable directory that is then used to quarantine the files instead. |
| On clam AV failure | If, for whatever reason, clamAV fails to run or scan files, you as the administrator will be alerted. Additionally, you can change the default setting Treat files as OK (the scanner is ignored) to Treat files like viruses (all files are deleted or moved, or moved to the quarantine directory if the scanner fails). |

# System Security

In this section we are dealing with configuration settings, login via secure HTTP, and module security.

# Configuration Security

There are a number of general configuration settings that potentially have an impact on the security of your system.

## Accessibility of Dataroot

In the Notifications screenshot at the beginning of the chapter, you probably spotted the warning that the **dataroot** directory is directly accessible via the Web. Moodle requires additional space on the server to store uploaded files such as course documents and user pictures. The directory is called dataroot and should not be accessible via the Web. If this directory is accessible directly, unauthorized users can get access to its content.

To prevent this, move your dataroot directory outside the web directory, and modify `config.php` by changing the `$CFG->dataroot` entry.

In externally hosted environments, it is often not possible to locate the directory outside the web directory. If this is the case, create a file called `.htaccess` in the data directory and add a line containing **deny from all**.

## Cron Process

We already described the cron process in Chapter 2, which covered the installation of Moodle. It is a script that runs regularly to perform certain operations such as sending emails, cleaning up temporary files, and so on. Scripts that run on the operating system level can potentially contain malicious code.

It is possible to run the script via a web browser by simply typing in this URL: `http://<your Moodle site>/admin/cron.php`. To prevent this, two mutually exclusive settings are located in **Security | Site policies**.

If you allow only the cron process to be executed from the command line, running the script via a web browser will be disabled and a message will be displayed saying: **Sorry, internet access to this page has been disabled by the administrator**. The cron process is still executed automatically if set up correctly.

By default, Moodle requires that running the cron script via a web browser requires the provision of a password in the form of a parameter, for example http://<your Moodle site>/admin/cron.php?password=yourpassword. If the password (default is the Moodle database name) is not provided, the error message **Sorry, you have not provided a valid password to access this page** is displayed.

| | |
|---|---|
| Cron execution via command line only *cronclionly* | ☐ Default: No<br>If this is set, then the cron script can only be run from the command line instead of via the web. This overrides the cron password setting below. |
| Cron password for remote access *cronremotepassword* | ••••• ☐ Unmask<br>This means that the cron.php script cannot be run from a web browser without supplying the password using the following form of URL:<br>http://site.example.com/admin/cron.php?password=opensesame<br>If this is left empty, no password is required. |

# HTTP Security

Moodle offers HTTPS support, which runs HTTP requests over SSL (a more secure, but significantly slower socket layer). The login of every system is a potential vulnerability and it is possible to **Use HTTPS for logins,** which is activated in **Security | HTTP security**:

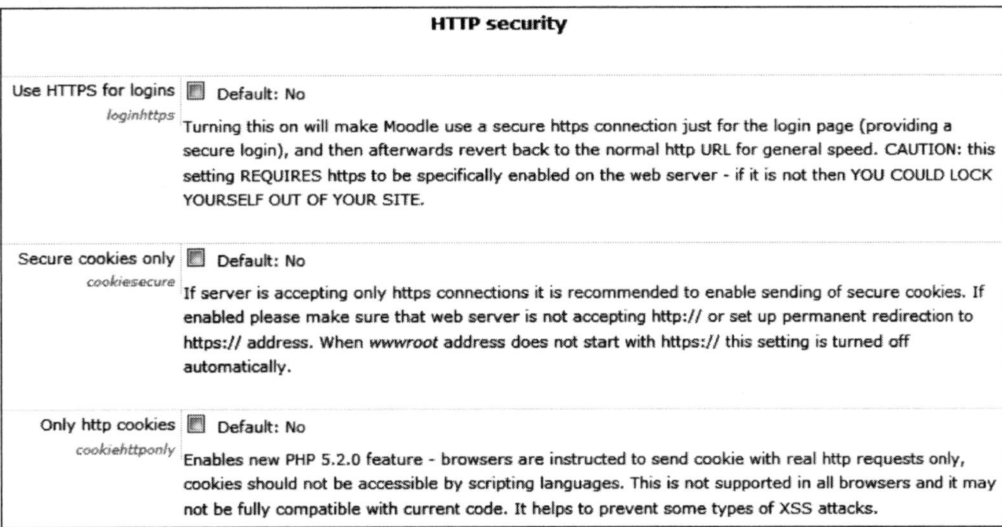

**HTTP security**

| | |
|---|---|
| Use HTTPS for logins *loginhttps* | ☐ Default: No<br>Turning this on will make Moodle use a secure https connection just for the login page (providing a secure login), and then afterwards revert back to the normal http URL for general speed. CAUTION: this setting REQUIRES https to be specifically enabled on the web server - if it is not then YOU COULD LOCK YOURSELF OUT OF YOUR SITE. |
| Secure cookies only *cookiesecure* | ☐ Default: No<br>If server is accepting only https connections it is recommended to enable sending of secure cookies. If enabled please make sure that web server is not accepting http:// or set up permanent redirection to https:// address. When *wwwroot* address does not start with https:// this setting is turned off automatically. |
| Only http cookies *cookiehttponly* | ☐ Default: No<br>Enables new PHP 5.2.0 feature - browsers are instructed to send cookie with real http requests only, cookies should not be accessible by scripting languages. This is not supported in all browsers and it may not be fully compatible with current code. It helps to prevent some types of XSS attacks. |

HTTPS encrypts the username and password before it is transferred from the user's browser to the server that hosts Moodle. HTTPS has to be enabled on your web server and you will have to purchase an SSL certificate. Every web server has a different method for enabling HTTPS, so you will have to refer the documentation of your server.

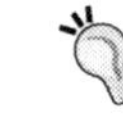

If you turn on HTTPS for logins without the relevant system components installed, you will lock yourself out of your system!

HTTPS is only used for the login procedure; once a user has logged in, Moodle reverts to HTTP. Running your entire Moodle system via HTTPS would cause severe performance problems.

Web servers can be configured so that they only accept HTTPS URLs. If this is the case on your system, it is recommended to allow only secure cookies.

Moodle already supports a new feature that instructs web browsers to send cookies only with real requests, which prevents some cross-scripting attacks. However, the feature requires PHP 5.2.0 and is not supported in all web browsers.

# Module Security

The objective of the module security feature is to restrict the usage of Moodle activities and resources in courses. If activated in **Security | Module security**, a separate "Restrict activity modules?" frame appears in the settings of certain courses:

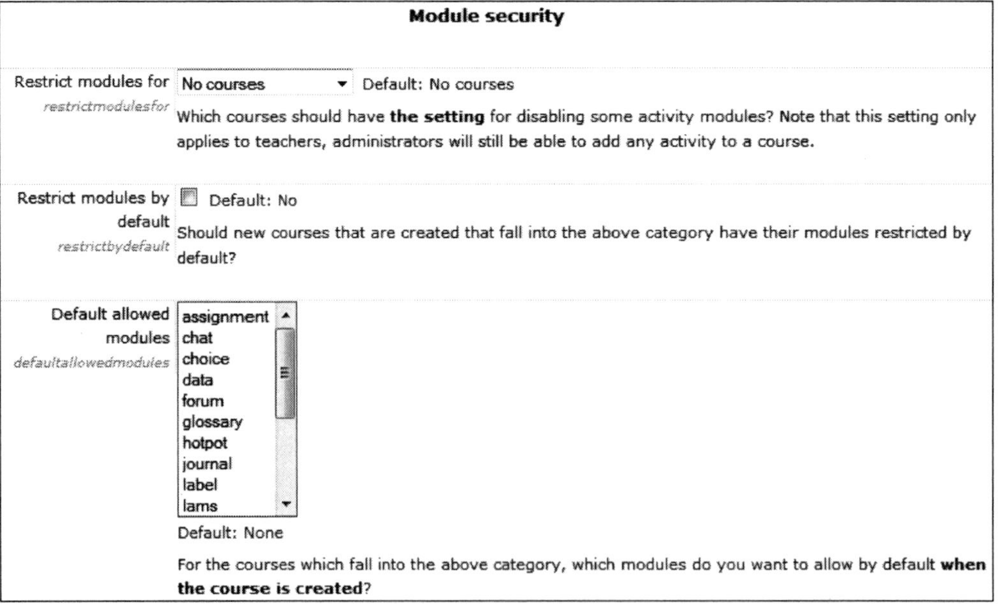


You can choose whether modules can be restricted between "All courses" and "Requested courses". The other two default settings specify whether modules are restricted, and which ones are selected.

# Summary

In this chapter you have learned how to protect your Moodle system against any misuse.

Moodle is based on the LAMP platform, which has proven to be very secure if configured correctly. Moodle developers are very conscious about security since they know it is vital when dealing with personal user data such as grades. Hence, the topic has been given highest priority. However, there is no guarantee that your system is 100% protected against misuse. New hacking techniques will emerge and users will continue to be careless with their credentials (you have all seen the post-it notes under the keyboard.). So, make sure the security patches and updates on your entire system, not just Moodle, are always up-to-date and keep educating your users about the dangers.

The Health Check in Appendix 1 includes a security section in which you will find some additional settings which will help to safeguard your system.

Now that you system is secure, let's make sure it performs to its full potential.

# 11
# Moodle Performance and Optimization

The performance of a web-based system is a critical issue and it is a key responsibility of the administrator to configure, monitor, and fine-tune the virtual learning environment for maximum speed. While Moodle has the potential to scale to thousands of simultaneous users, good performance management is required to guarantee adequate scalability.

After providing an overview, we will be covering the most relevant topics relating to Moodle performance and optimization.

- Moodle content

  We will look at how content creation, content volume, and different content types can impact the performance of your Moodle system.
- Moodle system settings

  A wide range of system-related performance settings are dealt with, namely:
  - Path settings
  - Caching settings
  - Module settings (gradebook, chat, forum, and cron)
  - Miscellaneous settings (languages, filters, and searches)

# Performance and Optimization Overview

LAMP software in general and Moodle in particular have very distinct application layers consisting of the operating system, web server, database server and the application developed in a programming language. Each layer has its own idiosyncrasies when it comes to optimization. We will mainly focus on the **application layer**, which is the focus of this book.

The following areas are not dealt with in any detail in the following pages, and it is necessary to refer to the respective documentation on performance and optimization issues:

- Operating system performance

  The choice of operating system and its configuration will have a major impact on how Moodle will perform. In principle, Linux or any other Unix derivative performs better than any other operating system. PHP applications such as Moodle run significantly slower in the Windows environment than on Linux. Some aspects of this have been covered in Chapter 2 when we dealt with the installation of Moodle.

- Database performance

  The database is not only a core element of Moodle but also a major bottleneck as it requires disk access, which is slower than memory access. Entire books have been dedicated to database optimization with indexing, caching, buffering, querying, and connection handling as the main candidates. The two optimizations that have a significant impact on your database performance are: enabling of query caching and the increase of buffer sizes. You might also want to consider running the database on a separate dedicated server.

- Web server performance

  Each web server offers an array of optimization settings that include memory handling, caching, process management, and other minor tweaks.

- PHP performance

  There are a number of ways with which PHP can be forced to execute a code faster. The key is the usage of a PHP accelerator (such as eAccelerator or APC) in combination with good memory management and caching techniques.

- Hardware performance

  We already covered some aspects of this in Chapter 2, where we mentioned that there is no one-size-fits-all approach when it comes to the ideal hardware setup. For single-server systems the key is RAM: the more, the better. Once the system size increases, it is recommended to use multiple servers, ideally in a load-balanced environment.

For each area mentioned, benchmark and stress tests are available that will help you to gauge what performance bottlenecks are present and, after optimization has been carried out, if they have been reduced. There are also add-ons available for most web browsers that display information about the time it takes to load pages, thus offering some indicative performance measurements.

An entire area has been dedicated to performance and optimization in the MoodleDocs. You will find most of the relevant information and links to related sites at `http://docs.moodle.org/en/Performance`.

# Moodle Content

The content that is created and uploaded by your course creators or front page designers will have an impact on the performance of your system. While you cannot dictate what learning sources are added to Moodle, the following pointers can provide explanations if certain aspects within courses behave sluggishly, or users on slower Internet connections experience difficulties accessing learning materials.

## Content Creation

Moodle is significantly slower when run in editing mode. Unless you or any other user is not modifying any content, it is recommended to turn editing off as it puts less strain on the system.

Some content is created quicker in a separate standalone application such as web development tools, word processors, or SCORM editors, as opposed to the built-in Moodle tools.

## Content Volume

The amount of content within a course can cause problems for student access. While each resource and activity is accessed individually, there are pedagogical limits on the number of learning objects that should be stored in a course. Furthermore, a course with hundreds of large resources is less likely to support a good learning experience than a number of courses broken down in more manageable chunks. It will also have slowed down backing up and importing of courses.

# Content Types

Moodle supports a large number of content types such as office documents, graphics, animation, audio, and video. In principal, there exists a trade-off between size, quality, and functionality. There are a number of precautions that can be taken for each type:

- Office documents
    - Save office files as PDF files (which are much smaller in size) unless editing is required.
    - Use online repositories, such as Google Docs, that put less strain on your server.
    - Scan text using OCR and not images.
- Graphics
    - Reduce the image resolution, especially when pictures have been taken with digital cameras.
    - Reduce image color depth.
    - Use a compression format.
    - When using Microsoft Word, insert images in text documents as metafiles (using the Paste Special command).
    - Only use formats that are supported directly by web browsers (GIF, JPG, and PNG).
- Audio files
    - Reduce the sample rate (especially for spoken content).
    - Mono recordings are often sufficient for spoken content.
    - Use a compression format such as MP3.
- Animations and video
    - Keep animation quality, dimension, and sample rate to a minimum.
    - Use Flash for performance.
    - Stream videos (from external sources such as `www.teachertube.com`) if possible.

These are just a few recommendations that will help to reduce the stress on your system. The better your course content creators are informed, the lesser resources will be taken up by the content per se. While the usage of different types of textual and multimedia resources should be encouraged, it is important to introduce a culture to provide information on how these content types are streamlined as much as possible.

A bigger problem is scalability, which is caused by concurrent users of the system. We will be devoting the rest of the chapter to this issue.

# Moodle System Settings

Moodle offers a wide range of system-related performance settings that are set at various places in the **Site Administration** block.

## Path Settings

There are three operations that Moodle performs regularly. They can either be run using Moodle's internal routines coded in PHP or, alternatively, by native versions of each function provided by the host operating system. The second approach is significantly faster as it reduces the load on your server, but is only supported in Unix environments. The three programs that can be run using external programs are:

- Zip (for compressing files)
  This will accelerate backups and manual zip operations.
- Unzip (for uncompressing files)
  This will accelerate restore and manual unzip operations.
- Du (for listing directories)

  This will accelerate the displaying of directory content, especially if it contains a lot of files.

To enter the system paths for the three programs, go to **Server | System Paths** in the **Site Administration** block:

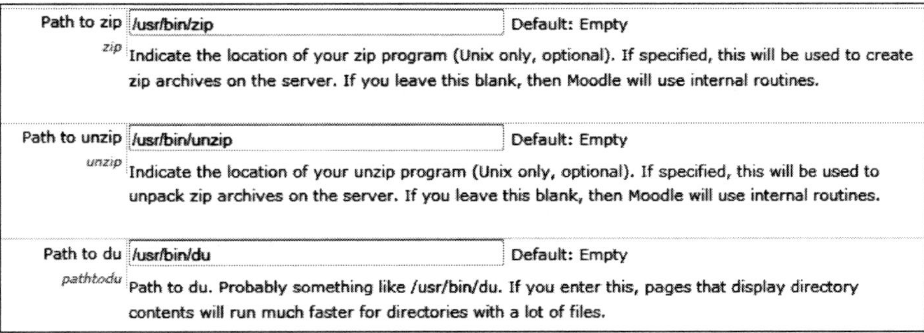

Path to zip
zip
/usr/bin/zip
Default: Empty
Indicate the location of your zip program (Unix only, optional). If specified, this will be used to create zip archives on the server. If you leave this blank, then Moodle will use internal routines.
Path to unzip
unzip
/usr/bin/unzip
Default: Empty
Indicate the location of your unzip program (Unix only, optional). If specified, this will be used to unpack zip archives on the server. If you leave this blank, then Moodle will use internal routines.
Path to du
pathtodu
/usr/bin/du
Default: Empty
Path to du. Probably something like /usr/bin/du. If you enter this, pages that display directory contents will run much faster for directories with a lot of files.

On most systems the location of the three executables is `/usr/bin/zip`, `/usr/bin/unzip` and `/usr/bin/du`, respectively. If this does not work, run the `which` command on the Unix shell to find out where the programs are located, for example, `which unzip`.

[  If any of the system paths are set incorrectly, Moodle will malfunction! ]

# Caching Settings

Caching stores frequently accessed data in a temporary storage, and expedites its access using the cached copy as opposed to the re-fetched (from disk) or re-computed (in memory) data. It has proven to be one of the most efficient performance optimization techniques and Moodle is no exception. There are a number of caching-related settings that you can access at **Server | Performance**:

| **Performance** | |
|---|---|
| Cache Type *cachetype* | None ▾ Default: None<br>Select a type of cache for Moodle to use. This will only configure the cache, remember to enable rcache so that the cache is used for something. Use **only** if you need to reduce the load on the database system -- otherwise Moodle will actually run slower. Medium-traffic sites may see benefits using 'internal'. A single webserver with eAccelerator or Turckmmcache installed *with the shared memory options enabled* should try 'eaccelerator'. If you have a multiple-server setup, and you have one or more memcached daemons running and the PHP-memcached extension, select 'memcached' and configure the memached options below.<br>**Note:** make sure you test performance under load and tune accordingly -- the caches can make your site slower. In high-traffic situations, eAccelerator and memcached can yield the most benefits, but have the higher costs in CPU usage on the webserver. |
| Record cache *rcache* | No ▾ Default: No<br>Use the cache to store database records. Remember to set 'cachetype' as well! |
| Record cache TTL *rcachettl* | 10 Default: 10<br>Time-to-live for cached records, in seconds. Use a short (<15) value here. |
| Int. cache max *intcachemax* | 10 Default: 10<br>For internal cache only. Maximum number of records to keep in the cache. Recommended value: 50. Use lower values to reduce memory usage. |
| memcached hosts *memcachedhosts* | Default: Empty<br>For memcached. Comma-separated list of hosts that are running the memcached daemon. Use IP addresses to avoid DNS latency. memcached does not behave well if you add/remove hosts on a running setup. |
| memcached use persistent connections *memcachedpconn* | No ▾ Default: No<br>For memcached. Use persistent connections. Use carefully -- it can make Apache/PHP crash after a restart of the memcached daemon. |

| Setting | Description |
|---|---|
| **Cache Type** | Moodle supports a number of caching types, as described in the explanation below the option.<br><br>By default, support for caching has been turned off (**None**), which is suitable for most small sites. If you have a separate caching system installed, you have to select its type (**eaccelerator** or **mmemcached** are supported. For the latter, you have to provide a comma seperated list of server IP addresses). If you do not have either system installed and wish to make use of caching, choose **internal** which makes use of the record/internal cache. |
| **Record cache** | If the **Cache Type** option has been set to **internal**, change this setting to **Yes** to support record caching. |
| **Record cache TTL** | The value specifies the time-to-live for cached records (in seconds). The default value is **10** and it is recommended that the value shouldn't exceed **15**. |
| **Int. cache max** | The **Int. cache max** specifies the maximum number of records that could be kept in the internal cache. This will enable a primary cache for database records without using the database engine cache.<br><br>This setting only works if the **Cache Type** has been set to **internal**. The lower the value, the lesser the memory used. The recommended value is **50**. |
| **memcached hosts** | A comma-separated list of hosts (use IP addresses, not URLs, to avoid DNS latency) that are running the memcached daemon. This setting only applies when **Cache type** is set to **memcached**. |
| **memcached use persistent connections** | Persistent connections are faster than transient ones. Choose **Yes** to use a persistent connection with **Cache Type** set to **memcached**. |

# Module Settings

A number of modules in Moodle offer settings that have an impact on the performance of your Moodle system.

# Gradebook Optimization

Up to version 1.8, Moodle's gradebook caused severe performance problems, especially on larger systems. With 1.9, where grade information is pushed into a central data area, as opposed to previous versions where data was pulled on demand from various courses, the performance has improved manifold.

A dedicated **Grades** menu can be found in the **Site Administration** block where you will find a number of settings that will have an impact on performance. In general, when more aggregation and other calculations have to be carried out, the population of the gradebook data store becomes slow. For example, the **Aggregate including subcategories** parameter in **Grades | Grade category settings** will add some minor overhead to the calculation of grades.

A second gradebook-related area that has some impact on performance is the Gradebook history, which forces Moodle to keep track of any changes in grades. Go to **Server | Cleanup** and you will see two Gradebook history settings at the bottom:

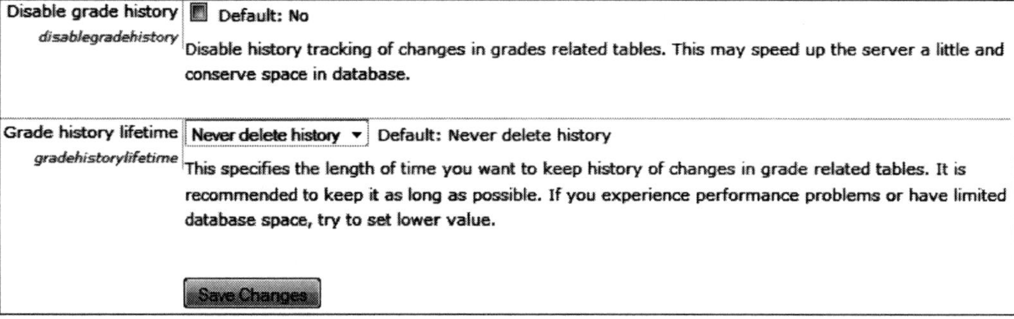

Disable grade history
disablegradehistory
Default: No
Disable history tracking of changes in grades related tables. This may speed up the server a little and conserve space in database.
Grade history lifetime
gradehistorylifetime
Never delete history
Default: Never delete history
This specifies the length of time you want to keep history of changes in grade related tables. It is recommended to keep it as long as possible. If you experience performance problems or have limited database space, try to set lower value.
Save Changes

The Gradebook history is turned on by default and values are kept forever. You can either turn the facility completely off, or limit the number of days you wish to keep grade entries.

# Chat Optimization

By default, the chat method in Moodle is set to **Normal chat,** which contacts all participating clients on a regular basis. The upside of this approach is that it requires no configuration and works on any system; the downside being that it has a significant performance impact on the server, especially when the chat activity is used very often. A solution is to use **Chat server daemon**, which ensures a scalable chat environment. However, the daemon, a small system-level program that runs in the background, has to be installed on the operating system level and only works on Unix (check your Unix administration guide on how to do this).

To change the chat method Moodle uses and to learn how to configure a number of performance parameters, go to **Modules | Activities | Chat**:

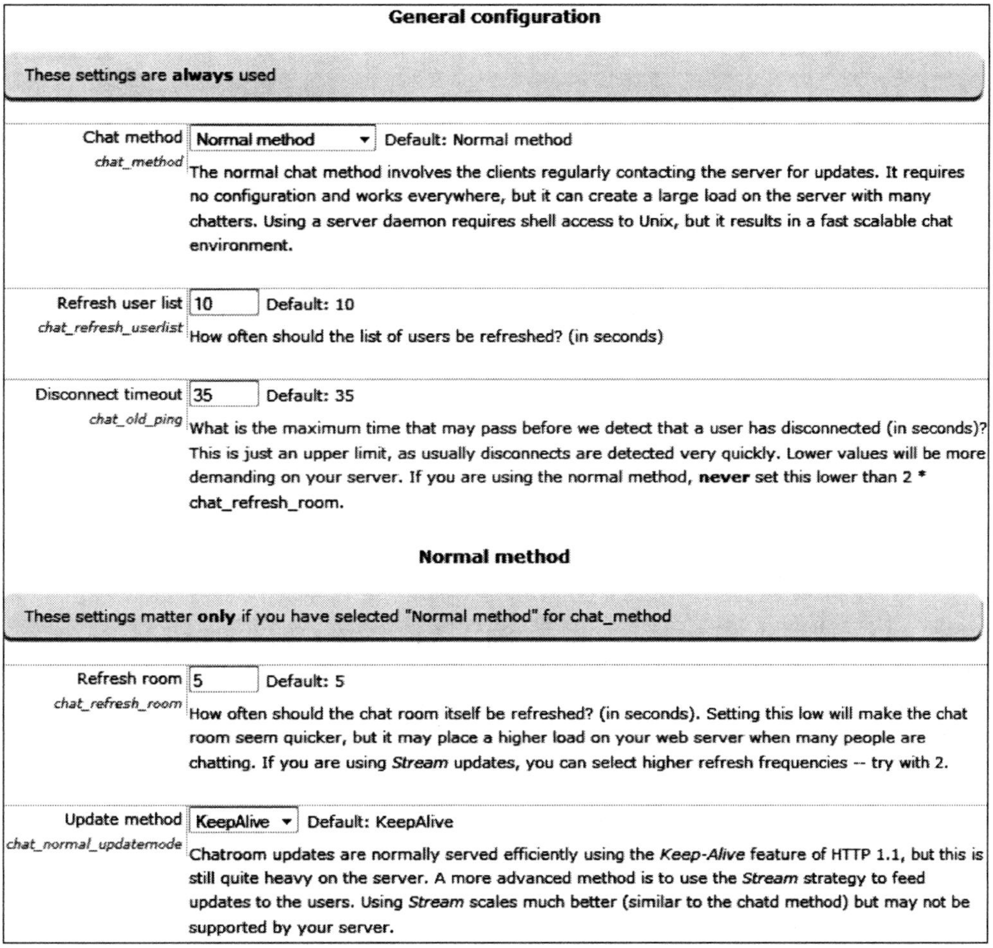

**General configuration**

These settings are **always** used

Chat method *chat_method* [Normal method] Default: Normal method
The normal chat method involves the clients regularly contacting the server for updates. It requires no configuration and works everywhere, but it can create a large load on the server with many chatters. Using a server daemon requires shell access to Unix, but it results in a fast scalable chat environment.

Refresh user list *chat_refresh_userlist* [10] Default: 10
How often should the list of users be refreshed? (in seconds)

Disconnect timeout *chat_old_ping* [35] Default: 35
What is the maximum time that may pass before we detect that a user has disconnected (in seconds)? This is just an upper limit, as usually disconnects are detected very quickly. Lower values will be more demanding on your server. If you are using the normal method, **never** set this lower than 2 * chat_refresh_room.

**Normal method**

These settings matter **only** if you have selected "Normal method" for chat_method

Refresh room *chat_refresh_room* [5] Default: 5
How often should the chat room itself be refreshed? (in seconds). Setting this low will make the chat room seem quicker, but it may place a higher load on your web server when many people are chatting. If you are using *Stream* updates, you can select higher refresh frequencies -- try with 2.

Update method *chat_normal_updatemode* [KeepAlive] Default: KeepAlive
Chatroom updates are normally served efficiently using the *Keep-Alive* feature of HTTP 1.1, but this is still quite heavy on the server. A more advanced method is to use the *Stream* strategy to feed updates to the users. Using *Stream* scales much better (similar to the chatd method) but may not be supported by your server.

Well-explained descriptions have been provided for each parameter. The following table lists the settings that are performance-related and the context (that is, the chat method used) in which they apply:

| | Normal Method | Server Daemon |
|---|---|---|
| Refresh user list | √ | √ |
| Disconnect timeout | √ | √ |
| Refresh room | √ | |
| Update method | √ | |
| Max users | | √ |

## Forums

On systems with very large forums, tracking unread posts can slow down the activity. Though the impact is rather minor, the tracking can be turned off in **Modules | Activities | Forum** where you will find the **Track unread posts** parameter.

# Miscellaneous Settings

Finally, we are dealing with a number of performance-related settings that do not belong to any category described so far.

## Language-Related Settings

We already dealt with localization in great detail in Chapter 8, where we covered the configuration of Moodle. Two issues arise when supporting multiple locales that can potentially have a negative impact on the performance of your Moodle system.

If you install a large number of language packs, performance will be reduced. Check if all installed languages are required; Go to **Languages | Language packs** and remove any obsolete ones.

Language packs are also cached in Moodle to speed up the retrieval of language strings. You find the **Cache language menu** parameter in **Languages | Language settings**. Unless you are modifying a language pack, it is highly recommended to leave this setting at **Yes**. It caches all language strings rather than loading them dynamically.

## Large Log files

In Chapter 9, one of the subjects we looked at was Moodle reporting and statistics. Keeping track of user behavior can potentially have a negative impact on your server.

Both monitoring facilities require a log file, which is populated in the background. In **Server | Cleanup**, you will see a **Keep logs for** parameter where you can specify the number of days for which user data is kept.

If you have enabled the statistics functionality, be aware that it is likely to have a profound impact on the performance of your system whenever the statistical information is updated. Go back to the section on **Statistics** settings in Chapter 9 (**Server | Statistics**) and make sure that the configuration is set to have minimum impact on the server.

# Filter Settings

Having too many active Moodle filters affects the server load, especially on lower end systems. The number of active filters will increase the time it takes to scan each page as filters are applied sequentially, and not in parallel. Go to **Modules | Filters | Manage filters** and hide all filters that are not required.

Caching is applied to pages that use text filters, that is, copies of text that are kept in memory. The trade-off is between refreshing the cache too often (small values), which slows down the server and not refreshing it often enough (larger values), which potentially means values are not updated on screen. Go to **Modules | Filters | Manage filters** and set **Text cache lifetime** parameter in the **Common settings** to **1 minutes** or **30 seconds**.

Additionally, turn on **Filter uploaded files** if required, and keep **Filter all strings** turned off as it is only required while using the **multilang** filter:

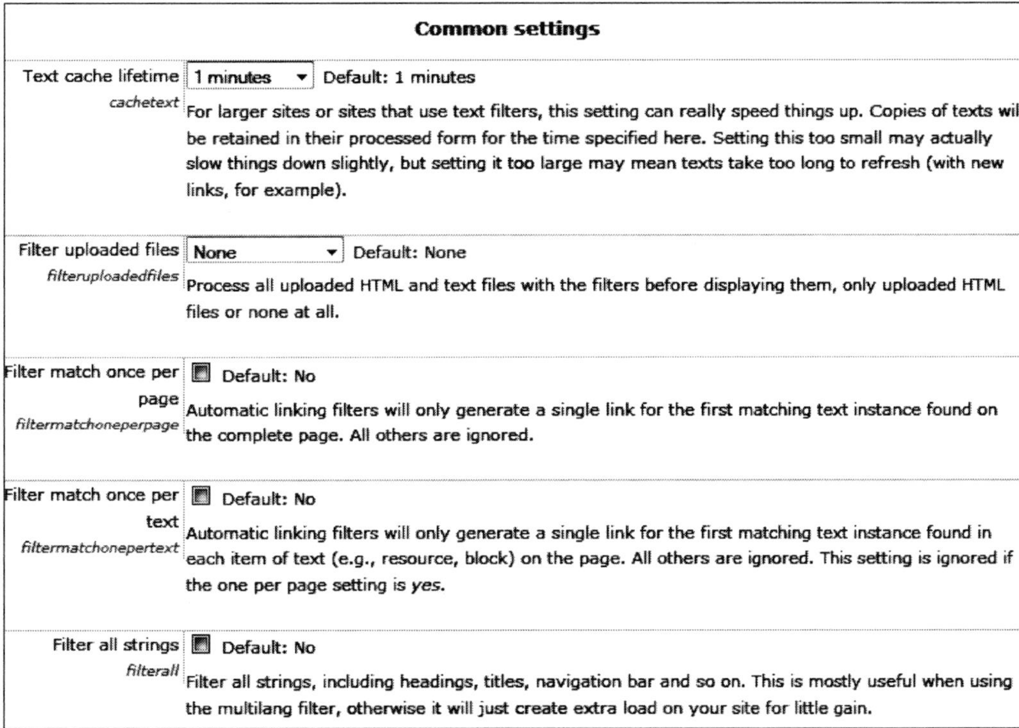
Common settings
Text cache lifetime
cachetext
1 minutes
Default: 1 minutes
For larger sites or sites that use text filters, this setting can really speed things up. Copies of texts will be retained in their processed form for the time specified here. Setting this too small may actually slow things down slightly, but setting it too large may mean texts take too long to refresh (with new links, for example).
Filter uploaded files
filteruploadedfiles
None
Default: None
Process all uploaded HTML and text files with the filters before displaying them, only uploaded HTML files or none at all.
Filter match once per page
filtermatchoneperpage
Default: No
Automatic linking filters will only generate a single link for the first matching text instance found on the complete page. All others are ignored.
Filter match once per text
filtermatchonepertext
Default: No
Automatic linking filters will only generate a single link for the first matching text instance found in each item of text (e.g., resource, block) on the page. All others are ignored. This setting is ignored if the one per page setting is yes.
Filter all strings
filterall
Default: No
Filter all strings, including headings, titles, navigation bar and so on. This is mostly useful when using the multilang filter, otherwise it will just create extra load on your site for little gain.

# Search Settings

There are two unrelated search settings in Moodle, both of which are still in an experimental stage. You can find them at **Miscellaneous | Experimental**:

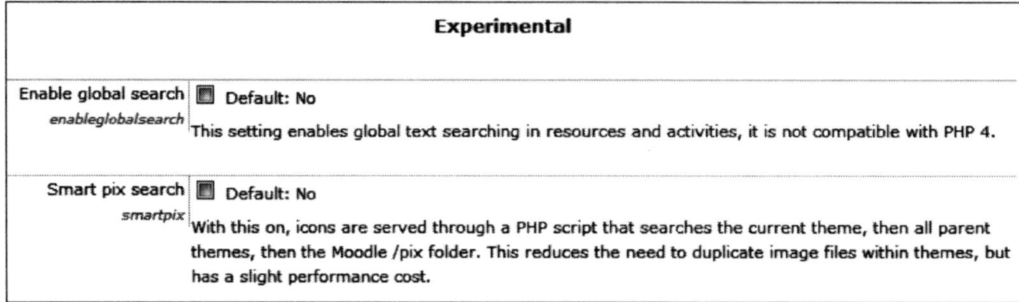

Experimental
Enable global search
enableglobalsearch
Default: No
This setting enables global text searching in resources and activities, it is not compatible with PHP 4.
Smart pix search
smartpix
Default: No
With this on, icons are served through a PHP script that searches the current theme, then all parent themes, then the Moodle /pix folder. This reduces the need to duplicate image files within themes, but has a slight performance cost.


By default, searches apply only within courses. Once you **Enable global search**, any searches spawn across courses and fully consider access rights. Global searches are not only computationally more expensive, but also require PHP 5 to be installed on your server.

If you enable **Smart pix search,** themes that use parent themes will use slightly less disk space and will simply use theme maintenance as images do not have to be duplicated, but loading can take a bit longer.

# Course Backups

As you will learn in the next chapter, course backups have a negative impact on the performance during their execution, especially on larger systems. If possible, schedule the backup procedure when the load on the overall system is low. If you turn off site-wide course backups and use system-level backups instead, you avoid the performance problems, but lose the ability to recover individual items.

# Cron Optimization

We already covered this as a part of the installation, but it is worth re-iterating that the method of how you call the Moodle cron job can have a significant impact on the performance of your system, especially on larger installations.

If the `cron.php` script is invoked over HTTP (either using `wget` or `curl`), more memory is used than calling directly via the `php -f` command.

If you run more than one instance of Moodle on the same server, it is recommended to run the crons in batch mode to avoid simultaneous executions.

## Roles

We dedicated an entire chapter to roles management. Its powerful flexibility comes at a price, which is some minor performance drop if a lot of lookups are required in the context hierarchy (avoid global roles), and if the override mechanisms is applied frequently.

There is also a performance-related setting **Don't return all default role users** in **Users | Permissions | User policies**. If you experience speed problems in courses with a large number of users, enable this option and monitor the performance. We will be dealing with this next.

# Moodle Performance Profiling and Monitoring

When you set up your Moodle system, you will be able to take some initial precautions to optimize the performance of your VLE. However, the real test is when Moodle is in full operation, that is, when the system is under load.

Moodle provides some basic profiling information that you turn on in **Server | Debugging**, where you have to enable the **Performance info** option. This will display information about execution time, RAM usage, number of files in use, CPU usage, and load as well as the record cache hit/miss ratio (less information will be shown on a Windows-based installation). The data will be displayed in the footer of Moodle as long as it is supported by the theme in use:

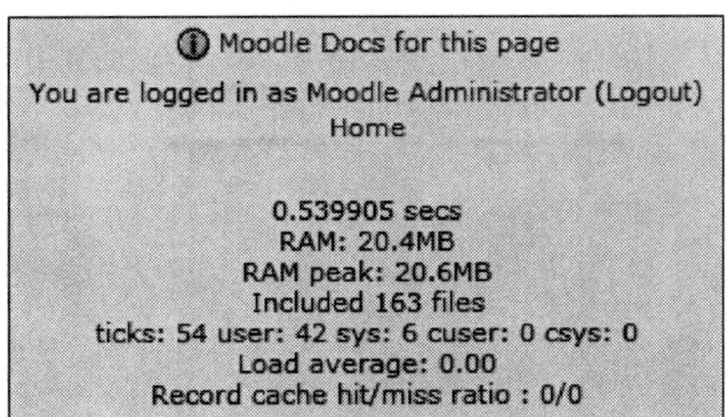


To get Moodle to display more granular profiling information and additional measures, add the following four lines to your `config.php` file:

```
define('MDL_PERF'    , true);
define('MDL_PERFDB'   , true);
define('MDL_PERFTOLOG'   , true);
define('MDL_PERFTOFOOT', true);
```

In addition to the profiling information Moodle provides, you can gather more data using a combination of system-level tools:

- Run a monitor to know what your system is doing (for example, Cacti, an open-source graphing tool).
- Run an alerts and notification monitor (for instance, Nagios).
- Test your network speed (using the `iperf` command).
- Check your disk usage statistics (using the `iostat` command).
- See what processes are doing (using `strace`).

All the mentioned systems and tools are for Linux only and you will find help in their respective documentations.

Now that you have been armed with a number of profiling and monitoring tools, you can change settings (as described throughout the chapter) and see what impact, either positive or negative, they have on the performance of your Moodle system.

# Summary

In this chapter you have learned how to optimize and monitor Moodle's performance.

As you have probably gathered from the content, system and application optimization is not always straightforward. It depends on a range of circumstances such as the system Moodle is running on, the hardware that it utilizes, the network, the number of concurrent users logged in to the system, the types of activities that are carried out, and so on. While the basic optimization is usually straightforward, fine-tuning can become a bit of an art in itself. A lot of trial and error (that is, profiling) will be required to achieve the ideal setup for your Moodle system.

The *Health Check* in *Appendix 1* includes a performance section in which you will find some additional settings that will help to optimize your system.

Now that your system should perform to its maximum potential, let's make sure that you have a professional backup and recovery strategy in place.

# 12 Backup and Restore

Your hosted Moodle will contain a lot of very important data such as coursework, assignments, grades, and all administrative data, for example users and roles. Therefore, it is vital that you have a good backup strategy in place.

Moodle supports two types of backups:

- Course-level backup

**Course backups** are usually run on an ad hoc basis, and only save the selected course. You will learn about how to create course backups, how to restore courses and the related course import facility.

- Site-level backup

The **site backup** option saves all courses and their related data to a specified location at regular intervals. You will learn how to set this up and recover data from it.

Both mechanisms will be covered in detail before we look at **system-level backups,** which includes Moodle backups (covering the Moodle software as well as the data stored in it) and snapshot creation (full system images).

## Course-Level Backup and Restore

We will first have a look at the backup procedure before going into details of how to recover data during the restore operation.

# Course Backup

To back up a course it is best if you are inside that course, where you have to select the **Backups** link in the **Administration** block. A list of all course elements will be shown. Alternatively, you can restore courses from within course categories. Go to **Courses | Add/edit courses** in the **Site Administration** block and select the category in which the course to be backed up resides. Select the **Backup** icon (by default a **yellow** box), which directs you to the same screen. The first backup screen contains three parts that will be dealt with separately.

## Backup Options

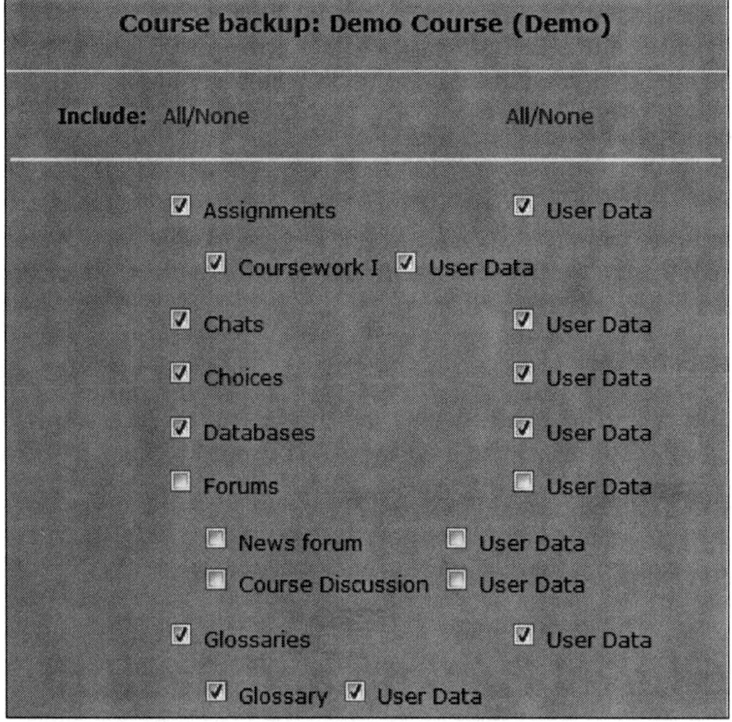


In the screenshot, all learning resources are shown to be grouped by activity and resource type. By default all elements are selected. If you wish to exclude any individual items, you have to deselect them. For instance, in the screenshot, **Forums** has been excluded from the backup.

Moodle distinguishes between course content and user data. For example, in a forum activity, the forum description and all settings are classified as course content whereas all posts to a forum are classified as user data. We will have a closer look at this shortly.

The **All** and **None** links above the course content and user data are shortcuts to select and deselect all tick boxes, respectively.

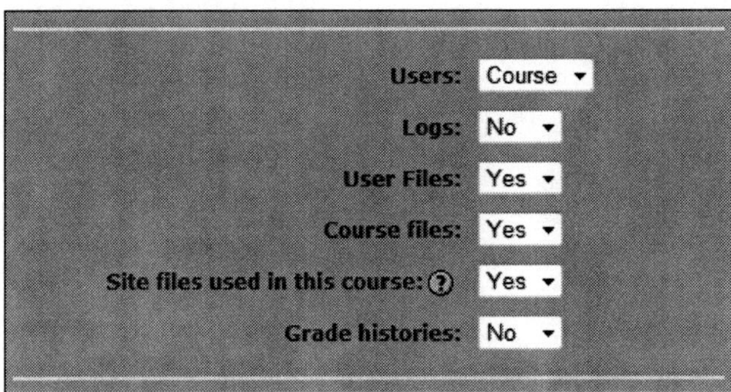


As can be seen in the preceding screenshot, the following settings are available:

| Setting | Description |
|---|---|
| **Users** | User records can be included in the backup. The following three options are available:<br>• All: Includes all users in your Moodle system<br>• Course: Includes only users who are enrolled to the course (default)<br>• None: Excludes user data |
| **Logs** | Specify whether log files should be excluded (default) or be stored in the archive. Beware that log files can enlarge the backup files significantly. |
| **User Files** | Specify whether user files should be included (default). This includes all student submissions for assignments and other file uploads. |
| **Course files** | Specify whether the content of the files area should be backed up. The `backupdata` folder is excluded from this inclusion. |
| **Site files used in this course** | Specify whether files located in the **Site files** area should be included (default). |
| **Grade histories** | Moodle keeps a grade history. Specify whether it should be included in the backup archive. |

If the course is a metacourse, an additional setting is displayed that allows you to specify whether the relationship with other courses is to be included in the backup:

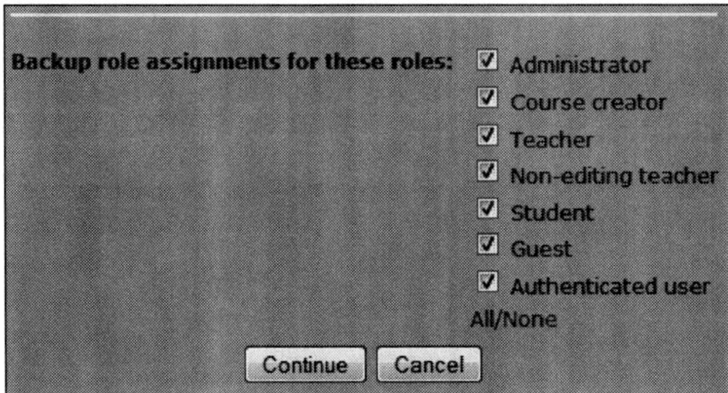


Within a course, either the administrator or the editing teacher(s) will have certain roles assigned. These can include standard enrollments to the course, as well as locally assigned roles (both for predefined and user-defined roles such as the **Parent** role in the screenshot). To include these role assignments in the backup, leave all roles ticked; otherwise deselect the ones you wish to exclude.

# Content-Only versus Full-Course Backups

There are two types of course backups that you are likely to perform:

- Content-only backups
- Full-course backups

If you wish to pass a course on to another user or make it available for download, **content-only backup** is the best option. As the name suggests, it only contains content that can be passed on to another person without transferring any information about users, roles, grades, and so on.

To perform a content-only backup, you have to select the **None** link on the top right corner of the "Backup options" page. This excludes all user data from the course. Additionally, you set the backup options to the following settings:

- **Users** = **None**
- **Logs** = **No**
- **User files** = **No**
- **Course files** = **Yes**
- **Site files used in this course** = **Yes**
- **Grade history** = **No**

If you wish to back up a course for potential recovery purposes, you should create a **full-course backup**, which includes user data (for example, forum posts), course data, and user information. To do this, leave all the settings at their default values, except **Grade histories**.

If you wish to back up the log information of the course as well, the **Logs** setting has to be changed to **Yes**. Bear in mind that logs can be extremely large and often exceed multiple gigabytes.

Whether you choose to create a content-only or a full-course backup, Moodle will automatically include the settings of a course, topic labels, as well as the positioning of blocks that have been added. However, sometimes there are problems with the content created by third-party add-ons. If you encounter any issues, you will have to exclude these items from the backup.

# Finalizing Backup

Once the **Continue** button has been pressed, you have to specify a name for the backup file. The default name is

`backup-<course short name>-<year><month><day>-<hour><minute>.zip.`

Additionally, a list of all elements included in the backup is listed on screen. Once you have confirmed this information, the actual archive is created in the `backupdata` folder of the course. This can take a few minutes depending on the amount of course content. After completion, a summary message is shown.

Moodle creates a customized file format for backups known as the `Moodle backup format`. A Moodle backup file is a compressed ZIP file consisting of an XML file (which describes the content of the file) and the actual data about user and course, and log information.

Backups sometimes fail on large courses, often silently. The cause is usually the backup process that runs out of time or memory. This usually happens on commercial web hosts that are not dedicated to Moodle. If this happens, increase the `max_execution_time` value in your `php.ini` file. Also make sure that your Path to zip is set in Server | System Paths if you use a Unix system (see path settings in previous Chapter).

# Course Restore

To restore an entire course or parts thereof, use the **Restore** link within a course or in the course category screen. Moodle recognizes backup files and only displays the **Restore** option when it finds an XML file in the above mentioned format inside the ZIP archive:

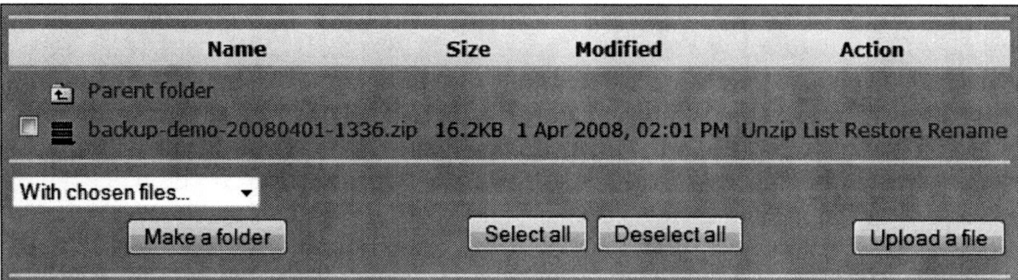


By default, all backup archives are stored in the `backupdata` directory in the course files. In the example shown in the preceding screenshot, a single course called **backup-demo-20080401-1336.zip** is present. From its name we already know that the course is called "demo" and was backed up on April 1st, 2008 at 13.36.

Backups from a different version of Moodle than the one you are using can cause difficulties. If you are experiencing difficulties, check out the FAQ covering backups at `http://docs.moodle.org/en/Backup_FAQ`.

Select **Restore** and confirm the start of the restore process. The next screen displays information about the course backup (course name, course summary, backup name, Moodle version, and backup date/time) as well as backup details. Once you have confirmed this screen, you are confronted with a number of upload settings:

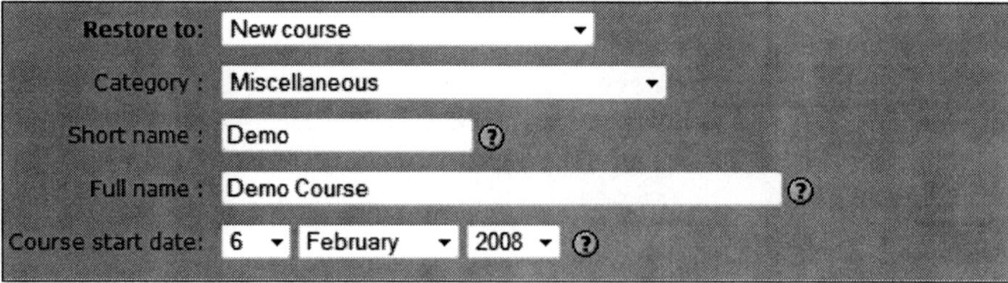

Restore to: New course
Category : Miscellaneous
Short name : Demo
Full name : Demo Course
Course start date: 6 February 2008

| Setting | Description |
|---|---|
| **Restore to** | • New course<br>A new course is created using the data in the backup file.<br>• Existing course, deleting it first<br>An existing course is replaced, deleting all data that was present.<br>• Existing course, adding data to it<br>Two courses are merged. If an activity or resource with the same name exists, one will not be overriden, but rather both will be kept intact. |
| **Category** | Specify the category in which the new course will be created, otherwise an existing course will be selected from. |
| **Short name** | Many organizations have a shorthand way of referring to a course. The field is compulsory as it will be used in several places where the full name is inappropriate (such as in the breadcrumb trail). |
| **Full name** | The full name of the course will be displayed at the top of the screen and in the course listings. |
| **Course start date** | Starting date of the course. |

The next part of the screen displays the course content and user data that has been stored in the archive. The format is identical to the backup screen. By default all data present is selected. If you wish to narrow down the data to be restored, you have to deselect items manually or via the familiar **All** and **None** shortcuts:

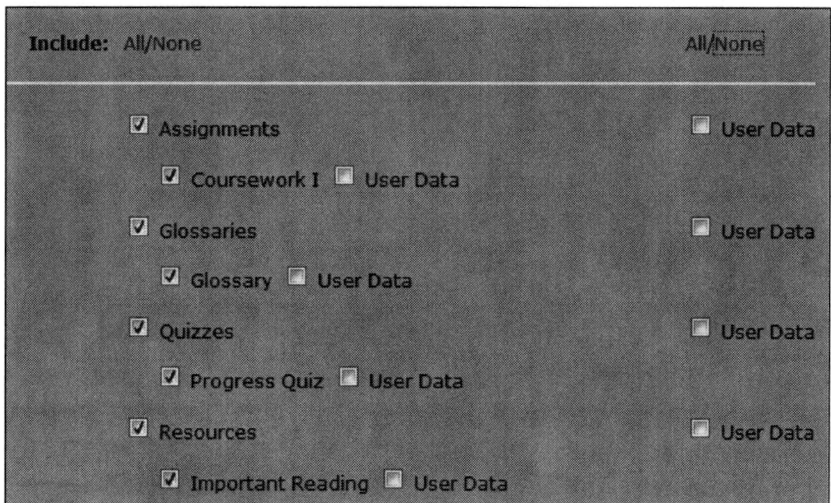

To upload a course or to copy a course shell into Moodle, only resource-related information should be selected (as in the screenshot). User data should only be included when restoring lost data or when transferring a course from one system to another, where user activity has to be preserved.

If data is added to an existing course and an item (for example, a forum) already exists, it will not be overridden with the data from the backup file. Instead, a second version with the same name will be created.

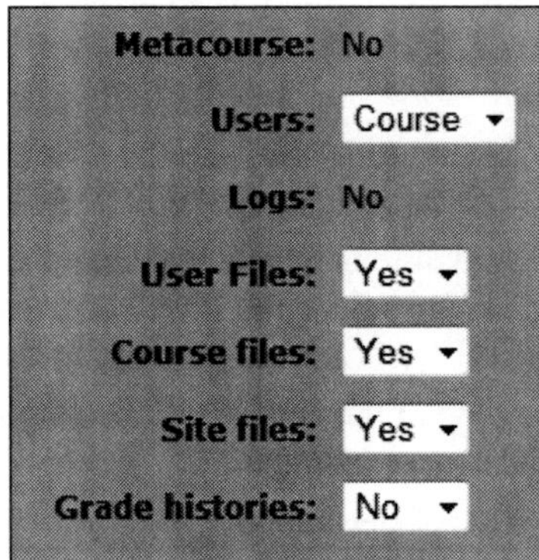


These settings are identical to the backup creation. Values can only be changed if they have been included in the backup in the first place. If groups and/or groupings data is present in the backup file, an additional option is displayed under the **Users settings**.

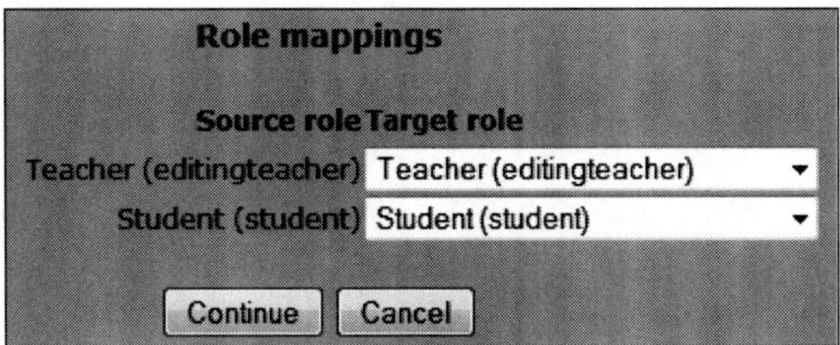


If user data has been stored in the backup, all roles are displayed and have to be mapped onto their counterparts in the new course. If you stay within your existing Moodle system, the mappings should be the same for the source and the target role. If you use custom roles, which do not exist on one of the systems, you will have to provide appropriate mappings.

Once the settings have been changed, press **Continue**. If you have selected the restore target to be an existing course, you have to select a course from the presented list:

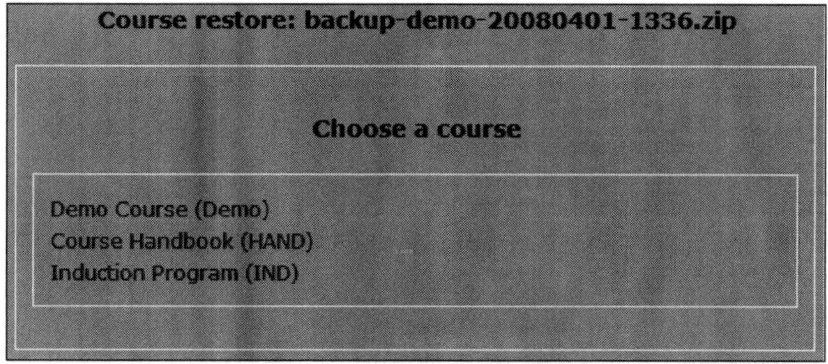


After one last confirmation screen, a final screen will display the result of the uploading exercise. The selected items will now be available in the new or existing course.

> If your Moodle is hosted on a Unix system, make sure **Path to unzip** is set in **Server | System Paths**, as this will speed up the backup process significantly. The default value on Linux systems is `/usr/bin/unzip`. The same should be kept in mind while "Finalizing Backup", which was the previous section we seen.

# Course Import

It is sometimes necessary to copy data from some other course. To achieve this, Moodle provides the **Import** course data feature. However, unlike the backup function, it will not import user data, such as assignment submissions or forum posts. It will only import the structure of activities. For example, you might want to import a single quiz from one course to another.

Teachers are allowed to import only those courses for which they have editing rights; as administrator this restriction does not apply. This mechanism bypasses the requirement for a backup and restore procedure, if you want to copy course content from one course to another and do not require the user data.

First, select the **Import** link from the **Administration** side-block. Ignore the **Import groups** panel at the bottom of the screen.

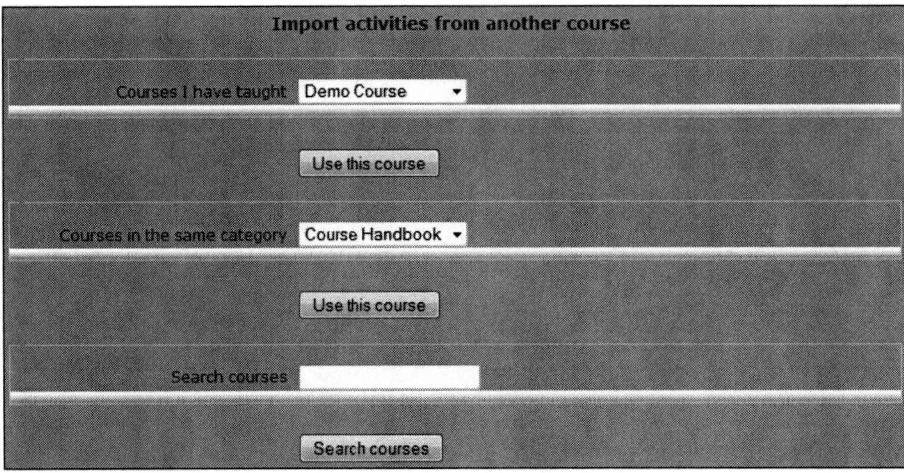


Next, select the course you wish to import either from courses you have taught, from courses that are in the same category, or via the search course facility.

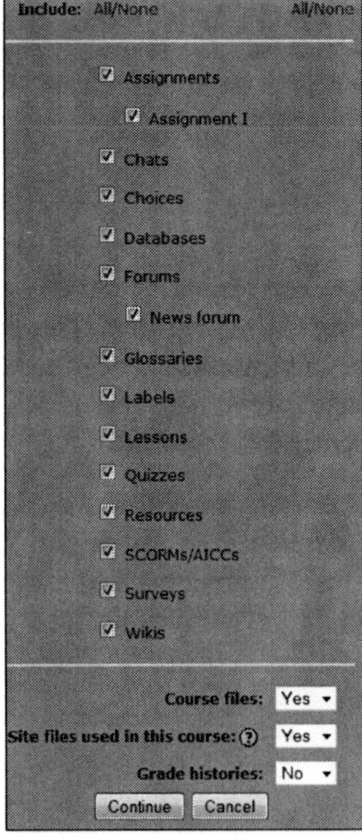

As seen in this screeshot you will then be presented with a check box list from which you can select any activities or resources you wish to import. The **Course files** option at the bottom dictates whether uploaded files are included in the import or not. The **Site file used in this course** and **Grade histories** options are the same as in backing up and restoring courses.

Finally, you have to click **Continue** three times to start the actual data import operation. The completion will be confirmed with a final information screen.

# Site-Level Backups

So far, we have covered how to back up a single course. The site-level backup performs the same operation for every course on the system, including the front page, which is also a course (the front page backup uses the site name).

# Backup Settings

To schedule site backups, go to **Courses | Backups** in the **Site Administration** block. You will see a number of settings:

| Setting | Description |
|---|---|
| **Include Modules** | Includes course modules (activities and resources) in backup archive. Sometimes there are problems with third-party add-ons. |
| **Include module user data** | Includes data added by users in modules such as assignments. |
| **Metacourse** | If selected, metacourse relationships to other courses will be included in the backup archive. |
| **Users** | User records are included in the backup. The following two options are available:<br>• All (default): Includes all users in your Moodle system.<br>• Course: Includes only users who are enrolled to the course. |
| **Logs** | Specify whether the log files should be excluded (default) or be stored in the archive. Beware that log files can enlarge the backup files significantly. |
| **User Files** | When switched on, user files such as assignment submissions and forum posts will be saved. |
| **Course Files** | When switched on, course files will be included. These are the files and directories located in the files area. |
| **Site files** | Specify if files located in the Site files area should be included. |

| Setting | Description |
|---|---|
| **Messages** | When switched on, any sent messages will be included. |
| **Blogs** | If enabled, blog entries will be included in the backup. |
| **Keep** | Specify the number of backups to be kept. Beware that a large number will have an impact on disk usage. Older versions will be deleted automatically. |
| **Active** | Turns automatic backup on and off (default). Make sure your backup is activated! |
| **Schedule** | Specify the days of the week on which the backup has to run. |
| **Execute at** | Specify the time of the day when the backup is to be executed. |
| **Save to** | If left blank (default), each course backup archive will be saved in the respective `backupdata` folders.<br><br>If you wish to keep all the backups at the same location, you have to specify the full (absolute) path to the directory. In hosted environments, there is likely to be a directory called something like `/srv/www/vhosts/.../httpdocs/moodledata`. |

For the backup to start automatically at the specified time, the **cron process** has to be set up correctly, which is already covered in Chapter 2.

The recovery of courses is identical to the way data is restored from course-level backup archives. The site-level backup creates a standard compressed ZIP file for each course in the Moodle XML backup format, and leaves the ZIP file in the `backupdata` folder of each course.

# Backup Strategy

There are a number of issues to consider when running automatic site-wide Moodle backups:

- Backup content

  Make sure that everything included in the archives is needed, and anything that is not required is excluded. For instance, do you have to back up the entire log file every night?

- Backup size

  The size of the backup files can be potentially huge (multiple gigabytes). Ensure that you only keep the backups that are required.

- Backup timing

  The backup operation is a CPU-and hard disk-intensive operation. Make sure to schedule it when the load on the site is relatively low. If you run multiple sites on the same server, it is a good idea to time-stagger the backups.

- Backup frequency

  Do you need daily backups or are weekly backups sufficient? Are there periods (such as summer holidays) when you can switch off the backup facility altogether?

- Backup location

  By default all backup files are saved to the respective courses, which means the backups are held on the same server as Moodle itself. If you have to recover multiple courses, you have to locate each archive separately, which is potentially a very time-consuming exercise.

  You might want to consider copying all files to a single directory, which is then backed up on an external device (tape, external disk, NAS drive, and so on). An even better alternative is to include the directory in the organization-wide backup.

# Drawbacks of Site-Level Backups

Site-level backups are a great way to automate course backups, and to make the life of individual teachers and instructors easier. However, there are a number of drawbacks that should be stressed:

- Course backups are potentially very expensive in terms of time and CPU usage. It is not uncommon that backups time out, especially on commercially hosted systems that are not dedicated to Moodle.
- If teachers and instructors run their own backups, there is a likelihood of duplication of archives, which should be avoided if possible.
- As the name suggests, you only back up courses, not the entire system. While this is sufficient if you have to recover a simple course or a number of activities, it does not provide a solution to the scenario when the entire system has to be restored.

If possible, you should not use the course backup facility as your primary backup system. Instead, system-level backups should be used, which we will look at next.

# System-Level Backups

System-level backups cannot be configured or executed from within Moodle. Instead, they will have to be set up on system (shell) level. If your system is hosted externally, there is a possibility that you will not have access to the system level, which will prevent you from performing this type of backup. That means it's time to change to another host!

There are two types of system backups that are not mutually exclusive:

- Moodle backups: They create an archive of Moodle, the course content, and the user data on shell level.
- Snapshots: They create an image of the system, which is used if a system has to be recovered in its totality.

# Moodle Backup

Moodle distinguishes between Moodle software and the data that is stored in it. The advantage of this separation becomes apparent when creating backups: A software backup is only required when an update has been installed, whereas the data has to be backed up more frequently.

## Moodle Software

Backing up the Moodle software is straightforward. All you have to do is create a copy of the directory and all its sub-directories where the Moodle software is installed (usually called `moodle`). Most administrators would create a single archive of the directory for easier handling (in Unix using the tar command with the -cvf parameters: `tar -cvf <backupfile> .`). This step is usually only required before a system upgrade or when you need to archive your entire system.

## Moodle Data

Moodle stores its data in two separate locations:

- Moodle database

  Most content is stored in the Moodle database. You can either use the export feature of phpMyAdmin (if installed) or use the following `mysqldump` shell command for MySQL to create a single backup file:

```
mysqldump -u <username> -p [-h <databasehost>] -C -Q -e -a
<database> > <backup-file>.sql
```

The `<username>` has to be replaced with the database username. `-p` will ask you for a password and the `<databasehost>` is only required if the database is located on a separate server. `<database>` is the name of the database and `<backup-file>` is the name of the archive to be created. It is common practice to use the `.sql` extension.

To recover the database dump, use the following `mysql` shell command:

```
mysql -p <database> < <backup-file>.sql
```

For more information on mysql and mysqldump, check out the reference sites at `http://www.mysql.com`.

- Moodle data directory (by default called moodledata)

  This is where all uploaded content resides, for instance, assignments, user profiles pictures, and so on. Like the Moodle system, all that has to be done is to create a copy of the directory and all its sub-directories. Most administrators would create a single archive of the directory for simpler handling (in Unix using the `tar` command with the `-cvf` parameters).

The advantage of this approach is that it is less resource-intensive and recovery of the full Moodle system is far more straightforward. However, it is almost impossible to retrieve individual activities as is possible with course backups.

# Snapshot Creation

The creation of snapshots is only briefly mentioned for completeness as it is not a Moodle administrator role, but a system administrator task. However, you should make sure that such a mechanism is set up in case of hardware failures.

A snapshot is basically an image of the entire partition on the hard disk that contains the Moodle software as well as all data (database and data directory). The advantage of the snapshot is that the entire system can be rolled back to the point when the image was created. However, any data that has been added or modified since this point will be overridden. Snapshots cannot be used to recover a single course or parts thereof, but can only be used for a full replacement of the system.

No matter what combination of backups you choose, frequently verify that the backup procedure is actually working. There is nothing worse than a false sense of security, that is, assuming that all your data is backed up when it isn't!

# Summary

In this chapter you have learned the various ways of backing up different types of data in Moodle. You learned how to create course-level, site-level, and system-level backups as well as data recovery from each type. It is important that your Moodle backup strategy fits in with your organization's overall disaster recovery plan.

Moodle offers a good range of backup and restore options. However, sometimes there are problems with some of the built-in backup and recovery operations. The common causes for problems are time-outs, memory overload, archives that cannot be read, and third-party add-ons. Be aware that these issues exist and run test recoveries to be on the safer side.

# 13
# Installing Third-Party Add-Ons

There exists a plethora of third-party Moodle software that add new functionalities, fix problems, or integrate Moodle with external systems. In this chapter you will learn the essentials about installing third-party add-ons.

- Good and bad third-party add-ons
  Since externally developed software is not scrutinized by Moodle's quality assurance process, you have to make a judgment about the trustworthiness of non-core add-ons. A checklist of criteria is provided to make this decision a bit easier.
- Popular third-party add-ons
  There are over 400 titles to choose from; for your convenience we discuss the most popular ones.
- Installation of third-party add-ons
  We describe the installation process using the popular Feedback activity module as an example.
- Uninstalling third-party add-ons
  Here we describe how to uninstall third-party add-ons.

Let's start with an overview of third-party software.

## Third-Party Software: An Overview

Moodle comes with a number of core modules that include activities (for example, quiz and assignments), filters (multimedia or algebra), and blocks (calendar) as well as other components such as enrolment and authentication plug-ins, grade reports, question types, and so on. While the provided functionality sufficiently satisfies the vast majority of users, there is a growing demand for additional software.

Due to the open-source nature of Moodle and its modularity (that's what the "M" in Moodle stands for after all), it is relatively straightforward for developers to add new functionality or modify existing features. These can range from minor modifications or hacks to full-blown modules. There is a **Modules and plugins** link from the main Moodle page at `http://moodle.org`, which directs you to the database of the available third-party software.

Each add-on has **Name**, **Type**, and **Status** (**Contributed**, **Core**, **Standard**, and **Third-Party**) minimum requirements (stated under heading **Requires**), and **Summary**. The list contains core modules and plug-ins in case you have deleted them from Moodle. The following types of add-ons are available for download, most of which are self-explanatory:

| Type | Description |
|---|---|
| **Activity Module** | New Moodle activity to be used in courses. |
| **Admin Report** | Additional site-wide reports. |
| **Assignment Type** | Either additional assignment types or additions to any of the four existing ones. |
| **Authentication Method** | New authentication plug-ins such as Google Apps, Joomla, and OpenID. |
| **Block** | (Plenty of) additional Moodle blocks. |
| **Course Format** | Different ways to organize courses. |
| **Course Report** | Additional course-level reports. |
| **Enrolment Method** | New enrolment plug-ins. |
| **Filter** | Extra filters to be applied to text written in the HTML editor. |
| **Integration** | Collection of add-ons to support external systems. |
| **Major Patch** | Significant code changes to core code. |
| **Other** | Add-ons that don't fit in any of the other categories. |
| **Question Import/Export Format** | Additional importers and exporters for questions from other quiz tools and VLEs. |
| **Question Type** | New question types to be used in question banks. |
| **Quiz Report** | The gradebook supports report plug-ins that are found in this category. |
| **Resource Type** | New Moodle resource type to be used in courses. |
| **Small Hack** | Minor code changes to the core code. |
| **SSO Plugin** | Single sign-on plug-ins. |
| **User Profile Field** | Changes to user profiles. Some of this functionality can be implemented via the **User profile fields** option. |

There are currently over 400 third-party Moodle software titles and the number is growing continuously. You will find everything, from the weird and wonderful to some very powerful add-ons. A search facility at the bottom allows you to apply filters to the database of modules:

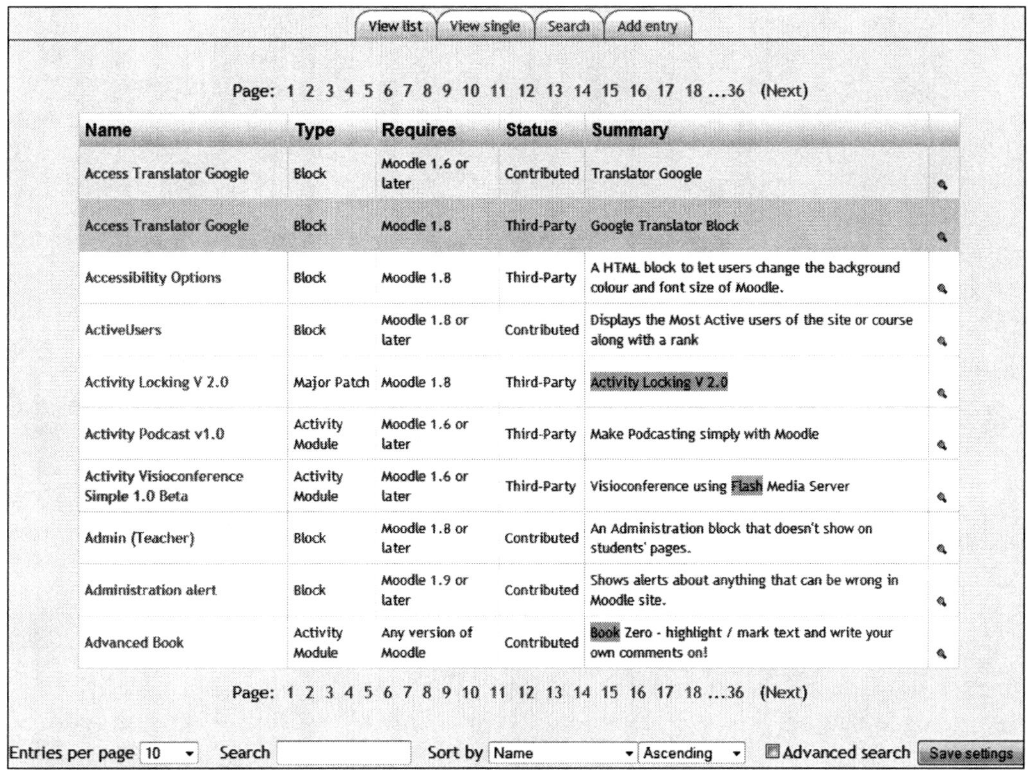

View list | View single | Search | Add entry

Page: 1 2 3 4 5 6 7 8 9 10 11 12 13 14 15 16 17 18 ...36 (Next)

| Name | Type | Requires | Status | Summary |
|---|---|---|---|---|
| Access Translator Google | Block | Moodle 1.6 or later | Contributed | Translator Google |
| Access Translator Google | Block | Moodle 1.8 | Third-Party | Google Translator Block |
| Accessibility Options | Block | Moodle 1.8 | Third-Party | A HTML block to let users change the background colour and font size of Moodle. |
| ActiveUsers | Block | Moodle 1.8 or later | Contributed | Displays the Most Active users of the site or course along with a rank |
| Activity Locking V 2.0 | Major Patch | Moodle 1.8 | Third-Party | Activity Locking V 2.0 |
| Activity Podcast v1.0 | Activity Module | Moodle 1.6 or later | Third-Party | Make Podcasting simply with Moodle |
| Activity Visioconference Simple 1.0 Beta | Activity Module | Moodle 1.6 or later | Third-Party | Visioconference using Flash Media Server |
| Admin (Teacher) | Block | Moodle 1.8 or later | Contributed | An Administration block that doesn't show on students' pages. |
| Administration alert | Block | Moodle 1.9 or later | Contributed | Shows alerts about anything that can be wrong in Moodle site. |
| Advanced Book | Activity Module | Any version of Moodle | Contributed | Book Zero - highlight / mark text and write your own comments on! |

Page: 1 2 3 4 5 6 7 8 9 10 11 12 13 14 15 16 17 18 ...36 (Next)

Entries per page 10 Search Sort by Name Ascending Advanced search Save settings

Once you click on an add-on, you will be directed to a dedicated page that provides additional information about the contributed piece of software, along with comments, documentation, ratings, discussions, and a link to download the software.

# Good Add-Ons and Bad Add-Ons

Every module that is part of the core Moodle has gone through a thorough quality assurance process. The potential problem with third-party add-ons is that you don't know anything about the quality of the software.

While it is possible to uninstall modules if they don't fit the purpose, you will have to make sure that you don't put barriers in place for future updates. If an add-on is not maintained, it is unlikely to support any forthcoming versions of Moodle and you will have to delete the module already in use or you won't be able to upgrade your system.

There are a number of criteria that indicate whether an add-on is trustworthy or not.

- Popularity

  Moodle keeps statistics about downloads from Moodle, which you can find at `download.moodle.org/stats.php`. At the bottom of the page you will see a table listing the top 50 plug-ins downloaded in the last 60 days. While this is no guarantee, the more popular a module, the more likely it is to be of a high standard.
- Ratings

  Each add-on page allows users to rate the software. Both, the quality and quantity of the ratings are relevant. Anything over 70% usually indicates a good add-on.
- Level of active support

  Some of the most valuable third-party (and even core modules such as Workshop) add-ons have vanished because they are unsupported. Your best bet is if the add-on is supported by a major stakeholder in Moodle such as the **Open University**, or a Moodle Partner such as **Synergy Learning**.
- Forum posts and comments

  Users are encouraged to post comments, problems, and good reviews about each module. Read through the posts to get an idea of what other users have experienced. Be suspicious about modules that are not talked about at all.
- Documentation

  Each add-on should have a dedicated page in MoodleDocs. It is usually not a good sign if the page does not exist or is only a wiki stub. Also, it is good practice to keep a change log for the developed software.
- Standalone

  It is a good practice that third-party add-ons do not modify any core code (known as patches supplied in the form of `diff` files). This is important as the changes will be overridden with every Moodle update and the modifications will have to be reapplied. While it is not always possible for a programmer to implement this principle, it should only be done if absolutely necessary.
- Supported versions

  Support for the current version and one or more previous versions is a sign that the software is being actively maintained.

- Code

  If you can read PHP code, have a look at the actual source code of the add-on. Try to find answers to the following questions:

  - Is the code well structured and easy to follow?
  - Is the source code well-commented on?
  - Does the module follow the Moodle coding guidelines (`docs.moodle.org/en/Coding`)?

- Developer

  Some developers are known to produce very well-written Moodle add-ons. Programmers affiliated with any of the **Moodle Partners** are usually a good bet.

# Popular Add-Ons

The following is a list of some popular third-party Moodle add-ons (in alphabetic order), available through **Modules and plugins link** at `http://moodle.org`, as well as a brief description for each plug-in:

- **Accessibility Options (Block)**

  The block allows students to change the font size and background color of their Moodle site.

- **ActiveUsers (Block)**

  The configurable block displays the most active users along with a ranking. Each user is a given a rank calculated as the Z score of the number of hits.

- **Book (Activity Module)**

  This activity allows users to create multi-page resources in a book-like format.

- **Certificate (Activity Module)**

  The fully customizable activity generates PDF certificates for students.

- **Feedback (Activity Module)**

  The activity module allows users to create and conduct surveys to collect feedback. The module is planned to be included in the core of Moodle 2.0. We will be using the **Feedback** module as an example for installing a third-party add-on later in this chapter.

- **Flash (Activity Module)**

  The module allows developers to embed their Flash movies in Moodle in an integrated way, so that they can take advantage of the gradebook, backup/restore facility, and so on.

- **Jmol (Filter)**

  The filter displays 3D chemical and biological molecular files directly, using the Java-based open-source Jmol molecule viewer (`www.jmol.org`).
- **Marking (Block)**

  The block displays a list of courses that contain assignments and require marking. Only assignments that have unassessed work are listed, and each assignment displays the number of pieces of work that need marking.
- **MRBS (Block)**

  The block integrates with the open-source **MRBS** (**Meeting Room Booking System**), which allows the allocation of physical resources and locations.
- **MySQL Admin (Other)**

  This module is a repackaged version of phpMyAdmin. Once installed, you will see a new item, namely, **Database** in the **Server** menu in the **Site Administration** block.
- **Quickmail (Block)**

  The block allows sending emails with an optional attachment to other users in the same course. A history of all your sent emails is recorded for later reference.

# Installing Third-Party Add-Ons

A good advice is to avoid experimenting with new add-ons on a production site. Most organizations set up a shadow of site of their live server that is used as a sandbox. Once the installation is successful, the procedure is re-applied on the production site.

Additionally, it is recommended that you make a complete site backup before installing any third-party software. That way you can roll back in case of a disaster.

The installation of third-party add-ons requires a number of steps that you should follow:

1. Download an add-on.
2. Put Moodle in maintenance mode.
3. Unzip files (either locally or on the server).
4. Copy files in appropriate location(s).
5. Start the Moodle admin page to run the installer.
6. Test the add-on (and remove if it does not work; refer the uninstall section ahead).
7. Put Moodle out of maintenance mode.

Most add-ons are structured in a similar way. However, some modules either don't follow this standardized approach or require other steps, especially when the module communicates with other software systems. Each plug-in should contain a file (usually called README) with the installation instructions. It is important that you read these first before installing a module.

# Installing the Feedback Module

Out of the available options to demonstrate the installation of a third-party add-on, we have chosen the **Feedback** module for a number of reasons. It satisfies all the criteria we just discussed: It is a very useful and popular activity, it is packaged in the standard format, and it will be added to the core of Moodle very soon.

After locating the add-on in the **Modules and plugins** database, download the latest version of the software.

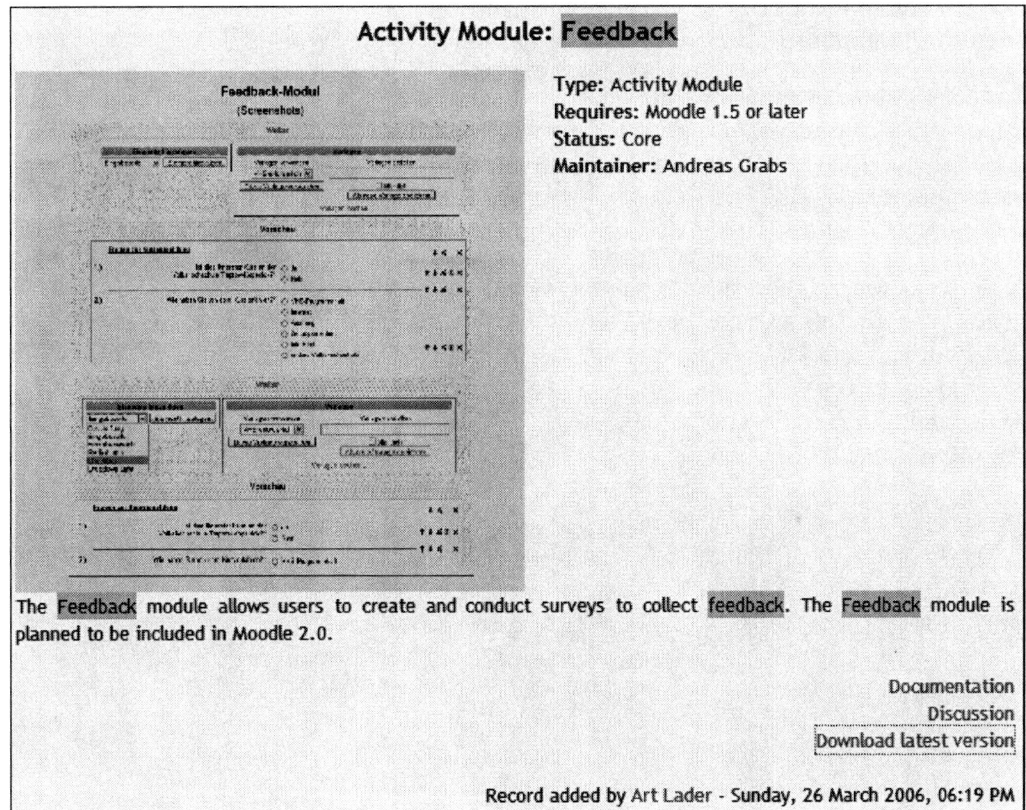

Next, put Moodle in maintenance mode (**Server | Maintenance mode** in the **Site Administration** block). While it is possible to add most modules while Moodle is in use, it is not recommended to do so as this can lead to some unforeseen problems.

The **Feedback** module follows the standardized structure of add-ons, that is, it includes the same directory hierarchy as Moodle. The ZIP file contains two folders: `mod` (the activity module) and `blocks` (an optional side block). After unzipping the downloaded file, you have to copy the files and directories in each folder to their corresponding directories on your Moodle site. That is, the content (a directory called `feedback`) in the `blocks` directory has to be copied to the Moodle `blocks` directory and the content (another directory called `feedback`) in the `mod` directory in the Moodle `mod` directory. You might have to change the user and group to the same as the folders in those directories.

Often, the ZIP file contains the same directory hierarchy as Moodle. If so, it is possible to simply unzip the files in the Moodle root directory. However, be careful that you are in the correct directory. The steps described in the previous paragraph are a bit more time-consuming, but usually safer.

Both components contain so-called `lang` files that contain the localization strings for multiple languages. In the case of activity modules, they can be left in the `mod/feedback/lang` folder. The `lang` file for the feedback block is called `block_feedback.php`, which has to be copied into the corresponding lang folder of `moodle/moodledata`. This is described in the `README.txt` file.

Now go to your Moodle admin page, which is located at `http://<yoursite>/admin`. The module behind this page will recognize that a new module has to be installed, and will kick off the installer. In the case of **Feedback** module, a number of database tables with fields are created and populated with values. The success of each database operation will be displayed as well as the overall success of the installation:

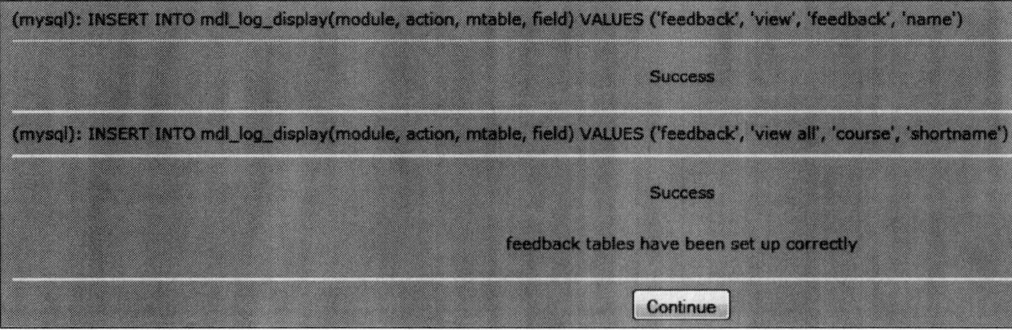

That's it! All you have to do now is to make sure the module works properly in Moodle. In the case of **Feedback** module, go to **Modules | Activities | Manage Activities** and you will see an entry for the activity. It is also worth adding the activity to a course to make sure everything is working properly:

| Activity module | Activities | Version | Hide/Show | Delete | Settings |
|---|---|---|---|---|---|
| Assignment | 8 | 2007101511 | | Delete | Settings |
| Chat | 2 | 2007101509 | | Delete | Settings |
| Choice | 4 | 2007101509 | | Delete | |
| Database | 0 | 2007101512 | | Delete | Settings |
| Exercise | 0 | 2007110500 | | Delete | |
| Feedback | 1 | 2008050106 | | Delete | |
| Forum | 13 | 2007101512 | | | Settings |

Finally, don't forget to disable Moodle's maintenance mode and let your users know that a new functionality is available.

# Installing Other Add-Ons

We demonstrated how to install the **Feedback** activity, which follows the typical installation process. Other add-ons have to be copied to their corresponding locations, for example filters are located in the `filter` directory. As mentioned before, the locations should be described in the `README` file. Any anomalies, such as the copying of the lang files in the **Feedback** block, will also be explained in the instructions.

Add-ons which usually require more installation effort are the ones that provide a link to other software systems, both open-source and commercial. These usually have the type of Integration. Examples are the Turnitin Plugin for plagiarism prevention and the MIS Upload Tool for importing user data from Capita SIMS and Serco CMIS.

If you are attempting to install these modules, make sure you have created a backup of Moodle and its database as some add-ons modify core code and the database. If this is the case, you have to re-apply the changes every time you update Moodle (unless you check out the Moodle source using CVS in which case changes will be automatically merged, and you would be asked to resolve them if any conflict arises).

# Uninstalling Third-Party Add-Ons

If you decide to uninstall a third-party add-on, and if the module is listed in the **Activities**, **Blocks**, or **Filters** section in the **Modules** menu, you have to use the provided **delete** option.

Deleting an add-on will also delete all user data associated with the module irreversibly!

The delete operation will remove all data associated with the module and display a message to confirm the success. To complete the deletion and prevent the module re-installing next time, go to the admin page and delete the directory from your server that is displayed on the screen:

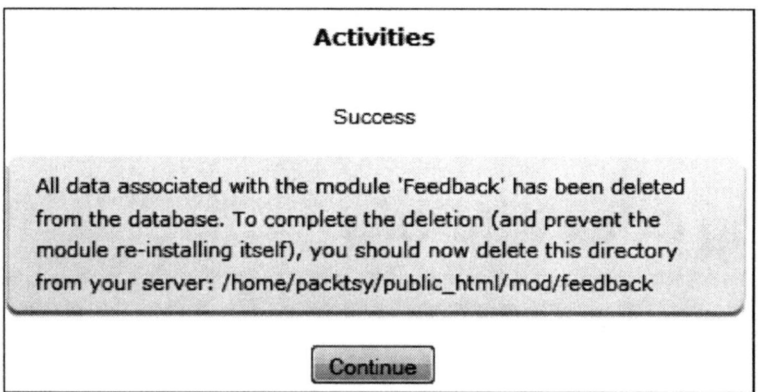

Activities
Success
All data associated with the module 'Feedback' has been deleted from the database. To complete the deletion (and prevent the module re-installing itself), you should now delete this directory from your server: /home/packtsy/public_html/mod/feedback
Continue


The message about deleting the directory only applies to blocks, activity modules, filters, question types, authorization, enrolment plug-ins, and other modular software components. It does not apply to other types of third-party software such as hacks, patches, and so on, which have to be removed manually.

# Summary

In this chapter you have learned the essentials about third-party Moodle add-ons.

You hopefully got a flavor of the breadth and depth of additional functionality that is available for your VLE. It not only demonstrates the extensibility and popularity of Moodle, but also shows a significant benefit of open-source software and its ability to programmatically enhance a program to a user's requirements.

Another form of extending the reach of Moodle is to network it with other Moodle systems. We will cover this in the following chapter.

# 14
# Moodle Networking

Moodle provides a unique functionality that lets you network multiple Moodle sites. This is useful in a number of contexts, for example when you want to share resources across VLEs, partner with another organization, or have a multi-campus setup where each site has its own Moodle.

After providing an overview of Moodle networking, you will learn about the following topics:

- Networking prerequisites and security

  You will learn which networking components are required and how security is guaranteed.
- Peer-to-peer networks

  You will learn how to link two Moodle sites.
- Community hubs

  You will learn how to connect multiple Moodle sites to a central hub.
- Mahara integration

  You will learn how to set up Moodle with Mahara, a popular open-source e-portfolio system that makes use of the networking functionality.

MoodleDocs contains a very well-written wiki on Moodle networking at `http://docs.moodle.org/en/Moodle_Network` and this chapter follows the document in part.

# Networking Overview

Virtual learning environments are usually standalone systems. But learning, in addition to doing, is primarily about communication and collaboration (social constructionist theory). Moodle networking overcomes this limitation and provides a powerful facility to establish logical links among multiple Moodle sites. The following two topologies are supported:

- Peer-to-peer

  This layout connects two Moodle systems directly. This topology is favorable if you have two partnering organizations or one site that offers courses in which students from another site wish to enrol.

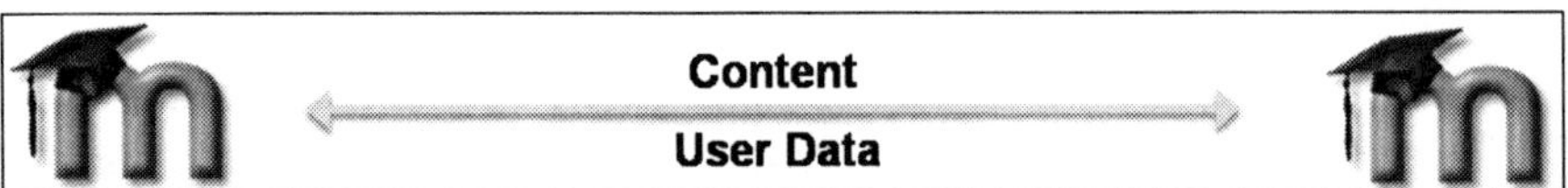


- Community hub

  A Community hub is a Moodle server that is configured to accept connections from other Moodle servers, and to provide a set of services to users of these other servers. This topology is favorable if you have a portal that is used for sharing learning resources or courses.

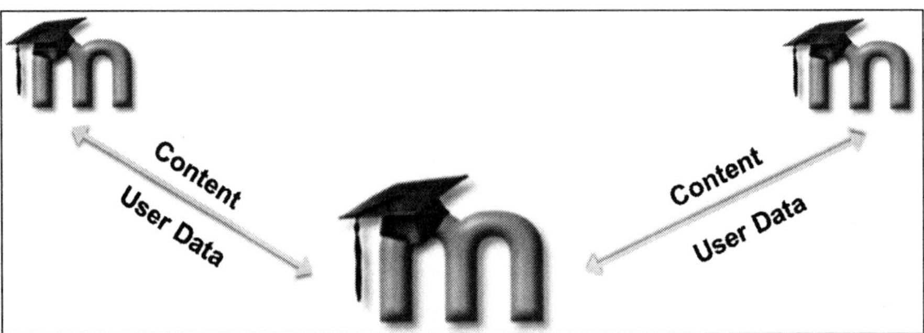


Moodle Networking supports **single sign-on (SSO)**, which provides a seamless integration of multiple Moodle systems. Security is guaranteed by fully encrypting authentication and content exchanges.

The two topologies are not mutually exclusive and can be mixed in the same network. It is even possible to create a network of networks! The following is an example of a large-scale Moodle network (courtesy of Wrexham County Borough Council), where all participating Moodle instances connect to a hub and some schools have established peer-to-peer connections:

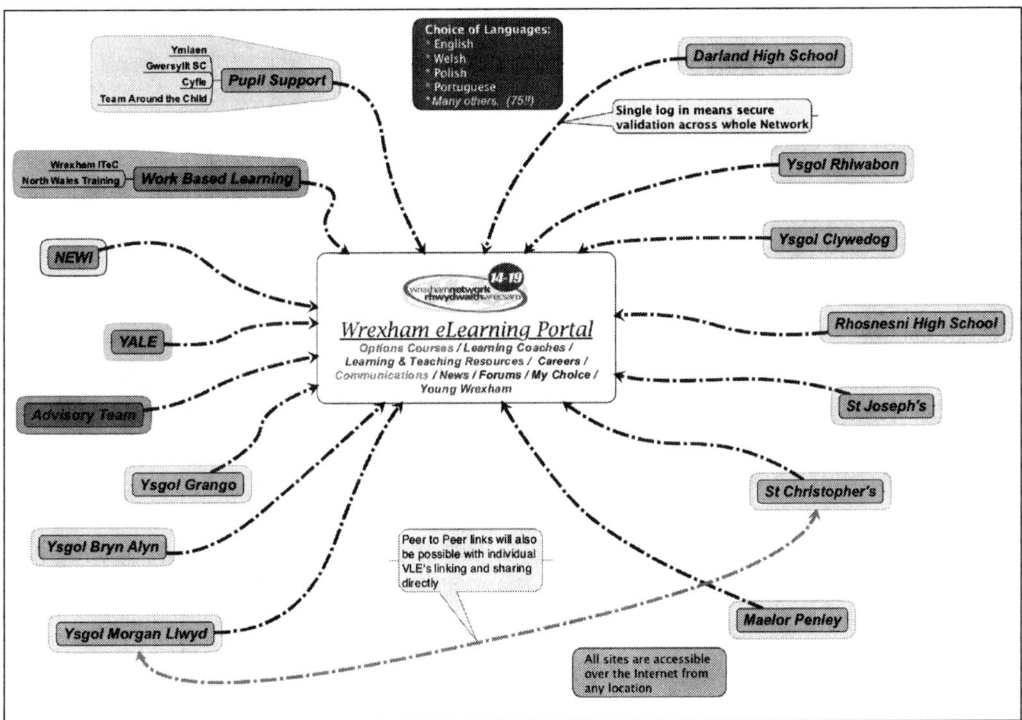


After covering some networking prerequisites and security issues, you will learn how to set up peer-to-peer networks and a community hub.

# Networking Prerequisites and Security

Moodle networking requires a number of additional components to be installed on your server that deal with secure communication and safe data exchange.

## Required PHP Extensions

The following elements are part of the network and have to be installed on all Moodle servers:

- cURL: A PHP library of calls that are specifically designed to safely fetch data from remote sites. If not installed, you have to recompile PHP and add `--with curl` while running `configure`.
- OpenSSL: Another PHP library that provides encryption functionality without the need of a purchased SSL certificate. If not installed, you have to recompile PHP and add `--with openssl` while running `configure`.
- XML-RPC: A PHP library that supports remote procedure calls via XML. If not installed, you have to recompile PHP and add --with `xmlrpc` while configuring. Some Linux distributions provide menu-driven XML-RPC support as a part of their package configuration.

  It is possible to add trusted XML-RPC hosts to Moodle, which allows them to execute calls via XML-RPC to any part of the Moodle API (**Networking | XML-RPC hosts**). This is potentially very dangerous and is only meant for developers. We will not be dealing with this functionality in this book.

To make sure whether the required PHP extensions have been installed, go to **Server | Environment** and make sure the status for all three components is **OK**:

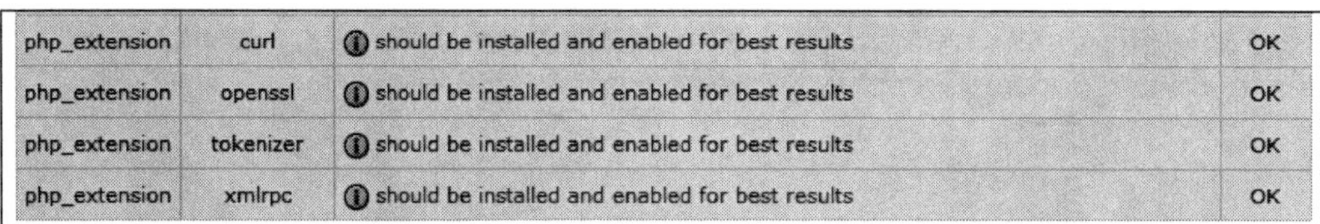

| | | | |
|---|---|---|---|
| php_extension | curl | should be installed and enabled for best results | OK |
| php_extension | openssl | should be installed and enabled for best results | OK |
| php_extension | tokenizer | should be installed and enabled for best results | OK |
| php_extension | xmlrpc | should be installed and enabled for best results | OK |

## Networking Security

The above PHP extensions guarantee the secure communication and safe transmission of data between participating sites. Unlike other secure web systems, neither HTTPS is required nor is the purchase of an SSL certificate. Once networking is turned on, you will immediately be confronted with Moodle's networking security measures.

To activate Moodle networking go to **Networking | Settings** and turn on networking. You will see the **Public key** that has been created by OpenSSL. Turning on networking has to be performed on all participating servers in the Moodle network.

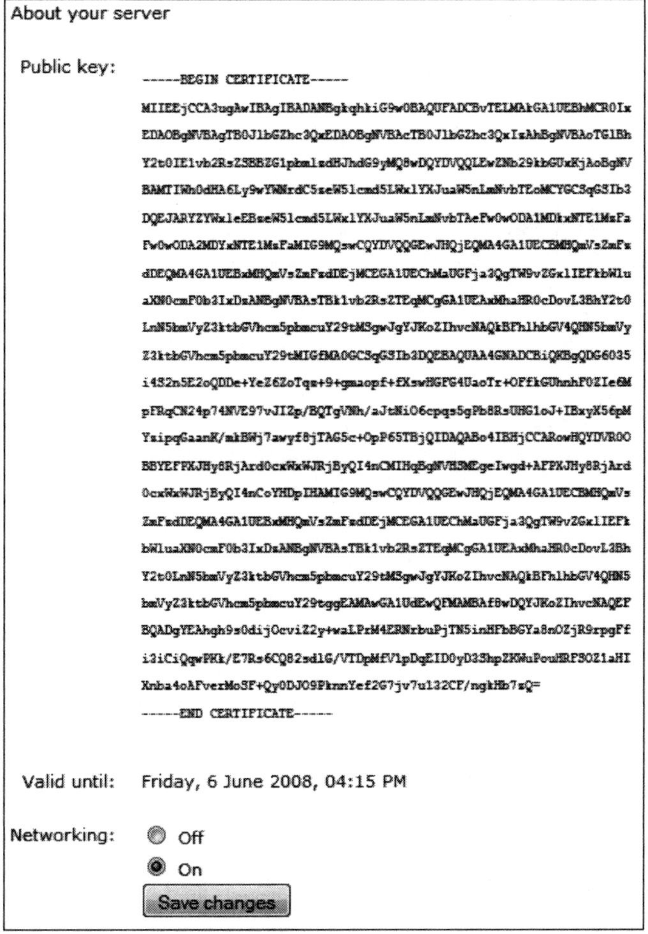


The key has an expiry date which is 28 days from creation, after which a new key is created (called key rotation). The key can be renewed manually using the key deletion option on the same screen.

The key expiry duration cannot be changed via a Moodle parameter. While this is justified from a security perspective, it can be irritating especially in larger networks when connections between servers have to be re-established every time a public key is renewed. If you wish to change this, modify the source code line `$days=28` in `mnet/lib.php` to a value that you feel is appropriate.

Now that Moodle networking has been enabled, it is time to get the servers talking to each other.

# Peer-To-Peer Networks

First, we deal with peer-to-peer networks where two Moodle servers are connected. For demonstration purposes we have set up two Moodle sites; one is located at `http://packt.synergy-learning.com` and the other at `http://packt1.synergy-learning.com`.

If both your sites are hosted in the same domain and you are accessing both sites from the same web browser simultaneously, change the cookie prefix of one site (**Server | Session Handling**) to avoid any conflicts.

# Adding a Peer

Go to **Networking | Peers** and add a new remote host you want to connect to. We are currently working on `http://packt.synergy-learning.com`, and to establish a link to the remote server we have to enter `http://packt1.synergy-learning.com`. Then perform the same step vice versa on the other host:

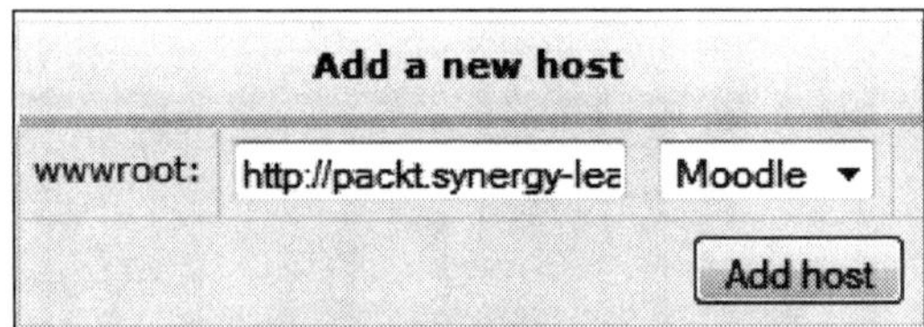


The pull-down menu on the right offers an additional host type "Mahara". **Mahara** is an open-source e-portfolio system that can be integrated via the Moodle networking mechanism. We will cover the integration at the end of the chapter. For now, let's leave this setting at **Moodle**.

Once the host has been added, the name of the site, its hostname, the public key, its expiry date and the IP address of the **Packt1** server are displayed:

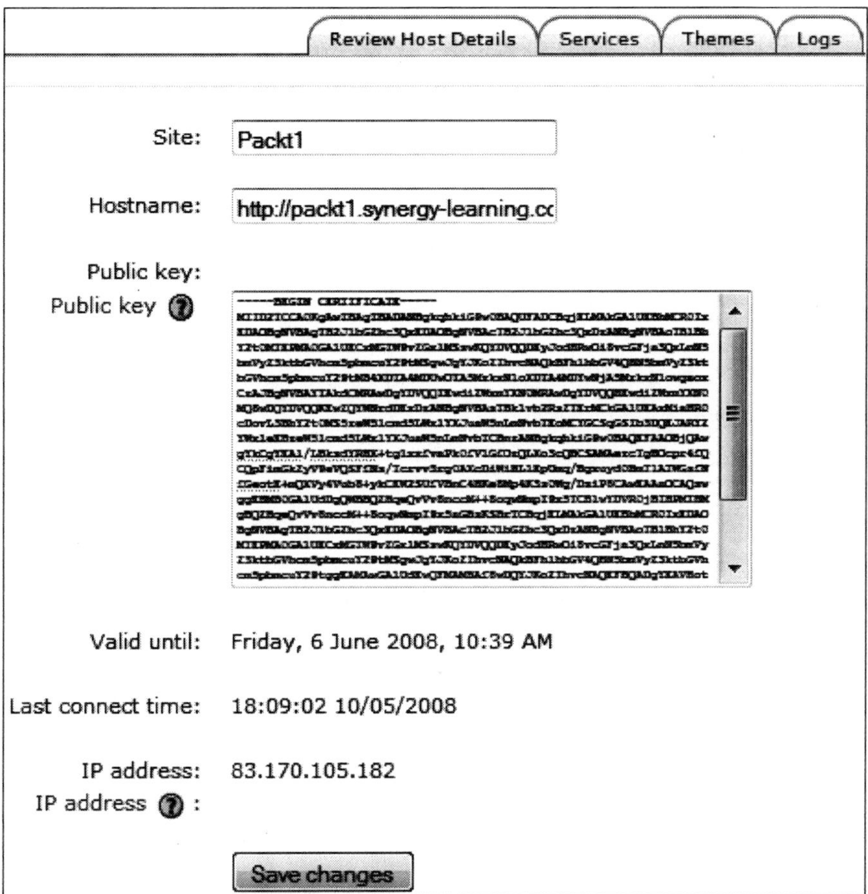


After you have saved the changes, you will see three additional tabs at the top of the screen that describe details of the peer connection. You can always come back to this screen by selecting the host in **Networking | Peers**, where it has been added automatically to the list of peers.

## Peer Services

The SSO supported by Moodle avoids the need for users to log in when roaming to a remote site. The **Services** tab contains three areas. We will currently focus only on the last two that deal with SSO. The enrolment service will be dealt with later on.

There are two SSO services that represent a two-way process, and both services have to be set up on both Moodle sites. Peer services can be published and subscribed.

**Publish** the **Identity Provider** service to allow your users to roam to the other site without needing to log in again. **Subscribe** to the **Identity Provider** service to allow authenticated users from the other site to access your site without having to re-login.

**Publish** the **Service Provider** service to allow authenticated users from the other site to access your site without having to re-login. **Subscribe** to the **Service Provider** service to allow your users to roam to the other site without having to re-login there:

| | **Your Users** | **Other Users** |
|---|---|---|
| Publish Identity Provider | Allow roaming | |
| Subscribe Service Provider | Allow roaming | |
| Subscribe Identity Provider | | Grant access |
| Publish Service Provider | | Grant access |

Each service has a reciprocal dependency on the other server as shown in the table. For example, the subscribed SSO (Service Provider) on the local site requires the SSO (Service Provider) to be published on the other site.

To allow roaming in both directions, check all four boxes on both peers in your Moodle network:

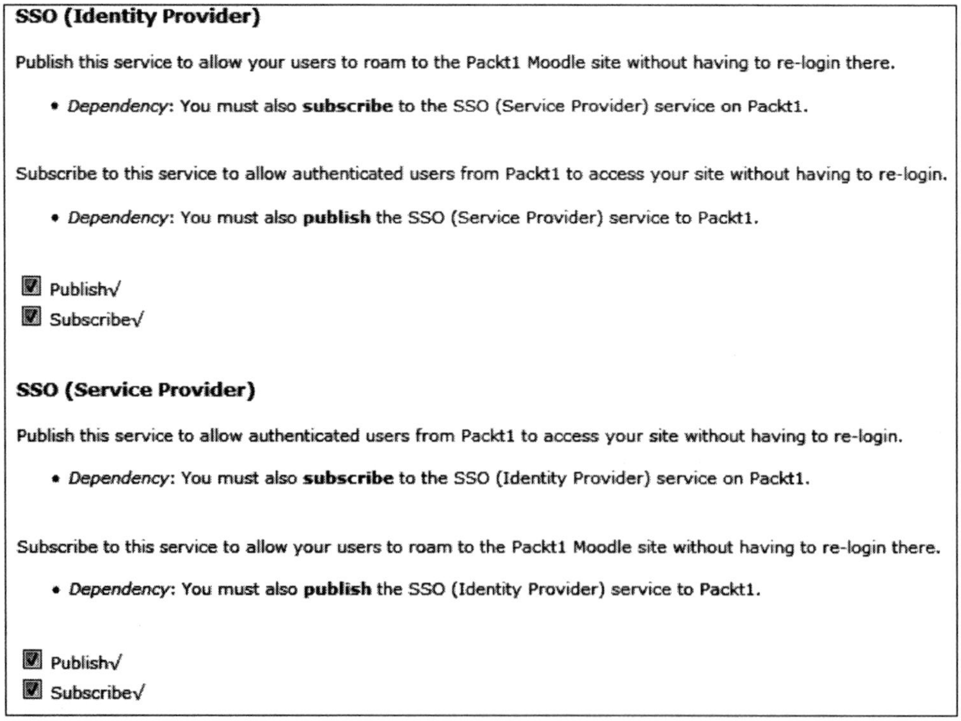

**SSO (Identity Provider)**

Publish this service to allow your users to roam to the Packt1 Moodle site without having to re-login there.

- *Dependency*: You must also **subscribe** to the SSO (Service Provider) service on Packt1.

Subscribe to this service to allow authenticated users from Packt1 to access your site without having to re-login.

- *Dependency*: You must also **publish** the SSO (Service Provider) service to Packt1.

☑ Publish√
☑ Subscribe√

**SSO (Service Provider)**

Publish this service to allow authenticated users from Packt1 to access your site without having to re-login.

- *Dependency*: You must also **subscribe** to the SSO (Identity Provider) service on Packt1.

Subscribe to this service to allow your users to roam to the Packt1 Moodle site without having to re-login there.

- *Dependency*: You must also **publish** the SSO (Identity Provider) service to Packt1.

☑ Publish√
☑ Subscribe√

# Peer Themes

When a user roams to another site, the theme of the remote site will be displayed. This is the expected behavior as the user realizes that s/he is on another site. However, sometimes you want to create a more seamless integration where it is less obvious to the user that s/he has entered a "foreign territory". This is similar to roaming with your cell phone when you go abroad. Your phone behaves in exactly the same way as at home-just your bill will be much higher!

By default, the remote site's default theme is used. However, you can select any other theme available on the remote site in the same way as described in Chapter 7 when we dealt with the Look and Feel of Moodle:

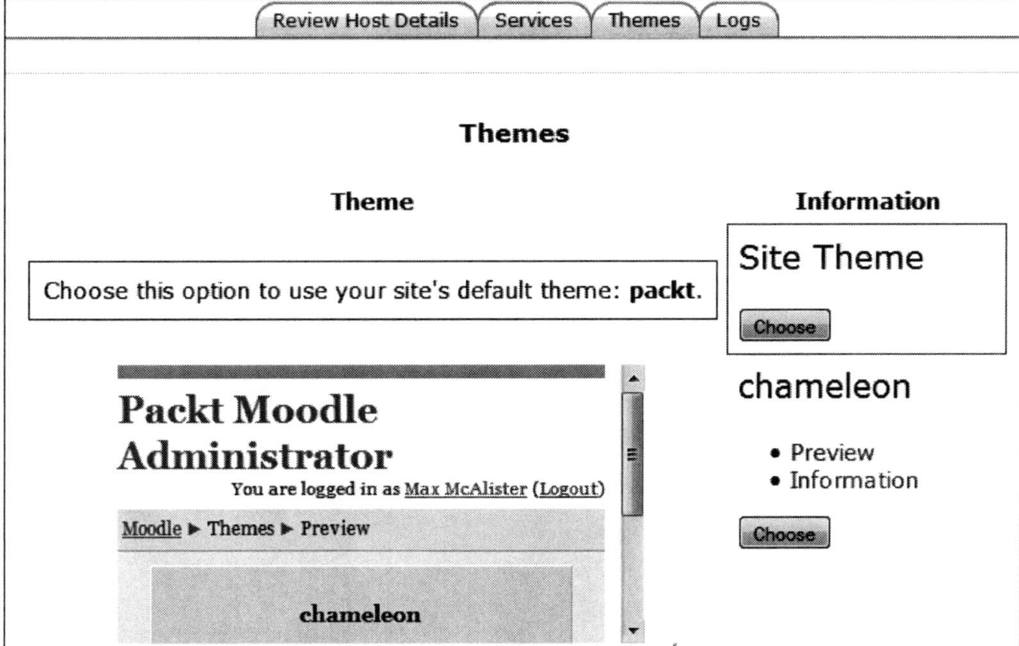


# Peer Logs

Moodle records detailed logging information about each action that takes place in its system. Each record or hit contains data about:

- Who (user) did
- What (action)
- When (date and time) and
- Where (IP address).

The monitoring and tracking works in exactly the same way as discussed in Chapter 9 when we looked at monitoring user activity. The only difference is that remote sites can be selected from the first pull-down menu of the available filters:

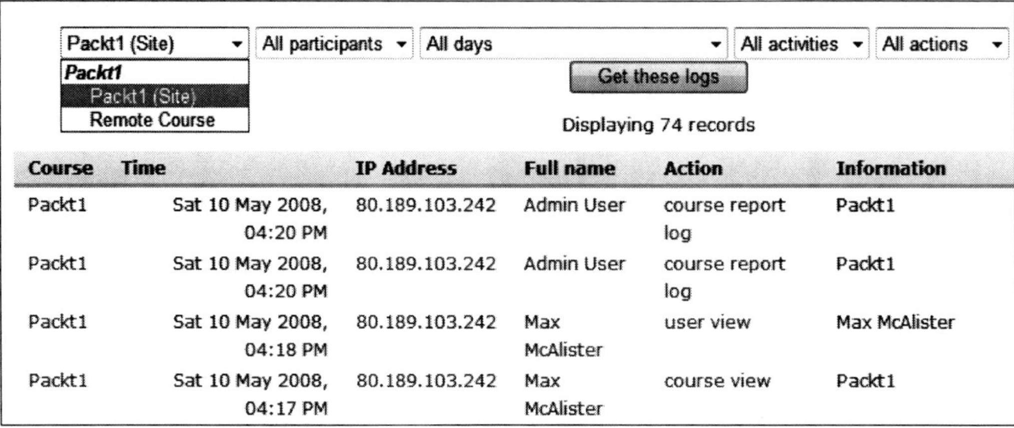

Packt1 (Site)
All participants
All days
All activities
All actions
Packt1
Packt1 (Site)
Remote Course
Get these logs
Displaying 74 records
Course Time IP Address Full name Action Information
Packt1 Sat 10 May 2008, 04:20 PM 80.189.103.242 Admin User course report log Packt1
Packt1 Sat 10 May 2008, 04:20 PM 80.189.103.242 Admin User course report log Packt1
Packt1 Sat 10 May 2008, 04:18 PM 80.189.103.242 Max McAlister user view Max McAlister
Packt1 Sat 10 May 2008, 04:17 PM 80.189.103.242 Max McAlister course view Packt1


# Network Authentication

To initiate roaming, you have to enable the Moodle network authentication plug-in on both sites. Go to **Users | Authentication | Manage authentication** and enable the **Moodle Network authentication** option. Then go to the settings page and change the **Auto add remote users** to **Yes**. Every time a new user from a remote site logs in to this site, a user record is created automatically:

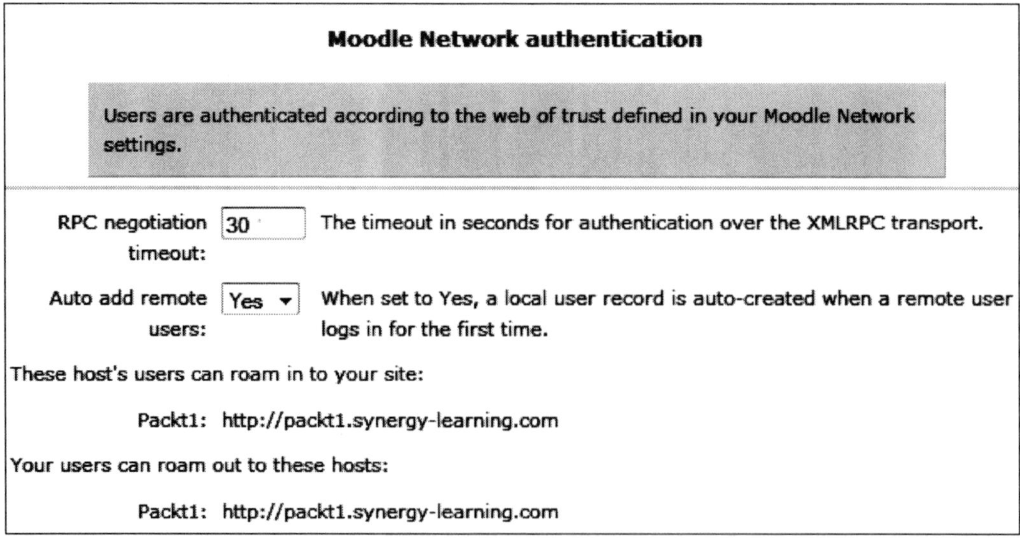

Moodle Network authentication
Users are authenticated according to the web of trust defined in your Moodle Network settings.
RPC negotiation timeout:
30
The timeout in seconds for authentication over the XMLRPC transport.
Auto add remote users:
Yes
When set to Yes, a local user record is auto-created when a remote user logs in for the first time.
These host's users can roam in to your site:
Packt1: http://packt1.synergy-learning.com
Your users can roam out to these hosts:
Packt1: http://packt1.synergy-learning.com

The two entries at the bottom of the screen list which host's users are allowed to roam in to your site and which local users are allowed to roam out will be displayed. Later, users who will have been added via SSO Access Control will also be displayed on this screen.

# Allow Roaming

So far only administrators and users with the `moodle/site:mnetlogintoremote` capability are allowed to roam to other sites. By default, this **Roam to a remote Moodle** capability is turned off and has to be allowed for each role. Go to **Users | Permissions | Define roles** or revisit Chapter 6 for details on how to do this.

Unless all teachers and/or students are allowed to roam, it is worth considering creating a separate roaming role. Alternatively, if you wish to grant (or deny) access to individual users from a remote host, go to **Networking | SSO Access Control**. You have to specify a username, a remote hub (hosts or all hosts, where the latter is relevant for community hub mode), and the access level (grant or deny).

The newly added username needn't exist in either Moodle site! In the list of users, the remote hub ID is displayed and not its name. This is the internal ID, similar to a user ID, group ID or role ID:

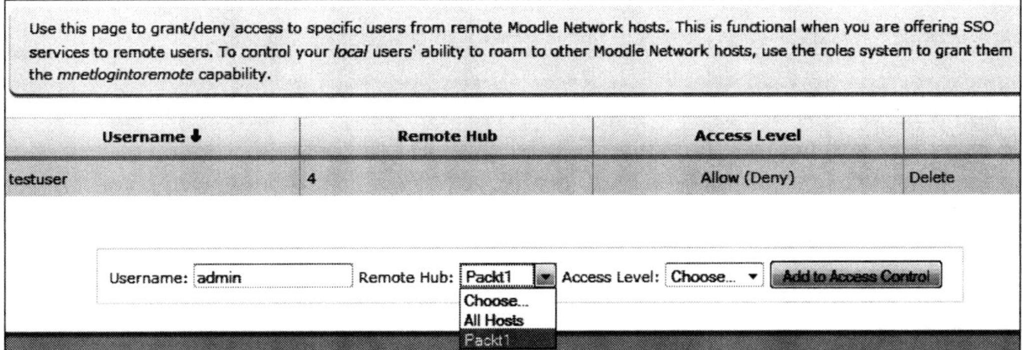
Use this page to grant/deny access to specific users from remote Moodle Network hosts. This is functional when you are offering SSO services to remote users. To control your local users' ability to roam to other Moodle Network hosts, use the roles system to grant them the mnetlogintoremote capability.
Username
Remote Hub
Access Level
testuser
4
Allow (Deny)
Delete
Username: admin
Remote Hub: Packt1
Choose...
All Hosts
Packt1
Access Level: Choose...
Add to Access Control

# Network Server Block

Moodle provides a **Network Servers** block, which has to be added to the front page. The block cannot be configured and is only displayed if the role of the logged in user has the `moodle/site:mnetlogintoremote` capability set to **Allow**:

Network Servers
Packt1

Once you click on the remote server, you will be re-directed to the selected peer where you can enrol to remote courses. Your first peer-to-peer network is set up!

Moodle displays a different logged in message in the header. Instead of **You are logged in as <user> (Logout)**, the message reads **You are logged in as <user> from <peer> (Logout)**. This is similar when you are logged in as another user. When you click on your name, you access the profile of the newly created user on the remote server, which cannot be changed.

You also see that the information in the **My courses** block includes all remote courses (in our case only one called **Remote Course**) and a link back to the local site where the user is enrolled in two courses:

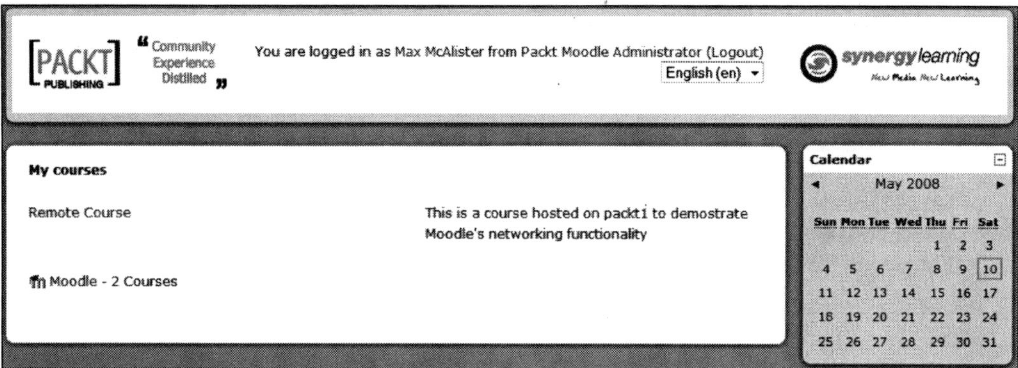


If you want to deny access by a remote user, go to **Users | Accounts | Browse list of users** and you will see that an additional column has been added to the list of users. Remote users cannot be edited locally, only their role is being displayed. In the right-hand column, you select **Deny access** to revoke access to the site. To reverse the operation, select **Allow access**:

| First name / Surname | Email address | City/town | Country | Last access | | |
|---|---|---|---|---|---|---|
| Admin User | alex@synergy-learning.com | belfast | United Kingdom | now | Edit | |
| Max McAlister | alex@synergy-learning.com | Belfast | United Kingdom | 7 mins 5 secs | Packt Moodle Administrator | Allow (Deny access) |

# Network Enrolment

This last step is optional and is required only if you wish to grant an administrator in one Moodle system the permission to enrol local users in remote courses, and the other way round.

## Networking Enrolment Plug-In

First of all, go to **Courses | Enrolments** and enable the **Moodle Networking** plug-in. Edit its settings by either changing the **allow_allcourses** parameter to **Yes** or selecting a set of courses or categories via the **Edit allowed courses and categories here** link:

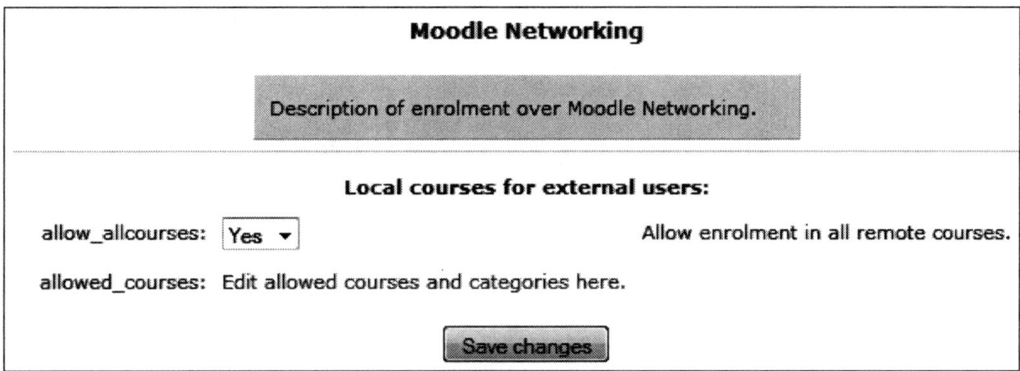
Moodle Networking
Description of enrolment over Moodle Networking.
Local courses for external users:
allow_allcourses: Yes
Allow enrolment in all remote courses.
allowed_courses: Edit allowed courses and categories here.
Save changes

## Network Enrolment Service

Now go back to **Networking | Peers**, select the remote host, and click on the **Services** tab. **Publish** and **Subscribe** to the **Moodle Networked Enrolment** service. This grants remote administrators the right to enrol students on your site and allows the local students to enrol in courses on the remote site, respectively. This step has to be repeated on the peer.

Both Moodle sites are now fully networked and new students can now be enrolled into courses. When you go to **Networking | Enrolments**, you will see a list of remote hosts where local users are enrolled. When you click on the host, courses offered for remote enrolment are displayed:

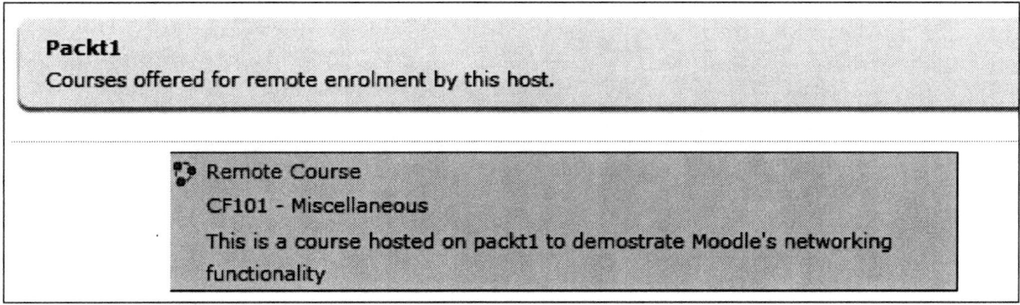
Packt1
Courses offered for remote enrolment by this host.
Remote Course
CF101 - Miscellaneous
This is a course hosted on packt1 to demostrate Moodle's networking functionality

# Community Hubs

A community hub is similar to the peer-to-peer network, with the only difference being that it accepts connections from multiple Moodle servers. While this could be set up manually using a number of peer-to-peer connections, the hub mode automatically accepts any hosts that try to connect to it.

A learning portal that contains resources to be shared across a number of sites is typically implemented using the hub mode.

Once networking has been turned on, choose the Moodle site that will act as a hub and go to **Networking | Peers** to turn on **Register all hosts (Hub mode)**.

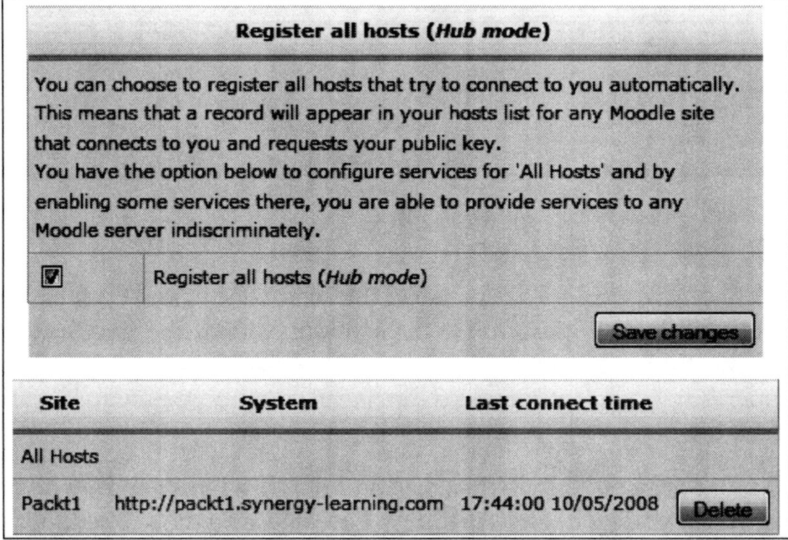


All the other settings are identical to the peer-to-peer parameters. You might decide that traffic (that is, authentication and enrolment) should only go one-way, that is from the different Moodle sites to the hub. You can control this by the **Publish** and **Subscribe** options, as seen before under the Peers Services section.

# Mahara Integration

According to its website (`www.mahara.org`), "*Mahara is an open source e-portfolio, weblog, resume builder and social networking system, connecting users and creating online learner communities. Mahara is designed to provide users with the tools to demonstrate their life-long learning, skills and development over time to selected audiences.*" It has recently become very popular in both vocational and academic settings.

## Mahoodle!

Moodle and Mahara (nicknamed Mahoodle) can be easily integrated via the network function. A very good setup guide can be downloaded from `http://docs.moodle.org/en/Mahoodle`. We only cover the basic networking-related settings required to establish a link between the two systems. More details can be found in the *Mahara documentation*.

It is assumed that Moodle networking (authentication, role permissions, and so on) has been configured as explained in previous sections. It is further assumed that a Mahara site has been set up and networking components have been installed.

Since both Mahara and Moodle use the SSO mechanism of the networking feature, you can configure Moodle so that logged-in Moodle users can navigate to the Mahara site and, without the need to log in, start using the e-portfolio system. If users don't have an account on Mahara, their user data will be imported from Moodle and used to populate their Mahara account.

# Mahara Networking

After logging in to Mahara as an administrator, go to **Site Administration | Networking** and enable networking. Once this has been confirmed, the screen looks very similar to its counterpart in Moodle. This is not surprising as both modules have been programmed by the same development team:

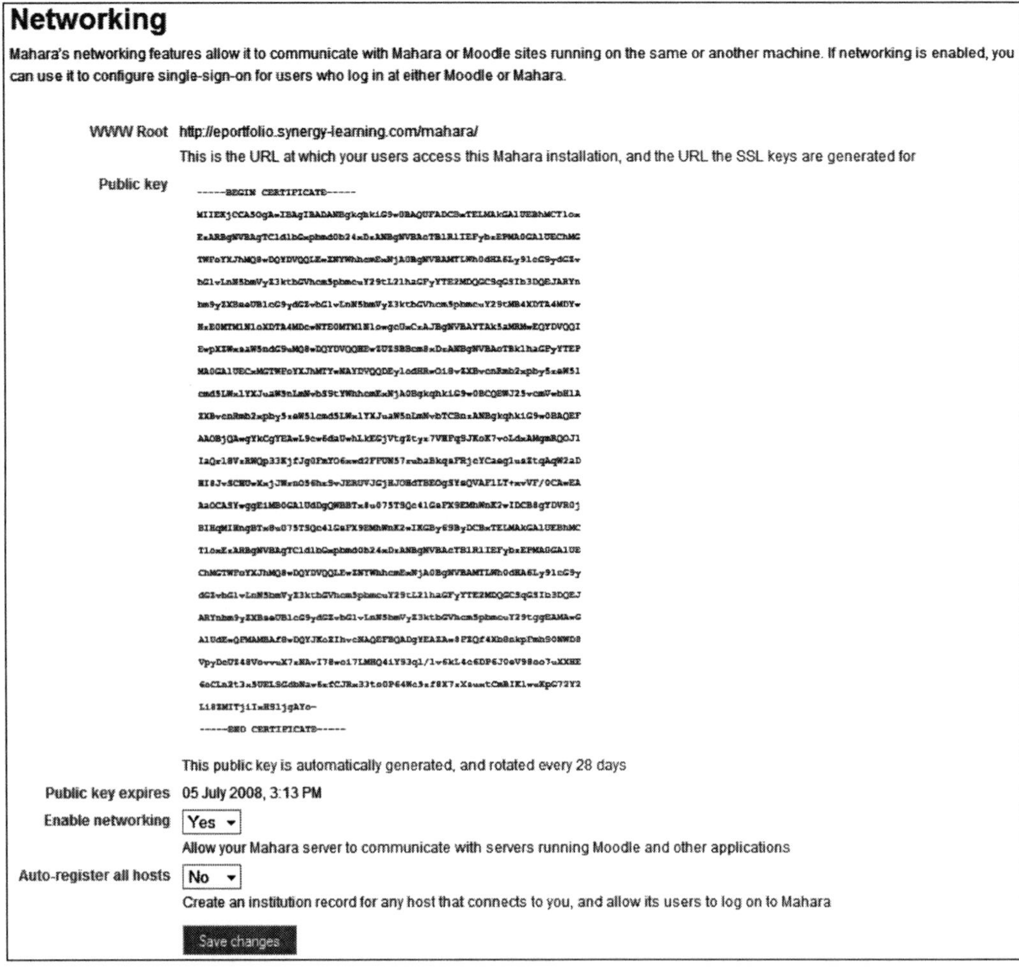

Networking
Mahara's networking features allow it to communicate with Mahara or Moodle sites running on the same or another machine. If networking is enabled, you can use it to configure single-sign-on for users who log in at either Moodle or Mahara.
WWW Root
http://eportfolio.synergy-learning.com/mahara/
This is the URL at which your users access this Mahara installation, and the URL the SSL keys are generated for
Public key
-----BEGIN CERTIFICATE-----
-----END CERTIFICATE-----
This public key is automatically generated, and rotated every 28 days
Public key expires
05 July 2008, 3:13 PM
Enable networking
Yes
Allow your Mahara server to communicate with servers running Moodle and other applications
Auto-register all hosts
No
Create an institution record for any host that connects to you, and allow its users to log on to Mahara
Save changes


Now that Mahara networking has been enabled, go to **Admin Home | Institutions,** which is required to allow SSO. Add a new institution, and enter its name and display name. At this stage you can leave all other entries, including the hidden locked fields, at their defaults.

Once you have submitted the values, you will be directed to a similar-looking screen where you have to select **XMLRPC–Authenticate by SSO from an external application** and add it (via the little plus symbol) to the list of supported authentication plug-ins. This will open a new window, where you have to enter the XML-RPC options. This is the equivalent of the **Peers** and **Services** settings in Moodle. A few of the important settings are listed next:

- **Authority name**: It acts as the descriptor of the service.
- **WWW root**: It is the URL of your Moodle system for which you also have to provide a descriptive **Site name**.
- **Application**: It has to be changed from **Mahara** to **Moodle** to reflect the type of external system.

The remaining self-explanatory fields describe the interdependencies with the other site. To allow two-way traffic (logging in from Moodle to Mahara and vice versa) all options have to be selected:

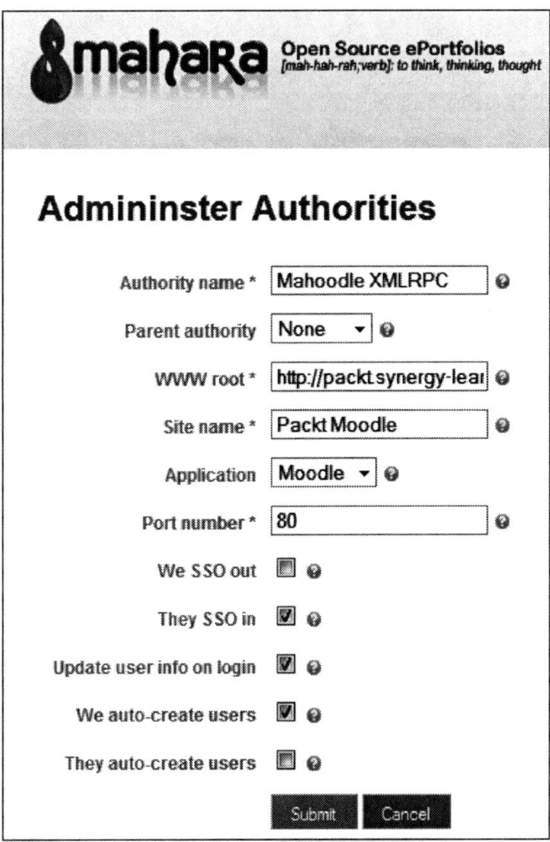

Once this is done, your **Administer Institutions** screen should look as follows:

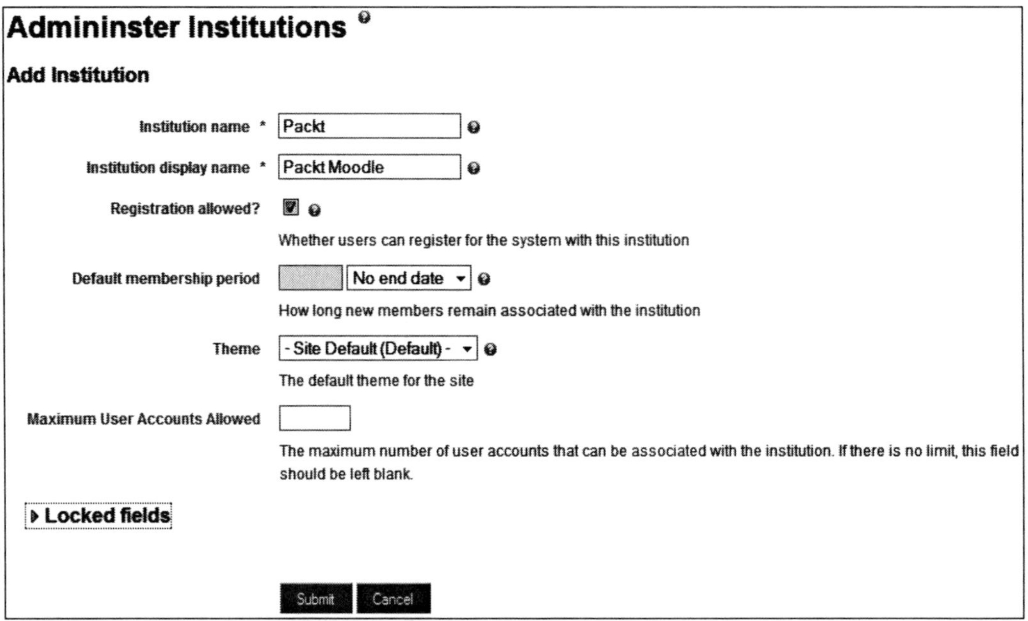


# Adding Mahara to Moodle

Now go back to your Moodle system and add a new host, but this time change the host type from **Moodle** to **Mahara**:

The host details (site name, hostname, public key, expiry date, and IP address) will be displayed and you will have to save them. Then you have to configure the SSO Identity and Service providers as you did earlier.

Once this has been successful, you will see that Mahara has been added to the **Network Servers** block on your front page:

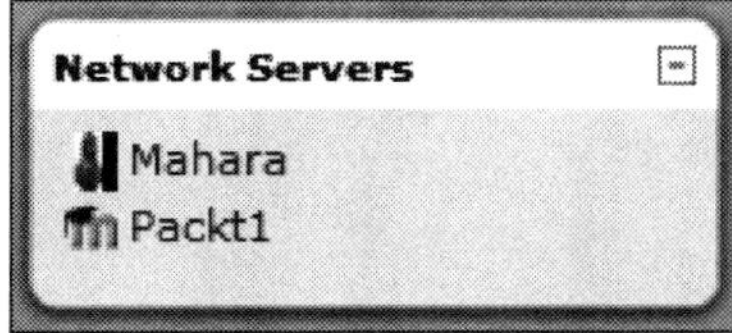


Here we have only covered the basics of connecting Moodle and Mahara via the networking interface. Additional features such as the theme used when roaming and the reverse mechanism of accessing Moodle from Mahara have not been covered.

The next version of Moodle will contain a **Portfolio API**, which will allow an even closer integration between Moodle and external e-portfolio systems such as Mahara. It will be possible to directly add artefacts from Moodle such as assignments and forum entries.

# Summary

In this chapter you have learned how to network disparate Moodle systems. After providing an overview of Moodle networking, we covered some pre-requisites and security issues, peer-to-peer networks, community hubs, and concluded with Mahara integration.

The networking facility that has recently been introduced to Moodle provides a new dimension to virtual learning environments. Disparate VLEs can be connected logically and roaming from one Moodle site to another can be facilitated. This opens up entirely new opportunities, whether it is among entities within your organization or with external sites.

It is expected that the community hub feature will be extended in the near future to simplify the process of finding and navigating external Moodle repositories. There will also be significant changes in the way you can interact with Mahara and other e-portfolio systems from within Moodle, once the forthcoming Portfolio API will have been implemented.

# Moodle Health Check

The objective of the Moodle Health Check is to provide you with a checklist of common problems and tips to improve your Moodle experience. The test comprises of over 120 individual checkups and covers the following four main areas:

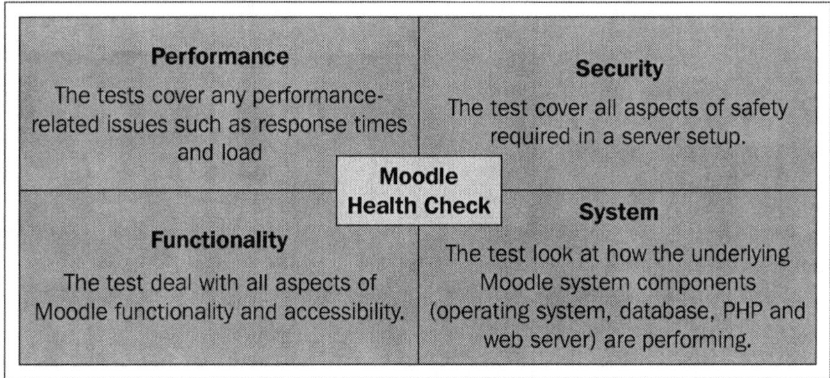

Performance
The tests cover any performance-related issues such as response times and load
Security
The test cover all aspects of safety required in a server setup.
Moodle Health Check
Functionality
The test deal with all aspects of Moodle functionality and accessibility.
System
The test look at how the underlying Moodle system components (operating system, database, PHP and web server) are performing.


Almost all areas have been covered in different chapters in the book. For each test, the following information is provided:

**ID Title (Chapter/s in which test is covered)**

Explanation (as per the parameter settings in Moodle)

Solution(s)

All tests are context-sensitive, that is, they only apply in certain circumstances. For example, some tests are only applicable in Windows environments whereas others only apply if you use networking.

# Moodle Health Check: Performance

Some of the performance-related information collated in this section has been derived from `http://docs.moodle.org/en/Performance`.

### P1 zip path set (Chapter 11)

Setting the path for compressing files accelerates backups and other zip operations. It further reduces the load on your server as the specified zip executable is used.

Go to **Server** settings and specify the **ZIP Path** location. On Unix systems, this is usually `/usr/bin/zip`.

### P2 unzip path set (Chapter 11)

Setting the path for uncompressing files accelerates restore and other unzip operations. It further reduces the load on your server as the specified unzip executable is used.

Go to **Server** Settings and specify the **UNZIP Path** location. On Unix systems this is usually `/usr/bin/unzip`.

### P3 du path set (Chapter 11)

This will accelerate the display of directory content, especially if it contains a lot of files. It reduces the load on your server as the specified executable is used.

Go to **Server** settings and specify the **du Path** location. On Unix systems, this is usually `/usr/bin/du`.

In all the three settings we just discussed, if you set the path incorrectly, Moodle will malfunction. Change this path to its correct location.

### P4 Enable language menu caching (Chapters 8 and 11)

This saves a lot of memory and processing power. If enabled, the language menu takes a few minutes to update after languages have been added or removed.

Go to **Language settings** and turn on **Cache language menu**.

### P5 Minimize installed language packs (Chapters 8 and 11)

Large number of installed language packs can potentially reduce performance.

Check if all installed languages are required and all language packs have been installed. Remove the ones that are not necessary.

## P6 Set appropriate Cache level (Chapter 11)

If load has to be reduced on the database, the cache should be activated. Internal caching is suitable for medium-traffic sites.

If you do not have eAccelerator or mmemcached installed, choose **internal** as your **cachetype**. It makes use of the record/internal cache.

If you have a single server and have compiled eAccelerator with shared memory support, set the **cachetype** to the **eaccelerator** option.

If you have a separate memcached server, then the cache type should be set to **memcached** and a CSV list of server IP addresses should be entered.

## P7 Enable record/internal cache (Chapter 11)

Use the cache to store database records. Cache type (the previous setting) should also be set for this setting to have an effect.

Go to **Performance** settings in the **Server** section and change the **Record cache** setting to **Yes**.

## P8 Record Cache TTL (Chapter 11)

The value specifies the time-to-live for cached records (in seconds). Default value is 10 and it is recommended that the value should not exceed 15.

Go to **Performance** settings in the **Server** section and change the **Record cache TTL** value to **10**.

## P9 Internal maximum cache (Chapter 11)

The value specifies the maximum number of records to keep in the internal cache. This will enable a primary cache for database records without using any database engine cache. The lower the value, the less the memory used. The recommended value is 50.

Go to **Performance** settings in the **Server** section and change the **Int. cache max** value to **50**.

## P10 memcached hosts set (Chapter 11)

It is a comma-separated list of hosts that are running the memcached daemon. This setting only applies when memcached is used.

Go to **Performance** settings in the **Server** section and specify a comma-separated list of hosts in the **memcached hosts** field.

### P11 memcached hosts naming (Chapter 11)

While specifying hosts, use IP addresses to avoid DNS latency. This setting only applies when memcached is used.

Go to **Performance** settings in the **Server** section and specify a comma-separated list of hosts in the **memcached hosts** field.

### P12 memcached use persistent connections (Chapter 11)

Use persistent connections for memcached servers. Use carefully as it can make Apache/PHP crash after a restart of the memcached daemon. This setting only applies when memcached is used.

Go to **Performance** settings in the **Server** section and change the **memcached use persistent connections** setting to **Yes**.

### P13 Large logfiles (Chapters 9 and 11)

Moodle collects usage data from all activities taking place once a user is logged in. Moodle records detailed logging information about each action that takes place in its system. Each record or hit contains data about who (user) did what (action) when (date and time) and where (IP address). While this information is valuable for monitoring and tracking activities, it can potentially create a huge log file.

Go to **Cleanup** settings in the **Server** section, and change **Keep logs for** from **Never** to a shorter value such as **365** days.

### P14 Avoid https for all Moodle pages (Chapters 10 and 11)

Using secure web connections (https rather than http) carries a higher processing burden; both for the web server and the client (caching cannot be used as effectively, so the number of file requests will increase dramatically). For this reason, using https for all Moodle pages is not recommended.

Change your web connection from https to http.

If you require a degree of security at the login stage, you can enable https just for the login screen by turning on **Use HTTPS for logins** in the **HTTP security** settings in the **Security** section.

### P15 Minimize active Moodle filters (Chapter 11)

Having too many Moodle filters active can have serious effects on server load, especially on lower-end systems. The number of active filters has a direct effect on the perceived latency (the time taken for each page impression) of your site.

Go to **Filters | Manage filters** in the **Modules** section and hide all filters that are not required.

### P16 Enable text cache (Chapters 8 and 11)

For larger sites or sites that use text filters, this setting will speed things up. Copies of texts will be retained here in their processed form for the time specified. Setting this too small may actually slow things down slightly, but setting it too large may mean texts taking too long to refresh (with new links, for example).

Go to in **Filter | Manage filters** in **Modules** and set **Text cache lifetime** to **1 minutes** or **30 seconds**.

### P17 Disable text cache for all strings (Chapters 8 and 11)

Filtering all strings, including headings, titles, navigation bar, and so on is only useful while using the **multilang** filter. Otherwise, it will just create extra load on your site for little gain.

Go to **Filter | Manage filters** in **Modules** and turn off **Filter all strings**.

### P18 Use chat server deamon

The normal chat method involves the clients regularly contacting the server for updates. It requires no configuration and works everywhere, but it can create a large load on the server with many clients. Using a server daemon requires shell access to Unix, but it results in a fast scalable chat environment.

Go to the **Chat** settings in the **Activities** section and change **chat_method** to **Chat server daemon**. Make sure that the chatd process is running on your operating system.

### P19 Use streamed chat if possible

Chatroom updates are normally served efficiently using the **Keep-Alive** feature of HTTP 1.1, but this is still quite heavy on the server. A more advanced method is to use the Stream strategy to feed updates to users. The Stream strategy is much better approach (similar to the chatd method).

Go to the **Chat** settings in the **Activities** section and change **chat_normal_updatemode** to **Stream**. Make sure that the feature is supported by your server.

### P20 Chat refresh parameter setting

The chat activity refreshes the list of users at regular intervals to detect who has joined the active chat. The smaller the value (in seconds), the bigger the load of traffic to the server.

Go to the **Chat** settings in the **Activities** section and change **chat_refresh_userlist** to **10** (default).

### P21 Chat old ping setting

The chat activity refreshes the list of users at regular intervals to detect who has disconnected. The value (in seconds) is an upper limit, as usually disconnects are detected very quickly. Lower values will be more demanding on the server. If you are using the normal method, never set this lower than `2 * chat_refresh_room`!

Go to the **Chat** settings in the **Activities** section and change **chat_old_ping** to **35** (default).

### P22 Chat refresh room setting

The chat activity has to refresh the chat room. Setting this to a lower value (in seconds) will make the chat room seem quicker, but it may place a higher load on your web server when many people are chatting.

Go to the **Chat** settings in the **Activities** section, and change **chat_refresh_room** to **5** (default) if the **Chat method** is **Normal**. It is set to **2** if the **Update method** is set to **Stream.**

### P23 Maximum chat clients

If a chat daemon is used, Moodle can limit the number of simultaneous clients connected to a chat. The lower the value, the lesser the load on the server.

Go to the **Chat** settings in the **Activities** section and change **chat_servermax** to **100** (default).

### P24 cron script calling method (Chapters 2 and 11)

The Moodle cron task is triggered by calling the script `cron.php`. If this is called over HTTP (either using wget or curl), it can take a large amount of memory on large installations. If it is called by directly invoking the php command (for example, `php -f /path/to/moodle/directory/admin/cron.php`) efficiency can be improved to a better level.

Change your crontab entry to invoke the cron task by using php.

### P25 Smart pix search (Chapter 8)

When enabled, icons are served through a PHP script that searches the current theme, then all parent themes, and finally the `Moodle /pix` folder. This reduces the need to duplicate image files within themes, but has a slight performance cost. The feature is still in an experimental stage and should be avoided in a production environment.

Go to the **Experimental** settings in the **Miscellaneous** section and turn off **Smart pix search**.

### P26 Statistics (Chapter 9)

If statistics is enabled, Moodle's cron job will process the logs and gather some statistics. Depending on the amount of traffic on your site, this can have a negative impact on performance.

Unless required, statistics should be disabled in the **Server** settings.

### P27 Use slash arguments (Chapter 11)

Files (images, uploads, and so on) are provided via a script using "slash arguments" (the second option under **HTTP** settings). This method allows files to be easily cached in web browsers, proxy servers, and so on.

Unless your PHP server does not allow slash arguments, this should be enabled in **HTTP** settings.

### P28 Don't return all default role users (Chapter 6)

This setting prevents all users from being returned from the database due to deprecated calls such as `get_course_user` for the site course if the default role provides that access. Check this if you suffer a performance hit.

Go to **User policies** setting in **Permissions** section and turn on **Don't return all default role users**.

### P29 Disable grade history (Chapter 8)

Disable history tracking of changes in grades-related tables. This may speed up the server a little and conserve space in database.

Go to **Cleanup** settings in the **Server** section and set **Disable grade history**. If you enable grade history, you might want to reduce the **Grade history lifetime**, which is specified underneath.

# Moodle Health Check: Security

Also check `http://docs.moodle.org/en/Security` for upcoming security-related issues.

### S1 dataroot directory directly accessible via the web (Chapters 2 and 10)

Moodle requires additional space on a server to store uploaded files such as course documents and user pictures. The directory is called `dataroot` and should not be accessible via the web.

Locate your `dataroot` directory outside the `web` directory and modify `config.php` accordingly (`$CFG->dataroot entry`).

If it is not possible to locate the directory outside the `web` directory, create a file `.htaccess` in the `data` directory and add a line containing **deny from all**.

### S2 Usernames are protected (Chapters 5 and 10)

By default, `forget_password.php` does not display any hints that would allow guessing of usernames or email addresses.

Go to **Site policies** settings in the **Security** section and turn on **Protect usernames**.

### S3 Guest access (Chapter 10)

Moodle provides a Guest role, which allows visitors to see certain content without being authenticated by the system. This should be avoided if possible.

Go to **Authentication** settings in the **Users** section and set **Guest login button** to **Hide**.

### S4 Auto-login guests (Chapters 5 and 10)

Visitors can be logged in as guests automatically while entering courses with guest access.

Go to **User Policies** settings in the **Permission** subsection in the **Users** section, and turn off **Auto-login guests**.

### S5 Open to Google (Chapter 10)

If you enable, Google bots will be allowed to enter your site as a Guest. Additionally, people coming in to your site via a Google search will automatically be logged in as Guests.

Go to **Site policies** settings in the **Security** section and turn off **Open to Google**.

### S6 Disable register globals (Chapter 10)

The `register_globals` directive will inject PHP scripts with a number of variables such as request variables from HTML forms, which allows writing of insecure scripts. Turning it off will help prevent against possible XSS problems in third-party scripts.

Add `php_flag register_globals 0` to `.htaccess`.

Add `register_globals = Off` to `php.ini`.

### S7 Force users to log in for profiles (Chapter 5)

It is recommended that users log in to a real (non-guest) account before being allowed to see the user profile pages.

Go to **Site policies** settings in the **Security** section and turn on **Force users to login for profiles**.

### S8 Allow EMBED and OBJECT tags (Chapters 8 and 10)

As a default security measure, normal users are not allowed to embed multimedia (such as Flash) within texts using explicit `EMBED` and `OBJECT` tags in their HTML (although it can still be done safely using the media plug-ins filter).

Go to **Site policies** settings in the **Security** section and turn off **Allow EMBED and OBJECT tags**.

### S9 Enable trusted content (Chapter 10)

By default, Moodle will always thoroughly clean the text that comes from users to remove any possible bad scripts, media, and so on that could be a security risk. **The Trusted Content System** is a way of giving your trusted users the ability to include these advanced features in their content without interference. To enable this system, you need to first enable this setting and then grant the Trusted Content permission to a specific Moodle role. Texts created or uploaded by such users will be marked as trusted and will not be cleaned before display.

Go to **Site policies** settings in the **Security** section and turn off **Enable Trusted Content**.

### S10 Blog visibility (Chapter 10)

Using this setting, the visibility of user blocks can be restricted to a particular level on this site. It is recommended to avoid the **The world can read entries set to be world-accessible** setting.

Go to **Site policies** settings in the **Security** section and set **Blog Visibility** to **All site users can see all blog entries** or less.

### S11 Email notification enabled (Chapter 10)

If login failures have been recorded, email notifications can be sent out. They can be an indication of somebody unauthorized trying to get access to the Moodle system.

Go to **Notifications** settings in the **Security** section and set **Email login failures to** to **Administrator** or **All administrators**.

### S12 Email or display notification threshold set (Chapter 10)

If notifications about failed logins are active, it is possible to specify the threshold of failed login attempts by one user or one IP address before an email is sent. The value should not be set to anything less than 10.

Go to **Notifications** settings in the **Security** section and set **Threshold for email notifications** to **10**.

### S13 Use strong Moodle admin password (Chapter 10)

Strong administrator password increases the security of your Moodle system.

Go to the user profile of each admin account and change the password to a strong version (mix upper- and lowercase characters, use numbers and special characters).

### S14 Use strong Moodle database password (Chapter 10)

A strong Moodle database password increases the security of your Moodle system.

Change the Moodle MySQL password to a strong version (mix upper- and lowercase characters, use numbers and special characters). Also update `config.php` (`$CFG->dbpass`).

### S15 Set MySQL root password (Chapter 10)

By default, the MySQL password is empty, which allows anybody with shell permission to get access to the Moodle database.

Go to your shell as superuser and use the following command to change the root password:

```
mysqladmin -u root password NEWPASSWORD
```

### S16 Set course manager to appropriate role (Chapter 6)

The course manager should be set to the Teacher role.

Go to **Course managers** setting in the **Appearance** section, and select **Teacher** from the **Course managers** list.

### S17 SWF Filter disabled (Chapters 8 and 10)

As a default security measure, normal users should not be allowed to embed swf flash files.

Go to **Filters** settings in the **Modules** section and select **Multimedia Plugins Settings** within these, and disable the **.swf filter**.

### S18 Visitor role (Chapters 6 and 10)

Users who are not logged in to the site will be treated as if they have this role granted to them at the site context. This should be set to Guest.

Go to **User policies** settings in the **Permissions** sub-section in the **Users** section and select **Guest** as **Role for visitors**.

### S19 Guest role (Chapters 6 and 10)

This role is automatically assigned to the guest user. It is also temporarily assigned to 'not enrolled users' when they enter a course that allows guests without a password. This should be set to Guest.

Go to **User policies** settings in the **Permissions** sub-section in the **Users** section and select **Guest** as **Role for guest**.

### S20 Default role for all users (Chapters 6 and 10)

All logged-in users will be given the capabilities of the role you specify here at the site level, in addition to any other roles they may have been given. This should be set to 'Authenticated'.

Go to **User policies** settings in the **Permissions** sub-section in the **Users** section and select **Authenticated user** as **Default role for all users**.

### S21 Default role for users in a course (Chapters 4, 6, and 10)

Users who enrol in a course will be automatically assigned this role. It should be set to "Student".

Go to **User policies** settings in the **Permissions** subsection in the **Users** section, and select **Student** for **Default role for users in a course**.

### S22 Creator's role in new courses (Chapters 6 and 10)

This role is automatically assigned to creators in new courses they created. It should be set to Teacher.

Go to **User policies** settings in the **Permissions** subsection in the **Users** section, and select **Teacher** for **Creators** role in new courses.

### S23 Minimize global roles assignments (Chapter 6)

Global roles will apply to the assigned users throughout the entire site, including the front page and all the courses. It is recommended to keep the number of global roles to a minimum.

Go to **Assign global roles** settings in the **Permissions** subsection in the **Users** section, and remove as many global roles as possible.

### S24 Networking turned off (Chapter 14)

Moodle supports very powerful networking that allows connecting multiple Moodle systems in a peer-to-peer style or a hub topology. If not needed, this feature should be turned off.

Go to **Networking | Settings** and turn off **Networking**.

### S25 XML-RPC hosts (Chapter 14)

The trusted hosts mechanism allows specific machines to execute calls via XML-RPC to any part of the Moodle API. This is available for scripts to control Moodle behavior and can be a very dangerous option to enable.

Go to **XML-RPC** hosts settings in the **Networking** section and delete any specified hosts, unless required.

### S26 Backups specified (Chapter 12)

Moodle provides a backup facility that creates backups automatically. It is recommended to be activated unless you have alternative backups in place.

Go to **Backups** settings in the **Courses** section and activate backups.

### S27 Block deleting files referenced by resources

Block deleting of files and directories referenced by resources. Please note that images and other files referenced from html are not protected.

Go to **Resource** settings in **Activities** in the **Modules** section, and set **resource_blockdeletingfile** to **Yes**.

### S28 HTML Purifier disabled (Chapter 8)

Use HTML Purifier instead of KSES for cleaning of untrusted text. HTML Purifier is actively developed and is believed to be more secure, but it is more resource intensive. Expect minor visual differences in the resulting html code. Please note that embed and object tags cannot be enabled, and that MathML tags and old lang tags are not supported.

*Go to Experimental settings in the Miscellaneous section and disable "Enabled HTML Purifier".*

### S29 Set password policy (Chapter 10)

A password policy may be set up to ensure that users choose passwords of certain length and so on.

Go to **Site policies** settings in the **Security** section and turn on **Password policy**.

Go to **Site policies** settings in the **Security** section and specify the following settings (minimum values):

- Password length: 8
- Digits: 1
- Lowercase letters: 1
- Uppercase letters: 1
- Non-alphanumeric characters: 1

**S30 Email change notification**

An email confirmation step is required when users change their email address in their profile.

Go to **Site policies** settings in the **Security** section and turn on **Email change confirmation**.

**S31 ReCAPTCHA support (Chapter 5)**

If you support email-based registration, it is advisable to turn on the **ReCAPTCHA** facility.

Go to the **Authentication** section in **Users** and provide **private** and **public ReCAPTCHA** keys.

Go to **Email-based self-registration** in the **Uses | Authentication** section, and enable turn on **Enable ReCAPTCHA element**.

# Functionality

## Core Functionality

This is really a potpourri of functionality-related tests that may or may not apply to your setup.

**F1 Moodle Version (Chapter 2)**

The latest stable Moodle version provides the full feature set and includes all available security patches and bug fixes.

An older version of Moodle can be used. Update to the latest version if possible (`http://download.moodle.org`).

An update of your current Moodle version is available. Upgrade if possible (`http://download.moodle.org`).

A beta version of Moodle is installed, which should not be used in a production environment (`http://download.moodle.org`).

### F2 GD Support (Chapter 2)

The GD library handles all images and graphical displays in Moodle. The GD library has to be included in the PHP installation and set GD support has to match GD version (usually 2.0 or higher)

Go to **System paths** settings in the **Server** section and select **GD 2.x is installed**.

### F3 cron.php maintenance process specified (Chapter 2)

Some of the Moodle's modules require continual checks to perform tasks that are performed by a script called `cron.php`. A cron process has to be specified to run the script automatically and regularly.

Specify crontab entry to run script (by invoking the php command) every 5 minutes.

### F4 aspell path set

The Moodle editor supports spellchecking. To use this feature, aspell 0.50 or later has to be installed on the server, and the correct path to access the aspell binary has to be set.

Go to **System paths** settings in the **Server** section and specify the aspell Path location. On Unix systems, this is usually `/usr/bin/aspell`.

The path, if set incorrectly, will cause Moodle to malfunction.

### F5 Site errors (Chapter 9)

Any site errors, apart from login errors, indicate that there is a problem with the Moodle setup.

Check errors and fix accordingly.

### F6 Problems in your question database

A test can be performed to check for possible problems in the Moodle question database.

Check errors and fix accordingly.

### F7 Unit tests

When you modify code in a module it might work well within that module but cause problems in other modules (known as side-effects). To tackle it Moodle allows running of a number of Moodle unit tests that check for proper working of and site-effects between modules.

Check errors and fix accordingly.

### F8 AJAX and Javascipt enabled (Chapter 5)

This setting allows you to control the use of AJAX (advanced client/server interfaces using Javascript) across the whole site. With this setting enabled, users can still make a choice in their profile, otherwise AJAX is disabled for everybody.

Go to **AJAX and Javascript** settings in the **Appearance** section and turn on **Enable AJAX**.

### F9 Global search (Chapter 11)

Global search enables global text searching in resources and activities. It is still in an experimental stage and also requires PHP 5 to work.

Unless you feel comfortable with early stage features, go to **Experimental** settings in the **Miscellaneous** section and turn off **Enable global search**.

### F10 Enable outcomes

Support for outcomes (also known as Competencies, Goals, Standards, or Criteria) means that assessments and other activities can be graded using one or more scales that are tied to outcome statements. Enabling outcomes makes such special grading possible throughout the site.

Go to **Outcomes** settings in the **Grades** section and turn on **Enable outcomes**.

### F11 Enable tags

Support for the tags functionality allows the tagging of user interests.

Go to the **Site policies** settings in the **Security** section, and turn on **Enable tags functionality**.

### F12 Enable groupings

Moodle 1.9 has introduced the concept of site-wide groups, also known as groupings that are effectively groups of groups. The feature is not yet fully implemented and should not be used yet.

Unless you feel comfortable with early stage features, go to **Experimental** settings in the **Miscellaneous** section and turn off **Enable groupings**.

### F13 Start of week set to appropriate value (Chapter 8)

The default start of week is Sunday, even if this is incorrect for the used locale.

Go to **Calendar** settings in the **Appearance** section and change **Start of Week** to **Monday**.

### F14 Moodle Docs location set properly (Chapter 3)

It defines the path to the MoodleDocs. The paths should be set to `http://docs.moodle.org` unless you provide your own documentation.

Go to **MoodleDocs** settings in the **Appearance** section, and change **MoodleDocs document root** to `http://docs.moodle.org`.

### F15 Debugger turned off

Moodle provides various debug modes that show PHP's error reporting. The setting is only useful for developers and should be deactivated.

Go to **Debugging** settings in the **Server** section, and change **Debug messages** to **MINIMAL** or **NONE**.

### F16 Deactivate any unused Moodle blocks (Chapter 8)

By default, Moodle has activated a number of blocks that are unlikely to be used (such as the Loan Calculator). These blocks should be turned off.

Go to **Blocks** in the **Modules** section and hide all blocks that are not required.

### F17 Deactivate any unused Moodle activities (Chapter 8)

By default, Moodle has activated a number of activities that are unlikely to be used (such as the Survey). These blocks should be turned off.

Go to **Activities** in the **Modules** section and hide all activities that are not required.

### F18 Check for untranslated words or phrases (Chapter 8)

If language packs other than English are used, some words and phrases might not have been translated. These strings can be identified and consequently edited.

Go to **Language editing** settings in the **Language** section, and check for **untranslated words or phrases**. Then edit words and phrases identified and provide the translations accordingly.

### F19 New multilang syntax (Chapter 8)

When authoring multi-language content, `<span lang="xx">` and `<lang>` should not be used anymore.

Your site is using old multi-language syntax. Run the multilang upgrade script at `http://moodle.yourorg.com/admin/multilangupgrade.php`.

### F20 PayPal Support (Chapter 5)

When PayPal is used as enrolment method, the email address of the receiving PayPal account has to be specified.

Go to the **PayPal** settings in the **Enrolments** settings in the **Course** section, and specify an email address in **enrol_paypalbusiness**.

### F21 Authorize.Net Support (Chapter 5)

When Authorize.Net is used as enrolment method, secure http has to be turned on.

Go to **HTTP security** settings in the **Security** section and turn on **Use HTTPS for logins**.

### F22 Third-party Moodle add-ons (Chapter 13)

Moodle can be extended through third-party add-ons (**Modules and Plugins** section at `http://moodle.org`). However, these plug-ins have not been verified for Moodle and are a potential risk.

One or more third-party Moodle add-ons have been installed on the system, and some are not compatible with the current version of Moodle.

## Accessibility

Also check out `http://docs.moodle.org/en/accessibility` and Chapter 8.

### A1 Validate HTML - Front Page Accessibility test (Chapter 8)

The W3C provides a markup validation service that checks whether your Moodle front page is XHTML 1.0 Strict.

Some warnings have been displayed during validation. To reproduce the messages go to `http://validator.w3.org/check?verbose=1&ss=1&uri=http://moodle.yourorg.com`.

### A2 Section 508 Check - Front Page Accessibility test (Chapter 8)

The test checks for all relevant criteria of the Section 508 standard.

Some warnings have been displayed during validation. To reproduce the messages go to: `http://www.contentquality.com/mynewtester/cynthia.exe?rptmode=-1&url1=http://moodle.yourorg.com`.

### A3 WCAG 1 (2,3) Check - Front Page Accessibility test (Chapter 8)

The test checks for all relevant criteria of the **Web Content Accessibility Guidelines** standard.

Some warnings have been displayed during validation. To reproduce the messages go to: `http://www.contentquality.com/mynewtester/cynthia.exe?rptmode=0&warnp2n3e=1&url1=http://moodle.yourorg.com`.

### A4 Front Page rich content (Chapter 8)

The front page of a Moodle system is the page that is loaded most frequently. There is a tradeoff between user experience and server load. It is recommended to avoid multimedia rich elements such as videos or large images. It is further recommended to avoid server-heavy components such as Java applets.

If multimedia rich content has been identified, it is recommended to reduce the size of the elements.

If Java applets have been found on your front page, it is recommended to remove these or replace them with non-Java equivalents.

### A5 Moodle Theme Browser Support (Chapter 8)

Moodle themes are based on **Cascaded Style Sheets** that drive the look and feel of different elements. They have proven to be inconsistent across browsers. The browsers that should be supported are Internet Explorer 6 and 7, Firefox 2 and 3, and Safari/Google Chrome. Keep in mind to:

- Adjust Moodle theme to support Internet Explorer versions 6.0 and 7.0.
- Adjust Moodle theme to support Firefox 2.0 and 3.0.
- Adjust Moodle theme to support Safari/Google Chrome.

# System

Some of the system-related information collated in this section has been derived from the performance section on MoodleDocs `http://docs.moodle.org/en/Performance` and also `http://docs.moodle.org/en/Installing_AMP`.

# Operating System

### OS1 Server dedicated to Moodle (Chapter 3)

Moodle performs best when run on a dedicated server, that is, no other applications are running in parallel on the same system. Examples that should be avoided are mail servers and other web servers.

Uninstall any software that is not required and turn off any services that are not needed.

### OS2 Non-Unix Operating System (Chapters 2 and 3)

Moodle has been developed and optimized for a LAMP platform (Linux, Apache, MySQL, and PHP/Perl). It, therefore, runs the most stable in such an environment. When run on a Windows server, approximately twice the hardware resources are required to achieve the same performance of a Moodle system.

Invest in a Unix/Linux server or sign up with a dedicated Moodle host that uses Unix as the operating system.

### OS3 Unicode support (Chapters 2 and 8)

Moodle supports multi-language character sets and, therefore, requires necessary Unicode libraries to be installed on operating system level.

Install Unicode libraries on your system. Apply the Moodle Unicode migration script at: `http://moodle.yourorg.com/admin/utfdbmigrate.html`.

### OS4 Optimize Network Applications (Chapter 2)

A Windows server should be set to be optimized for network applications. This setting is available at:

**Control Panel | Network Connections | LAN Connection | Properties | File and Print Sharing for Microsoft Networks | Properties | Optimization**

# Database

### DB1 MySQL Version (Chapters 2 and 3)

Moodle requires MySQL version 4.1.16.

Upgrade your database system MySQL to version 4.1.16 or greater.

### DB2 Query caching enabled

The query cache stores query statements, which increases performance when the same query is run multiple times. Keep the following things in mind:

- Set query cache using the `query_cache_size` parameter in `my.cnf` to 36M.
- Set the `query_cache_type` parameter in `my.cnf` to 1.
- Set the `query_cache_min_res_unit` parameter in `my.cnf` to 2K.

### DB3 Table caching enabled

The table cache stores table-related information for re-usage.

Set table cache using the `table_cache` parameter in `my.cnf` to a minimum of 256 (Moodle 1.6) and 512 (for all greater versions), respectively.

### DB4 Thread caching enabled

The thread cache keeps connections alive instead of closing them, which costs time and allows the re-usage at a later stage. This is not to be confused with connection-pooling.

Adjust the value in `my.cnf` so that the thread cache utilization is as close to 100% as possible (`thread cache utilization (%) = (threads_created / connections) * 100`).

### DB5 Enabled key buffering

The key buffer can improve the access speed to Moodle's SELECT queries. The correct size depends on the size of the index files (`.myi`).

Set the key buffer size using the `key_buffer_size` parameter in `my.cnf` to 32M, and a higher value if additional modules and plug-ins are installed.

### DB6 Turn off InnoDB

"InnoDB is a storage engine which provides MySQL with a transaction-safe (ACID compliant) storage engine that has commit, rollback, and crash recovery capabilities. InnoDB does locking on the row level and also provides an Oracle-style consistent non-locking read in SELECT statements. These features increase multi-user concurrency and performance.

Moodle tables are in the MyISAM format, so InnoDB can be turned off as there is no performance gain."

To turn off InnoDB in MySQL, please consult: `http://dev.mysql.com/doc/refman/5.0/en/innodb-configuration.html`.

If you have to use InnoDB, all tables that are used by Moodle have to be converted from the current MyISAM format using the `http://moodle.yourorg.com/admin/innodb.php` script.

### DB7 Cache hit ratio >90%

The MyISAM cache hit ratio should be at least 90%. A value of less than 90% is a strong indication of the fact that the database isn't performing to its fullest.

Adjust caching parameters until the ratio reaches a minimum of 90%.

### DB8 Run XMLDB Test

XMLDB is Moodle's database abstraction layer, that is, the library of code that lets Moodle interact with and access the database. It provides a test feature that shows any anomalies in the database structure.

Check errors and fix accordingly.

### DB9 Database Index Test

A search for potential missing indexes in your Moodle server can be carried out.

Check errors and fix accordingly.

### DB10 Database Bigints Test

A search for potential wrong integer fields in your Moodle server can be carried out.

Check errors and fix accordingly.

### DB11 Database and all tables have to be Unicode (Chapters 2 and 8)

The database and all the used tables have to be Unicode (collation `utf8_unicode_ci` or `utf8_general_ci`, for example).

Check all your tables and make sure none are in non-Unicode collation order such as latin1.

If the entire database is still in non-Unicode format, apply the Moodle Unicode migration script at `http://moodle.yourorg.com/admin/utfdbmigrate.html`.

# PHP

### PHP1 PHP Accelerator installed (Chapter 3)

A PHP accelerator boosts the performance of PHP code by caching compiled bytecode from PHP scripts. Moodle uses PHP as underlying programming language and a PHP accelerator is vital to achieve acceptable performance.

A PHP accelerator should be installed. Recommended optimizers are APC or Zend.

### PHP2 PHP Version (Chapter 2)

Moodle uses PHP as underlying programming language. Depending on which version of PHP is used, it requires a minimum release to work properly.

- Version 4.3.0 is required if PHP4 is used.
- Version 5.1.0 is required if PHP5 is used.
- Version 5.2.0 is required for forthcoming version Moodle 2.0.

### PHP3 PHP extension iconv (Chapter 2)

The iconv PHP extension provides functionality to convert characters from one character set to another. It is required in Moodle.

Install the PHP iconv extension on your system.

### PHP4 PHP extension mbstring (Chapter 2)

The mbstring PHP extension provides multibyte specific string functions and encodings. It is required for Moodle Unicode support.

Install the PHP mbstring extension on your system.

### PHP5 PHP extension curl (Chapters 2 and 14)

The curl PHP extension provides functionality to securely fetch data from remote sites. It is required for Moodle networking features.

Install the PHP curl extension on your system.

### PHP6 PHP extension openssl (Chapters 2 and 14)

The openssl PHP extension provides functionality to employ asynchronous encryption techniques (PKI encryption). It is required for Moodle networking features.

Install the PHP openssl extension on your system.

### PHP7 PHP extension tokenizer (Chapter 2)

The tokenizer PHP extension provides an interface to the PHP tokenizer embedded in the Zend engine. It is required in Moodle for PHP acceleration.

Install the PHP tokenizer extension on your system.

### PHP8 Configure PHP as Apache / IIS ISAPI module

The performance of PHP is significantly better when installed as an Apache/IIS ISAPI module, rather than a CGI binary.

Install PHP as Apache module on a Unix server. It is best to uninstall PHP as CGI first.

Install PHP as Apache module on a Windows server. It is best to uninstall PHP as CGI first.

If you have to install PHP as CGI, enable the `fastcgi` option.

### PHP9 memory_limit set to appropriate value (Chapter 11)

The memory limit specified has an impact on the performance of PHP code.

Set the memory limit to 40M using the `memory_limit` parameter in php.

# Web Server

### WS1 Apache Version

Apache 2 has an improved memory model, which reduces memory usage and should be used for any Moodle system.

Install Apache 2 on your server.

### WS2 Number of Apache modules

Reducing the number of modules that Apache loads to the minimum necessary will reduce the memory needed, which should be taken care of while loading modules in the `httpd.conf` file.

### WS3 MaxClients Directive

The MaxClients parameter sets the limit of maximum simultaneous requests that can be supported by the server (maximum number of spawned child processes). It shouldn't be set too low, otherwise an ever-increasing number of connections are deferred to the queue and they eventually time-out while the server resources are left unused. Setting this too high, on the other hand, will cause the server to start swapping. This will cause the response time to degrade drastically.

MaxClients = Total RAM dedicated to the web server / Max child process size

Set the MaxClients directive in `httpd.conf` to its appropriate value.

### WS4 MaxRequestsPerChild Directive

The MaxRequestsPerChild parameter sets the limit on the number of requests that an individual child server process will handle. After MaxRequestsPerChild requests, the child process will die and will never expire if set to its default value of 0.

Set the MaxRequestsPerChild directive in `httpd.conf` to a value between 20 and 30.

### WS5 KeepAlive and KeepAliveTimeout Directives

The KeepAlive directive allows multiple requests to be sent over the same TCP connection. This is particularly useful while serving image-rich HTML pages. If KeepAlive is set to Off, then for each image a separate TCP connection has to be made. Overhead, due to the establishment of a TCP connection, can be eliminated by turning On KeepAlive.

KeepAliveTimeout determines how long to wait for the next request. It is recommended to set this to a value between 2 and 5 seconds. If it is set too high, child processes are tied up waiting for the client when they could be used for serving new clients.

Set the KeepAlive directive in `httpd.conf` to On.

Set the KeepAliveTimeout directive in `httpd.conf` to a value between 2 and 5.

### WS6 DirectoryIndex Directive

The DirectoryIndex parameter sets the list of resources to look for when the client requests an index of the directory by specifying a / at the end of a directory name. If set incorrectly, a time-consuming content negotiation will occur.

Set the DirectoryIndex directive in `httpd.conf` to `index.php index.html index.htm`.

### WS7 ExtendedStatus Directive

The ExtendedStatus parameter controls whether the server keeps track of extended status information for each request. This is only useful if the status module is enabled on the server. This is only required while development work is carried out.

Set the ExtendedStatus directive in `httpd.conf` to Off.

### WS8 HostnameLookups Directive

The HostnameLookups parameter enables DNS lookups so that host names can be logged. Lookups are expensive and should be avoided if possible.

Set the HostnameLookups directive in `httpd.conf` to Off.

### WS9 TimeOut Directive

The TimeOut parameter defines the amount of time Apache will wait from the total amount of time it takes to receive a GET request, the amount of time between receipt of TCP packets on a POST or PUT request, and the amount of time between ACKs on transmissions of TCP packets in responses.

Unless the server is used for other web applications, set the TimeOut directive in `httpd.conf` to a value between 30 and 60.

### WS10 Option Directive

Avoid Option Multiview as this performs a directory scan, which can be I/O expensive.

Set the Option directive in `httpd.conf` to All.

### WS11 AcceptPathInfo Directive

The AcceptPathInfo parameter allows scripts to be passed as arguments that are essential to allow relative links between your resources.

Set the AcceptPathInfo directive in `httpd.conf` to On.

### WS12 Caching

Apache can be told to load pages faster by specifying that the browser should cache some page elements such as images, and reuse them from local memory rather than reload them every time a page is requested.

Configure Apache so that everything stays in the browser cache except HTML and XML content. The procedure differs for various operating systems.

# B

# Configuration Settings Reference

The objective of the Configuration Settings Reference is to provide you with a list of parameters that can be modified in `config.php` and the impact that each of the values will have.

We will first look at `config.php` and what types of parameters are supported by Moodle. After providing this overview, we will look at three types of configurations settings:

- Administration settings

  These are settings that are available via the **Site Administration** block, but can be locked with values specified in `config.php`.
- System settings

  These are compulsory configuration values that have been created by the installer and are required for Moodle to function.
- Theme settings

  These are settings that influence the look and feel of Moodle.

## Configuration Reference: An Overview

The configuration file `config.php` contains a number of settings that heavily influence how Moodle operates. It is located in the main directory of your Moodle system, and can be edited with any text editor.

Be careful while modifying `config.php`! Moodle depends heavily on its content and any fault can cause the software to malfunction.

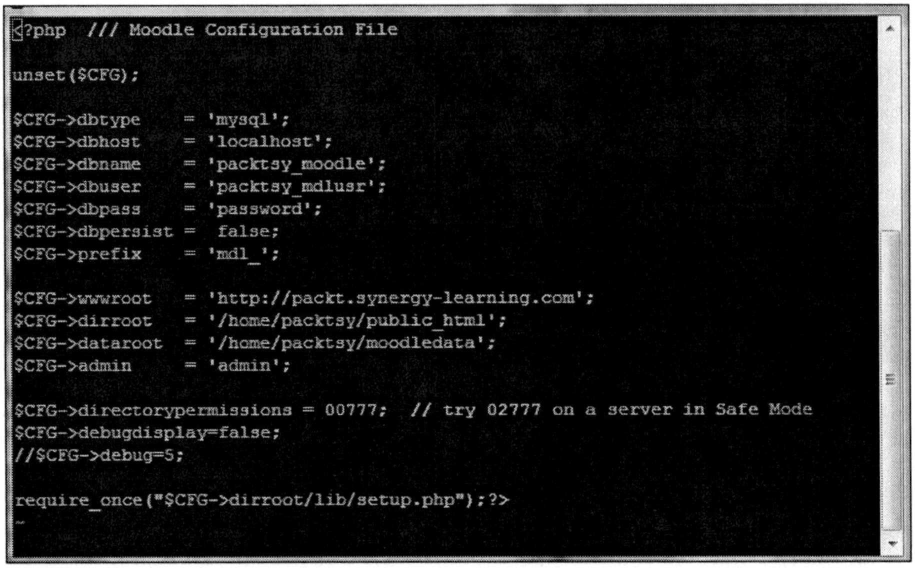

```
<?php  /// Moodle Configuration File

unset($CFG);

$CFG->dbtype    = 'mysql';
$CFG->dbhost    = 'localhost';
$CFG->dbname    = 'packtsy_moodle';
$CFG->dbuser    = 'packtsy_mdlusr';
$CFG->dbpass    = 'password';
$CFG->dbpersist =  false;
$CFG->prefix    = 'mdl_';

$CFG->wwwroot   = 'http://packt.synergy-learning.com';
$CFG->dirroot   = '/home/packtsy/public_html';
$CFG->dataroot  = '/home/packtsy/moodledata';
$CFG->admin     = 'admin';

$CFG->directorypermissions = 00777;  // try 02777 on a server in Safe Mode
$CFG->debugdisplay=false;
//$CFG->debug=5;

require_once("$CFG->dirroot/lib/setup.php");?>
```

The values in the `config.php` file we are interested in are the ones that start with a dollar symbol. Each parameter has the following information format:

```
$<object>-><parameter> = <value>;
```

`<object>` is the part of Moodle in which the parameter is used, for example `$CFG` or `$THEME`.

`<parameter>` is the name of the configuration setting. Each setting has a unique identifier.

`<value>` is the type of values the parameter accepts, for example true or false.

Each parameter has to be terminated by a semicolon. To comment out a parameter, precede it with two forward slashes. Make sure that there are no spaces or line breaks after the final `"?>"` in the `config.php` file.

# Configuration Reference: Administration Settings

Each parameter in the **Site Administration** block menus can be configured via the `config.php` file. If a value has been set via this method, it is effectively hardcoded and cannot be changed via the Moodle interface; not even by the administrator.

For example, you might want to make sure that an administrator does not, even by accident, turn on https for logins. Turning this on would lock everybody out of the site if no SSL certificate is installed. To do this, enter the following line in `config.php`:

```
$CFG->loginhttps=false;
```

How do you know what the parameter is called? Go to the respective setting in Moodle (in this case **Security | HTTP security**) and you will see the name of the parameter underneath the label.

If value is specified in `config.php`, Moodle will display **Defined in config.php** besides the parameter, which indicates that the setting cannot be changed by the user. Invalid values are also shown for these hardcoded settings. In the following screenshot, the **Debug messages** value is incorrect while the **Display debug messages** value is correct:

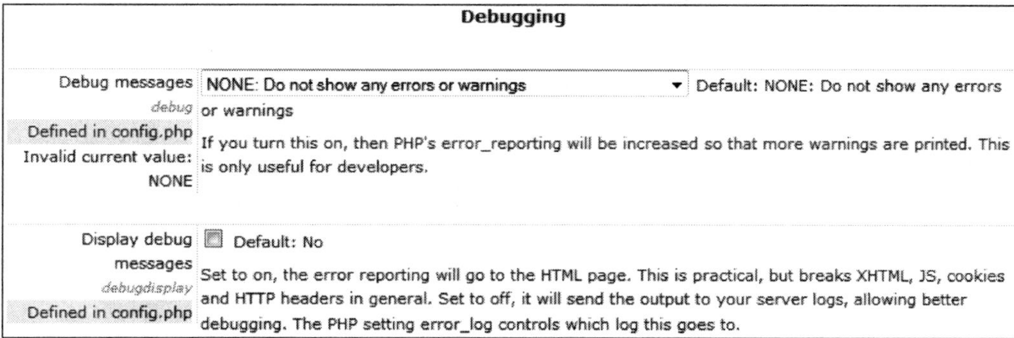


The value that a parameter accepts depends on the type of setting. The table provides information for each type:

| Type | Moodle Field | Values |
|---|---|---|
| Binary | Checkbox | True or 0 and false or 0. |
| Numeric | Number Field | The number. |
| String | Text Field | Text has to be surrounded by single quotes. |
| Password | Password Field | Passwords have to be surrounded by single quotes. |

| Type | Moodle Field | Values |
|---|---|---|
| List | Pull-Down Menu | Each value is represented by a number. Unfortunately, there is no consistency for the allocation. For example, while the debug parameter accepts the values 0, 5, 15, 6143, and 38911, the sitemailcharset parameter accepts 0, EUC-JP, and GB18030! The easiest way to find out what values are valid is to check the database. Go to `mdl_config`, browse for the field with the same name as the parameter, and use that value in the configuration file. |
| Array | Multi-select Menu | The same applies as for the list type. Values are separated by commas. Again, check `mdl_config` to be on the safe side. |

There are some other special types that are mentioned when applicable. For each parameter, the type is put in brackets in the reference part of this appendix.

# Configuration Reference: System Settings

These parameters are listed in the order in which they appear by default in `config.php`.

## Compulsory Parameters

**$CFG->dbtype (String)**

The database system that is used, **MySQL** is the default. For all other values such as postgres7 or oci8po, check the values given during the database setup in the installer.

**$CFG->dbhost (String)**

The name of the database host: localhost or 127.0.0.1 if the database is located on the server as Moodle, or any other URL (resolved or unresolved) if located on another server.

**$CFG->dbname (String)**

The name of the database.

**$CFG->dbuser (String)**

The username of the database account.

### $CFG->dbpass (String)

The password of the database account.

### $CFG->dbpersist (Binary)

This specifies whether an existing database connection should be reused. This can improve performance, but is potentially less stable.

### $CFG->prefix (String)

By default, all tables in Moodle are prefixed with `mdl_`. This should be changed only if you run multiple Moodle installations using the same database.

### $CFG->wwwroot (String)

This is the full web address (including `http://`) where Moodle has been installed.

### $CFG->dirroot (String)

This is the absolute directory name where Moodle has been installed.

### $CFG->dataroot (String)

This is the absolute directory name where Moodle's data dictionary is located. The directory has to be readable and writable, but must not be accessible via the Web.

### $CFG->admin (String)

The admin pages in Moodle are located in the admin directory. If this has to be changed then specify the new directory here as some ISPs don't allow its usage because it conflicts with their internal setup.

### $CFG->directorypermissions (Special)

These are the permissions in Unix format that are applied for directories Moodle is creating. Default is 00777.

## Optional Parameters

There exist a significant number of parameters that are neither set by the installer, nor can be modified via the Moodle administrator interface. These optional parameters allow you to modify the behavior of Moodle. Explanations have been taken from the dedicated configuration page at `http://docs.moodle.org/en/Configuration_file`. The parameters have been listed in alphabetical order.

### $CFG->admineditalways (Binary)

Setting this to true will enable administrators to edit any post at any time.

### $CFG->allowvisiblecoursesinhiddencategories

Restore pre-1.6 behavior where courses could still be available even if the category they were in was hidden.

### $CFG->apacheloguser (Menu)

The setting will turn on username logging into Apache log. Accepted values are 0 (feature turned off), 1 (log user ID), 2 (log full name), and 3 (log username).

### $CFG->dblogerror (Binary)

The setting will turn **SQL Error logging** on. This will output an entry in Apache error log indicating the position of the error and the statement called. This option will surely take action disregarding the `error_reporting` setting.

### $CFG-> bounceratio (Numeric)

Refer $CFG->handlebounces.

### $CFG->customscripts (String)

Enabling this will allow custom scripts to replace existing Moodle scripts. For example, if `$CFG->customscripts/course/view.php` exists then it will be used instead of `$CFG->wwwroot/course/view.php`. At present, this will only work for files that include `config.php` and are called as part of the URL (`index.php` is implied). Custom scripts should not include `config.php`.

> Warning: Replacing standard Moodle scripts may pose security risks, and/or may not be compatible with upgrades. Use this option only if you are aware of the risks involved. Specify the full directory path to the custom scripts.

### $CFG->docroot (String)

By default, Moodle documentation is provided via the MoodleDocs at `http://docs.moodle.org`. If you wish to replace the documentation with your own, you will have to change the link to the homepage of your alternative documentation. Bear in mind that the directory structure and file naming has to be identical to the default documentation.

### $CFG->defaultblocks (Array)

These blocks are used when no other default setting for blocks is found. Accepted values are: participants, activity_modules, search_forums, admin, course_list, news_items, calendar_upcoming, and recent_activity.

**$CFG->defaultblocks_override (Array)**

If this parameter is set, it overrides all other DEFAULT block variables and is the only one used. Array values are: participants, activity_modules, search_forums, admin, course_list, news_items, calendar_upcoming, and recent_activity.

These following variables define the specific settings for defined course formats. They override any settings defined in the format's `config` file:

**$CFG->defaultblocks_site (Array)**

Accepted values are: site_main_menu, admin, course_list, course_summary, and calendar_month.

**$CFG->defaultblocks_social (Array)**

Accepted values are: participants, search_forums, calendar_month, calendar_upcoming, social_activities, recent_activity, admin, and course_list.

**$CFG->defaultblocks_topics (Array)**

Accepted values are: participants, activity_modules, search_forums, admin, course_list, news_items, calendar_upcoming, and recent_activity.

**$CFG->defaultblocks_weeks (Array)**

Accepted values are: participants, activity_modules, search_forums, admin, course_list, news_items, calendar_upcoming, and recent_activity.

**$CFG->disablemycourses (Binary)**

This setting will prevent the **My Courses** page from being displayed when a student logs in. The site's front page will always show the same (logged out) view.

**$CFG->disablescheduledbackups (Binary)**

Prevent scheduled backups from operating (and hide the GUI for them). This is useful for webhost operators who have alternate methods of backups.

**$CFG->disablestatsprocessing (Binary)**

Prevent stats processing and hide the GUI.

**$CFG->emailconnectionerrorsto (String)**

Email database connection errors to someone. If Moodle cannot connect to the database, then email this address with a notice.

### $CFG->filelifetime (Numeric)

Time in seconds for files to remain in caches (default is 86400, which equals 24 hours). Decrease this if you are worried about students being served outdated versions of uploaded files.

### $CFG->forcefirstname (String)

Use this to anonymize usernames for all students. If set, then all non-teachers will always see this for every person.

### $CFG->forcelastname (String)

To anonymize usernames for all students. If set, then all non-teachers will always see this for every person.

### $CFG->handlebounces (Binary)

This is for handling email bounces. It should be used in conjunction with `$CFG->minbounces` (Numeric, default 10) and `$CFG->bounceratio` (Numeric, default 20). Also check `$CFG->mailprefix`, `$CFG->mailprefix` and `$CFG->maildomain`.

### $CFG->mailprefix (String)

`mdl+` is the separator for Exim and Postfix, `mdl-` is the separator for qmail.

### $CFG->maildomain (String)

Indicates your email domain.

### $CFG->loginaspassword (Password)

Set global password for login as teacher is prompted only once in each session. Set your own password and tell it only to teachers who should have access to this feature.

### $CFG->minbounces (Numeric)

Refer $CFG->handlebounces.

### $CFG->nofixday (Binary)

This setting will cause the `userdate()` function not to fix `%d` in date strings, and just let them show with a zero prefix.

### $CFG->preferlinegraphs (Binary)

This setting will make some graphs (for example, user logs). Preferably, use lines instead of bars.

### $CFG->respectsessionsettings (Binary)

The setting will tell Moodle to respect your PHP session settings. Use this if you want to control session configuration from `php.ini`, `httpd.conf`, or `.htaccess` files.

### $CFG->tracksessionip (Binary)

If this setting is set to true, then Moodle will track the IP of the current user to make sure it hasn't changed during a session. This will prevent the possibility of sessions being hijacked via XSS. But it may break things for users logging in with proxies that change all the time such as AOL.

### $CFG->unicodedb (Binary)

This setting will put Moodle in Unicode mode. Please note that your database must support it. Do not enable this if your database is not converted to UTF-8.

### $CFG->unicodecleanfilename (Binary)

Allow Unicode characters in uploaded files, generated reports, and so on. This setting is new and not much tested. There are known problems with backup/restore that will not be solved because native infozip binaries are doing some weird conversions; use internal PHP zipping instead.

Please note that this is not recommended for production sites.

# Configuration Reference: Theme Settings

These are the theme-related parameters, some of which have been used in Chapter 7, Moodle Look and Feel.

There are two parameters that are set in the `config.php` file:

### $CFG-> allowthemechangeonurl (Binary)

This activates session themes.

### $CFG-> themeorder (Array)

To change the priority of page themes, modify the parameter to reflect the new order. The default is set to ('page', 'course', 'category', 'session', 'user', and 'site').

The remaining values, which are listed next, are set within the `config.php` file of a particular theme.

**$THEME->blockssheets (Binary)**

If set to 'true', `styles.php` will be used for all block modules. Disable this only if needed.

**$THEME->customcorners (Binary)**

If set to 'true', rounded corners for blocks will be supported.

**$THEME->custompix (Binary)**

If changed to 'true', a pix directory is required containing copies of `moodle/pix` and `pix/mod` containing custom icons for activities.

**$THEME->filter_mediaplugin_colors (Settings)**

Settings of the built-in Moodle media player:

- Colors (same as explained in the previous point)
- Player (waitForPlay)

**$THEME->langsheets (Binary)**

If changed to 'true', `styles.php` will be used for each language. That way, different styles can be used for different languages.

**$THEME->makenavmenulist (Binary)**

If changed to 'true', a variable called `$navmenulist` will be available in `header.html`, which is used for creating pop-up navigation menus such as the **Jump to...** menu.

**$THEME->modsheets (Binary)**

If set to 'true', `styles.php` will be used for all activity modules. Disable this only if needed.

**$THEME->navmenuwidth (Numeric)**

Number of characters displayed in the 'Jump to...' menu inside modules (default is 50).

**$THEME->parent (String)**

Name of the parent theme.

### $THEME->parentsheets (Array)

List of styles used from the parent theme.

### $THEME->resource_mp3_player_colors (Settings)

Settings of the built-in Moodle MP3 player:

- Colors (bgColour, btnColour, btnBorderColour, iconColour, iconOverColour, trackColour, handleColour, loaderColour)
- Fonts (font and fontColour)
- Player (buffer, waitForPlay and autoPlay)

### $THEME->sheets (Array)

This is the order in which included stylesheet files are used in the theme.

### $THEME->standardsheets (Array)

List of styles used from the standard theme.

# Index

## A



## B



## C

## N



## O



## P

## R

## S

## T



## U

# V



# W

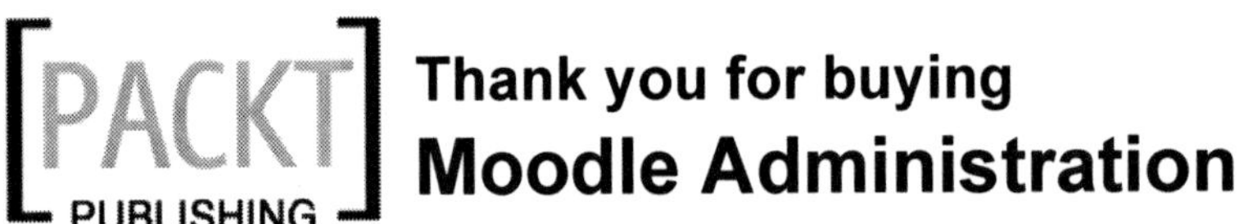


# Packt Open Source Project Royalties

When we sell a book written on an Open Source project, we pay a royalty directly to that project. Therefore by purchasing Moodle Administration, Packt will have given some of the money received to the Moodle Project.

In the long term, we see ourselves and you—customers and readers of our books—as part of the Open Source ecosystem, providing sustainable revenue for the projects we publish on. Our aim at Packt is to establish publishing royalties as an essential part of the service and support a business model that sustains Open Source.

If you're working with an Open Source project that you would like us to publish on, and subsequently pay royalties to, please get in touch with us.

# Writing for Packt

We welcome all inquiries from people who are interested in authoring. Book proposals should be sent to `authors@packtpub.com`. If your book idea is still at an early stage and you would like to discuss it first before writing a formal book proposal, contact us; one of our commissioning editors will get in touch with you.

We're not just looking for published authors; if you have strong technical skills but no writing experience, our experienced editors can help you develop a writing career, or simply get some additional reward for your expertise.

# About Packt Publishing

Packt, pronounced 'packed', published its first book "Mastering phpMyAdmin for Effective MySQL Management" in April 2004 and subsequently continued to specialize in publishing highly focused books on specific technologies and solutions.

Our books and publications share the experiences of your fellow IT professionals in adapting and customizing today's systems, applications, and frameworks. Our solution-based books give you the knowledge and power to customize the software and technologies you're using to get the job done. Packt books are more specific and less general than the IT books you have seen in the past. Our unique business model allows us to bring you more focused information, giving you more of what you need to know, and less of what you don't.

Packt is a modern, yet unique publishing company, which focuses on producing quality, cutting-edge books for communities of developers, administrators, and newbies alike. For more information, please visit our website: `www.PacktPub.com`.

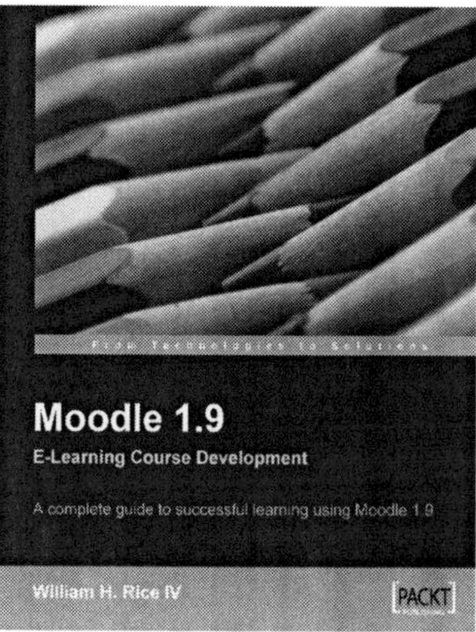


## Moodle 1.9 E-Learning Course Development

ISBN: 978-1-847193-53-7 Paperback: 360 pages

A complete guide to successful learning using Moodle

1. Updated for Moodle version 1.9
2. Straightforward coverage of installing and using the Moodle system
3. Working with Moodle features in all learning environments
4. A unique course-based approach focuses your attention on designing well-structured, interactive, and successful courses
5. Configure site settings, set up the front page, create user accounts, and create courses

---

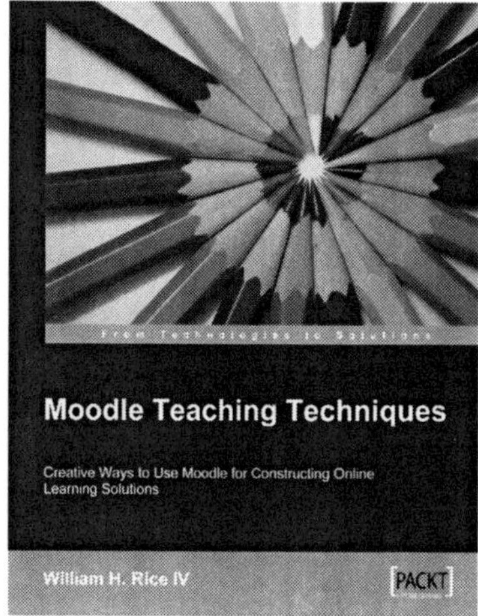


## Moodle Teaching Techniques

ISBN: 978-1-847192-84-4 Paperback: 200 pages

Creative Ways to Use Moodle for Constructing Online Learning Solutions

1. Applying your teaching techniques through Moodle
2. Creative uses for Moodle's standard features
3. Workarounds, providing alternative solutions
4. Abundantly illustrated with screenshots of the solutions you'll build
5. When and how to apply the different learning solutions
6. Especially good for university and professional teachers

Please check **www.PacktPub.com** for information on our titles

CPSIA information can be obtained at www.ICGtesting.com
226899LV00003B/94/P

9 781847 195623